The Philosopher, or On Faith

GRAPHAI

Graphai: Writings from Byzantium and Its Neighbors presents texts and translations from the Byzantine world. Ideal for scholars and students, these elegant volumes publish written material never before seen in translation and offer exciting new translations of well-known works. The series encompasses all periods and genres, and is not limited by the political boundaries of the Byzantine Empire.

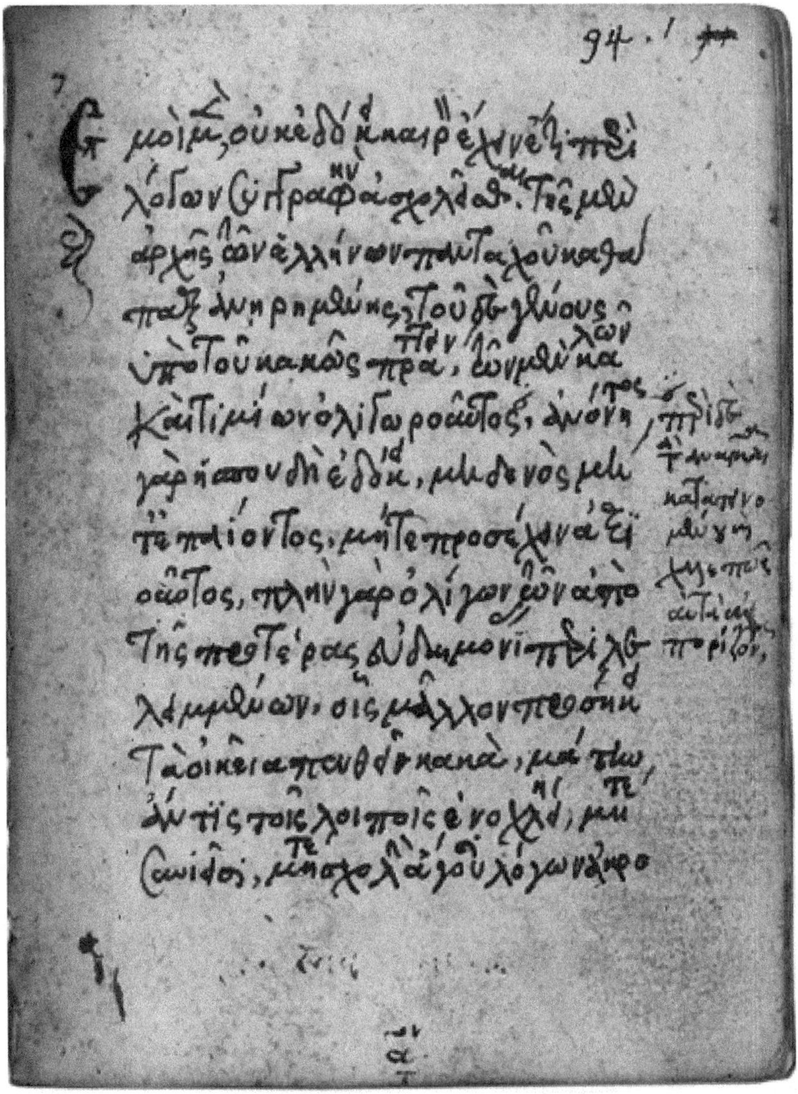

Figure 1. Biblioteca de la Catedral de Toledo, cod. 96-37, f. 94r/1r. Photo courtesy the Archivo y Biblioteca Capitulares, Catedral de Toledo.

GRAPHAI

The Philosopher, or On Faith

GEORGE AMIROUTZES

Edited and Translated by

JOHN MONFASANI

DUMBARTON OAKS ✠ TRUSTEES FOR HARVARD UNIVERSITY

WASHINGTON, DC

Printed in the United States of America.

Library of Congress Cataloging-in-Publication Data

Names: Amoiroutzēs, Georgiōs, approximately 1400-1470, author. | Mehmed II, Sultan of the Turks, 1432–1481. | Amoiroutzēs, Georgiōs, approximately 1400–1470. Dialogus de fide in Christum habitus cum rege Turcarum. Greek. | Amoiroutzēs, Georgiōs, approximately 1400–1470. Dialogus de fide in Christum habitus cum rege Turcarum. English. | Monfasani, John, editor, translator.

Title: The philosopher, or, On faith / George Amiroutzes ; edited and translated by John Monfasani.

Other titles: Graphai.

Description: Washington, DC : Dumbarton Oaks, Trustees for Harvard University, [2021] | Series: Graphai: writings from Byzantium and its neighbors | Includes bibliographical references and indexes. | Greek text with English translation on facing pages; introduction in English.

Summary: "'God necessarily exists, since it is not possible for things to be otherwise, as Aristotle shows in the Metaphysics.' So Mehmed II, the Ottoman conqueror of both Constantinople and Trebizond, tells George Amiroutzes, the Byzantine scholar and native of Trebizond, in the beginning of Amiroutzes' dialogue *The Philosopher, or On Faith*. The dialogue is a literary recreation of the conversations between Mehmed, a Muslim, and Amiroutzes, a Christian. In the course of *The Philosopher*, the two debate the role of logic and rationality in religious debate, the nature of God, and the fate of the body and soul in the afterlife. Surprisingly complex and subtle arguments emerge, firmly situated in their fifteenth-century context but steeped in the long Greek philosophical tradition. Previously known only from a sixteenth-century Latin translation, *The Philosopher* was recently rediscovered in a Greek manuscript in Toledo. In this volume, John Monfasani presents both the editio princeps of this manuscript and the first translation of the text from the Greek, with an introduction that discusses the life of Amiroutzes and the text as well as two appendixes that offer texts and translations of two additional documents related to Amiroutzes and *The Philosopher*."—Provided by publisher.

Identifiers: LCCN 2021013521 | ISBN 9780884024859 (hardcover)

Subjects: LCSH: Christianity and other religions—Islam—Early works to 1800. | Apologetics—Early works to 1800.

Classification: LCC BP172 .A47513 2021 | DDC 239/.2—dc23

LC record available at https://lccn.loc.gov/2021013521

www.doaks.org/publications

For John A. Demetracopoulos

CONTENTS

PREFACE

I consider my scholarly career a series of happy accidents. The present volume is a case in point. As explained in the Introduction, I quite serendipitously stumbled upon the text edited here in 2004, but, amid the press of other responsibilities and projects, only now have I been able to give the public an edition and translation of it. The delay has proved profitable, however, in that the intervening period allowed me to meet many scholars who in one way or another contributed to the edition. One especially deserves mention: John A. Demetracopoulos of the University of Patras, whose suggestions have been invaluable and whose friendship a great support for more than a decade. To him I dedicate the volume. I am indebted to the University of Albany, State University of New York, for a travel grant that allowed me to see the manuscript of the treatise in situ in Toledo for the first time in 2005. I also thank my Albany colleague Dmitry Korobeynikov and Jules Janssens in Leuven for their help. Once I submitted the manuscript to Dumbarton Oaks, the two readers for the press saved me from an embarrassing number of errors. For their benefaction I am enormously grateful. Finally, I owe a large debt to my editor Colin Whiting, whose erudition and good judgment improved the edition in ways large and small.

INTRODUCTION

I. George Amiroutzes

This is the *editio princeps* of a Greek text that had been lost since the sixteenth century. Before we can discuss it and its history, however, we need to gain an understanding of its author, George Amiroutzes.[1]

Born about 1400 and dying in or a little before 1470, Amiroutzes was part of that last great generation of Byzantine intellectuals before the Turkish conquest brought the Palaeologan Renaissance to an end.[2] As multiple contemporary witnesses attest, in his own day Amiroutzes enjoyed the sobriquet "the

1. For the multiple ways one finds his family name spelled, see Janssens and Van Deun, "George Amiroutzes and His Poetical Oeuvre," 297, n. 1.

2. I summarize what is known of his life and cite the relevant literature in Monfasani, *George Amiroutzes the Philosopher*, 5–12; see also idem, "A Note on George Amiroutzes." The most important comprehensive studies are, in chronological order, Tomadakis's 1948 article "Ἐτούρκευσεν ὁ Γεώργιος Ἀμιρούτζης," followed by Argyriou and Lagarrigue, "Georges Amiroutzès et son 'Dialogue sur la foi,'" and Janssens and Van Deun, "George Amiroutzes and His Poetical Oeuvre." Not included in these studies is the evidence for Amiroutzes' Pontic property reported by Beldiceanu, "Biens des Grands Comnènes," 26, 41 (doc. III), and Beldiceanu and Beldiceanu-Steinherr, "Biens des Amiroutzés," 65–66, 73 (doc. 2), 74 (doc. 4), 78 (doc. 10). Bryer ("Rural Society in Matzouka," 85) comments that "his income seems to have been modest . . . and Beldiceanu is right to ask if Trapezuntine ministers were in fact largely rewarded by tax farms and 'biens incorporels.'" Two important recent contributions are Kaldellis, "Interpolations in the *Histories*," and Mondrain, "Jean Argyropoulos professeur à Constantinople." One bit of information I overlooked previously is the fact that John Eugenicus sometime before 1427 addressed to Amiroutzes an early draft of his exhortation to the monastic life before revising it and addressing it to Theodore Palaeologus, the despot of Mistra; see Mercati, "Sopra alcuni autografi di Giovanni Eugenico," 155–56.

Philosopher." Amiroutzes rose to high administrative status in his native Trebizond on the Black Sea coast of modern Turkey before Mehmed II subjugated the city on 15 August 1461, eight years after having conquered Constantinople. Trebizond had been the last independent Greek state. Amiroutzes' role in the surrender of the city to Mehmed is controversial, in part because he seems to have been a cousin of Mahmoud Pasha,[3] the Ottoman official who negotiated the surrender of the city for Mehmed. Two hostile sixteenth-century chronicles accuse him of tricking the Emperor of Trebizond, David Comnenus, into surrendering.[4] Amiroutzes' contemporary Laonicus Chalcocondyles simply records in his *Histories* that Amiroutzes negotiated the surrender of Trebizond with his cousin Mahmoud Pasha without any suggestion of treachery.[5] But

3. The fullest discussion of the possibility and exact nature of this relationship is Stavrides, *Sultan of Vezirs*, 78–79, 86–87. The Byzantine sources that assert this relationship are Chalcocondyles (*Histories* 9.79), who says that they were cousins; the *Ecthesis chronica* (ed. Lambros, 26; ed. and trans. Philippides, 70–71), which explains that Amiroutzes' mother and the mother of Mahmoud Pasha were sisters, daughters of one Iagaris, probably Marcus Palaeologus Iagaris, a prominent figure at the court of Constantinople in the first four decades of the fifteenth century; the *Historia politica* (38) repeats the claim of the *Ecthesis chronica* and probably derives from it. Bryer, "Trebizond and Serbia," 37, provides a genealogical chart graphically representing the relationship.

4. See the previous note for the *Ecthesis chronica* and the *Historia politica*. Both also accuse Amiroutzes of getting Mahmoud Pasha to depose the patriarch and slit the nose of the Grand Ecclesiarch for refusing to allow him to put away his wife and marry the widow of the Duke of Athens (*Ecthesis chronica*, ed. Lambros, 27–28; ed. and trans. Philippides, 72–73; *Historia politica* 38–39). But it is not clear that Amiroutzes was married at the time. In the letter to Bessarion after the fall of Trebizond (see Appendix I), he voiced his anguish at the suffering of his son and son-in-law, but never mentions his wife, who, if alive, would have certainly and conspicuously shared in the anguish. Furthermore, as other scholars have pointed out, if Amiroutzes wanted the approval of the patriarch to remarry, he must have still been a Christian and not an apostate as the two chronicles charge.

5. See n. 3. Critobulus, who as a fellow member of Mehmed's court clearly was friendly with Amiroutzes, does not mention Amiroutzes at all when relating the surrender of Trebizond and instead identifies Mahmoud Pasha's intermediary as Mehmed's Greek secretary Thomas Katavolenos (see Critobulus, *Histories* 4.7.4; on Katavolenos, see Patrinelis, *Ὁ Θεόδωρος Ἀγαλλιανός*, 71–74). Bryer and Winfield (*Byzantine Monuments*, 64), on the basis of the Turkish chronicle of Tursun, assert that "David himself [Emperor of Trebizond] abandoned his city and realm and negotiated terms only for his family household."

later on in the *Histories*, Chalcocondyles tells us that Amiroutzes revealed to the Turkish authorities that after David Comnenus and his family were moved to Adrianople, they engaged in compromising correspondence with Mehmed's enemy, Uzun Hasan, the Turkoman ruler in eastern Asia Minor.[6] This revelation quickly led Mehmed to order the execution of Emperor David and his sons. The strangest aspect of this report is that the most recent student and translator of Chalcocondyles' *Histories*, Anthony Kaldellis, believes not only that this report in the *Histories* is an interpolation, but also that the interpolator was none other than George Amiroutzes himself. The report goes on to say that Amiroutzes was fearful of his Ottoman master thinking he had anything to do with such plotting.[7]

Whatever the truth of this report, it is certain is that a year or two after the surrender of Trebizond, Amiroutzes had become a member of Mehmed II's household and that his two sons, Alexander and Basil, at some point entered into the service of Mehmed's government.[8] So he and his family prospered after the surrender, thus lending credence to the idea that he had betrayed for his own private advantage the public trust of his position as *protovestiarius*, that is, the chief or one of the chief administrative officers of Trebizond.[9] Indeed, the two hostile sixteenth-century Byzantine chronicles accuse him and

6. Chalcocondyles, *Histories* 9.80.

7. See Kaldellis, "Interpolations in the *Histories*," 272–76, and the notes on the text in his edition of Chalcocondyles, *Histories* 2.481–82.

8. See nn. 27–30.

9. Apart from his position as *protovestiarius*, the only other governmental job performed by Amiroutzes that we know of is his failed 1449 legation to Genoa to negotiate a tariff dispute; see Bănescu, "Le conflit entre Gênes et l'empire de Trébizonde"; Iorga, *Notes et extraits*, 3:245–47; Karpov, *L'impero di Trebisonda*, 168–70; idem, *Ιστορία της αυτοκρατορίας της Τραπεζούντας*, 337–39. George Scholarius (*Oeuvres complètes*, 4:453–54) spoke of this embassy and praised Amiroutzes in a letter of 1449/50 to the emperor of Trebizond. Karpov calls Amiroutzes *protovestiarius* in discussing the legation, but the Genoese document quoted by Iorga only calls him *spectatus miles et comes palatinus*. Iorga (*Notes et extraits*, 2:16) edits a papal financial document of 24 October 1439 recording a payment of 96 florins to the *megas logariastes*, the ambassador (*orator*) of Trebizond, but this person does not seem to be Amiroutzes, since the payment was partially in compensation of the costs incurred by the ambassador and four familiars in traveling from Florence to Venice, which would make no sense if he were Amiroutzes, who was present in Florence for the whole time of the council.

his sons of being apostates to Islam.[10] But the only contemporary who actually accused Amiroutzes of apostatizing was a Greek émigré to Renaissance Italy, George of Trebizond. In his *Martyrium Beati Andreae de Chio*, written in Rome in 1468, three years after he had visited Constantinople and spoken with Amiroutzes, George reported that there was a certain Aristotelian philosopher from Trebizond, whom he would not name *honoris causa*, who had denied the cross of Christ and converted to Islam.[11] He also reports that while he was in Constantinople, a Greek military man imprisoned and pressured to convert to Islam by Mehmed II declared that he would not apostatize as had his fellow citizen "the Philosopher."[12] Nonetheless, George was surely mistaken, basing himself on common gossip rather than anything Amiroutzes had said to him. In 1468, while George was writing his *Martyrium Beati Andreae de Chio* in Rome, Bishop Theophanes of Media (i.e., Theodore Agallianos before changing his name upon entering the office of bishop) initiated a correspondence with Amiroutzes concerning Theophanes' treatise on divine providence.[13] The good bishop certainly would not have entered into such a discussion with an

10. See nn. 27–30.

11. On the *Martyrium*, see Monfasani, *Collectanea Trapezuntiana*, 597–99. The only source for the text was a lost manuscript used in truncated form in 1577 by Peter Canisius in his *De Maria Virgine incomparabili* and then in full by Laurentius Surius in his *De probatis sanctorum historiis* of 1579. Leone Allacci (Leo Allatius) in his *De ecclesiae occidentalis atque orientalis perpetua consensione* of 1648 (col. 915) first identified Amiroutzes as the subject of George's accusation, but it was not until 1866, when Migne reprinted George's text from the *Acta Sanctorum* in volume 161 of the Patrologia Graeca, that Allacci's identification appeared with the text. I take my text from Surius, *De probatis sanctorum historiis* 3:493 (PG 161:880): *Quidam enim, quem honoris causa non nomino, ex Trapezuntana ortus urbe, Peripateticorum philosophiae professor, sive sua sponte, ut multi aiunt, sive impulsus, nescio, nec si sciam, dicere ausim, crucem domini negavit et Mahumeto adhaesit.*

12. Surius, *De probatis sanctorum historiis* 3:493 (PG 161:880): when the Sultan demanded that the military man *philosophum concivem suum volens nolensve imitaretur*, he responded that *philosophus… in deliciis educatus maiore spe ipsarum Christi crucem negavit*; he himself would accept the earthly death *quam fugiendam censuit philosophus.*

13. See Patrinelis, *Ὁ Θεόδωρος Ἀγαλλιανός*, 41–42, 48; Stéphanou, "Théophane de Médie." Theophanes' predecessor as bishop of Media was still alive in January 1467. Moreover, in early 1468, while he was still Theodore, he sent the treatise to the former patriarch Gennadius II (George Scholarius).

apostate. Nor do we have the slightest evidence that Amiroutzes ever changed his name, which would have been the case had he converted to Islam. In *The Philosopher* itself, Amiroutzes declared that he would rather die than surrender his Christian faith (XLIII.1.21–22).[14] We also have poignant textual evidence of Amiroutzes' Christian faith before he became an Ottoman courtier in a letter he sent Cardinal Bessarion in Italy dated 10 December 1461, that is, four months after the surrender of Trebizond.[15] Amiroutzes wrote from Adrianople, where he, along with Emperor David Comnenus and the imperial family, were being detained. He appealed in desperation to Bessarion to ransom him and one of his sons, Basil. While George himself was being detained in Adrianople as part of the human booty of Trebizond, Basil had not only been reduced to the status of a slave, but was now also being pressured by no less a personage than Mehmed II to convert to Islam by means of arguments, gifts, and blows.[16] He was being driven nearly out of mind, Amiroutzes exclaimed, at what was happening to his son.[17]

We learn a great deal else from this letter concerning the relationship between Amiroutzes and Bessarion. Amiroutzes had grounds to stress in the letter that his ties to Bessarion ran deep and stretched far back. Bessarion, it turns out, was Basil's godfather. Bessarion's mother held the baby at the baptismal font in Bessarion's stead, since as a Roman cardinal Bessarion was already living in Italy at the time.[18] We also learn that Bessarion's mother was interred in the monastery of Paraskeve in Trebizond, which she had entered after becoming a widow.[19] Indeed, the man who carried Amiroutzes' letter to Bessarion, Amiroutzes noted, was a relative of Bessarion's and some sort of lay official of the monastery. We know next to nothing about Amiroutzes' education and academic activity, but it is reasonable to suppose that he and Bessarion shared some of the same teachers and friends when the latter was attending school in Constantinople in the 1420s, quite apart from familial links between the two

14. The organizer of the Greek manuscript of *The Philosopher*, it should be noted, also believed that Amiroutzes eventually apostatized; see *The Philosopher* XXI.12.2.

15. I edit and translate the relevant part of the letter in Appendix I.

16. Appendix I, §§12–13.

17. Ibid., §11.

18. Ibid., §6.

19. Ibid., §23. See Monfasani, "Bessarion Missal Revisited"; "Bessarionea," 90–91.

back in Trebizond.[20] Certainly at the Council of Ferrara–Florence in 1438–39, Bessarion and Amiroutzes were allies in support of the union of the Greek and Latin churches.[21]

More significant for our understanding of *The Philosopher* are other aspects of the letter. First of all, if we are to take Amiroutzes at his word, Mehmed II himself had already identified young Basil as a prize slave. Since earlier in the letter Amiroutzes had explained that in divvying up the booty of Trebizond, Mehmed reserved as sex slaves the boys and girls who had reached puberty or were near puberty,[22] Amiroutzes' concern was not merely the fear of apostasy for the boy. Also, despite complaining about his "slavery," Amiroutzes himself and the rest of his family, save for Basil and his son-in-law, who were potential sex slaves,[23] were not so much slaves as much as prisoners of war being held for ransom and interned in Adrianople. Amiroutzes even told Bessarion that if he sent ransom money, he, Amiroutzes, would be free to race to Constantinople to collect it.[24]

We do not know whether Bessarion ever did ransom George Amiroutzes and his son Basil. In *The Philosopher*, Amiroutzes says nothing about his son and attributes his own rescue from internment to Mehmed II hearing of his fame and, after an interview, ordering him to stay in attendance for conversation.[25] As for his sons,[26] the Byzantine chronicles make it clear that eventually Basil became an Ottoman official with the name Mehmed Bey and was known as a translator from Greek into Arabic and Turkish,[27] while another of

20. See Monfasani, *George Amiroutzes the Philosopher*, 11–12.

21. Ibid., 7. As a layman, he did not sign the decree of union, but he did put in writing a formal profession of his agreement with it; see *Orientalium documenta minora* 3.3, 36–39 (doc. 32).

22. Appendix I, §5.

23. Ibid., §7: "because he is young and handsome."

24. Ibid., §22. Amiroutzes had already begged Bessarion to ransom him in an earlier letter; see §§2 and 16.

25. *The Philosopher* I.4.1–3.

26. Janssens and Van Deun, "George Amiroutzes and His Poetical Oeuvre," 302, n. 23, collect the literature on his sons, Alexander/Skender Bey and Basil/Mehmed Bey.

27. See Critobulus, *Histories* 5.10.5–8, on how he translated for Mehmed II in 1465 a synopsis of Ptolemy's *Geography* made by his father; and the *Ecthesis chronica* (ed. Lambros, 36; ed. and trans. Philippides, 86–87) and the *Historia politica* 117 and 124 on how he translated Christian religious texts for Mehmed.

Amiroutzes' sons, Alexander, became a high Ottoman financial administrator with the name Skender Bey.[28] When did Amiroutzes' sons become Muslims? Even the Byzantine chronicles acknowledge that for a time they remained Christians.[29] We have a fascinating but frustratingly obscure letter of the Greek copyist and scholar Michael Apostolis to Amiroutzes in which he congratulates Amiroutzes on how his sons had successfully answered a question Mehmed II had put to them but without telling us exactly what the question was. In the same letter, Apostolis recommended a policy of crypto-Christianity, that is, seeming to be Muslim while in actuality remaining Christian.[30]

Apostolis's letter as well as the hostile Greek chronicles and George of Trebizond's report of apostasy, if nothing else, attest to the general perception that Amiroutzes was well ensconced in the Ottoman court. Francesco Filelfo, the distinguished humanist of the Sforza court in Milan, confirms this perception. In 1465, he wrote Amiroutzes to recommend the architect Antonio Averlino, better known as Filarete, who was planning to travel to Constantinople.[31] In the event, Filarete never did go to Constantinople, but Filelfo's recommendation makes no sense unless he believed that Amiroutzes had the influence to facilitate Filarete's stay in the city. Similiarly, and again in 1465, it was on Amiroutzes' recommendation that, as he himself tells us, George of Trebizond dedicated to Mehmed II his Greek introduction to Ptolemy's

28. Both Greek chronicles (*Ecthesis chronica* [ed. Lambros, 46–47; ed. and trans. Philippides, 102–3]; *Historia politica* 130–31) accuse Alexander/Skender Bey of expropriating 180,000 aspers from the patriarchate and having Patriarch Nephon II expelled under Sultan Bayezid II (1488?).

29. Argyriou and Lagarrigue ("Georges Amiroutzès et son 'Dialogue sur la foi,'" 45) plausibly suggest that the two did not convert until early in the reign of Mehmed II's successor, Bayezid II (1481–1512), to keep their positions at court under the religiously more rigid ruler. Alexander/Skender Bey was a high financial officer, but it is not clear what official position Basil/Mehmed Bey held.

30. See Frangedaki, "On Fifteenth-Century Cryptochristianity," who calls attention to a document of John Kalekas as Patriarch John XIV (1334–47) condemning crypto-Christianity (*Acta et diplomata graeca* 1:183–84, no. LXXXII). The most recent editor of the letter, Stefec (*Die Briefe des Michael Apostoles*, 89–90 [text], 154 [comment]), dates the letter simply to sometime after 1461. Noiret (*Lettres inédites de Michel Apostolis*, 13, 46–47) places it in 1467 because it falls within a group of letters written that year or the year before.

31. See Filelfo, *Ep.* 3:1134–35: book 25, letter 49, dated (in Greek) 30 July 1465.

Almagest.[32] Amiroutzes knew Mehmed well enough to believe that he might be interested. Not surprisingly, therefore, the court historian Critobulus gave over a section of his *Histories* to explain how after the sultan had become interested in Ptolemy's *Geography*, he commanded Amiroutzes to prepare a world map and also an epitome that explained how to calculate distances. Both of those works Amiroutzes' son Basil translated into Arabic (perhaps Turkish is meant).[33] Earlier in the *Histories*, Critobulus explained how Amiroutzes entered the Sultan's entourage:

> **Of the philosopher George Amiroukis and how the Sultan received him and honored him.**
> Among the companions of the ruler of Trebizond [after the city had been captured] was a man named George Amiroukis, a great philosopher learned both in the studies of physics and dogmatics[34] and mathematics and geometry and the analogy of numbers, and also in the philosophy of the Peripatetics and Stoics. He was also full of encyclopedic knowledge, and was an orator and a poet as well.
>
> The Sultan learned about this man and sent for him. On getting well acquainted with his training and wisdom, through contact and conversation, he admired him more than anyone else.[35] He gave him a suitable position in his court and honored him with frequent audiences and conversations, questioning him on the teachings of the ancients and on philosophical problems and their discussion and solution. For the Sultan himself was one of the most acute philosophers.[36]

Until these dramatic events in the last decade of his life, Amiroutzes' fame, or, if one wishes, notoriety, rested on a completely different set of achievements. As

32. See Monfasani, *Collectanea Trapezuntiana*, 282, 283, 677.

33. See n. 9.

34. By "dogmatics," Critobulus apparently means medical knowledge; he used the same word listing the accomplishments of Mehmed's II's physician Iacopo da Gaeta (Ja'qūb-Pasha); see his *Histories* 4.5.4.

35. Riggs's translation "more than anyone else" for διαφερόντως is overly strong; something like "highly" or "immensely" would be fairer.

36. Critobulus, *Histories* 4.9.3, as translated by Riggs, 177.

we noted at the start, Amiroutzes was viewed as one of the most learned men of his day, enjoying the sobriquet "the Philosopher." Along with the famous Platonist George Gemistus Pletho and the Aristotelian and future patriarch George Scholarius, Amiroutzes was one of the three learned laymen whom the Greeks took with them when in late 1437 they sailed from Constantinople to the Council of Ferrara–Florence (1438–39).[37] In Florence, the chancellor of the city, Leonardo Bruni, addressed to Amiroutzes his treatise, written in Greek, on the constitution of Florence.[38] Unlike Pletho and Scholarius, however, Amiroutzes adhered to the union of the Greek and Latin churches proclaimed at the council. As we have seen, he was back in Italy a decade later, leading a delegation from Trebizond to Genoa in 1449, and when Trebizond fell in 1461, he held a high administrative position in the state, that of *protovestiarius* (though in the later rubric to *The Philosopher* he gave himself the different title of *logothetes*). But this status did not prevent him from becoming part of the human booty that the Turks claimed in the fall of Trebizond.

The strange thing about Amiroutzes is that despite his contemporary fame—a fame, it needs to be noted, that eventually brought him to the attention of Mehmed II—until quite recently we in fact have had precious little evidence of Amiroutzes as a philosopher. In 1906 Spyridon Lambros published a philosophical prayer of supplication to God by Amiroutzes,[39] but it would be more than another hundred years, in 2009, to be precise, before Caroline Macé and Peter Van Deun published a second philosophical piece by Amiroutzes, namely, a brief essay refuting the notion that there is one common intellect for all men.[40] Finally, in 2011, from the same manuscript that preserves *The Philosopher*, I published a group of fifteen philosophical tractates by Amiroutzes.[41] Apart from these writings, what we have from Amiroutzes are various poems, two erotic, five in praise of Mehmed II,[42] five letters (one to Bessarion,[43] three to

37. Monfasani, *George Amiroutzes the Philosopher*, 6–7.

38. See Moulakis, "Leonardo Bruni's Constitution of Florence."

39. "Γεωργίου Ἀμηρούτζη ἀνέκδοτος εὐχή," 51–55.

40. "L'intellect n'est pas commun."

41. Monfasani, *George Amiroutzes the Philosopher*.

42. Now edited by Janssens and Van Deun, "George Amiroutzes and His Poetical Oeuvre."

43. See Appendix I.

Theophanes of Media,[44] and one to Critobulus[45]) and a short geographical work that survives only in a Latin translation printed at Nuremberg in 1514, which we shall discuss shortly.[46]

II. *The Philosopher, or On Faith*

A. TEXTUAL HISTORY

The text has had a curious history. No Greek source mentions it. Yet in 1518 in Rome Zenobio Acciaiuoli, the head of the Vatican Library, translated it into Latin.[47] Then, despite copies having been made that still survive in the Vatican Library, not only the Latin translation, but also the Greek original disappeared from sight. Given its content, one can understand why Acciaiuoli would have wanted to translate the work, but how it made its way from Ottoman Constantinople to Rome is a mystery. The publication four years earlier, however, of a Latin translation of Amiroutzes' geographical opuscule for Mehmed II may provide a clue.

In his *Histories*, Critobulus describes the epitome of Ptolemy that Amiroutzes prepared for Mehmed II in the summer of 1465, translated "into Arabic" (Turkish?) by his son Basil, consisting of a map of the whole world laid out on a single large panel with all the seas, rivers, mountains, islands, and cities marked on it with an accompanying table of *canona*, *metra*, and *apostaseis* that allowed one by virtue of these coordinates to establish the distances between them.[48] The treatise of "Georgius Amirucius" published by Johannes Werner

44. First published by Papadopoulos-Kerameus, "Θεοφάνους Μηδείας καὶ Γεωργ. Ἀμηρούτση [sic]:᾿Επιστολαί," and then again by Spyridon and Eustratiades, *Catalogue of the Greek Manuscripts*, 412–16 (in both editions, letters 1, 4, 7, and 9 are from Theophanes to Amiroutzes, and letters 2, 6, and 8 are from Amiroutzes to Theophanes).

45. In the same two editions cited in the previous note, as letter 3.

46. See Monfasani, *Georges Amiroutzes the Philosopher*, 9–10, n. 23.

47. On Acciaiuoli, who was once a disciple of Girolamo Savonarola in Florence, see Monfasani, "'Lost' Final Part," for the relevant literature, to which should be added Daneloni, "Nuovi contributi su Zanobi Acciaiuoli," and Maiorino, "Il bibliotecario-archivista di Leone X."

48. *Histories* 5.10.6 (ed. Reinsch, 195.19–23): πᾶσαν τὴν τῆς οἰκουμένης περίοδον ἐν ἑνὶ πέπλῳ καὶ πίνακι γῆς καὶ θαλάσσης ὁμοῦ, ποταμούς τέ φημι καὶ λίμνας καὶ νήσους

(1468–1522) in 1514 as part of his volume containing his own translation of the first book of Ptolemy's *Geography* includes no map or epitome, but it does offer a method for establishing distances based on accompanying tables and it was clearly addressed to Mehmed II, explaining how the method it revealed would assist in military campaigns.[49] Werner explained that he received the text from Johannes Stabius (1460–1522), the humanist, geographer, and astronomer associated with the imperial court in Vienna.[50] Stabius provided Werner the text already rendered into Latin by an unnamed scholar. Werner himself did not know who Amiroutzes was, apart from the fact that he was a near contemporary. On Stabius's urging, however, he corrected errors in Amiroutzes' text and added an appendix to clarify and remove what he viewed as imprecisions in what Amiroutzes had to say. Given their interests, it is understandable that Werner and Stabius would seize upon Amiroutzes' scientific opuscule, just as Acciaiuoli did *The Philosopher*. The same manuscript that preserves the Greek text of *The Philosopher* also contains fifteen philosophical tractates by Amiroutzes in various states of completion that never attracted a translator. This was not the same manuscript used by Acciaiuoli since it does not identify the author of the dialogue while Acciaiuoli's copy did. Manuscripts of Amiroutzes' writings were clearly circulating in the Latin West by the early sixteenth century. Somehow after his death the papers that Amiroutzes left behind, or least copies of them, had made their way to the West. But how could Stabius in Vienna seemingly know of Amiroutzes' geographical opuscule well before Acciaiuoli learned of *The Philosopher* in Rome, unless Amiroutzes' writings entered the Latin world via Central Europe rather than Italy, which was the more common route for Greek manuscripts at the time? A major center of humanist activity beginning in the late fifteenth century, Vienna, especially under the leadership of Johannes Cuspinian (1473–1529), would have been very receptive to new Greek texts and manuscripts emanating from Constantinople.[51]

καὶ ὄρη καὶ πόλεις καὶ πάντα ἁπλῶς, παραδοὺς ἐν τούτῳ καὶ κανόνας καὶ μέτρα καὶ ἀποστάσεις καὶ τἄλλα πάντα εἰδέναι καλῶς.

49. See Appendix II.

50. On Werner, see Worstbrock, "Werner (Vernerus, Bernerus), Johannes"; on Stabius, see Grössing, "Stabius (Stöbere), Johannes."

51. See, for instance, how in 1514–16 Cuspinian arranged for the translation of books 16–17 of Diodorus Siculus from a manuscript in Vienna: Monfasani, "Diodorus

However Amiroutzes' writings arrived in the West, they soon disappeared from sight after the early sixteenth century. In his *De ecclesiae occidentalis atque orientalis perpetua consensione* of 1648, that indefatigable student of matters Byzantine, Leone Allacci, reported a work of Amiroutzes' criticizing the Council of Ferrara–Florence.[52] Unfortunately for Allacci, he had been duped. George Coressios, a contemporary anti-Latin polemicist and forger from Allacci's own native island of Chios, had fabricated this attack on the fifteenth-century council of union.[53] So not until the eighteenth century did an authentic work of Amiroutzes once again come to the fore. In 1745, as part of a graduate program at the University of Göttingen, Magnus Crusius (1697–1751) published a synopsis of Zenobio Acciaiuoli's translation, the *Dialogus de fide*, based on the translation he found in a manuscript in Paris. This manuscript is Bibliothèque nationale de France (= BnF), lat. 3395. The manuscript is special: it is an autograph; it also contains the translation twice over, first as a working copy with corrections and deletions, and then in fine copy. But while identifying Amiroutzes as the author of the dialogue, it fails to name the translator. In making the translation, Acciaiuoli had no need to provide this detail to himself. So in more recent times, when it was edited not once but twice, first by Argyriou and Lagarrigue in 1997, and then by de la Cruz Palma in 2000, it remained

Siculus," 75–77, 128–29, 133. On Cuspinian, see Stelzer, "Cuspinianus (Spieshaymer, Spieß-, -heimer), Johannes"; Stelzer notes Cuspinian's interest in cartography (535–36). On humanism in Vienna, see Strnad, "Die Rezeption von Humanismus."

52. *De ecclesiae occidentalis atque orientalis perpetua consensione*, col. 935.

53. See Gill, "Tractate about the Council of Florence"; for a similar case in which Coressios duped a modern scholar, see Monfasani, "Pletone, Bessarione e la processione dello Spirito Santo." I suspect that Coressios is still duping modern scholars. Janssens and Van Deun ("George Amiroutzes and His Poetical Oeuvre," 306) have promised to edit Amiroutzes' letter to one Michael Correses of Thessalonica found in the University of Illinois, Urbana (Pre-1650 MS 0002, ff. 186r–188v), which argues for the impermissibility of additions to the Creed. Not only the clear anti-Latin purpose of the letter, i.e., opposition to the *Filioque* clause, but the name of the addressee, and the fact that the texts immediately preceding it in the miscellaneous manuscripts have seventeenth-century dates (1656 and 1671), should give one pause; for a description, see C. G. Lowe, "Byzantine Manuscript"; for a reproduction, see https://hdl.handle.net/2027/uiuc.5192307, p. 11; see also Monfasani, *George Amiroutzes the Philosopher*, 5, n. 1.

anonymous.[54] It also suffered the loss of the last part of the dialogue (XLI–XLV), which makes up about a fifth of the whole, because the folios containing this last part had fallen out of BnF lat. 3395 since the time Crusius had seen it.[55]

Then came a series of serendipitous events. First, in 2004 *Speculum* asked me to review de la Cruz Palma's 2000 edition of Acciaiuoli's *Dialogus de fide*. Reading the text, I recalled having already seen it in the Vatican in 1970 or 1971 when a graduate student working on my dissertation.[56] Volume II (1977) of Paul Oskar Kristeller's *Iter Italicum* even reports three Vatican manuscripts of the work, including the excellent Vat. lat. 3469, prepared for Cardinal Gian Pietro Carafa, the future Pope Paul IV (1555–59).[57] Since in the colophon the anonymous translator of the Parisian manuscript declared that he completed the translation on "XII Juli 1518 in Oratorio S. Sylvestri Montis Caballini," one immediately knew that the translator was a Dominican, since S. Silvestro a Montecavallo in Rome was a Dominican monastery until the 1540s.[58] But the most prominent expert in Greek of the Dominicans at S. Silvestro was Zenobio Acciaiuoli, the librarian of the Vatican Library. A comparison of the hand of BnF lat. 3395 with signed autographs of Acciaiuoli confirmed that he was indeed the anonymous translator. The result was an article that appeared in 2006, publishing the supposed lost part of the dialogue and identifying Acciaiuoli as the translator.

54. Argyriou and Lagarrigue reproduced the fine copy of the translation found in BnF lat. 3395, ff. 83r–144r; de la Cruz Palma incorporated the working copy that follows in the manuscript, ff. 146r–176v, with its corrections and deletions, into his apparatus.

55. As explained in Monfasani, "'Lost' Final Part," 208, Acciaiuoli stopped transcribing the fine copy at 184.13 of de la Cruz Palma's edition, while the working copy, which was complete, stops at 182.2 of de la Cruz Palma's edition because the folios with the rest of the text in BnF lat. 3395 have dropped out.

56. See Monfasani, *George of Trebizond*, 131–32. I even rashly promised to edit the work (ibid., n. 98) and acquired a microfilm of MS Vat. lat. 3469 in 1983.

57. See Kristeller, *Iter Italicum*, 2:320 for Vat. lat. 3469, 2:335 for Vat. lat. 5619, and 2:345 for Vat. lat. 8603.

58. Argyriou and Lagarrigue, followed by de la Cruz Palma, were misled into thinking that the translator lived in a Theatine oratory by the mistaken explication of the colophon as "Rome, oratoire des Théatins, Montecavallo" in the modern Bibliothèque nationale de France; the Theatines, however, took over site in the 1540s. See Monfasani, "'Lost' Final Part," 199 and 203.

The second serendipitous event occurred three days after I had sent off the article.[59] One evening in August 2004, I was looking at a photocopy of pages of Graux and Martin's 1892 catalogue of Greek manuscripts in the cathedral library of Toledo, *Notices sommaires des manuscrits grecs d'Espagne et de Portugal*, because they had suggested that an anonymous text in one of the manuscripts might be ascribed to Theodore Gaza. They provided an *incipit*, and, having just sent off the article on Acciauoli's translation, I immediately recognized it as the beginning of the dialogue Acciauoli had translated. Amiroutzes' Greek text was lost no longer.

Cod. 96-37 of the Biblioteca Capitolare of Toledo (henceforth = **T**) is an extraordinary manuscript on multiple counts.[60] A miscellany of 312 folios, transcribed by two hands of the late fifteenth or early sixteenth century (distinguished in the apparatus as **T** and **T**^{1}),[61] it begins with a series of fifteen tractates of varying sizes by "the philosopher" (ff. 1r–90r). As the sobriquet would suggest and the contents of the tractates confirm, Amiroutzes is the author of these previously unknown works. I published these text in 2011.[62] Next comes *The Philosopher*, but without the identification of the author (ff. 94r–219v, and with a separate numeration, ff. 1r–126v). The remaining third of the manuscripts is very miscellaneous, with Isaac Argyrus's treatise on geodesy (was it also found among Amiroutzes' papers along with Amiroutzes' geographic opuscule on determining distances between points on a map?), Ps.-Justin's *Expositio rectae fidei*, Patriarch Peter of Antioch's letter to Michael Cerularius, and, most interestingly of all, a series of anonymous works on confession, the

59. Relying on memory, I give a mistaken time line in Monfasani, *George Amiroutzes the Philosopher*, 13. Retrieving my old emails, I now see that I received de la Cruz Palma's edition to review 20 November 2003; I send off on 13 August 2004 my article, "'Lost' Final Part"; and on 17 August 2004, I requested a microfilm of cod. 96-37 at the Biblioteca Capitolare of Toledo, which means that I made the discovery the evening before. I first saw the manuscript in situ on 21 February 2005.

60. For a full description, see Monfasani, *George Amiroutzes the Philosopher*, 18–23.

61. Mark Sosower believed the hands were sixteenth century, as I reported in *George Amiroutzes the Philosopher*, 14; but David Speranzi with *cautela necessaria* on the basis of sample images informs me that they could also be hands of the second half of the fifteenth century.

62. Accompanied by an English translation: Monfasani, *George Amiroutzes the Philosopher*, 56–199.

sacraments, the articles of the faith, and on the Holy Spirit, decidedly reflecting Latin influence. One of these opuscules (ff. 239v–247v) is in fact an anonymous translation of Thomas Aquinas's *Summa theologiae* 2-2.14.1, and some of the others may also be translations of Latin texts. So, overall, the creator of **T**, who is clearly the second hand in the manuscript (ff. 220r–306r), the corrector in the prior folios (i.e., T¹ in the apparatus of *The Philosopher*), and the person who wrote the mysterious ex-libris on f. 1r ("ἐκ τῶν τοῦ φρανχελλουκκίου"; Fra Angelluccio?), was a philo-Latin, if not in fact a Latin.[63] Since Amiroutzes is not named as the author of his tractates or of *The Philosopher*, the organizer of **T** compiled what is overwhelmingly a collection of anonymous unique or little known texts. How and why he did so are questions one would dearly like to be able to answer.

B. OUTLINE

Although not an especially long work, Amiroutzes' dialogue is surprisingly complex and subtle in its argument. So, before analyzing it, it would be best to outline its development:

(A. = Amiroutzes; M. = Mehmed II)

I.1–4. A. bemoans the fate of the Greeks, now slaves of the Turks, and explains (I.4.7–8) that the dialogue is a literary recreation of conversations he had with M. (note that at XV.1.1 A. refers to what he had said "yesterday"). M. lays down the parameters of the conversation, namely, that A. cannot say anything about Islam, but is free to say what he wishes about Christianity (I.4.4–5). The discussion will be based on "common conceptions" (I.4.6), as M. confirms (II.1.3). (Later on [X.1.2], M. demands scientific demonstration, and A. responds [XXI.11.3 and XXII.1.4] that matters such as these are not susceptible to scientific demonstration.)

II–III. M. raises the issue of the Incarnation. How can the necessary combine with what admits possibility? A. responds that the union of God and man involved no change in God since they did not share a common genus, just as the union of soul and body involves no change in soul since it does not share the same genus as body.

63. An interesting hint suggesting a philo-Latin Greek are the marginal annotations at XXI.10.2 (calling attention to Amiroutzes here following Latin logical usage) and XXXVII.3.3 (attributing the opinion expressed there to the Latins, Basil the Great, and Gregory of Nazianzus).

IV–V. M. asks: How can such a union take place without some form of modification? A. responds: Since God transcends nature, the Incarnation does not conform to natural processes. The divine remained unaltered just as light does when joined to the translucent, but human nature was elevated in the hypostatic union.

VI–VII. M. asks: How is it not blasphemy to say God entered the belly of a woman and was defiled by bloody substances? A. responds: Because of his infinite power God can be everywhere and in a particular place at the same time. It was not divine nature, but the man whom divine nature assumed that was defiled by bloody substances.

VIII–IX. M. asks: If God is everywhere, what was special about his being in Mary's belly? A. responds: He was not a fetus in Mary as he would have been in other women, because in Mary he was fulfilling an ineffable and unique act of the divine dispensation.

X–XI. M. observes: You are asserting absurdities unhinged from rational premises. A. answers: Geometric and physical proofs are not suitable to matters outside their genus, as is the case here. Here it suffices that the assertions do not contradict common notions. For truth cannot be in conflict with truth. Scientific premises treat universally occurring phenomena. But unique divine acts cannot be demonstrated by scientific principles or common notions.

XII–XIII. M. asks: So, from where do you draw your assumptions while deserting logic? The principles of all sciences are interrelated. A. responds: My assertions conform to what the prophets asserted, which are impossible to prove on the basis of logic and common opinions.

XIV–XV. M. comments: We think that the prophets agree with common notions, just as Avicenna said. A. responds: The First Principle began the procession of being *ex nihilo*, something that cannot be scientifically demonstrated from common notions. I hear that Avicenna thought the First Principle was responsible only for the First Mind, which was then the first in a series of creators (i.e., implicitly he contradicts Revelation). All the miracles God performed at different times cannot be proved on the basis of common notions. To the common people these miracles carry more conviction than do scientific demonstrations. Divine miracles and truth should be accepted as premises outside the realm of physics.

XVI–XVII. M. asks: How do pagans, Jews, Christians, and Muslims prove anything to each other on the basis of their own peculiar assumptions? Each have miracles and divine truths they believe in. We are back to Protagoras's dictum (i.e., uncertainty on whether the gods exist or not). A. responds: It is hard to prove the truth of these miracles since the visual evidence no longer exists, but we should try to do so on the basis of memory and written evidence and not cede the field to fraudsters.

XVIII–XIX. M. asks: But since you deny the law of the Hebrews, how can you make use of their prophets? A. responds: We honor the whole law of Moses and the prophets. Christ's law fulfills Moses's, the purpose of which the Hebrews misunderstand. For instance, Christ's law commands not only that we not commit adultery, but also that we not lust. Christ's law leads men to God not by threats but by admonition and demonstration of the truth.

XX–XXI. M. comments: You have corrupted the book of the prophets just as you have corrupted the Gospel to suit your views. So what good is your proof? A.: How can that be so if we accept the same text of the prophets as do the Hebrews? And how could the evangelists have corrupted the message of Christ if they were willing to publish so much that was shocking and unacceptable to the world rather than to seek to curry favor? If the apostles, ignorant fishermen, preached lies, would they have been willing to die even at the hands of their own kinsmen for what they knew were lies? How could the Gospels subsequently be corrupted when there are so many copies in circulation in so many different languages, and yet they all agree? Even the heretics when teaching their heresies never suggested that the Gospels were corrupt.

XXII–XXV. M. comments: All very unscientific, but if I concede all this for the sake of argument, why would God consent to an absurd deed such as becoming man to accomplish his goals? How does the omnipotent become impotent? A. responds: I am well aware that in this matter arguments of logical necessity and geometric exactness are impossible. God had no need of creation, but out of his goodness he made man the noblest creature and the reason for creation. Man, however, revolted against God's will and rendered vain the purpose of his being created. God sent the law, but those who obeyed it were small in number, were restricted to Palestine, and obeyed poorly. Again, out of goodness, God would not abandon man, and so the Word of God became man to unite virtue and right knowledge with human life. We assert that this was the only way to save man and that Jesus's divine nature remained completely unmixed with his human nature in a way we cannot imagine. Moses and the prophets educated only the Jews; Jesus came to save the whole world. It was a greater feat for God to have drawn back man to his true end by condescending to become man than to have created *ex nihilo* in the first place.

XXVI–XXVII. M. comments: Even if we grant the monstrosity of the Incarnation, the fact remains that Jesus failed. The largest nation, the Indians, are not Christians, and there are more Muslims than Christians. God is not this impotent. A. responds: God could not command conversion if he was to respect our free will. But Christian churches all over the world prove his success. Even you Muslims have not been able to destroy all of them (where you rule). And some Indians and Africans, namely, the Ethiopians, have accepted the Gospel. The real question is not about Jesus's supposed failure, but why there is evil if Providence exists. The followers of your prophet converted out of fear of death or slavery. But God wants conversion freely chosen. Otherwise what would have been the point of God giving us free will? Hence not everyone converts to the truth. If you say that this is a disgrace, you are blaming God. Anything compelled is not virtue.

XXVIII–XXXI. M. comments: Your childish arguments call for physical punishment rather than rebuttal. But tell me, which of the prophets said that God would become man? Be careful what you say since Jacob here (Mehmed's physician) was once a Hebrew and can read the Hebrew text on the spot. If you take offense at what I have just said, blame the translator. A. responds: If you do not wish to hear me out, I shall remain silent. In any case, different prophets prophesized different aspects of Christ; one his birth, another his suffering, another his resurrection, as in Genesis 49:8–10, where Jacob predicts that the expectation of the nations will come from Judah's thighs. And look at Psalm 44, where David predicts the Messiah.

XXXII–XXXVII. M. comments: I agree that the prophets predicted that Jesus would be the son of the Virgin Mary of the tribe of David, but not that he is God. For what David said applies to men as men. When David spoke of existing before the moon and the sun, he meant not Jesus, but the angels, since God would not create the imperfect before the perfect in the order of creation. Nor can anything caused be eternal. A. responds: Well argued, but eternal things can be caused. Noetic forms once created are eternal, but since the movement of the heavens is the measure of time, as Aristotle says, and since noetic forms exist in time, they did not precede the moon and the sun. In the case of things that occur in time, one particular thing follows another, but the First Cause does not work in time. So everything emanated from it together as an ordered whole without time. It is not right to group noetic forms (i.e., angels) with souls since the former are completely removed from matter while the latter are the forms of a body and live eternally after being released from the body. The Platonists believe that (preexistent) souls are born into this world so that God can punish them, which is unworthy of God. It would make the accidental prior to the essential, since man is an essence and this punishment accidental. Why is generation (birth) necessary if these forms preexist? But there is no problem if the soul is generated at the same time as the body. But what about predestination and divine foreknowledge? We consider predestination to be divine foreknowledge of what the predestined themselves choose. For God does not predestine by lottery or arbitrarily. Otherwise God's punishment of evildoers would have no justice to it. Lastly, since what potentially exists does not actually exist, Christ always actually existed and not merely potentially in divine foreknowledge. Therefore the prophets knew Christ was God, as when David speaks of the actions of Christ.

XXXVIII–XXXIX. M. comments: Everything you have said is refutable, but let me ask: Is God one or many? If many, you have fallen into intolerable error; if one, how do you explain your "father, son, and holy spirit"? A. responds: Christians believe in a God that is radically one. But God's essence is the substratum of his properties, and it is these properties that have brought abuse upon us. The rules of physics do not apply to God. God is both a mind and a noetic being. The Platonists say he is beyond mind. He is the one itself and beyond all predication, while mind is in some way below the one. But of necessity the First Principle is the best mind and knows itself and all that exists. As Aristotle says, God is the best mind. The Platonic position entails all sorts of absurdities. The only logical conclusion is that God as the best mind and first cause creates and orders all things to himself as their end. Knowing all things is, as Aristotle says, God knowing himself. But if God is always happy knowing himself, as Aristotle says, he must also will in order to choose this happiness. Nor does it make sense in thinking that God does not will. We thus have three things: mind, thought, and will. Mind we call Father, since thought proceeds from it; thought, Word; and will, Holy Spirit, because this is what the prophets called it and because he goes forth following the Word. But the three are one in substance. The three properties arise not from definitions but from the nature of their reality.

XL–XLI. M. comments: With your logic, you can equally say God is substance, goodness, truth, life, and many other things. Furthermore, it is not true that God is mind. For the divine is ineffable and nameless. If thought is a product of God as mind, it would be both a self-caused and a caused substance; and if not a substance, then it is an accident. You believe in imbecilities. A. responds: We affirm that God is substance, goodness, truth, life, and so on, but there is a difference: mind, thought, and will are distinct from each other and divide him. God is goodness, life, etc., but mind, thought, and will are in him. We grant that God is ineffable and ungraspable. What we predicate of him signifies only his actions. But recognizing inasmuch as God is the First Principle, the perfections of his creatures must be eminently and primordially his. For the things we predicate of the divine essence are taken from its works. Necessarily then something in itself, befitting God, corresponds to them. But mind thinking itself is not two substances, but one; the difference is a numerical one of relationship.

XLII–XLIII. M. comments: All this is just fancy words. Aristotle says that habit explains the retention of puerilities in law. But explain to me the resurrection of the dead. What kind of resurrected life do they have? A. responds: We often come to faith through the prophets and the Gospel. If the lives of the prophets and evangelists agree with their words, how can we doubt? Did not people in every land desert their ancestral worship for Christ through the agency of ignorant, poor nobodies persecuted by the Roman Emperors? I therefore consider myself blameless in adhering to what seems the truth, for which I am ready to die. We believe the resurrected life will not be like the present one. The resurrected life will not be one of animal sensation, and so we shall not need nourishment. It will be the life of the mind as we become immortal and God-like.

XLIV–XLV. M. comments: But then the resurrected body would be superfluous and mind would be pointless and without pleasure. A. responds: Your arguments do not reflect what we believe about the resurrected. We both believe that the resurrected do not dwell in their place of birth: the blessed are in heaven, the impious in hell. The vegetative soul does not exist in the afterlife, and therefore neither do its activities, and neither do motion and change, as the motion of the first heavenly sphere will disappear. The body will be the mind's luminous vehicle rather than its organ. In heaven, the mind enjoys the first truth and the body enjoys freedom from suffering and being eternal. The body of the wicked will not be glorious and it will pay the price for their wanton insolence. This is our faith, and we have not arrived at it through philosophy, but have demonstrated its consequences through philosophy.

C. STRUCTURE AND SETTING

As is apparent from the outline, Amiroutzes wrote a catechism, with Mehmed II asking the questions and Amiroutzes answering them. But rather than being purely a literary artifice, the catechetical structure probably approximates to a considerable degree how Mehmed conducted his conversations with Amiroutzes. They certainly discussed topics other than religion. As we have seen, Critobulus tells us that Mehmed "honored [Amiroutzes] with frequent audiences and conversations, questioning him on the teachings of the ancients and on philosophical problems and their discussion and solution."[64] Furthermore, Critobulus relates how Mehmed became interested in Ptolemy's *Geography* and how Amiroutzes prepared a world map, some sort of summary of the *Geography*, and a treatise on calculating distances between locations, which led to his instructing the Sultan on his new method.[65] So Amiroutzes' literary artifice involved limiting the dialogue to explaining Christian doctrine, though it is also probably the case that Mehmed and Amiroutzes had a series of conversations that focused exclusively on religion and that it was these discussions that Amiroutzes chose to put into literary form.

Mehmed II certainly wished to understand Christian beliefs. In the years immediately after the conquest he famously he held three discussions with Patriarch Gennadius II (George Scholarius) concerning Christian doctrine, which resulted in Scholarius summarizing the substance of his claims at the sultan's request in a treatise entitled *On the Sole Way for Man's Salvation*.[66] Finding this treatise overly verbose and challenging, the sultan then asked for a more concise summary. Scholarius complied with a second treatise, his *Confession of Faith*.[67] Christos Patrinelis points out that the sixteenth-century *Historia politica* records how Mehmed asked Patriarch Maxim II (1476–82) to write an exegesis of

64. See n. 36.

65. See n. 48.

66. George Scholarius, *Oeuvres complètes*, 3:434–52; see Jugie, "Écrits apologétiques," 295–98; Tinnefeld, "Georgios Gennadios Scholarios," 502, no. 49.

67. George Scholarius, *Oeuvres complètes*, 3:453–58; see Jugie, "Écrits apologétiques," 302–11; Tinnefeld, "Georgios Gennadios Scholarios," 502–3, no. 50.

the Christian creed.[68] The earlier sixteenth-century chronicle, the *Ecthesis chronica*, tells us that Mehmed always used to ask "about the doctrines of our faith," and when confronted with a miracle confirming the Orthodox doctrine on the condition of the corpses of excommunicated sinners, he came to believe "that the faith of the Christians was true."[69] Though we should take the last part of this report with a large grain of salt, it is therefore no surprise that Mehmed used Amiroutzes to satisfy his curiosity about Christianity. In fact, we have an extraordinary report of Mehmed's interest in Christianity from George of Hungary, a Christian captive who spent twenty years as a slave apparently in Bursa and, after gaining freedom, an indefinite amount of time in Constantinople:

> Thus the friars in Pera [the town opposite Constantinople on the Golden Horn] said that he entered their church and sat in the choir to watch the ceremonies and manner of liturgy. Thus they even celebrated mass in front of him as he wished and in the elevation [of the host] showed him a non-consecrated host, wishing to satisfy his curiosity without nevertheless casting pearls before swine [Matt. 7:6]. When he had a discussion with them about the law and ritual of Christians and had heard that bishops presided over their churches, he even wanted them for the consolation of Christians to bring forward some bishop upon whom he promised to bestow without stint his favor, aid, and all that was necessary for his station.[70]

What is surprising, however, is that a sultan would indulge in religious discussions with a Christian. Literary documentation of similar instances is hard to

68. Patrinelis, "Mehmed II the Conqueror," 353, citing *Historia politica* 47.21–48.7.

69. Ed. and trans. Philippides, 86–89; ed. Lambros, 35–38.

70. George of Hungary, *Tractatus de moribus, condictionibus et nequicia Turcorum* 224–26 (11a15–21), my translation of: *Unde fratres in Pera dixerunt eum intrasse ecclesiam eorum et sedisse in choro ad videndum cerimonias et modum officii. Unde etiam ipsi missam coram eo ipso sic volente celebraverunt et hostiam non consecratam in elevatione demonstraverunt, volentes eius cuiriositati satisfacere nec tamen margaritas porcis prodere. Qui etiam, dum cum eis de lege et ritu Christianorum colloquium habuisset et audisset, quod episcopi preessent ecclesiis, voluit, ut ad consolationem Christianorum aliquem episcopum adducerent; cui ad omnia suo statui necessaria promisit se favorem et auxilium sine defectu prestiturum.*

come by. Early on we have a brief letter of the monophysite (Jacobite) patriarch in Syria, John I, relating a discussion he had with the Muslim general Amir in 639,[71] the dialogue that the Melkite Syrian bishop of Harran, Theodore Abū Qurrah (c. 750–820/25), had with a high government official of Emesa,[72] and a substantial text written by the Nestorian patriarch Timothy I recreating the dialogue he had over a two-day period with Caliph Mahdi in Baghdad around 781.[73] But then there is nothing until we come to Amiroutzes, though Muslim rulers must have had such discussions at various places and times.[74] Scholarius's two treatises are accounts of Christian doctrine rather than of his discussions with the sultan.

Although he acted as a punctiliously orthodox Sunni in his public behavior, Mehmed II, in Franz Babinger's words, "in his private associations . . . had considerable sympathy for heretical ideas."[75] His contacts with Italian artists and humanists bespeak more than narrow cultural interests and taste.[76] Given the evidence of *The Philosopher*, I see no reason to doubt Critobulus' claim that

71. Nau, "Un colloque du patriarche Jean"; Newman, *Early Christian-Muslim Dialogue*, 1–55 (trans. E. Pietras). See also Suermann, "Copts and the Islam of the Seventh Century," 104–6; White and Hauser, *Monasteries of the Wadi 'n Natrûn*, 1:171–75.

72. See Khoury, *Les théologiens byzantins et l'Islam*, 83–95; PG 97:1491–1504.

73. Caspar, "Les versions arabes du dialogue," 107; Newman, *Early Christian-Muslim Dialogue*, 355–545; Swanson, "Folly to the Hunafā," 248–55.

74. One such religious discussion that took place rather near in time was that between Sultan Murad I (d. 1389) and Emperor John V Palaeologus (d. 1391), mentioned by Emperor Manuel II (d. 1425) in the second of his twenty-six dialogues with a Muslim scholar (1391); see Manuel II, *Dialogue with a Persian*, ed. Trapp, 17; ed. and trans. Khoury, 32; ed. and trans. Förstel, 42–43; and see also Balivet, "Le soufi et le basileus," 25. A somewhat similar case involves the discussions in the vicinity of Brusa in 1354 that the great leader of the hesychasts and archbishop of Thessalonica, Gregory Palamas, had with the grandson of the Turkish emir Orchan and then, by order of Orchan, with his "wise men," the *Chiones* (apparently Jewish converts to Islam); see Arnakis, "Gregory Palamas among the Turks"; Philippidis-Braat, "La captivité de Palamas chez les Turcs"; Sahas, "Captivity and Dialogue."

75. Babinger, *Mehmed the Conqueror*, 411.

76. See Babinger, "Maometto il Conquistatore"; idem, "Mehmed II., der Eroberer, und Italien"; idem, *Mehmed the Conqueror*, 377–38, 426 ("he boldly transgressed the Islamic prohibition of images"), 496–98, 504–7; idem, "Notes on Cyriac of Ancona"; Campbell and Chong, *Bellini and the East*, 66–97; Raby, "Mehmed the Conqueror's Greek Scriptorium"; idem, "Pride and Prejudice."

> [Mehmed] occupied himself with philosophy, such as that of the Arabs and Persians and Greeks, especially that translated into Arabic. He associated daily with the leaders and teachers among these, and had not a few of them around him and conversed with them. He held philosophical discussions with them about the principles of philosophy, particularly those of the Peripatetics and the Stoics.[77]

Critobulus's report suggests that Mehmed fancied himself as something of a philosophic savant. The numerous references to the rules of logic and science attributed to Mehmed in Amiroutzes' dialogue suggest the same, and a citation by Mehmed in the dialogue (XIV.1.2) of a text of Avicenna that Amiroutzes could not have known from Greek or Latin sources confirms that Mehmed had picked up some philosophic lore, even if in this case it was merely the assertion of Islam's superiority as a religion.

The verisimilitude of the dialogue extends beyond Mehmed II's seeming intellectual curiosity, his willingness to entertain arguments in defense of Christianity, and his familiarity with philosophy. The presence at the discussions of his well-known personal physician Iacopo da Gaeta (Jaʿqūb-Pasha after his conversion to Islam) could hardly be a fiction.[78] Nor can the brusque tone of Mehmed's questions and comments. Indeed, it is startling to see him excusing himself at one point in the dialogue (XXX.1.1) by blaming the translator for making him seem overly rude. I cannot imagine Amiroutzes inserting such an exchange into the dialogue if something similar had not in fact taken place. This exchange is also important as confirmation that Mehmed did not have any real facility in Greek.[79]

77. Critobulus, *Histories* 5.4, as translated by Riggs, 209.

78. See *The Philosopher* XXVIII.1.8–9. On Iacopo, who was killed by a mob in 1481 upon the death of Mehmed, see Babinger, "Jaʿqūb-Pascha, ein Leibarzt Mehmeds II"; Jacoby, "Un agent juif," 72, 75–77, 91–92; and Lewis, "Privilege Granted by Meḥmed II."

79. This was the conclusion of Patrinelis, "Mehmed II the Conqueror." I, for one, had once argued that Mehmed did know Greek on the basis of George of Trebizond's assertion in a letter he wrote in 1466 after returning from Constantinople; see Monfasani, *George of Trebizond*, 186, n. 34, and 359, which led Raby ("Mehmed the Conqueror's Greek Scriptorium," 24) to argue the same. But George actually never had a chance to talk to Mehmed when in Constantinople. I now suspect that he wrongly assumed that

We have no way of precisely dating the dialogue. Amiroutzes could not have written it before he had become securely ensconced in the sultan's entourage for an extended period of time. So its *terminus post quem* cannot be earlier than 1463. Its *terminus ante quem* is obviously Amiroutzes' death, ca. 1469. The dialogue has no proper conclusion. This suggests that Amiroutzes had not yet decided how to bring it to a close before he died, which in turn points to a date close to 1469.

While it is clear that Amiroutzes never really finished the dialogue, one may also ask why he began it in the first place. He is openly apologetic at the start for embarking on such a literary work when his people are suffering and laid so low. We have the answer, I believe, in his assertion towards the end of the dialogue (XLIII.1.21) of his willingness to suffer martyrdom rather than give up his faith. Amiroutzes could not but have been aware of the rumors that circulated about his apostatizing to Islam. The dialogue was in effect his answer to these rumors. I also think that Mehmed's questions about Christianity caused Amiroutzes to ruminate on how one justifies Christian doctrine to a nonbeliever. We do not have to believe that all the answers Amiroutzes provides in the dialogue are those he actually gave on the spot in talking with the sultan, but they certainly are the best answers he could think of when considering the issues afterward. Wishing to preserve his consideration of the matter, he put his ideas to paper in the form of a dialogue. *The Philosopher* is therefore Amiroutzes' *Apologia pro fide sua*.

D. ANALYSIS

As a defense of Christianity against Muslim criticism, the dialogue treats the traditionally contested topics of the Incarnation and the Trinity. But it does considerably more. To start, there is the one issue that runs through the dialogue from beginning to end, namely, the epistemological problem of finding a common ground upon which Christians and Muslims could productively debate rather than fruitlessly speak past each other. Early on, scripture, both Jewish and Christian, was assumed to provide this common ground, even if Muslims insisted that authentic scripture conformed to the indubitable

---

Mehmed knew Greek because Amiroutzes had told him that it would be acceptable for him to write his epitome of Ptolemy's *Almagest* in Greek for the sultan; see n. 32.

truth of the Koran. But as Sidney H. Griffith has succinctly put it, after a certain time "and certainly after the time of Ibn Taymiyyah (1269–1328), for the rest of the Middle Ages, Muslim authors seem to have lost interest in any possible authoritative or probative value in the texts of the scriptures of the Jews or Christians… Rather, the emphasis seems to have shifted in this period to demonstrating the untrustworthiness of the Bible."[80] In short, after a certain point the key Muslim tool for refuting Jewish and Christian arguments from scripture was *tahrīf*, that is, the accusation that Jews and Christians had falsified their scriptures either by textual corruption or misinterpretation.[81] How else could one explain the failure of either testament to prophesize or indicate in any way the coming of Muhammad, the supreme and final prophet?[82] How could Old Testament accounts about persons and events differ so much from what one reads in the Koran? How could the New Testament be so definitive about the crucifixion and death of Christ, something that the Koran denies?[83] This is not to speak of all the New Testament passages that suggest the divinity of Christ and the Christian Trinity.[84] Interestingly enough, the great Muslim philosopher Avicenna (980–1037) accepted the argument of Jews and Christians that they could not have altered the Hebrew Bible since it was already so widely diffused among diverse peoples already in conflict with each other before the coming of Muhammad.[85] Amiroutzes makes the same point (XXI.3), but then he goes on to make a similar argument for the New Testament, pointing out

80. Griffith, "Arguing from Scripture," 33. On Ibn Taymiyyah, see Michel, *Muslim Theologian's Response*, esp. 89–119, 210–40, on *taḥrīf*.

81. See Accad, "Corruption and/or Misinterpretation of the Bible"; Bouamama, *La littérature polémique musulmane*, 120–31; Di Matteo, "Il 'taḥrīf' od alterazione della Bibbia"; Gaudeul and Caspar, "Textes de la tradition musulmane concernant le taḥrîf"; Sirry, *Scriptural Polemics*, 100–32; Said Reynolds, "On the Qur'anic Accusation of Scriptural Falsification"; Toenies Keating, "Revisiting the Charge of *Taḥrīf*." Even a Muslim scholar such as Al-Biqāʿī who defended the veracity of the Hebrew Torah conceded a degree of corruption; see Saleh, "Fifteenth-Century Muslim Hebraist."

82. See Lazarus-Yafeh, *Intertwined Worlds*, 75–110.

83. See Ayoub, "Towards an Islamic Christology, II."

84. See Di Matteo, "Confutazione contro i cristiani"; idem, *La divinità di Cristo*.

85. Avicenna, *Epistola sulla vita futura* (trans. Lucchetta, 58): "E come potrebbe essere falsificato tutto un libro divulgato tra popolazioni innumerevoli, i cui paesi sono tra loro distanti, le cui mentalità sone diverse, poiché alcune sono Ebrei, altri Cristiani, ed [anzi] sono due popoli nemici tra loro?"; see also idem, *De Almahad*, 45r. For a Christian

that it was disseminated in many languages to different peoples, and that heretics and orthodox, though enemies, never accused each other of corrupting the text (XXI.21–22). He also adds as proof of the authenticity of the New Testament the fact that in condemning Jesus, the Jews confirmed that he claimed to be God (XXI.5.5–8); another proof is that the apostles preached a Gospel that showed them to have acted shamefully at times and Jesus himself to have evinced fear and weakness, things they would not have done if they were dissembling, least of all when certainly no one is willing to suffer and die (as they were) for what one knows to be lies, and when the severe moral transformation the apostles preached was the wrong way to curry favor among the elites as well as the masses (XXI.8, 12, 17–19).

Amiroutzes does appeal to the witness of the Old Testament in the dialogue (VII.4, XV.2, XIX.4–6 and 9, XXVII.17, XXXI), and at one point (XXI) he gives an extended defense of the authenticity of the Old and New Testaments (see also XIX.6–10). He even has Mehmed acknowledge the validity of arguments drawn from the Hebrew Bible (XXVIII) and then go on to argue against Amiroutzes about the correct interpretation of Psalm 71 (XXXII). But from the beginning Amiroutzes especially seeks rational grounds for defending Christian doctrine against Mehmed II's criticisms. Thus, at the start, he has Mehmed announce that "common notions" (*koinai ennoiai*) would be the criterion for judging each statement. "Common notions" have a long history in classical and patristic literature, and they remained popular as an argumentative tool for the Byzantines.[86] They were even used by Muslims in debate with Christians.[87] So it is not implausible to suppose that in his conversations with Amiroutzes Mehmed knew about common notions and agreed to base the discussions on them. But what is most interesting about Amiroutzes' utilization of common notions is his frank admission of their limitation as a means of proof in matters religious. What is beyond nature cannot be demonstrated by common notions or the rules of natural

enunciation of this argument, see early on Nicetas Byzantius, *Refutation of the Koran* 24; and in the Latin world, Ramón Martí, *De secta Machometi*, 58–60.

86. See Monfasani, *George Amiroutzes the Philosopher*, 28–29; Podskalsky, *Theologie und Philosophie in Byzanz*, 134–36, 152–53.

87. See Griffith, "Arguing from Scripture," 34, quoting the Christian Theodore Abū Qurrah (ca. 750–ca. 830), who has his Muslim opponent demand proof from common notions.

science and logic (see V.1–4, XI.1–2, XV.1.3, XXI.11.3, XXIII.1.4, XXXIX.1.8–20). One has to accept as true a premise that is beyond nature and common notions and then argue to the consequences of that premise. We may descry here the influence of some of the opening assertions of Thomas Aquinas's *Summa contra gentiles*.[88] Thomas's work had been translated into Greek by Demetrius Cydones a century earlier and was well known to Byzantine intellectuals.[89] But, as is true with Amiroutzes' philosophical tractates, proving the influence of Thomas on Amiroutzes is somewhat problematic given the absence of direct citation or quotation. Though there are other points of possible contact,[90] the clearest is Amiroutzes' knowledge of Avicenna in *The Philosopher*,[91] knowledge that he could only have gained from Thomas since Thomas's writings were the only ones translated into Greek that spoke of Avicenna.[92]

Whatever the influence of Thomas Aquinas on Amiroutzes' thinking on what could be the basis of proof in a dialogue with a Muslim interlocutor, Amiroutzes certainly agreed with Thomas on constantly citing Aristotle and criticizing Platonists in discussing theological issues.[93] Hence, he refutes Plato on the transmigration of souls (XXXVII.7–11 and XLV.2.30) and argues against the Neoplatonic notion of God as the One beyond being and mind (XXXIX.2.4–8). He even seems to have consciously taken Thomas's side in the scholastic debate on the priority of the mind to the will (XXXIX.14). Therefore, it is quite startling to see him, when discussing the soul's life after the death

88. Cf. *Summa contra gentiles* I.2.11b: *Unde necesse est ad naturalem rationem recurrere, cui omnes assentire coguntur. Quae tamen in rebus divinis deficiens est*; I.3.3: *nimiae stultitiae est homo si ea quae divinitus angelorum ministerio revelantur falsa esse suspicatur ex hoc quod ratione investigari non possunt*; I.5.30: *solum deum vere cognoscimus quando ipsum esse credimus supra omne id quod de deo cogitari ab homine possible est: eo quod naturalem hominis cognitionem divina substantia excedit, ut supra ostensum est.*

89. See Demetracopoulos, "Demetrius Cydones' Translation of Bernardus Guidonis' List"; Fyrigos, "Tomismo e antitomismo a Bisanzio"; Podskalsky, "Die Rezeption der thomistischen Theologie"; idem, *Theologie und Philosophie in Byzanz*, 173–230, passim.

90. See Monfasani, *George Amiroutzes the Philosopher*, 32–38.

91. See XV.1.5–7.

92. On translations of Latin scholastics into Greek, see Demetracopoulos, "Latin Philosophical Works."

93. One does not need to document Thomas's use of Aristotle, but for an inventory of his criticism of Platonism and Platonists, see Henle, *Saint Thomas and Platonism*.

of the body, appropriate without acknowledgment the Neoplatonic doctrine of the vehicle of the soul (ὄχημα) to explain the function of the resurrected body (XLV.2.23). This final section of the dialogue is extraordinary in another respect. To be sure, since patristic times, through the Middle Ages, Christians had given considerable thought to the resurrected body.[94] And Christians constantly criticized the carnality of the Muslim conception of paradise,[95] though, it should be pointed out, Avicenna argued that the sensual pleasures promised by the Koran are merely a device to explain the spiritual joys of heaven to the masses.[96] But rarely, if ever, did Christian anti-Muslim polemics enter into such philosophical deep water to answer, as does Amiroutzes, the charge that the Christian conception of the afterlife rendered the body superfluous. Another example of Amiroutzes' philosophical orientation is his treatment of free will. Not only does he make free will the basis of his rebuttal of Mehmed II's denial of Jesus's divinity (on the grounds that Jesus had failed to convert the world [XXVI–XXVII]), but he also takes pains to explain what divine providence is in terms that very much approximate the argument of Boethius in the *De consolatione philosophiae*, which had been translated into Greek by Maximus Planudes at the end of the thirteenth century (XXXVII.12–14).[97]

Thus, from his exploration of the dialectical validity of common notions and scientific demonstration to his discussion of the resurrected body, Amiroutzes consciously casts his dialogue as an exercise in philosophy. He signals this with the very title he gave his dialogue: *The Philosopher, or On Faith*. Even when he answers Mehmed II's critique of his interpretation of Psalm 71, he launches into lengthy philosophical analysis rather than biblical exegesis (XXXIII–XXXVII, with a brief textual exegesis at XXXVII.16–17). It is not coincidental that citations of Aristotle far exceed citations of scripture in the dialogue. As he says at the end, Christians do not come to a belief in the resurrection through

94. See Bynum, *Resurrection of the Body*; Greshake and Kremer, *Resurrectio mortuorum*; Michel, "Résurrection des morts"; and Pelikan, *The Shape of Death*.

95. See, for instance, Khoury, *Polémique byzantine contre l'Islam*, 300–14.

96. Avicenna, *De Almahad*, ff. 45r–50r; *Epistola sulla vita futura* 50–62. On Muslim refutation of Christian criticism here, see Fritsch, *Islam und Christentum im Mittelalter*, 136–38.

97. The fact that Theophanes of Media solicited Amiroutzes' opinion on his treatise on providence suggests that he had developed some sort of reputation as a thinker on the subject of free will and divine providence; see n. 44.

philosophy, but now, taking Christian belief as a premise, he himself is attempting to draw out the consequences of that belief through philosophy (XLIII.3). At the basis of Amiroutzes' whole approach is the axiom that premises can be neither contradictory nor irrational (XLIII.3.5–6). Amiroutzes never defines "irrational" in the dialogue, but he seems to mean that the irrational is whatever violates the rules of logic once a premise is accepted.

In a way it is not so odd that Amiroutzes waits until the last lines of the dialogue to enunciate its underlying principles. These last sentences are in fact a sort of conclusion answering the question raised at the start, namely, how one might prove the mysteries of the Christian faith to a Muslim. In that sense, these lines are a fitting conclusion. Since the dialogue as we have it is a polished literary work, we might take them as Amiroutzes' final choice on how to end the dialogue. Yet one still notices the lack of a passage that brings the work to an explicit end. So, though the work may have reached its intellectual conclusion in Amiroutzes' mind, I suspect that he never published it, and instead left it among his *Nachlass* because he never found before dying a propitious moment in his relationship with Mehmed II that would have allowed him to give the work a suitable ending.

III. The Text and Translation

Since the text and translation are based on a *codex unicus*, choosing between variant readings would not seem to be an issue. We have, however, Zenobio Acciaiuoli's sixteenth-century Latin translation, which was clearly based on a Greek exemplar different from **T**, since unlike **T**, it had a rubric identifying the author and giving the title of the dialogue. In Acciaiuoli's translation, the title runs as follows (as found in the edition of de la Cruz Palma):

> GEORGII AMERVZAE MAGNI TRAPEZVNTIS LOGOTHETAE DIALOGVS DE FIDE IN CHRISTVM HABITVS CVM REGE TVRCARVM. TITVLVS DIALOGI: PHILOSOPHVS VEL DE FIDE

The ending of the rubric in Acciaiuoli's translation assures us of the exact title of the dialogue as Amiroutztes intended it. The rest of the Latin rubric no doubt reflects what Acciaiuoli found in his Greek exemplar, but we cannot be sure of either the exact wording of the Greek or of the sequence of words in the Greek title. So I have accepted as the title in the Greek edition only Acciaiuoli's *Philosophus vel de fide*, retro-translated into Greek and placed between pointed brackets. The remainder of the Latin title I have rendered in the English translation as the subtitle of the dialogue without attempting a retro-translation in the facing Greek edition.

Fortunately, Acciaiuoli's exemplar otherwise seems not to have differed significantly from **T**. Acciaiuoli on occasion glossed when translating,[98] but his glosses are easily identifiable as such and do not suggest he had a fuller text in these passages. I have followed de la Cruz Palma's Roman numerals to mark the sequence of exchanges between Amiroutzes and Mehmed II (with Amiroutzes' introduction, when he is speaking in his own voice, marked as number "I") and Arabic numerals to mark paragraphs into which I have divided each speaker's response. I have also added a second set of Arabic numbers in a small font to mark the sentences and sometimes clauses within a paragraph. Maintaining de la Cruz Palma's Roman numerals makes it easy to compare his edition of Acciaiuoli's Latin translation with the Greek text.

Since we are dealing with a *codex unicus*, I have recorded in the margins of the edition of the Greek text the sequence of folio numbers in the manuscript. The text of the dialogue begins on f. 94r of the manuscript and has a double numeration until f. 96r (i.e., ff. 94–96 are also numbered ff. 1–3), but thereafter has only the second set of numbers peculiar to the dialogue alone, that is, ff. 1–126, until f. 126, which is also correctly numbered as f. 219 of the manuscript as a whole. I have placed the second set of folio numbers, 1–126, in the margins of the edition because it gives an accurate sense of the extent of the text at any given point and also because it is the only numeration in the manuscript for the whole length of the dialogue.

Since **T** is our only witness, I have maintained its orthography, accentuation, and word division save in the case of obvious error or of inconsistency (e.g., fluctuating between Ἰοῦδα and Ἰούδα). **T**'s orthography is quite good by modern standards, save that I regularly had to insert omitted iota subscripts. The

98. E.g., at I.5.1, he adds *falsam* when translating τῆς ἐκείνων θρησκείας as *illorum falsam religionem*.

accentuation of ἐστί does not always follow modern rules, but given the possibility that T reflects Amiroutzes' preferences, I have retained its accentuation.

One conspicuous difference between Acciaiuoli's Latin translation and the English rendering below is the verbal marker for Mehmed II's parts in the dialogue. Acciaiuoli writes *rex*, which would make one suppose that the Greek reads *basileus*, but Amiroutzes in fact consistently writes *kratōn* as the verbal marker for Mehmed. Amiroutzes does address Mehmed once in the dialogue as *basileus*,[99] but this one instance confirms that *kratōn* had a different significance for him than *basileus*. *Kratōn* can conceivably be translated as "conqueror," rather than the more common "master" or "ruler," in other words, as the Greek equivalent to the Turkish *fatih*, the sobriquet Mehmed received after taking Constantinople.[100] But did Amiroutzes understand *kratōn* in that way?[101] In his letter of 10 December 1461 to Bessarion, Amiroutzes first refers to Mehmed indifferently as *mega dunamenos*, *archōn*, or *basileus*, but then toward the end of the letter he twice prefers *kratōn*.[102] True, one may point to Amiroutzes' four poems in praise of Mehmed,[103] where he calls Mehmed *basileus* and *anax* numerous times, *autokratōr* twice,[104] and *archēgos* and even *khan* once;[105] but in poetry the needs of meter, euphony, and variety come into play in choosing sobriquets and titles. As already mentioned, Anthony Kaldellis considers the practice of referring to Mehmed as *kratōn* one of the signatures of the

99. *The Philosopher* XVII.1.1.

100. See Babinger, *Mehmed the Conqueror*, 94. My colleague, Dmitry Korobeynikov, reminds me that Mahmoud Pasha and Mehmed's secretary Tursun Beg produced a memoir entitled *Tarih-i Ebü'l Feth* ("History of the Conqueror"). See the summary translation and edition by Inalcik and Murphey: Tursun Beg, *History of Mehmed the Conqueror.*

101. Reinsch, "Reichsidee und Sprache," 331–32, has a useful discussion of the terms Amiroutzes used, even though *kratōn* is not mentioned.

102. See the Greek text in Appendix I.

103. The poems are edited in Janssens and Van Deun, "George Amiroutzes and His Poetrical Oeuvre," 314–18, as nos. I, II, III, and VII. All four had been previously edited. Reinsch ("Byzantinisches Herrscherlob") first edited poem VII and attributed it to Amiroutzes.

104. Poems II.15 and III.1 in Janssens and Van Deun, "George Amiroutzes and His Poetical Oeuvre."

105. Poem VII.20 for *archēgos* and III.2 for *khan* in Janssens and Van Deun, "George Amiroutzes and His Poetical Oeuvre."

knowledgeable Trapezuntine interpolator who introduced substantial passages into Laonicus Chalcocondyles' *Histories* in the later 1460s and who, Kaldellis suggests, was probably Amiroutzes. By that date Amiroutzes' sons doubtlessly had learned Turkish and would have been able to inform their father of Mehmed's sobriquet of *fatih*. Supporting this interpretation is the fact that at the very start of the dialogue (I.1.10), Amiroutzes uses the participle *kratōn* in the aorist plural (κρατήσαντες) to mean precisely "conquer" when recalling how the Macedonians conquered the Greeks. So a preferred but still merely variant term in referring to Mehmed in Amiroutzes' letter of 1461 could have gained a much more specific connotation in Amiroutzes' mind by the time he wrote the *The Philosopher* in the later 1460s. Consequently, though I cannot prove that Amiroutzes understood *ho kratōn* as meaning "The Conqueror," if he is in fact the interpolator of Chalcocondyles of the late 1460s, then such an understanding would explain the deliberate use of *kratōn* in the interpolations and in *The Philosopher*. This is why I have translated it as "conqueror" rather than as "ruler" or, as did Acciaiuoli, "king."

The Philosopher, or On Faith

TEXT AND TRANSLATION

<ΦΙΛΟΣΟΦΟΣ, Η ΠΕΡΙ ΠΙΣΤΕΩΣ>

I 1 1. Ἐμοὶ μὲν οὐκ ἐδόκει καιρὸν ἔχειν ἔτι περὶ λόγων συγγραφὴν ἀσχολεῖσθαι, 1r
τῆς μὲν ἀρχῆς τῶν Ἑλλήνων πανταχοῦ καθάπαξ ἀνῃρημένης, 2. τοῦ δὲ γένους
ὑπὸ τοῦ κακῶς πράττειν τῶν μὲν καλῶν καὶ τιμίων ὀλιγωροῦντος, περὶ δὲ τὰ
ἀναγκαῖα κατατεινομένου καὶ χαλεπῶς αὐτὰ ἀεὶ πορίζοντος. 3. ἀνόνητος γὰρ
‹οὐχ› ἧσσον δὴ ἐδόκει, μηδενὸς μήτ' ἐπαΐοντος μήτε προσέχειν ἀξιοῦντος.
4. πλὴν γὰρ ὀλίγων τῶν ἀπὸ τῆς προτέρας εὐδαιμονίας περιλελειμμένων, οἷς
μᾶλλον προσήκει τὰ οἰκεῖα πενθεῖν κακά, μάτην ἄν τις τοῖς λοιποῖς ἐνοχλείη.
5. μήτε συνιεῖσι μήτε σχολὴν ἄγουσι λόγων ἀκρο|άσει προσέχειν. 6. τότε μᾶλλον 1v
οὗ ἄν τις προνοούμενος οὐδὲν ἀπεικὸς ἐποίει περὶ λόγων τόκον σπουδάζων,
οὐδὲν χρηστότερον τῶν παρόντων ἐλπίζειν δίδωσι. 7. δέος μὲν οὖν μὴ καὶ
Σκυθίσαντες τελέως οὐδὲ Ἕλληνες ἔτι ὦσιν, ὃ πεπόνθασιν οἱ τὴν Ἀσίαν οἰκοῦν-
τες, 8. χαλεπῆς ἐκ πολλῶν χρόνων πεπειραμένοι δουλείας. οὕτω καθάπαξ

---

1 ΦΙΛΟΣΟΦΟΣ . . . ΠΙΣΤΕΩΣ] om. T; titulus ex translatione Latina Acciaiuoli **4–5** περὶ . . . πορίζοντος] in marg. add. T **6** οὐχ] supplevi || ἧσσον] ἥσσον T **11** οὐδὲν] in marg. iterat T[1] et έν in textu supra lin. scr.

THE PHILOSOPHER, OR ON FAITH

The Dialogue on Faith in Christ that George Amiroutzes, the Grand Logothete of Trebizond, Had with the Ruler of the Turks[1]

I 1 1. I did not think that the time was yet right for me to occupy myself with producing a work of literature, not with Greek rule utterly eradicated everywhere, 2. and the Greek people suffering so badly and paying little heed to higher and nobler pursuits because of the harsh conditions as they strain for the basic necessities of life and are invariably having a hard time obtaining them. 3. Such an endeavor seemed to me no less a fool's errand for the fact that there would be no one to praise it or even deign to pay any attention to it. 4. For apart from a few survivors of earlier happy days, who are themselves better served lamenting their own misfortune, one would pointlessly become a nuisance to everybody else. 5. People have neither the understanding nor the leisure to spend their time listening to works of literature. 6. In such circumstances, someone with literary ambitions would be acting all the more sensibly by anticipating this reaction and conceding that there is no hope of better things in the present situation. 7. We face the frightful prospect, then, that the Greeks will ultimately become Scythians, no longer remaining Greek, which is the fate suffered by those living in Asia.[2] 8. They have endured a harsh slavery for many years. Good

1. For the title and subtitle, see pp. 30–31.

2. This fear of the barbarization of the Greeks was already voiced by Emperor Theodore II Ducas Lascaris (r. 1254–58) in a letter to Nicephorus Blemmydes during the time when the capital of the Byzantine state had become Nicaea; see Lascaris, *Ep.* 8.15–20, for the choice between destruction or barbarization. Amiroutzes' contemporary, Cardinal Bessarion, shared the same fear; see two of his letters to Theodore Gaza (not to Michael Apostolis, as the editor, Mohler, supposed) after the fall of Constantinople in 1453: Mohler, *Kardinal Bessarion*, 3:479.20–21, for the fear of becoming no different from barbarians and slaves; 480.11–19, for the fear of the obliteration of the race and the statement that "we are the last of the Greeks" (ἔσχατοι τῶν Ἑλλήνων ἡμεῖς). Gennadius II (George Scholarius) voiced the same concerns in a patriarchal letter he published in 1454 shortly before his resignation from the office; see Angelou, "'*Who am I?*,'" 6; and George Scholarius, *Oeuvres complètes*, 4:220.9–11.

Ἕλληνας ἀπολέλοιπεν ἡ ἀγαθὴ τύχη. 9. καίτοι καὶ ἄλλοτε μέχρι δουλείας αὐτοῖς
ὑπῆρξε τὸ δυσπραγεῖν, καὶ οὐ νῦν πρῶτον αὐτοῦ πεπείραντες. 10. Μακεδόνες τε
γὰρ ἀλλόφυλοι πρῶτοι | τοῖς ὅπλοις κρατήσαντες κατηκόους αὐτοὺς ἐποίησαν, 2r
11. καὶ μετὰ ταῦτα Ῥωμαῖοι αὐτούς τε Μακεδόνας καὶ Ἕλληνας ὑπὸ τὴν αὐτὴν
τύχην ἤγαγον. 12. ἀλλὰ λόγων ὅμως οὐκ ἠμέλουν οὐδὲ φιλοσοφίας τότε,
τοὐναντίον μὲν οὖν. 13. παυσάμενοι τῆς πρὸς ἀλλήλους ὑπὲρ τῆς ἀρχῆς φιλονει-
κίας, εἰρήνης οὔσης, περὶ λόγους τὴν πᾶσαν σπουδὴν ἐποιήσαντο, 14. καὶ
ἤκμασέ γε τοὺς χρόνους τούτους ἐν Ἕλλησι φιλοσοφία.

2 1. Νῦν δὲ τὸ περιὸν τῆς τύχης, ᾗ κέχρηνται, καὶ τὴν ἐν τοῖς καλοῖς ἀφεῖλε
φιλοτιμίαν, πάντων ἀναγκαζομένων τὰ οἰκεῖα πενθεῖν | κακά. 2. οἱ μὲν γὰρ ψιλὸν 2v
μόνον τὸ τῆς δουλείας τοῖς Ἕλλησιν ἐπέθεσαν ὄνομα, τέως ἀφόρητον αὐτοῖς ὄν,
3. ἔργῳ δὲ τήν τε ἀρετὴν αὐτῶν καὶ τὴν σοφίαν αἰδούμενοι ἐλευθέρους καὶ
αὐτονόμους εἴων, 4. Ῥωμαῖοι δὲ οὕτως ἑάλωσαν τῶν προσόντων αὐτοῖς καλῶν
ὥστε καὶ μετεβάλλοντο, καὶ Ἕλληνες γενόμενοι τὴν τῆς οἰκουμένης ἀρχὴν
αὐτοῖς ἀπέλιπον. 5. νῦν δὲ τῷ φύσει πολεμίῳ τὸ τῆς θρησκείας διάφορον
προσγενόμενον χαλεπὴν δουλείαν αὐτοῖς ἐπήνεγκεν.

3 1. Οὔκουν ἐδόκει λόγων ἐπίδειξιν πρὸς οὕτω δυσπραγοῦντας ἀνθρώπους
ποιεῖσθαι, οὐδὲ σοφίας δόξαν θηρώμενον | εὐηθείας ἀπενέγκασθαι μᾶλλον. 3r

4 1. Ἐπεὶ δὲ μετὰ πάντας Ἕλληνας καὶ τῆς ἐμῆς πατρίδος ἑαλωκυίας δοῦλος
τοῦ τῶν Ῥωμαίων τε καὶ Ἑλλήνων ἐγενόμην δεσπότου, 2. ὁ δὲ λόγοις χαίρων καὶ
φιλοσοφίᾳ πυθόμενός τι περὶ ἐμοῦ εἰς λόγους ἦλθε, 3. καὶ ἀποδεξάμενος προσέ-

7 ἐποιήσαντο] γράφεται, ἐποιοῦντο in marg. scr. T[1] **18** ἀπενέγκασθαι] ἀπηνέγκασθαι corr. T

fortune has thus completely deserted the Greeks. 9. And yet, the misfortune that approaches slavery began for them at another time, and the present is not the first time they have tasted such misfortune. 10. For the Macedonians were the first foreign nation to conquer them by dint of arms and reduce them to a subject people. 11. Next, the Romans inflicted this very same misfortune on the Macedonians themselves and on the Greeks. 12. Nonetheless, people in those times did not lose interest in literature or philosophy. Quite the opposite, in fact. 13. With the rivalry among themselves for supremacy finally put to an end, nations lived in peace and poured all their energy into letters. 14. Amongst the Greeks, philosophy reached a pinnacle during those years.

2 1. Now, however, the surfeit of misfortune that the Greeks have experienced has deprived them of ambition for the finer things as they are all compelled to bewail their own suffering. 2. For the Romans imposed slavery upon the Greeks in name only, even if at the time the Greeks found the name intolerable. 3. In actual practice, however, the Romans were awed by the virtue and wisdom of the Greeks and allowed them to be free and autonomous. 4. The Romans were in effect captured by the fine things that came their way.[3] The result was that they changed; they themselves became Greeks and left their world empire to the Greeks. 5 Now, on the other hand, a difference of religion has conspired with the bellicose nature [of the Turks] to impose a harsh slavery upon the Greeks.

3 1. Hence I did not think it right to make a display of literary activity before a people suffering so grievously nor to pursue a reputation for wisdom at a time when it would be better to gain one for simple goodness.

4 1. After I had become, along with all the Greeks, the slave of the Despot of the Romans and Greeks through his conquest of my homeland,[4] 2. he heard something about me; and because he took delight in debates and in philosophy, he engaged me in discussions, 3. and having approved of me, he ordered that I be

3. As de la Cruz Palma notes (*Diálogo de la Fe*, 4), Acciaiuoli in his translation (*Romani autem ita capti sunt iis quae inesse Graecis ornamenta conspexerunt*) suggests Horace, *Ep.* 2.1.156–57 (*Graecia capta ferum uictorem cepit et artes intulit agresti Latio*).

4. On Amiroutzes' capture by the Turks at the fall of Trebizond, see pp. 2–9.

ταξεν ἀεὶ προσιέναι καὶ ἕπεσθαι ἐπὶ στρατιᾶς, καὶ πολλάκις μὲν ἐπὶ φιλοσοφίᾳ
συνεγένετο, 4. οὐδὲν δὲ ἧττον καὶ ἐπὶ τῇ τῆς δόξης διαφορᾷ, ἐν οἷς ἡ ἡμετέρα
μόνον ἐξητάζετο πίστις, εἰ συμβαίνει τοῖς κοινοῖς λογισμοῖς. 5. περὶ δὲ τῆς
ἐκείνου οὐδὲ με|μνῆσθαι συνεχωρεῖτο, καὶ πολλοὶ μὲν ὑπ᾽ ἐκείνου καὶ οὐδὲ 3v
ἀγεννεῖς ἔνιοι προετάθησαν λόγοι. 6. πολλοὶ δὲ αὖ ὑπ᾽ ἐμοῦ ἐλέγχοντος, μὲν τὰ
ἐπαγόμενα δεικνοῦντος, δὲ τὰ ἡμῖν δοκοῦντα οὐδὲ ταῖς κοιναῖς ἐννοίαις
μαχόμενα. 7. ἔδοξέ μοι αὐτὰ ταῦτα τὰ κατὰ διαφόρους συνουσίας εἰρημένα
συνθέντα ἐκδοῦναι, 8. ὅπως ἔχωσιν οἱ εὐσεβεῖς πρὸς τοὺς ἀντιπίπτοντας λόγους
καλῶς ἵστασθαι καὶ μὴ ἧττον ἡ ἀλήθεια τοῦ ψεύδους φέρηται.

5 1. Κατὰ μὲν γὰρ τῆς ἐκείνων θρησκείας πολλοὶ συνέγραψαν καὶ οὐδὲ ἔδει
προσθεῖναι, 2. πρὸς δὲ τὰ νῦν κατὰ τῆς ἡμετέρας δόξης ἐπαγόμενα | οὐδεὶς 4r

---

5 ἀγεννεῖς] ἀγενεῖς T **8** συνθέντα] ad συντεθέντα perperam mut. T^1

in constant attendance and follow in the train of the army,[5] as he often entered into conversation with me on philosophy.[6] 4. Nonetheless, wherever a difference in belief was at issue, only our faith was to be examined and only if the examination conformed to common reasoning.[7] 5. As far as his own faith was concerned, however, no reference to it would be permitted. He advanced many arguments, some of which were anything but ignoble. 6. I too, in turn, ventured many arguments in rebuttal, offering rational inferences and plausibilities not in conflict with common conceptions. 7. It seemed worthwhile to me to publish in synthetic form what we said in the course of these different conversations 8. so that the pious might effectively hold their own against contrary arguments and that the truth to no less a degree might win out over falsehood.

5 1. Inasmuch as many have written against the religion of the Muslims, there was no need for me to add to their critiques.[8] 2. But no one is speaking with

5. It is impossible to say to which campaigns Amiroutzes is referring. Mehmed II campaigned in the Balkans each summer between 1462 and 1464 and then again between 1466 and 1468. He also campaigned against Lesbos in 1462. See Babinger, *Mehmed the Conqueror*, 203–71. Amiroutzes may have already been dead when Mehmed attacked Negroponte in 1470.

6. See XV.1.1 for a reference to a discussion that Amiroutzes and Mehmed II had "yesterday."

7. The use of "common notions" is a mainstay of Amiroutzes' argumentative arsenal, much used in the dialogue, especially in its early sections (see I.4.6, II.2.5, II. 3.1, VI.1.5, VII.4.2, XI.2.6, XIV.1.1–2, XV.1.3, XV.1.8, XVI.1.5, XVI.1.8, XXXVII.13.2, XXXIX.13.1, and XLI.4.10) and is just as frequently employed in his tractates. "Common notions" is something one finds widely cited in Greek and Byzantine philosophy and theology into the fifteenth century (see Monfasani, *George Amiroutzes the Philosopher*, 28–29). But it also reflects a Muslim demand; Griffith ("Arguing from Scripture," 34) quotes the ninth-century Christian apologist Theodore Abū Qurrah (ca. 755–830), who explained that his Muslim adversary made the following demand: "Persuade me not from your Isaiah or Matthew, for whom I have not the slightest regard, but from compelling, acknowledged, common notions." But Amiroutzes recognized the limitations of common notions; see XI.2.6–8, after which he has the Conqueror challenge him on the criterion of truth and the danger of departing from common notions and universal principles (XII.1.1–12, XIV.1.1–2, XVI.1.1–8). Amiroutzes then argues (XV.1.1–4.5, XVII.1.1–8, XXIII.1.1–5) that common notions cannot explain what is beyond nature, i.e., the supernatural working of the divine.

8. Nor in his conversations with Mehmed II was he permitted to voice any criticism of Islam, as he himself admitts in I.4.5.

ἀποδεικτικῶς εἶπεν, οὐδὲ ἐκ τῶν ἀρχῶν ὧν προσήκει. 3. οὐ γὰρ ὁμοίως ἀποδεικτέον πρός τε τοὺς ὁμοδόξους διαλεγόμενον καὶ πρὸς τοὺς διαφερομένους, 4. ἀλλ᾽ ἐκ τῶν ἑκάστῳ δοκούντων τόν γε ὡς δεῖ ἀποδεικνύντα τοὺς λόγους ἀνάγκη προάγειν.

6 1. Διὰ ταῦτα τοὺς λόγους τούτους συνεθέμην, οὕς τε ἐκεῖνος εἶπεν ἐπὶ τῆς οἰκείας ἰσχύος καὶ οὓς αὖ πρὸς τούτους ἐγώ. 2. ἐλέχθησαν δὲ οὐκ ἐν μιᾷ συνουσίᾳ, ἀλλ᾽ ἐν πλείοσιν. 3. ἐπειδὴ τοίνυν ἔμελλε περὶ τοιούτων ἐρεῖν, θαρρεῖν κελεύσας καὶ προειπὼν περὶ ὧν εἰπεῖν ἐβούλετο, | 4. ἀπὸ τοιούτου λόγου τὴν 4v ἀρχὴν ἐποιήσατο.

II 1 1. **Ὁ Κρατῶν.** Ὁ θεός, ἔφη, ἐξ ἀνάγκης ἔστιν, ὅτι μὴ ἐνδέχεται ἄλλως ἔχειν, ὡς Ἀριστοτέλης ἐν τοῖς Μετὰ τὰ Φυσικὰ δείκνυσι. 2. τὸ δὲ ἐξ ἀνάγκης ὂν οὔτε μεταβάλλειν ἐνδέχεται οὔτε μὴν ὕλῃ συνῆφθαι. 3. διότι τὸ μεταβάλλον ἅπαν ἔστι δυνάμει πρὸς ὃ μεταβάλλει, 4. τὸ δὲ δυνάμει ἐνδέχεται ἄλλως ἔχειν «ἢ ἁπλῶς ἢ τοῦτο αὐτὸ ὃ λέγεται» δυνάμει, ὅπερ ἀντίκειται τῷ λόγῳ τοῦ ἀναγκαίου. 5. ὃ τοίνυν ἔστιν ἐξ ἀνάγκης οὐ μεταβάλλει, ἀλλ᾽ οὐδὲ τῇ ὕλῃ δυνατὸν ἑνωθῆναι. 6. διότι ἡ ὕλη ἀρχή ἐστι τοῦ ἐνδεχομένου, τὸ δὲ ἀναγκαῖον οὐ δύναται συνελθεῖν τῷ | ἐνδεχομένῳ. 7. οὐκ ἄρα τὸ ἀναγκαῖον δύναται τῇ ὕλῃ 5r συνῆφθαι.

2 1. Πῶς οὖν ὑμεῖς οἱ Χριστιανοί φατε ὅτι ὁ θεὸς γέγονεν ἄνθρωπος; οὐ γὰρ ἐνδέχεται μὴ μεταβάλλειν γινόμενον ἄνθρωπον ἢ μὴ συνελθεῖν τῷ ἐνδεχομένῳ.

---

6 αὖ] supra lin. scr. T **10** Ὁ Κρατῶν] in marg. T **12** μεταβάλλειν] μετὰ βάλλειν T **19** οὖν] supra lin. scr. T/T[1] || ὑμεῖς] ἡμεῖς T || Χριστιανοί φατε] Χριστιανοί φατὲ T, et similiter postea, ut si φημί non est encliticum

rigorous logic in response to the rational arguments that the Muslims today adduce against our beliefs, nor is there anyone speaking on the basis of the principles proper to the debate. 3. For in discussions with those of a different belief we should not seek to make demonstrations like those we make in discussions with those who share our belief. 4. Rather, one must necessarily put forward arguments, as is required, that make a case on the basis of what is plausible to each party in the debate.[9]

6 1. Consequently, I have synthesized the arguments he made in support of his position and those I made in turn responding to them. 2. These things were said not in a single conversation, but in the course of numerous conversations. 3. Whenever, therefore, he felt like talking about these matters, he bade me to be bold and then announced the subject about which he wanted to speak. 4. He used to begin discussions with an argument such as the following.

II 1 1. **The Conqueror.**[10] God, he said, necessarily exists, since it is not possible for things to be otherwise, as Aristotle shows in the *Metaphysics*.[11] 2. What, however, necessarily exists can neither accept change nor, indeed, be joined to matter. 3. Hence everything that changes is potentially that to which it changes. 4. What potentially can be otherwise "either absolutely or in the particular sense in which it is said"[12] potentially <can change>. This is the opposite of the definition of what is necessary. 5. What exists necessarily, therefore, does not change, but neither does it have the potential to be united with matter. 6. Hence matter is the principle of what admits possibility. But what is necessary cannot combine with what admits possibility. 7. What is necessary therefore cannot be joined to matter.

2 1. How, then, can you Christians say that God became man? It is not possible for God, if he became man, not to change or not to join with what

9. In II.3.1–2, Amiroutzes has Mehmed II make explicit that common notions constitute the first principles of the discussion. The origin of Amiroutzes' position goes back to Aristotle's *Topics* 1.100a29–b23, where *endoxa* ("generally accepted opinions," in the translation of E. M. Forster) are explained. Cf. *Metaphysics*, 11.1061b19: "even the mathematician uses the common axioms (*tois koinois*)" (trans. Tredennick).

10. For translating ὁ κρατῶν as "the conqueror," cf. κρατήσαντες in I.1.10, and see pp. 32–33.

11. This seems to be a generic reference to book 12 of the *Metaphysics*.

12. Aristotle, *Metaphysics* 9.1050b15–16 (trans. Tredennick).

2. ὅπερ ἔτι καὶ μᾶλλον ἐστὶν ἀδύνατον ὅτι δὲ οὐκ ἐνδέχεται μὴ μεταβάλλειν γινόμενον ἄνθρωπον. 3. δῆλον ὅτι μὴ ἀεὶ τοῦτο ἦν, ἀλλά ποτε ἐπὶ τοῦτο ἦλθεν. ὃ δὲ μὴ ἀεὶ ὂν ὁ ὕστερόν ἐστι γέγονε. 4. τὸ δὲ γεγονὸς ἀνάγκη μεταβάλλειν τοὐλάχιστον ἐξ οὗ [μὴ] ἦν εἰς ὃ γέγονεν. 5. ἀλλὰ τοῦτο ἀδύνατον λέγειν ἐπὶ θεοῦ. μάχεται γὰρ καὶ ταῖς κοιναῖς ἐννοίαις, | καὶ ἀνάξιον ἄλλως ἐστὶν αὐτοῦ. 5v

3 1. Εἰ μὲν οὖν καὶ τὰ μαχόμενα τοῖς κοινοῖς λογισμοῖς προσίεσθε, οὐ κἂν εἴη πρὸς ὑμᾶς διαλέγεσθαι, πάσης ἀρχῆς ἀνῃρημένης. 2. εἰ δὲ τοῦτο, γοῦν σωφρονοῦντες οὐ προσίεσθε. θαυμάζοιμ᾽ ἂν εἴ τι πρὸς τὰ εἰρημένα λέγειν ἔχοιτε.

III 1 1. **Ὁ Φιλόσοφος**. Ὅτι μὲν ὁ θεὸς ἐξ ἀνάγκης ἐστίν, ἔφην ἐγώ, καὶ μεταβολὴν ἡ τοιαύτη φύσις οὐδεμίαν ἐπιδέχεται, οὐδεὶς ἀντερεῖ. 2. τὸ δὲ ἐπαγόμενον ἀρνούμεθα, εἰ γέγονεν ἄνθρωπος, μετέβαλλεν. 3. τοῦτο γὰρ οὔτε αὐτοί φαμεν οὔτε οἷς λέγομεν ἕπεται. δίχα γὰρ τροπῆς ἢ ἀλλοιώσεως ἢ ὅλως μεταβολῆς ὁ τοῦ θεοῦ λόγος | γεγόνεν ἄνθρωπος. 4. οὐ γάρ φαμεν ἄνθρωπον γενέσθαι 6r ἀποβαλόντα τὴν ἀίδιον φύσιν, ἀλλ᾽ ἐκείνης ἀκινήτου μενούσης ἐν τῷ οἰκείῳ ὕψει τὴν ἄρρητον ταύτην οἰκονομίαν γενέσθαι. 5. ὅτι δὲ οὐκ ἀδύνατον ἄνευ μεταβολῆς οἰκείας τοῦτο τὸν θεὸν δυνηθῆναι πολλαχόθεν δῆλον. 6. ἐκεῖνα γὰρ μεταβάλλει τῶν εἴς τινος ὑπόστασιν συνιόντων ὅσα ἑνός ἐστιν γένους καὶ τῆς αὐτῆς ὕλης κοινωνεῖ, 7. καθάπερ τά τε στοιχεῖα καὶ πάντα ἁπλῶς τὰ σώματα συνιόντα ἐπὶ τῷ ἕν τι εἶδος ὑποστῆσαι. 8. ἐπεὶ γὰρ τῆς αὐτῆς ὕλης κοινωνεῖ, εἰκότως τά γε τοιαῦτα | καὶ ποιεῖ καὶ πάσχει εἰς ἄλληλα. 9. ὅσα δὲ μηδενὸς 6v γένους κοινωνεῖ μήτε ὕλην ἔχει συνιόντα εἴς τινος ὑπόστασιν, οὐ μεταβάλλει. 10. τὸ γὰρ εἶδος, καὶ ᾧ τι ἁπλῶς καὶ ᾧ τοιόνδε ἢ τοσόνδε ἤ τι ἄλλο τοιοῦτον γίνεται, 11. οὐ μεταβάλλει ἐν τῇ τῆς ὕλης ἑνώσει, ὡς Ἀριστοτέλης δείκνυσιν ἐν τῷ ὀγδόῳ τῶν Μετὰ τὰ Φυσικά. 12. εἰ γὰρ μεταβάλλει, ἀνάγκη σύνθετον εἶναι,

1 καὶ] supra lin. scr. T **3** ὁ] supra lin. scr. T/T^1 **4** μὴ] seclusi (v. III.4.2 infra) **9** Ὁ Φιλόσοφος] in marg. T **14** ἀκινήτου] ἀκένώτου T **16** ἐκεῖνα γὰρ] ἐκεῖνα γὰρ ἐκεῖνα T **17** μεταβάλλει] μεταβάλλειν corr. T/T^1 || εἴς τινος] ad εἴ τινος mut. T^1 sed usus auctoris esse videtur (v. III.1.9 infra) **19** εἶδος] τὸ ante in marg. perperam add. T^1 **22** ἢ] supra lin. scr. T, deleto aliquo **24** τῷ] supra lin. scr. T

admits possibility. 2. This is all the more impossible because he cannot but change in the very act of becoming man. 3. Clearly he was not always that, but at a certain moment turned into that. What is not eternal becomes the last thing it is. 4. What has become, however, necessarily changes, at the very least from what it was into what it has become. 5. But that is impossible to say about God; it contradicts common conceptions and it is otherwise unworthy of him.

3 1. If, then, you propose things that contradict common reasoning, we shall have nothing further to discuss with you, since you will have eliminated the whole principle of our discussion. 2. If this is the case, certainly as an intelligent person, you do not believe such things. I would be amazed if you had anything to say in response to what I have just said.

III 1 1. **The Philosopher.** I said: No one denies that God necessarily exists and that as such his nature does not admit a single change. 2. We deny, however, the inference that if he became man, he changed. 3. For neither do we ourselves say that God changed nor does it follow from what we say. The Word of God became man without change, alteration, or any sort of transformation, 4. and we do not say he became man and discarded his eternal nature, but that this ineffable dispensation took place with the divine nature remaining undisturbed in its own majesty. 5. On multiple grounds it is clear that God can do this without any change in himself. 6. For those things that belong to a single genus and share the same matter change when they coalesce in the subsistence of something, 7. just as do the elements and just as do absolutely all bodies that coalesce in the subsistence of some single form. 8. When such things share the same matter, they plausibly affect and are affected by each other. 9. On the other hand, things that share no common genus and that do not have matter that coalesces into the subsistence of something do not change. 10. For form, both that by which something comes to be in an absolute sense or that by which something comes to be of such a nature, such a size, or some such something or another, 11. does not change in its union with matter, as Aristotle shows in the eighth book of the *Metaphysics*.[13] 12. For if a thing does change, it necessarily is a

13. Uncertain reference. De la Cruz Palma (Amiroutzes, *Diálogo de la Fe*, 12) cites *Metaphysics* 8.1042b3–6 and 1044b21–29, but the former is not applicable and the latter weakly so; more apt, but not perfect, would be the discussion of the Ideas and Forms in book 8, especially 1038b10–34 and 1039b20–1040a7.

καὶ τὸ μὲν αὐτοῦ ὕλην, τὸ δὲ εἶδος εἶναι. 13. εἰ μὲν οὖν καὶ τοῦτο τὸ εἶδος σύνθετον εἴη, εἰς ἄπειρον πρόεισιν. εἰ δὲ ἁπλοῦν, δῆλον ὅτι ἑνοῦται τῇ ὕλῃ δίχα μεταβολῆς.

2 1. Δηλοῖ δὲ | τοῦτο γε οὐδὲν ἧττον καὶ ἡ λογικὴ ψυχή. καὶ γὰρ αὕτη ἑνοῦται 7r
τῷ σώματι δίχα μεταβολῆς τῆς οἰκείας οὐσίας. 2. οὐ γὰρ ἀποβάλλει τὴν αὐτῆς φύσιν ἐν τῇ τοῦ σώματος ἑνώσει, ἀλλὰ τὴν ἐνέργειαν μεταβάλλει μόνον ὅτι μετὰ φαντασίας θεωρεῖ. 3. καὶ τοῦτο δέ, ὡς ἔνι μάλιστα, προϊοῦσα καταλείπει· 4. καὶ χωριστὴν πειρᾶται τὴν ἐνέργειαν ἔχειν καθάπερ καὶ τὴν οὐσίαν.

3 1. Τὰ μηδενὸς ἄρα γένους ᾧ συνέρχονται κοινωνοῦντα μήτε ὕλην ἔχοντα συνιόντα, ᾗπερ εἴρηται, οὐ μεταβάλλει. 2. ὁ δὲ θεὸς οὐδενὶ τοῦ αὐτοῦ γένους
κοινωνεῖ. οὐδαμῶς τε ἔχει ὕλην, | ὥς ἐστιν ἀφ᾽ ἑαυτοῦ φανερόν. 3. οὐκ ἄρα 7v
μεταβάλλει γινόμενος ἐν ὕλῃ. εἰ γὰρ τὸ εἶδος, ὅ ἐστιν ἀρχὴ ἐν τῷ συνθέτῳ καὶ οὐδὲ ἄνευ ὑποκειμένου ἅπαν ὑποστῆναι δυνάμενον, 4. οὐ μεταβάλλει τῇ ὕλῃ συνιὸν εἰς τινὸς ὑπόστασιν, πῶς ἂν ἐκεῖνο μεταβάλλοι ὃ μὴ μόνον ἐστὶ καθ᾽ αὑτὸ ὑφεστώς, 5. ἀλλὰ καὶ παντὸς τοῦ εἶναι ἀρχὴν καὶ ὃ αὐτό ἐστι τὸ εἶναι αὐτοῦ; 6. ὅ γε μὴ δὲ ὡς εἶδος ἡνώθη τῷ ἀνθρώπῳ, ἀλλά τινα τρόπον ἕτερον ἄληπτον ἡμῖν, τῷ δὲ θεῷ μόνον γνώριμον, 7. ὅτι μὲν οὖν οὐκ ἀδύνατον ἄνευ
μεταβολῆς οἰκείας τὸν τοῦ θεοῦ λόγον ἀνθρωπίνην φύσιν ἀναλαβεῖν φανερόν. | 8r

4 1. Τὰς δὲ προτάσεις αἷς τοὐναντίον ἐδείκνυτο λύειν οὐ χαλεπόν. ἐλέγετο τοίνυν ὡς «ὃ μὴ ἀεὶ ὂν ὃ ὕστερόν ἐστι γέγονε»· 2. «τὸ δὲ γεγονὸς ἀνάγκη μεταβάλλειν τοὐλάχιστον ἐξ οὗ ἦν εἰς ὃ γέγονε». 3. τοῦτο δὲ ἐγώ φημι μήτε ἀληθὲς καθ᾽ αὑτὸ εἶναι μήτε οἷς προὔργου τίθεσθαι συμβαίνειν.

5 1. Πρῶτον δὲ καθ᾽ αὑτὸ σκεπτέον δυοῖν τοίνυν ὄντοιν ἐν σχέσει τινί. 2. εἰ

---

9 μηδενὸς] μη- supra lin. scr. T || ᾧ] οἷς T **11** ἔχει] ἔχειν corr. T/T^{1} **20** ὃ^{2}] in marg. add. T sed perperam post ὕστερον **22** προὔργου] -ρ^{2}- supra lin. scr. T^{1} (v. III.6.2 infra) **23** τοίνυν] τοί νυν T

composite, and is both its matter and its form. 13. If this form, then, is a composite, it will go on changing into infinity. If the form is simple, however, it clearly unites with matter without changing.

2 1. Obviously this is no less true for the rational soul. For it is united to the body without changing its own substance. 2. It does not cast off its nature in uniting with the body,[14] but only changes its activity, since it thinks with phantasms. 3. Also, it leaves the body behind as much as possible when it is functioning well, 4. and when it is separated from the body, it seeks to maintain its activity just as it seeks to maintain its substance.

3 1. Things that neither share a common genus that joins them together, nor share a common matter in the way we explained above, do not therefore change. 2. God does not share a genus in common with anything. In no way does he have matter, as is obvious from his very nature. 3. Therefore he does not change when he has entered matter. For if form, which is the principle in a composite and without which acting as substrate the composite cannot at all subsist, 4. does not change when it unites with matter to make something subsist, how would that thing change which is not only self-subsistent 5. but also the principle of all existence, and which is itself its own existence? 6. God did not unite to man as a form, but in some other way incomprehensible to us and known to God alone, 7. since it is obvious that the Word of God could in fact assume human nature without any change in himself.

4 1. It is easy to refute propositions whose contraries have been demonstrated to be true. Therefore, when you say that "what is not eternal becomes the last thing it is,"[15] 2. and "what has become, however, necessarily changes at the very least from what it was into what it has become,"[16] 3. I say that these statements are not in themselves true nor do they accord with what you have stipulated to good effect.

5 1. First of all, let us examine the essence of the argument in the case of two entities that are in some sort of relationship.[17] 2. If either entity changes, then the

14. Amiroutzes' phrasing here suggests metempsychosis, though this is not his intent.

15. See II.2.3.

16. See II.2.4.

17. For what follows, cf. Thomas Aquinas, *Summa contra gentiles* 2.12–14, concerning the relationship between God and creatures, though Aquinas does not bring up the issue of changing relationships nor use the example of light and the object lit.

θάτερον μεταβάλλει, ἡ μὲν σχέσις ἑτέρα γίνεται. θάτερον δὲ οὐκ ἀνάγκη μεταβάλλειν καίτοι τῆς σχέσεως ἑτέρας αὐτῷ γινομένης. 3. οὐ γὰρ ἐκ τοῦ δυνάμει καθ᾽ αὑτὸ πρόεισιν εἰς τὸ ἐνεργείᾳ. | 8v οὐδὲ προσγίνεται αὐτῷ διὰ μεταβολῆς οἰκείας οὐδέν· 4. ἀλλὰ τῷ λοιπῷ προσγίνεται διὰ μεταβολῆς. αὐτὸ δὲ ἕστηκεν ἀπαθὲς ταύτῃ καὶ ἀκίνητον καὶ ἀμετάβλητον. 5. οὔκουν ἀνάγκη μεταβάλλειν ᾧ τί ποτε ὁπωσοῦν ὑπάρξει μὴ ἀεὶ τοῦτο προόν. 6. ἔτι εἴ τι προσίοι τῷ φωτὶ, αὐτὸ μὲν ἀνάγκη μεταβάλλειν καὶ προσγενέσθαί τι αὐτῷ φωτιζομένῳ, 7. τὸ δὲ φῶς οὐ μεταβάλλει. καίτοι ὑπῆρξεν αὐτῷ τὸ νῦν τόδε φωτίζειν μὴ ἀεὶ τοῦτο προσόν. 8. οὔκουν ἀνάγκη μεταβάλλειν οἷς τί ποτε ὁπωσοῦν ὑπάρξει. 9. καὶ πάντων ἥκιστα τὴν πρώτην ἀρχὴν ᾗ πάντα ἐξῃρημένως | 9r πρόσεστι, καὶ ἄμεινον ἀπείρως ἢ τοῖς ἄλλοις ἅπασιν.

6 1. Ὅτι μὲν οὖν καθ᾽ αὑτὸ θεωροῦσιν οὐκ ἀνάγκη συμβαίνειν μεταβολήν, δῆλον. 2. ὅτι δὲ οὐδὲ τοῖς ὑφ᾽ ὑμῶν προὔργου τιθεμένοις συμβαίνειν εἰσόμεθα ὧδε. 3. ἡ πρόοδος τοίνυν τῶν ὄντων ἀπὸ τῆς πρώτης ἀρχῆς σχέσιν ἐπιφέρουσά ποτε τῇ αἰτίᾳ μεταβολὴν οὐκ ἐπάγει 4. ὅτι μήτε τὰ ὄντα ἐξ αὐτῆς διὰ κινήσεως πρόεισι μήτε αὕτη κινεῖ τῷ κινεῖσθαι. 5. εἰ γὰρ ἐπάγει τοῦτο μεταβολὴν αὐτῇ, οὐκ

6 τί ποτε] τὶ ποτὲ T (v. III.5.7 infra) || προόν] προὼν corr. in textu et marg. T[1] **9** τί ποτε] τὶ ποτὲ T, sed ad τι ποτὲ mut. T/T[1] **13** προὔργου] -ρ²- supra lin. scr. T[1] (v. III.4.3 supra) **16** πρόεισι] πρό εἰσι T

relationship is altered. But one of the entities does not necessarily change when the relationship is altered in respect to it. 3. For potency in itself does not result in actualization. Nothing happens to the entity, since this is not a case of it itself changing. 4. Instead, change happens to the other entity because it is the one that changed. The former entity has itself remained unaffected, unmoved, and unchanged. 5. Therefore a thing does not necessarily change if something that is not always present should somehow befall it. 6. Yet, if something comes into the light, it itself necessarily changes. Something has accrued to the thing inasmuch as it is lit. 7. The light, however, does not change. Hence what befell the light is that it now illuminates this particular object, which had not always been present to it. 8. Therefore, things that something has in some way befallen do not necessarily change. 9. And the First Principle is the very last of all things to which change can happen, since all things are transcendentally present to it and it is infinitely superior to all other things.

6 1. If we look at the essence of your argument, we therefore clearly see that it is not necessary for change to occur. 2. As we shall now see, your argument does not agree with what you have stipulated to good effect. 3. The procession of beings from the First Principle entails a relationship, then, but this procession never leads to a change in the cause, 4. since it is not by the First Principle's motion that beings proceed from the First Principle, nor is it the case that the First Principle moves them by itself being in motion.[18] 5. For if the procession brought change to it, the First Principle would not be unmoved either essentially

18. The word *proodos*, procession, is a characteristic Neoplatonic term, specifically in the sense of the procession from the One. It is not found in the Aristotelian corpus save at *On Plants* 2.9.829a30, a text that is a retro-translation from the Latin, which is itself in turn a translation from the Arabic, and in a quotation of Empedocles by Aristotle at *On Sense and Sensible Objects* 2.437b26. Among the Greek Fathers, the TLG shows that Gregory Nazianzenus and Gregory of Nyssa use the term in discussions of the Trinity, but not for the relationship of the creatures to their creator. Canonized for Christians, however, by its use in the writings of Pseudo-Dionysius, the metaphysical sense of the term came into vogue (see Perl, "Pseudo-Dionysius the Areopagite," 773–77, and Lilla, "Introduzione allo studio dello Ps. Dionigi l'Areopagita," 543, 545, 550). In the Latin West, where the word *processus* was used, Albert the Great wrote a treatise *De causis et processu universitatis a prima causa* that paraphrased the Neoplatonic *Liber de causis*. Thomas Aquinas used the term often; at *Summa contra gentiles* 1.9, he speaks *de processu creaturarum ab ipso* [*deo*], and at 2.42, of the *processus autem entium a primo ente*.

ἂν εἴη ἀκίνητος καὶ καθ᾽ αὑτὸ καὶ κατὰ συμβεβηκός, 6. οὐδ᾽ ἐνέργεια εἰλικρινὴς καὶ ἄμικτος τοῦ δυνάμει. οὕτω γὰρ ἂν | ἐνδέχοιτο μηδὲν εἶναι τῶν ὄντων, ὅπερ 9v ἀδύνατον.

7 1. Οὐκ ἄρα μεταβάλλει προάγουσα, οὐδὲ ἐργαζομένη οὐδέν. καίτοι σχέσις αὐτῇ παρ᾽ ἡμῶν ἐπιγίνεται, προελθόντων τῶν ὄντων. 2. τὸ αὐτὸ δέ ἐστιν εἰπεῖν καὶ ἐπὶ τῶν κατὰ πρόνοιαν ἄλλοτε ἄλλως γινομένων· 3. ἐν ἅπασι γὰρ σχέσις τίς ἐπιγίνεται τῇ αἰτίᾳ; οὗτος οὖν ὁ λόγος καὶ τὴν πρόοδον ἀναιρεῖ τῶν κτισμάτων καὶ πάντα τὰ κατὰ πρόνοιαν γινόμενα. 4. ἀλλ᾽ οὔτε ὑμεῖς αὐτὸ φαίη τ᾽ ἄν ποτε, οὔτ᾽ ἀληθές ἐστι. ἀναιρετέον ἄρα τὸν λόγον ᾧ ταῦτα τὰ ἄτοπα ἀκολουθεῖ. 5. ἀλλὰ μὴν οὐδὲ ἐκεῖνο συμβαίνει τὸ ἀναγκαῖον συνελθεῖν τῷ | ἐνδεχομένῳ εἰ 10r γέγονεν ἄνθρωπος ὁ τοῦ θεοῦ λόγος. 6. τὸ μὲν γὰρ ἀναγκαῖον αὐτὸ γενέσθαι ἐνδεχόμενον ἀδύνατον. εἰ δέ τι οὐσία ὄν, ἐξ ἀνάγκης εἴη. 7. ἔπειτα ἔν τινι ὑποκειμένῳ γένοιτο, οὐκ ἀδύνατον τούτῳ τῷ ὑποκειμένῳ καὶ τὸ ἐνδεχόμενον ὑπάρχειν. 8. οὐ γὰρ ἐνδεχόμενον οὕτω γίνεται τὸ ἀναγκαῖον, ἀλλ᾽ ἐν ἑνὶ ὑποκειμένῳ ἥ τ᾽ ἐξ ἀνάγκης οὐσία καὶ τὸ ἐνδεχόμενον. 9. τοῦτο δὲ οὐκ ἀδύνατον. εἰ μὲν γὰρ ἐγένετο τὸ ὑποκείμενον αὐτὸ τὸ προσελθὸν εἰς ἕνωσιν ὥστε μηδεμίαν εἶναι ἔτι διαφορὰν συνέβαινεν, ἀληθῶς τὸ ἀδύνατον. 10. εἰ δὲ τὸ ὑποκείμενον τὴν οἰ|κείαν οὐκ ἀποβάλλει φύσιν ἐν τῇ τῆς οὐσίας ἐκείνης ἑνώσει, οὐδὲν ἀδύνατον 10v ὑποκεῖσθαι καὶ τῷ ἐνδεχομένῳ. 11. οὐ γὰρ ᾗ ἓν γέγονεν μετὰ τῆς οὐσίας ἐκείνης ὑπόκειται τῷ ἐνδεχομένῳ, ἀλλ᾽ ᾗ σώζει τὴν οἰκείαν φύσιν καὶ μετὰ τὴν ἕνωσιν.

8 1. Ἡμεῖς τοίνυν οὕτως ἑνωθῆναι τὸν τοῦ θεοῦ λόγον τῇ τοῦ ἀνθρώπου φύσει φαμὲν ἐν τῷ Ἰησοῦ, 2. ὡς καὶ μετὰ τὴν ἕνωσιν τὴν φύσιν ταύτην ἔτι μένειν ἐν τῷ οἰκείῳ εἶναι. 3. οὐ γὰρ ἀπέβαλε τὸ ἄνθρωπος ἀληθὴς εἶναι Ἰησοῦς εἰ καὶ μία ὑπόστασις γέγονε μετὰ τοῦ θεοῦ λόγου, 4. ἀλλὰ τῆς ἑνώσεως ὑπερφυῶς γεγενημένης αἱ δύο φύσεις ἄτρεπτοι μεμενήκασι. 5. πεπονθέναι τε γὰρ αὐτόν φαμεν καὶ τεθνηκέναι ἃ τῆς ἀνθρωπίνης σαφῶς. οὐ τῆς θείας ἐστὶ φύσεως. 6. οὔκουν ἕπεται | τὸ ἀναγκαῖον συνελθεῖν τῷ ἐνδεχομένῳ εἰ γέγονεν ἄνθρωπος 11r ὁ θεὸς. οὐδὲ περιέχει τι ἀδύνατον ἡ ὑπόθεσις. 7. ἔτι δὲ οὐδ᾽ ἄμεσος ἡ ἕνωσις

2 ἐνδέχοιτο] ἐνδέχετο corr. T[1] **15** ἐξ] ἐεξ T **16** προσελθὸν] εἰ supra προ (= εἰσελθὸν) scr. T/T[1] **19** ᾗ] supra lin. scr. T **21** τοῦ θεοῦ] in marg. add. T **24** ὑπερφυῶς] ὑπὲρ φυῶς T **25** τε] τὲ T **28** τι] τί T

or accidentally, 6. and it would be neither pure act nor unmixed with potency. In the latter case, it would be possible that nothing exists, which is an impossibility.

7 1. Therefore the First Principle does not change when it produces nor is it impacted in any way. Hence, once things have come into existence, a relationship to the cause follows for us. 2. This is the same as saying that a relationship follows for things that in different ways at different times are brought about by providence. 3. For in all instances, what relationship would follow for the cause? Therefore this argument of yours abolishes both the procession of creatures and everything brought about by providence. 4. But you would never say this, nor is it true. Consequently, we must do away with the argument that results in these absurdities. 5. Nor, in fact, does it follow that the necessary had combined with the contingent if the Word of God became man. 6. It is impossible for the necessary itself to become contingent. If, however, something is a substance, it would exist of necessity. 7. Therefore, if it enters into some substrate, it is possible for the contingent also to belong to that substrate. 8. For in such a case the necessary does not become the contingent. Rather, the necessary substance and the contingent exist in a single substrate. 9. This is not impossible. For if the substrate that entered into the union were itself to become such that no difference remained [between the necessary and the contingent], that truly would be impossible. 10. If, on the other hand, the substrate were not to surrender its own nature in its unification with the substance of the contingent, it is not impossible for it to be also the substrate of the contingent. 11. For the necessary is not the substrate of the contingent by virtue of becoming one with the substance of the contingent, but by virtue of preserving its own nature even after the unification.

8 1. We say, then, that this is how in Jesus, the Word of God was united to the nature of man. 2. Consequently, the latter nature still retains its own existence after the union. 3. For Jesus did not cease being truly man by becoming a single hypostasis with the Word of God. 4. Rather, when this union supernaturally came about, the two natures remained unaltered. 5. For we say that what was human [in him] clearly suffered and died. This is not true as far as his divine nature is concerned. 6. Hence it does not follow that the necessary bonded with the contingent if God became man. Nor does this hypothesis contain any impossibility. 7. Yet, the union of the Word of God with matter was not without media-

γέγονε τοῦ θείου λόγου μετὰ τῆς ὕλης. τὸν γὰρ Ἰησοῦν ἄνθρωπον ἀληθῶς πιστεύομεν γεγενῆσθαι, ψυχὴν ἔχοντα λογικὴν καὶ νοῦν ἴδιον. 8. τούτῳ γοῦν τῷ νῷ ἀμέσως ἡνώθη ὁ τοῦ θεοῦ λόγος. 9. δι᾽ αὐτοῦ δὲ καὶ τῷ τοῦ Ἰησοῦ σώματι οὔκουν συνῆλθε, τὸ ἄυλον τῇ ὕλῃ, ἀλλὰ τῷ ἀΰλῳ πρῶτον, 10. δι᾽ αὐτοῦ δὲ ἤδη τῇ ὕλῃ. οὐκ ἄρα ἀδύνατον, οὐδ᾽ ἄτοπον τὸν τοῦ θεοῦ λόγον δίχα μεταβολῆς ἢ πάθους γενέσθαι ἄνθρωπον.

IV 1 1. **Ὁ Κρατῶν**. Καὶ τίς ἡ τοιαύτη γέγονεν | ἕνωσις, ἔφη, εἰ μηδὲ μίαν 11v
ὑπέστη μεταβολὴν μήτε ὡς εἶδος ἡνώθη σώματι; 2. οὐ γὰρ ἐνδέχεται ἕνωσις γενέσθαι μὴ κατά τινα τρόπον μεταβολῆς· 3. ἢ τοῦτο ἀρνουμένους εἰδέναι δοκεῖν εἰκότως λέγειν ἃ μὴ ἴσασιν.

V 1 1. **Ὁ Φιλόσοφος**. Ὅσα μὲν κατὰ τὸν φυσικὸν γίνεται τρόπον, ἔφην ἐγώ, ἔστιν ἐπί τινα τρόπον ἐγνωσμένον ἀνενεγκεῖν. 2. ὅσα δὲ ἡ πρώτη ἀρχὴ ἀμέσως ποιεῖ, ταῦτα οὐκ ἔστιν ἐπ᾽ ἄλλο τι ἀνενεγκεῖν, ἐπεὶ πῶς ὑπέστησεν ὁ θεὸς τὰ ὄντα; 3. εἰ μὲν γὰρ κατά τινα τῶν φυσικῶν τρόπων, φυσικὸν ἔσται καὶ τὸ παράγον καὶ αὐτὴ ἡ πρόοδος. 4. τοιοῦτον δὲ ὄν, κινούμενον πάντως κινήσει, καὶ ἡ πρόοδος ἐν χρόνῳ. 5. ἀλλ᾽ ἡ πρώτη ἀρχὴ ἀκίνητός ἐστι καὶ καθ᾽ αὐτὸ καὶ
κατὰ συμβεβηκός, | ἥ τε πρόοδος οὐκ ἐν χρόνῳ. 6. εἰ δὲ κατὰ μηδένας τῶν 12r
ἐγνωσμένων ἡμῖν τρόπων, δῆλον ὅτι οὐκ ἀνάγκη ἐπὶ τῆς πρώτης ἀρχῆς ζητεῖν τὸ γινόμενον ἐπί τι ἕτερον ἀναφέρειν.

2 1. Μᾶλλον δὲ καθόλου ἄτοπον τοῦτο ζητεῖν. οὐ γὰρ ἐνδέχεται ἐπί τι ἕτερον ἀναφέρειν παράδειγμα· 2. ἢ οὐκ ἔσται πρώτη ἀρχή, οὐδὲ διοίσει τῶν φυσικῶν οὐδέν. 3. ὅπερ οἱ πάλαι φιλοσοφήσαντες ἠγνοηκότες ἐξ ὑποκειμένου παράγειν αὐτὴν ἔθεντο, ἐπείπερ καὶ τὰ ἄλλα πάντα τοῦτον παράγειν τὸν τρόπον. 4. καὶ
ὕλην ἀγένητον καὶ ἀναίτιον ὑπέθεντο τῇ πρώτῃ ἀρχῇ, δυναμένην | δέξασθαι τὴν 12v

1 ἀληθῶς] ἀληθῶ T **2** τῷ] νεῷ T[1] **9** μεταβολῆς] scripsi: ἑνώσεως T

tion.[19] For we believe that Jesus was truly born a man who had a rational soul and his own proper intellect. 8. The Word of God was united with that intellect without mediation. 9. It was, therefore, through this union [with Jesus's intellect] that the Word of God joined with Jesus's body, the immaterial with the material—but first the immaterial with the immaterial, 10. and only then, through this union, with the material. Hence it is neither impossible nor absurd that the Word of God became man without change or without being affected.

IV 1 1. **The Conqueror.** And what sort of union was that, he said, if it did not allow a single change or did not result in a form being united to a body? 2. For a union cannot take place save through some form of modification,[20] 3. or those who deny knowing how this union happens can be fairly seen as talking about that of which they know nothing.

V 1 1. **The Philosopher.** I responded: Whatever comes about through the process of nature, we can refer back to some sort of known process. 2. Whatever the First Principle directly produces, on the other hand, we cannot refer back to something else, since [how are we to know] how God makes them subsist? 3. For if he made them subsist through some natural processes, their production and procession would be natural phenomena. 4. If such is the case, then if he moves them, he himself is quite certainly moved and their procession takes place in time. 5. But the First Principle is immovable essentially and accidentally, and their procession is not in time. 6. If, however, the procession takes place in accordance with no ways known to us, then we clearly are not required in the case of the First Principle to try to refer the event back to something else.

2 1. Rather, it is totally absurd to seek that. For it is not possible to refer the exemplar [in this instance] back to something else. 2. Otherwise it will not be the First Principle nor will it differ in any way from the things of nature. 3. Since the ancient philosophers were ignorant of this fact, they held that the First Principle produced things from out of a substrate, since everything else is produced in this manner. 4. And they assumed that matter, as something capable of receiving the

19. Cf. Thomas Aquinas, *Summa theologiae* 3.6.1: *Si ergo attendamus gradum dignitatis, anima media invenitur inter deum et carnem. Et secundum hoc, potest dici quod filius dei univit sibi carnem mediante anima.*

20. T reads "of unification," but this must be either a scribal confusion or a *lapsus auctoris*. The latter is more likely since Acciaiuoli's Greek exemplar also had ἑνώσεως (*unionis* in Acciaiuoli's translation).

ταύτης ἐνέργειαν. 5. εἰ γὰρ ὁμοίως παράγει, τί διοίσει τῶν ἄλλων; τί δὲ ἔσται αὐτῇ καὶ τὸ πρώτῃ εἶναι, εἰ μή τινα τρόπον ἐξῃρήμενον ποιεῖ ἅττ᾽ ἂν ποιῇ; 6. ὅλως γὰρ ἅπαντα τῆς πρώτης ἀρχῆς ἐξῃρῆσθαι δεῖ τῶν ἄλλων εἰ μέλλει σώζεσθαι αὐτῇ τὸ πρῶτον, 7. ἢ ταῖς λοιπαῖς ὁμοταγὴς ἔσται. πῶς οὖν μία τῶν ὄντων ἀρχή; 8. πῶς δὲ πάντα ἐπέστραπται πρὸς αὐτὴν καὶ αὐτῆς ἐφίεται καὶ πρὸς αὐτὴν τέτακται φυσικῶς; 9. ἀλλὰ δῆλον ὅτι ἐξῄρηται πάντων ἡ πρώτη ἀρχή. ἐπεὶ καὶ ὅσα αὐτῆς καταφάσκομεν, οὐ κατὰ τὸν τρόπον ἐκεῖνον τοῦτο ποιοῦμεν, καθ᾽ ὃν | καὶ ἐπὶ τῶν ἄλλων. 13r

3 1. Οὐ γάρ ἐστιν ἡ θεία φύσις ὑποκειμένη τινὶ οὔτε οὐσιώδει οὔτε συμβεβηκότι ὅτι μὴ ἔστιν ἐν τῷ θεῷ ἄλλοτι παρ᾽ αὐτόν. 2. ἀλλ᾽ ἔστι καθάπαξ ἁπλοῦς καὶ ἀσύνθετος καὶ ἓν αὐτὸ ὅ τί ποτε ὄν. 3. τοσοῦτον δὲ μόνον ἴσμεν ἐπὶ πάντων τῶν τοῦ θεοῦ, ὅτι ἔστι, πῶς δὲ ἐστὶν ἀγνοοῦμεν. 4. καίτοι ἴσμεν ὅτι οὐ κατὰ τὸν φυσικὸν τρόπον, οὐδ᾽ ὃν ἡμεῖς νοεῖν δυνάμεθα. 5. ἀφαιροῦμεν γὰρ πανταχοῦ τὸ φυσικὸν εἶναι. καὶ οὕτω γινώσκομεν πάντα ἐπὶ θεοῦ. 6. ἐπεὶ καὶ Ἀριστοτέλης περὶ ταύτης διαλεγόμενος τῆς ἀρχῆς, τὸν αὐτὸν μέτεισι τρόπον. 7. «ἀκίνητον» | 13v γάρ φησι καὶ «ἀδιαίρετον» καὶ «μηδὲν ἔχειν μέγεθος». τί δ᾽ ἐστιν οὐδ᾽ αὐτὸς ἐτόλμησεν εἰπεῖν. 8. ἐν γοῦν τῷ δωδεκάτῳ τῶν Μετὰ τὰ Φυσικὰ «νοῦν τὸν ἄριστον» τὸν θεὸν λέγεται. οὐχ οἷος ὁ ἡμέτερος προστίθησιν· 9. «οὐ γὰρ ἔχει, φησίν, ἔν τινι χρόνῳ τὸ εὖ ὥσπερ ὁ τῶν συνθέτων». 10. οὐδὲν ἄρα τῶν τοῦ θεοῦ

2 ἅττ᾽] ἀτ᾽ corr. T

action of the First Principle, was ungenerated and not caused by the First Principle. 5. For if the First Principle produces in the same way as other things produce, how would it differ from them? What would it mean for it to be the First Principle if it does not make whatever it makes in some transcendent way? 6. For everything about the First Principle must completely transcend other beings if it is going to preserve itself as the First. 7. Otherwise it would belong to the same order as the rest [of nature]. How, then, would there be a single principle for what exists? 8. Moreover, how does everything turn back to it and desire it, and how is everything is ordered by nature toward it?[21] 9. But it is clear that the First Principle transcends everything. And when we affirm so many such things about it, we do not do so in the same way that we do for other things.

3 1. The divine nature is the subject of nothing, either substantively or accidentally, because there is nothing in God other than himself. 2. Rather, he is utterly simple and uncompounded, and is whatever the One itself is. 3. Moreover, concerning God, everything we know is only this much: that he exists. How he exists, however, we do not know. 4. And yet we know that he does not exist in the manner of a thing in nature. Nor can we even think of him existing [in this way]. 5. For we totally rule out that he is of the natural order. And thus we recognize that everything depends on God. 6. When Aristotle discusses this [First] Principle, he has the same approach. 7. For he says that it is "unmoved" and "indivisible" and "has no magnitude."[22] What it is, he did not dare to say. 8. Indeed, in book 12 of the *Metaphysics* God is called "the best mind."[23] It does not proceed incrementally as do our minds. 9. "For it does not possess," he says, "the good in a certain space of time, as the mind of composite beings does."[24] 10. Hence there

21. The counterpart of the Neoplatonic concept of the procession from the One is the reversion to the One, as expressed here by Amiroutzes; see Bussanich, "Plotinus's Metaphysics," 55–57; and Wallis, *Neoplatonism*, 65–66, 87–88, and 132–33.

22. Cf. Aristotle, *Metaphysics* 12.7.1073a4–7: . . . ἀκίνητος . . . καὶ ὅτι μέγεθος οὐδὲν ἔχειν . . . καὶ ἀδιαίρετος . . .

23. Not exactly what Aristotle says (ibid. 12.9.1074b33–35): . . . οὐκ ἂν εἴη τὸ ἄριστον ἡ νόησις. αὑτὸν ἄρα νοεῖ, εἴπερ ἐστὶ τὸ κράτιστον, καὶ ἔστιν ἡ νόησις νοήσεως νόησις (trans. Tredennick: ". . . thinking cannot be the supreme good. Therefore Mind thinks itself, if it is that which is best; and its thinking is a thinking of thinking").

24. Cf. ibid. 12.9.1075a8–9: ὥσπερ ὁ ἀνθρώπινος νοῦς, ἢ ὅ γε τῶν συνθέτων ἔχει ἔν τινι χρόνῳ (οὐ γὰρ ἔχει τὸ εὖ ἐν τῳδὶ ἢ ἐν τῳδί . . .). My translation is an adaptation of Tredennick's.

ἔστιν ἐπί τι ἄλλο παράδειγμα ἀνενεγκεῖν φυσικόν.

4 1. Οὕτως οὖν οὐδὲ περὶ τῆς ἐνανθρωπήσεως τοῦ θείου λόγου ζητεῖν ἐστι τίς ἡ ἕνωσις γέγονεν. ἔστι γὰρ μοναδική. 2. τοσοῦτον δὲ μόνον ἴσμεν περὶ αὐτῆς, ὅτι γέγονεν· οὔτε δὲ ὡς ὕλη καὶ εἶδος οὔτε ὡς κινοῦν καὶ κινούμενον οὔτε κατά τινα τρόπον ἕτερον ἐγνωσμένον ἡμῖν, 3. πλὴν | ὅτι ἡ ἕνωσις αὕτη ἕνα Χριστόν, τὸν 14r
τοῦ θεοῦ λόγον, καὶ τὴν ἀνθρωπίνην ἀνέλαβε φύσιν, πεποίηκε. 4. καὶ εἴη ἂν ἕνωσις ὑποστατικὴ ὅτι μίαν ὑπόστασιν ἀπετέλεσεν καὶ ἓν πρόσωπον ἢ ἄτομον. 5. ἡ δὲ τοιαύτη ἕνωσις τῇ μὲν θείᾳ φύσει οὐδὲ σκιὰν ἐπάγει μεταβολῆς, ἀλλ᾽ ἕστηκεν ἀκίνητος αὕτη καὶ ἀμετάβλητος. 6. ᾗ δὲ ἥνωται φύσει, ταύτην ἐπὶ τὸν ἄμεινον μετέβαλε καὶ θειότερον. 7. ἀνεῖλε δὲ οὐδὲ ταύτης τὰς ἰδιότητας ὥσπερ τὸ φῶς ἑνούμενον τῷ διαφανεῖ αὐτὸ μὲν οὐδὲν πάσχει. 8. οὐδὲ μεταβάλλει, τὸ μέν τι διαφανὲς φωτεινὸν ἐργάζεται ἀχρόνως φωτίζον αὐτό.

VI 1 1. **Ὁ Κρατῶν**. Καὶ πῶς ἐστι φάναι, ἔφη, μὴ βλασφημοῦντας τὸν | θεὸν 14v
αὐτὸν εἰς γυναικὸς εἰσελθεῖν γαστέρα καὶ αἵμασι πεφύρθαι καὶ τεθράφθαι, καὶ κυηθῆναι καὶ τετέχθαι; 2. ταῦτα γὰρ ἀνάξια θεοῦ. μᾶλλον δὲ βλάσφημα καὶ εὐσεβῶν ἀκοαῖς ἀφόρητα. 3. ἔτι, πότερον ὅλος ἦν ἐν τῇ νηδύι τῆς Μαριὰμ ἢ μή; εἰ μὲν γὰρ ὅλος ἦν ἐκεῖ, τίς ἦν ἐν τῷ οὐρανῷ; 4. εἰ δὲ μὴ ὅλος, δῆλον ὅτι τὸ μὲν

---

2 ἐστι] supra lin. scr. T/T^1; in marg. δεῖ add. T^1, sed deinde del. **10** ταύτης] ταύτας corr. T **14** γαστέρα] γαστερά T **16** νηδύι] νηδύῃ T

is nothing in God that can be referred back to some other exemplar in the natural order.

4 1. Thus, then, it is not the case, as far as the Word of God becoming man is concerned, that we need to inquire into what union occurred. For it was unique. 2. We only know this about it: that it happened not as a union of matter and form, nor as the conjunction of mover and moved, nor in accordance with some other way known to us. 3. We only know that this union produced the one Christ, the Word of God, and that the Word assumed human nature. 4. We also know that this union was hypostatic, since it brought about a single hypostasis and a single person or indivisible entity. 5. Such a union, however, did not induce even the shadow of change in the divine nature. Rather, the divine nature remained unmoved and unchanged. 6. The nature to which it was united, on the other hand, changed for the better and became more divine. 7. The union did not, however, destroy the divine nature's[25] individual properties, just as light, when it is united with the translucent, suffers nothing itself. 8. Nor does it change. It makes some transparent object luminous as it itself illuminates in a timeless instant.[26]

VI 1 1. **The Conqueror.** And how, he said, are you not blaspheming when you say that God himself entered the stomach of a woman, became intermingled with and nourished by bloody substances, experienced conception in the womb, and was born? 2. For these things are unworthy of God. Rather, they are blasphemies and insufferable to the ears of the pious. 3. Furthermore, was he wholly in the belly of Mary or was he not? For if he was wholly there, who was in heaven? 4. If, on the other hand, he was not wholly there, then clearly part of him

25. The Greek pronoun here, ταύτης, would seems to refer back to human nature ("the latter"), but the sense of the passage requires the reference to be to divine nature.

26. For light being ἀχρόνως (not an Aristotelian word), Amiroutzes seems to be repeating Alexander of Aphrodisias; see the latter's *On the Soul* 43.11: οὐ γάρ σῶμα τὸ φῶς. διὸ καὶ ἀχρόνως; and *Mantissa* 143.38–30: καὶ γὰρ ἅμα ἐξ ἅπαντος τοῦ διαφανοῦς ἄπεισιν τὸ φῶς καὶ ἅμα ἐν παντὶ γίνεται. διὰ τοῦτο δὴ καὶ ἀχρόνως δείκνυσιν ὁ Ἀριστοτέλης γινόμενον τὸ ὁρᾶν. Sharples (Alexander of Aphrodisias, *Supplement*, 133) translates: "Light departs from all the transparent at the same time and comes to be in it all at the same time. And on account of this Aristotle shows that seeing comes about timelessly." At n. 449, Sharples points out that Alexander of Aphrodisias's nineteenth-century editor, Ivo Bruns, had already noted "that Alexander is here expressing his own interpretation of what Aristotle says, rather than citing him directly."

αὐτοῦ γέγονεν ἄνθρωπος, τὸ δὲ οὔ. οὕτω δὲ μεριστὸν ἔσται τὸ θεῖον ἀμερὲς ὄν. 5. ἀλλ᾽ ἀμήχανον ταῦτα ἀληθῆ εἶναι ἢ ταῖς κοιναῖς περὶ τοῦ θείου δόξαις συνᾴδειν.

VII 1 1. **Ὁ Φιλόσοφος.** Ταῦτα ἔφην ἐγώ· τοῖς μὲν ἀπείροις τῆς φύσεως, ἔτι δὲ τῆς θείας δυνάμεως, μορμολύκεια ἂν εἴη, καὶ δέος ἐμποιεῖν ἱκανά. | 2. οἵπερ 15r οἴονται χρασμὸν ἕπεσθαι παντὶ τρόπῳ ἐν τοῖς τοιούτοις καὶ μολύνεσθαι τὸ γινόμενον ἐν αὐτοῖς, ὅ τί ποτ᾽ ἂν ᾖ. 3. τοῖς δὲ ἐπεσκεμμένοις τήν τε θείαν φύσιν καὶ τί τὸ χραίνεσθαί ἐστι καὶ τίνα τὰ τοῦτο πάσχειν δυνάμενα οὐδὲν παράδοξον δοκεῖ, οὐδὲ ἄτοπον.

2 1. Πρῶτον δὲ ἔρωμαι ὑμᾶς εἰ πανταχοῦ ἐστιν ὁ θεὸς ἢ μή. εἰ μὲν γὰρ μὴ πανταχοῦ, πότερον καὶ οὐδαμοῦ ἢ πῆ; 2. εἰ μὲν οὖν μηδαμοῦ, ἐστερημένα ἔσται τὰ ὄντα πάντα τῆς πρώτης ἀρχῆς. μᾶλλον δὲ τῆς μιᾶς. 3. καὶ τί λοιπόν; τὸ συνέχον αὐτά; ἢ ἐν τίνι ἔσονται; εἰ μὴ ἐν τῇ ἀρχῇ, ἧς εἰ στερηθείη, οὐδ᾽ εἶναι δυνήσεται ὁπωσοῦν. 4. εἰ δέ που ἔστιν ὁ θεὸς καὶ μὴ πανταχοῦ, | σῶμά τι ἔσται 15v καὶ ὅλως περιγραπτόν. μὴ δυνάμενον εἶναι εἰ μὴ ὅπου ἔστι μοναχοῦ. οὕτω δὲ ὡρισμένον τι εἶδος ἔσται. 5. τὸ δὲ τοιοῦτον οὐκ ἂν εἴη ἡ πρώτη ἀρχή. πρῶτον μὲν γὰρ οὐ πάντῃ ἔσται ἁπλοῦν. 6. διότι ἕτερον ἀνάγκη τὸ ὁριζόμενον εἶναι καὶ ᾧ ὁρίζεται. ἔπειτα ὑφ᾽ ἑτέρου πείσεται τὸ ὁρίζεσθαι. 7. τὸ γοῦν ἐπάγον τὸν ὅρον ἐκεῖνο πρῶτον. εἰς ἄπειρον οὖν εἶσιν εἰ μή τι ἔσται ὑπὸ μηδενὸς ὁριζόμενον. 8. ἁπλῶς καὶ ἀπολύτως εἵς τι ὄν, ἀλλὰ καθόλου. 9. τοῦτο δὲ οὐκ ἀνάγκη που εἶναι. λείπεται δὲ πανταχοῦ.

3 1. Ἔτι, ὁ θεὸς ἀμερής ἐστι καὶ ἄποσος. τοῦ δὲ ἀμεροῦς οὐ τὸ μὲν ἐνταῦθα τυγχάνει, τὸ δὲ ἄλλοθι. 2. (οὐ γὰρ ἂν ἔτι ἀμερὲς εἴη), ἀλλ᾽ ὅ|λον ἔστιν. ἔνθα ἂν 16r

---

10 ἔρωμαι] ad ἔομαι mut. T^1 **11** οὐδαμοῦ] οὐδαμῶς primum scribere videtur T || μηδαμοῦ] μὴ δαμοῦ corr. T/T^1 **14** ἔσται] ἔστω corr. T^1 **15** καὶ] ἢ T, sed corr. in marg. T^1 (v. proximam notam) || ὅλως] ὅλος corr. T^1, et deinde in marg. super σωμάτι [sic] ἔσται καὶ ὅλως scr. || περιγραπτόν] symbolum interpositionis (/\) sub linea post περιγραπτόν scr. T^1, sed nihil in marg. est praeter signum crucis **16** ἡ] supplevi || πρώτη] in marg. scr. T **18** πείσεται] η super -ει- scr. T/T^1 **20** που] ποῦ in textu et in marg. corr. T^1

became man and part of him not. Thus the indivisible deity would be a divisible being. 5. But it is impossible that these things are true or that they agree with common opinions concerning the deity.

VII 1 1. **The Philosopher.** I responded as follows. These things would seem like horrors to those ignorant of nature, let alone of the power of God. They are sufficient to induce complete consternation. 2. Such people think defilement occurred in every possible way in events such as these and that what took place in them was a befouling, whatever it was that took place. 3. But to those who have reflected upon the divine nature, and what defilement is and which things can suffer defilement, these events do not seem paradoxical or absurd.

2 1. First, however, let me ask you whether God is everywhere or not. And if he is not everywhere, is he nowhere or somewhere? 2. If, then, he is nowhere, all existents would be deprived of their First Principle. More to the point, they would be deprived of their sole principle. 3. What is left? That he encompasses them? Or that they are in something? If they are not in their principle (if they have been deprived of it), they will not be able to exist in any way whatsoever. 4. If, however, God is somewhere but not everywhere, he will be some sort of body and wholly circumscribed. But this is not possible if he is not exclusively someplace. In that case, he would be some delimited form. 5. Such a thing, however, would not be the First Principle. For it would not be absolutely the first in all respects, 6. since what is delimited is necessarily other than that by which it is delimited. Then the latter will succumb to being delimited by another. 7. What imposes the delimitation in fact precedes [what is delimited]. The process then would go on *ad infinitum* if there is not something which is not delimited by anything. 8. The process absolutely and unconditionally has to end in some being, but it has to be a being that is a universal. 9. The universal being necessarily is not in some particular place.[27] By elimination therefore it is everywhere.

3 1. Furthermore, God is without parts and non-quantitative. But what is without parts cannot be here and then someplace else. 2. For then it would not still be without parts. Rather it would be a concrete whole.[28] It would be in a

27. The negative precedes "necessarily" in the Greek, but sense requires that we attach it to "is in some particular place."

28. Cf. Aristotle, *Physics* 1.1.184a25, for ὅλον as translated by Wicksteed and Cornford.

ᾖ. 3. λέγω δὲ ὅτι καὶ πανταχοῦ. εἰ μὲν γὰρ εἴη τι ἀμερὲς μέν, ὡρισμένον δὲ ὅμως ἔχον τὸ εἶναι, 4. οὐκ ἀνάγκη καὶ πανταχοῦ αὐτὸ εἶναι. καίτοι ὅλον ὂν ἔνθα ἂν ᾖ. 5. λέγω δὲ ὡρισμένον ἔχειν τὸ εἶναι τὸ εἰδικὸν τρόπον τοῦ εἶναι συστελλόμενον. 6. τοῦτο γὰρ ὥρισται αὐτό τε καὶ τὸ εἶδος ᾧ ἐστιν, αὐτὸ μὲν τῷ εἴδει, ἐκεῖνο δὲ τῷ εἰδικῷ τρόπῳ τοῦ εἶναι. 7. ἐπεὶ ἐν τοῖς παρὰ τὴν πρώτην ἀρχὴν πᾶσι διαφέρει, ὅ τέ εἰσι καὶ ᾧ εἰσί, 8. εἰ δέ τι πρὸς τῷ ἀμερὲς εἶναι οὐδὲ ὡρισμένον ἔχει τὸ εἶναι, οὐδὲ συστελλόμενον ὁπωσοῦν, παντός τε εἴη τοῦ εἶναι ἀρχή. 9. τοῦτο ἀνάγκη καὶ πανταχοῦ εἶναι ὅπως ὑπὸ μηδενὸς ὁρίζηται, μὴ δὲ συ|στέλληται. ὁ δὲ θεός 16v ἐστι τοιοῦτος.

4 1. Ἀνάγκη ἄρα ὅλον τε εἶναι ἔνθα ἂν ᾖ καὶ πανταχοῦ τῇ τε οὐσίᾳ καὶ τῇ δυνάμει. 2. τοῦτο δὲ καὶ ταῖς κοιναῖς ἐννοίαις συνᾴδει καὶ τοῖς τῶν προφητῶν λόγοις. «οὐχὶ τὸν οὐρανόν», γάρ φησι, «καὶ τὴν γῆν ἐγὼ πληρῶ; λέγει κύριος». 3. καὶ πάλιν, «ποῦ πορευθῶ ἀπὸ τοῦ πνεύματός σου καὶ ἀπὸ τοῦ προσώπου σου ποῦ φύγω; ἐὰν ἀναβῶ εἰς τὸν οὐρανόν, σὺ ἐκεῖ εἶ. ἐὰν καταβῶ εἰς τὸν ᾅδην, πάρει». 4. δι᾽ ὧν ἀριδηλότατα φαίνεται τὸν θεὸν πανταχοῦ εἶναι. εἰ δὲ πανταχοῦ, οὐκ ἔστιν ὅπου μή ἐστιν, ὥστε καὶ ἐν τοῖς δοκοῦσιν αἰσχροῖς καὶ ἀτιμωτάτοις. 5. ἀλλ᾽ οὐδεὶς ἐκ τούτου προσγίνεται χρασμὸς τῇ θείᾳ φύσει. ἐκεῖνα γὰρ μόνα πάσχει τοῦτο ὅσα τῆς αὐτῆς ὕλης κοινωνεῖ. | 6. ταῦτα γὰρ εἰκὸς ποιεῖν καὶ 17r πάσχειν ὑπ᾽ ἀλλήλων. 7. ὅσα δὲ ἢ μὴ ἔχει ὕλην ἢ μὴ τὴν αὐτήν, ταῦτα ἑνούμενα τοῖς τοιούτοις καθάπαξ φυλάττεται ἀπαθῆ, καθάπερ τὸ φῶς ἑνούμενον τῷ βορβόρῳ μένει καθάπαξ ἀμόλυντον. 8. εἰ δέ τί ἐστιν ἄυλον, τοῦτο καθόλου τυγχάνει ἀπὸ τῶν τοιούτων ἀπαθὲς κἂν ἀεὶ τούτοις συνῇ.

5 1. Τί δὴ καινὸν ἢ μὴ προσῆκον τῇ θείᾳ φύσει συμβαίνει εἰ γέγονεν ἐν γαστρί, ἥπερ τυγχάνει, ὡς δέδεικται, οὖσα πανταχοῦ; 2. καίτοι καὶ ὑμῖν ἀκούω δοκεῖν, ὥσπερ δῆτα καὶ ἡμῖν, τὸν θεὸν αὐτουργὸν γενέσθαι τῶν ἔργων τούτων

---

1 τι] τί T **3** τὸ^{2}] τὸν corr. T/T^1 **4** τοῦτο] τούτῳ corr. T/T^1 et τοῦτο in marg. iterat || αὐτό τε] αὐτὸ τὲ T **6** τῷ] τὸ corr. T^1 || οὐδὲ] ὃ super -οὐ- scr. T^1 sed deinde del. **7** παντός τε] παντὸς τέ T; παντὸς ad παντός corr. T^1 **17** προσγίνεται] γίνεται corr. T^1 **18** τῆς . . . ὕλης] τοῖς ἑαυτοῦ ὕλης T, sed in marg. infer. scr. T^1 τῆς αὐτῆς ὕλης **19** ἔχει] ἔχειν corr. T/T^1 || ἑνούμενα] δὲ ante del. T **24** καίτοι] καὶ τοί T

particular place. 3. I say, however, that God is everywhere. For if something were without parts but delimited, even though it would still have being, 4. its being would not be necessary nor would it be everywhere. And yet, as a concrete whole, it would have the capacity of being in a particular place. 5. I say that what is delimited has the reduced sort of existence that a form has. 6. For it will be delimited and so too would the form by which it exists be delimited. It would be delimited by its form, and the form by existing in the way a form exists. 7. Since both differ from the First Principle in every detail, namely, in what they are and by virtue of that by which they exist, 8. if there is something that in addition to being without parts does not have a delimited existence nor an existence constricted in any way whatsoever, it would be the principle of all existence. 9. It would necessarily exist everywhere, because it is not delimited by anything or constricted. God is such a thing.

4 1. Necessarily, therefore, God as a concrete whole would be in a particular place and also everywhere, by virtue of his substance and his power. 2. That accords with common conceptions and with the words of the prophets. *Do I not*, he says, *fill heaven and earth? says the Lord.*[29] 3. And again, *Where can I go from your spirit, and where can I flee from your face? If I ascend into heaven, you are there. If I descend into hell, you are there.*[30] 4. It is crystal clear from these passages that God is everywhere. If, however, he is everywhere, there is no place where he is not, including, therefore, in seemingly shameful and disreputable places. 5. But no defilement accrues to the divine nature from that fact. For only those things suffer defilement that share in the same matter. 6. For these things, it is fair to say, affect and are affected by each other. 7. Things, however, that lack matter or do not have the same matter remain utterly unaffected when united with such foul things, just like light united to muck remains utterly undefiled. 8. If something is immaterial, it completely experiences no effect from such foul things, even if it were joined to them eternally.

5 1. Since, as been shown, the divine nature is everywhere, what new or unworthy thing befalls it if it happens to be in a stomach? 2. Nonetheless, I appreciate how this would strike you. Indeed, I share your concern about God becoming the product of these actions and of other ignominious activities.

29. Jer. 23:24.
30. Ps. 138:7–8.

καὶ τῶν ἄλλων τῶν ἀτιμωτάτων. 3. πῶς οὖν παρήγαγεν αὐτὰ εἰ τῇ φύσει ἦν αἰσχρά; | 4. πῶς δὲ προυπέστησεν ἐν τῷ νῷ; οὐ γὰρ ἐξ αὐτομάτου τοιαῦτα 17v γέγονεν εἰ τυγχάνει μιαρά. 5. τέθραπται δὲ κἀκ τῶν αἱμάτων ἐκείνων οὐχ ἡ θεία φύσις, ἀλλ᾽ ὁ ἄνθρωπος ὃν ἀνείληφε. 6. καὶ τὸ κυηθὲν δέ, καὶ τὸ τεχθὲν τοῦτο ἦν, ἀναληφθὲν μέντοι ὑπὸ τοῦ θείου λόγου. διὸ καὶ λέγεται τετέχθαι ὁ θεῖος λόγος. 7. ὅτι ἡ φύσις ἥνωται, ὑποστατικῶς τοῦτο πέπονθεν. 8. οὐχ ὅτι καθ᾽ αὑτὸν ἐκεῖνος ἐτέχθη, ἀλλ᾽ ὅτι τὸ πρόσλημμα. 9. οὔτε μολυσμὸς ἦν οὔτε κύησις καθ᾽ αὑτὸ οὔτε τόκος οὔτε τις ἀλλοίωσις ἐξ ὧν λέγομεν συμβαίνει τῇ θείᾳ φύσει. 10. πάντα γὰρ ταῦτα τοῦ ἀνθρώπου ἐστὶν ὃν ἀνείληφεν. πρὸς μὲν οὖν τὰ ἐπαγόμενα ἡμῖν μορμολύκεια ἐκ τοῦ χρασμοῦ οὕτως ἱστάμεθα.

6 1. Ὃ δὲ λέγετε, | «εἰ ἦν τῇ γαστρὶ τῆς Μαριάμ, τίς ἦν ἐν τῷ οὐρανῷ;», οὐ 18r δεῖται λοιπὸν ἀπολογίας, δεδειγμένου ὅτι ὁ θεὸς ὅλος ἐστὶ πανταχοῦ καὶ ἀπερίγραπτος. 2. τὸ γὰρ εἶναι ἐνθαδὶ καὶ μὴ εἶναι πανταχοῦ τῶν σωμάτων ἐστὶ μόνων καὶ τῶν ἐχόντων ἄλλως περιγραφήν. 3. εἰ δέ τι πανταχοῦ καὶ ἀπερίγραπτον εἴη ἀμερὲς ὄν, καὶ ὅλον ἔστιν ἐνταυθὶ καὶ ὅλον ἐστὶ πανταχοῦ. 4. οὐ γὰρ ὅ ἐστι ποσὸν ἄπειρον ἔστι, καὶ πανταχοῦ. τοῦτο γὰρ κατὰ συμβεβηκὸς ἂν ἦν πανταχοῦ τοῖς μορίοις. 5. ὁ δὲ θεὸς καθ᾽ αὑτό ἐστι πανταχοῦ. οὐ γὰρ συνεκτείνεται τοῖς διαστήμασι. πάντα δὲ αὐτὸς περιέχει καθάπερ στιγμήν. 6. εἰ δὲ ἀναγκαῖος ἦν (ὁ ὑμέτερος ἐκεῖνος λόγος), ἔδει τὸν θεὸν | ἐν τῷ οὐρανῷ ὄντα, 18v 7. μὴ εἶναι ἄλλοθι καὶ ἐν τούτῳ μὴ παντὶ ἢ ἰσομήκη εἶναι καὶ διάστασιν ἔχειν ἅπαντα ἄτοπα. 8. ἦν ἄρα καὶ ἐν τῇ τῆς παρθένου γαστρὶ καὶ οὐδαμόθεν ἀπῆν.

VIII 1 1. **Ὁ Κρατῶν**. Καὶ εἰ οὕτως ἦν ἐν αὐτῇ ὥσπερ κἀν τοῖς ἄλλοις, ἔφη, τί μεῖζον ἔσχεν ἡ Μαριάμ; 2. πῶς δὲ ἐκυοφόρησε μόνη; διὰ τί δὲ μὴ καὶ νῦν τοιοῦτόν τι γίνεται; 3. ἔοικε καπνὸν φεύγων ἄνθραξι περιπεσεῖν. τὸ γὰρ ἄτοπον ἐνταῦθα μεῖζον.

IX 1 1. **Ὁ Φιλόσοφος**. Οὐ τοῦτο φαμέν, ὅτι τὸν αὐτὸν τρόπον ἦν ἐν τῇ Μαριὰμ κυοφορούμενος ὅνπερ κἀν τοῖς ἄλλοις, 2. ἀλλ᾽ ὅτι οὐκ ἐκωλύετο καὶ

7 πρόσλημμα] πρόσλημα T **8** οὔτε τις] οὔτέ τις T **11** εἰ ἦν] οὖν in marg. infer. scr. T[1] **15** ἐνταυθὶ] οι supra -ι- scr. T[1] (sc. ἐνταυθοί) **15–16** ὅ . . . πανταχοῦ] in marg. scr. T[1], deleto in textu ὅς τι ποσὸν ἄπειρον ἐστι πανταχοῦ **22** Ὁ Κρατῶν] om. T, sed signo novum caput indicat || οὕτως] ἦν ante supra lin. scr. T[1] sed deinde del. || ἦν] del. T[1] sed sub marg. iterat **26** Ὁ Φιλόσοφος] om. T, sed signo novum caput indicat **27** ὅνπερ] ἥπερ corr. T[1]

3. How, then, did he bring them about if they are an affront to his nature? 4. How did he foreordain them in his mind? For such things did not happen spontaneously if they were defiling. 5. It is not the divine nature, however, but the man whom the divine nature assumed that was nurtured by those bloody substances. 6. The man conceived in the womb then, that is to say, the begotten, was assumed by the Word of God. This is the reason why we say that the Word of God was begotten. 7. Since his nature was united to the begotten, he hypostatically experienced that begetting. 8. Not because he was begotten in his own self, but because what was assumed was begotten. 9. No defilement befalls the divine nature, nor does conception *per se* or parturition or some alteration coming out of the things we are talking about. 10. For all these things appertain to the nature of the man whom he assumed. This is the way, then, that we stand up to the horrors raised against us on the issue of defilement.

6 1. The question you pose, namely, "If God was in Mary's stomach, who was in heaven?," does not require further rebuttal, since we have established that God as a concrete whole is everywhere and is uncircumscribed. 2. For to be in a particular place and not to be everywhere is characteristic only of bodies and of things otherwise possessing a circumference. 3. If, however, something is everywhere and uncircumscribed, since it is without parts, it is a concrete whole in a particular place and also a concrete whole everywhere. 4. For it is not the case that whatever is of an infinite quantity is also everywhere. For such a thing would be everywhere accidentally through its parts. 5. God, on the other hand, is everywhere by his essence. For he is not extended by [three-dimensional] places. He encompasses the universe just like it were a dot. 6. If, however, he was a necessary being (that is your phrase), he must be the God who was in heaven. 7. His being elsewhere, his not being everywhere in this world here, and his occupying [three dimensional] space are all absurdities. 8. He was therefore in the stomach of the Virgin while not being absent from anywhere else.

VIII 1 1. **The Conqueror.** And if he was in her, he asked, just the same way he was in other things, what privilege did Mary have over others? 2. How was it, moreover, that only she was pregnant with him? Why does not some such thing happen now? 3. This is like fleeing the smoke to fall into the coals. You have fallen into a greater absurdity.

IX 1 1. **The Philosopher.** We do not say that he was a fetus in Mary in the same way as he would have been in other women. 2. Rather, we say that he was

ὅλος ἐν αὐτῇ εἶναι καὶ ὅλος πανταχοῦ. 3. ἐν δὲ τῇ Μαριὰμ οὐχ ἁπλῶς μόνον
ὅλος ἦν, ἀλλὰ καὶ τὴν ἄρρητον | οἰκονομίαν πληρῶν κυοφορούμενος. τοῦτο δὲ 19r
οὐκ ἀπὸ τοῦ παρεῖναι περιγίνεται. 4. ἐγίνετο γὰρ ἂν ἀεί, ἀλλ᾽ ἀπὸ τοῦ †...† ὅπερ
οὐδαμοῦ οὔτ᾽ ἦν οὔτ᾽ ἔσται. 5. εἰ μὴ ἐν τῇ Μαριὰμ μόνον τότε, ἐπεὶ καὶ νῦν καὶ
ἀεὶ πανταχοῦ ὤν, οὐ πανταχοῦ ποιεῖ ἅττ᾽ ἂν ποιῇ, ἀλλ᾽ ὅπῃ βούλετο μόνον.

X 1 1. **Ὁ Κρατῶν**. Καὶ πόθεν, ἔφη, τὸ καινότατον τοῦτο καὶ ἀτοπώτατον
δείκνυται, ὅτι ὁ θεὸς γέγονεν ἄνθρωπος; 2. οὐ γὰρ δεῖ τὰ τυχόντα πιστεύειν οὐδ᾽
οὕτως ἄλογόν τινα δόξαν τίθεσθαι, ἀλλὰ καὶ ἀπόδειξιν φέρειν καὶ πίστιν τῶν
τιθεμένων. 3. ὁ δὲ τὴν πρώτην ὑπόθεσιν μὴ ἔχων δεικνύειν ἐπὶ σαθροῦ θεμελίου
τὰ λοιπὰ συνάπτει κἂν μὴ παντάπασιν ἄλογα ταῦτα φαίνηται; | 4. ἱκανὸν γὰρ τὸ 19v
τῆς ὑποθέσεως ἄτοπον τοιαῦτα πάντα ποιεῖν δοκεῖν. 5. ποίοις οὖν λόγοις δεικνύειν ἔχετε ὡς ἀληθὴς ἡ τῆς πίστεως ὑμῶν ὑπόθεσις; 6. εἰ γὰρ ἄνευ λόγου παντὸς ταύτην τίθεσθε, οὐκ ἂν φθάνοιτε καὶ μύθοις πιστεύοντες καὶ λόγοις πεπλασμένοις ἀριδηλότατα· 7. ἀρκεῖ δὲ καὶ τὸ μόνον ἐνστῆναι πρὸς τὰς τοιαύτας ὑποθέσεις καὶ μηδὲν ἔτι πολυπραγμονεῖν. 8. οὐ γὰρ ἕξουσιν ἀποδεικνύειν οἱ τούτοις πεπεισμένοι, ἀλλ᾽ αὐτοὶ μόνοι καθ᾽ ἑαυτοὺς τίθεσθαι δόξουσι τὰ πάντα ἄτοπα.

XI 1 1. **Ὁ Φιλόσοφος**. Ὅτι μὲν ἔφην ἐγώ, τὰ ἐπενεχθέντα ἄτοπα τῇ τῆς
πίστεως ὑποθέσει οὐδ᾽ ὅλως ἕπεται φανερόν. | 2. τὸ δὲ ἀπόδειξιν ταύτης ζητεῖν 20r
εὔλογον, καὶ οἰκείαν τῷ γένει, οὐ γεωμετρικὴν οὐδὲ φυσικήν. 3. οὔτε γὰρ πανταχοῦ τὴν γεωμετρικὴν ἀνάγκην ἐπιζητεῖν χρή, οὔτ᾽ ἔστι τὰ γεωμετρικὰ φυσικῶς ἀποδεικνύειν οὔτε τὰ φυσικὰ γεωμετρικῶς, ἀλλ᾽ ἐκ τῶν οἰκείων ἀρχῶν ἕκαστα δείκνυται καὶ προσφυῶν. 4. τὰ μὲν οὖν φυσικὰ ἐκ τῶν φυσικῶν ἀρχῶν ἀποδει-

1 αὐτῇ] αὐτῷ in textu et in marg. corr. T[1] **3** ὅπερ] spatium ante relinq. T; in marg. scr. T[1] ἴσθι· οἰκονομεῖν ἢ ἐνεργεῖν ἢ ποεῖν ἢ προνοεῖν **5** ἅττ᾽] ἅτ᾽ corr. T[1] **6** Ὁ Κρατῶν] om. T, sed signo novum caput indicat **10** γὰρ] supra lin. scr. T/T[1] **14** τοιαύτας] τοιαῦτας corr. T/T[1] **15** μηδὲν] μὴδὲν T **17** Ὁ Φιλόσοφος] om. T, sed signo novum caput indicat **19** καὶ οἰκείαν] ἀλλ᾽ supra lin. scr. T[1] sed deinde del. et in marg. scr. ἀλλ᾽ οἰκείαν

not prevented from being a concrete whole in her and a concrete whole everywhere. 3. In Mary, however, he was not only a concrete whole, but as a fetus, he was fulfilling the ineffable dispensation. This was not the consequence of his being present [in Mary]. 4. For he always existed. Rather, it was the consequence of the [divine arrangement?][31] that had never been before nor would ever be again. 5. Even if he was not only in Mary at that moment, because he is everywhere now and always, he does not do everywhere whatever he has the capacity of doing, but only what he may wish to do in some way.

X 1 1. **The Conqueror.** And how do you propose to prove, he asked, this totally novel absurdity, that God became man? 2. For we should neither believe something just because we happen upon it, nor assert any irrational doctrine. Rather we should produce scientific demonstration and proof for what is asserted. 3. If someone, however, cannot prove his first premise and constructs the rest of his argument upon a rotten foundation, how will his other assertions not seem totally irrational? 4. For the absurdity of the premise is enough to make all its consequences appear equally absurd. 5. What kinds of arguments do you have to show that your faith rests on a true premise? 6. For if you are going to postulate that your faith completely lacks a rational base, you could not more quickly make it crystal clear that you believe in myths and specious arguments. 7. It is sufficient for me simply to reject outright these sorts of premises and not fuss any further. 8. For those who believe in these premises will not be able to present demonstrations. Rather, they will be seen as only asserting all this nonsense among themselves.

XI 1 1. **The Philosopher.** The absurdities you allege, I said, clearly do not follow in any way from the premise of faith. 2. But it would be reasonable to seek a demonstration in this matter, a demonstration, however, that is proper to the genus and is not a geometric demonstration or a physical demonstration. 3. For it is not necessary to strive for geometric necessity in everything, nor to demonstrate geometry through physics nor physics through geometry, but rather to prove each on the basis of principles proper and suitable to it.[32] 4. Let physical

31. I am assuming that the missing word here is οἰκονομεῖν or a variant, as the marginal note in T seems to imply.

32. Cf. Aristotle, *Nicomachean Ethics* 1.2.1094b11–27; and *Posterior Analytics* 1.12.77a40–41.

κτέον. 5. εἰ δέ τι μὴ κατὰ τὸν φυσικὸν γίνεται λόγον, ἀλλ᾽ ὑπ᾽ ἕτερόν τινα τρόπον ὑπὸ τῆς πρώτης ἀρχῆς προνοίᾳ τινί, οὐκ ἂν εἴη τοῦτο ἐκ τῶν ἀρχῶν δεικνύειν τῶν φυσικῶν. 6. τὰ μὲν γὰρ φυσικὰ ἢ ἀεὶ ὡσαύτως ἢ ὡς ἐπιτοπολὺ γίνεται. τὰ δὲ προνοίᾳ τινὶ ὑπὸ | τῆς πρώτης ἀρχῆς γινόμενα οὔτ᾽ ἀεὶ οὔτ᾽ ὡς 20v ἐπιτοπολύ. 7. οὔκουν ἔστιν αὐτὰ δεικνύειν οὔτε ἐκ τῶν φυσικῶν ἀρχῶν οὔθ᾽ ὅλως ἐκ τῶν τοῦ λόγου.

2 1. Ἱκανὸν δὲ ἐν τοῖς τοιούτοις ὅτι μὴ ἀντίκειται ταῖς κοιναῖς ἐννοίαις δεικνύειν. μάχεσθαι γὰρ ἴσως ἀλήθειαν οὐκ ἐνδέχεται ἀληθείᾳ. 2. εἰ δέ τις οἴεται τὰ οὕτως ὑπὸ τῆς πρώτης ἀρχῆς γινόμενα οἷόν τε εἶναι ταῖς τοῦ λόγου δεικνύειν ἀρχαῖς, ἀπατᾶται νομίζων ἐξ ἄλλου γένους ἄλλο τι δεικνύειν ἐνεῖναι. 3. οὐ γὰρ ἐφαρμόζει τὸ καθόλου, ὃ δεῖ λαβεῖν ἐν τῇ ἀποδείξει. 4. ἢ ὑπὸ τὸ αὐτὸ γένος ἔσται. ἀλλὰ τὰ ἰδίως ὑπὸ τῆς πρώτης ἀρχῆς κατὰ πρόνοιαν γινόμενα οὐκ εἰσὶν ἐν | τῷ γένει τῆς τοῦ λόγου ἀρχῆς. 5. ἢ γὰρ ὡσαύτως ἀεὶ ἐγίνετο ἄν, καὶ ἦν 21r προειπεῖν ὅτι τε ἔσται καὶ ὅτε, ὥσπερ ὅτι ἔσται ἔκλειψις, καὶ ὅτε ἢ ὡς ἐπιτοπολύ, ὧν οὐδέτερον ἔστιν. 6. οὐκ ἄρα ἔστιν ἐκ τῶν κοινῶν ἐννοιῶν τὰ τοιαῦτα δεικνύ-

5 αὐτὰ] αὐ supra lin. scr. T/T[1] quoniam υ non plane liquet in textu **10** ἄλλο τι] ἀλλό τι T **14** τε] τέ T || ἔκλειψις καὶ] in marg. iterat T[1]

matters be demonstrated from physical principles. 5. If, however, something happens not in accordance with physical principles, but is brought about in some other fashion through the exercise of the providence of the First Principle, we would not demonstrate it on the basis of physical principles. 6. For physical phenomena always or usually happen in the same way. Things, however, that come about by an exercise of the providence of the First Principle do not always or usually happen. 7. Consequently, it is not a question of proving these things on the basis of physical principles or completely on the basis of logic.

2 1. Instead, for phenomena of this sort, it is sufficient to show that they do not contradict common notions. For truth, it is fair to say, cannot to be in conflict with truth.[33] 2. If, however, someone thinks that it is possible to show on the basis of logical principles that things are made to occur in a certain way by the First Principle, he is fooling himself, thinking that he can prove on the basis of one genus some other thing in another genus. 3. For the universal, which one must assume in a scientific demonstration, does not fit here. 4. Alternatively, suppose that the universal does fall under the same genus. Nonetheless, it is still the case that phenomena peculiarly brought about by the First Principle in accord with its providence are not in the genus of logical principles. 5. For then these phenomena would happen in the same way all the time, and we would be in the position to predict their occurrence, just as we predict that there will be an eclipse at a specific moment or most times, neither of which is the case here. 6. It

33. Amiroutzes enunciates a common scholastic tag, *verum vero consonat*, that is Aristotelian in origin (*Nicomachean Ethics* 1.8.1098b11–12: τῷ μὲν γὰρ ἀληθεῖ πάντα συνάδει τὰ ὑπάρχοντα, τῷ δὲ ψευδεῖ ταχὺ διαφωνεῖ [τἀληθές]; see Goddu, "Medieval Natural Philosophy," 226) and was expressed in various ways in the Middle Ages (John of Salisbury, *Policraticus* 2.29: *verum vero nequit esse contrarium*; Thomas Aquinas, *Summa contra gentiles* 1.7.2; Henry of Ghent, *Summa quaestionum ordinariarum* 10.3.4, as quoted by Wulf, *Philosophy and Civilization*, 168, n. 18), but most notably in the famous formulation *Cumque verum vero minime contradicat* of the papal bull *Apostolici regiminis* published at the Fifth Lateran Council in 1513 in opposition to the theory of a double truth (see, in general, Bianchi, *Pour une histoire de la "double vérité"*). George of Trebizond used precisely this passage in the Aristotelian *Nicomachean Ethics* as the "Aristotelian canon" for the establishment of truth in his 1466 treatise *On the Eternal Glory of the Autocrat*, contemporaneously with Amiroutzes (see Monfasani, *Collectanea Trapezuntiana*, 492–93, 531–32). On the theme *verum vero consonat*, see now the papers gathered in *Freiburger Zeitschrift für Philosophie und Theologie* 64 (2017): 5–109.

ειν. 7. ἀλλὰ μὴν οὐδὲ δείκνυται ὅλως. ἡ μὲν γὰρ ἀπόδειξις τοῦ καθόλου ἐστὶ πᾶσα. τὰ δὲ ἐκείνως γινόμενα οὐκ ἔστιν ὑπό τι καθόλου τοιοῦτον ἀνενεγκεῖν. 8. εἰσὶ γὰρ μερικὰ καὶ ἄλλοτε ἄλλως γινόμενα. καθὼς ἂν τῇ θείᾳ προνοίᾳ δοκῇ.

XII 1 1. **Ὁ Κρατῶν**. Καὶ πόθεν ἄλλοθεν, ἔφη, ὑπολαβών, ἔσται τι δεικνύειν ἔτι ἀναιρουμένων τῶν ἀρχῶν αἷς ἐπὶ τ' ἄλλα φύσει ἵεμεν; 2. ποῖον δὲ ἄλλο κριτήριον | ἀληθείας ἡμῖν καταλείπεται τοῦ κατὰ φύσιν ἐκβαλλομένου; 3. οὐ γὰρ 21v δήπου ἀπὸ τῶν αἰσθήσεων ἐπὶ τὴν ἀλήθειαν ἰέναι ἡγεῖσθαι δεῖν. οὕτω γὰρ τῶν ἀλόγων οὐδὲν διοίσεται. 4. ἔτι οὐδ' ἔσται σύνεσις τῶν λεγομένων, ᾧ φύσει συνίεμεν ἐκβαλλομένου. 5. ἀλλὰ βόμβος ἔσται τὰ λεγόμενα ἢ ψόφος ἄλλως, ἐπεὶ ἡ σύνεσις ἀρχὴ τυγχάνει τῆς ἀποδείξεως. 6. ἢ γὰρ ὅτι ἔστι προγινάσκειν ἀναγκαῖον ἐν τῇ ἀποδείξει ἢ τί τὸ λεγόμενον ἐστὶ ξυνιέναι δεῖ. 7. ὁ τοίνυν πᾶσαν ἀρχὴν ἀναιρῶν συναναιρεῖ δήπου καὶ τὸ συνιέναι. 8. τὸ δὲ τῶν διαφόρων ἐπιστημῶν διαφόρους εἶναι τὰς ἀρχὰς ἀληθὲς μέν, ἀλλ' ἀνάγκη ταύτας ὑπὸ τὰς πρώτας καὶ κοινο|τάτας εἶναι, αἷς ἐστιν ἐπὶ πάντας ἰέναι. 9. οὐ γάρ εἰσιν αἱ ἀρχαὶ 22r τῶν ἐπιστημῶν διῳκισμέναι, 10. ἀλλ' οὐδὲ ἀλλότριαι. ἀλλὰ ξυνῳδοὶ καὶ συγγενεῖς. καὶ αἱ τοῦ ὄντος, ᾗ τοιούτου, περιέχουσι πάσας. 11. ὁ δὲ τὰς φυσικὰς ἀρχὰς ἐκποδὼν τιθεὶς καὶ τὰς τοῦ λόγου καὶ ταύτας συνεκβάλλει δήπου. 12. ὁρᾷς οἷς ἀξιοῖς ὅσα τὰ ἄτοπα ἐπακουλουθεῖ;

XIII 1 1. **Ὁ Φιλόσοφος**. Εἰ μὲν ἕπεται ταῦτα οἷς εἶπον ἢ μή, ὕστερον ἐπισκεψόμεθα, ἔφην. 2. οἶμαι μέντοι τοὺς τοιούσδε λόγους ἥκιστα τῇ ἡμετέρᾳ περὶ τοῦ

---

4 Ὁ Κρατῶν] om. T, sed signo novum caput indicat **5** ἵεμεν] in marg. iterat T^1 **6** κριτήριον] in marg. iterat T^1 || ἐκβαλλομένου] ἐκ- in marg. iterat T^1 **7** ἡγεῖσθαι] ἡγεῖσθε T **13** ἀληθὲς] ἀληθὴς corr. T^1 **14** κοινοτάτας] κοινονοτάτας T **17** ὁρᾷς] signum novi capitis ante scribere incipit sed del. T/T^1 **18** ἐπακουλουθεῖ] ἀκουλουθεῖ corr. T, scrivendo ἐπα- in marg. **19** Ὁ Φιλόσοφος] om. T, sed signo novum caput indicat

is not possible therefore to prove such phenomena on the basis of common notions. 7. Indeed, they cannot be demonstrated at all. For every scientific demonstration depends on a universal. But phenomena occurring in this way cannot be referred back to some such universal. 8. For they are particulars, occurring in different times in different ways. This seems to be the way things happen through the agency of divine providence.

XII 1 1. **The Conqueror.** And, he said, from where else will you draw your assumptions to prove something if you have eliminated the first principles by which we proceed naturally to other conclusions? 2. What other kind of criterion of truth is left to us once the one according to nature is discarded? 3. For you do not think, it seems, that it is necessary to proceed from the senses to the truth. Thus your approach will not differ from irrational actions. 4. Furthermore, it involves no logical combination of statements, since you have discarded the way by which we proceed naturally. 5. Rather, the statements are just bombast or otherwise meaningless sound, inasmuch as scientific demonstration starts with the logical combination of statements. 6. For in a demonstration, either "it is necessary to assume the fact beforehand or one must understand the meaning of the term."[34] 7. He who eliminates every principle of logical conclusion eliminates, in effect, understanding. 8. While it is true that the different sciences have different principles, nonetheless, these different principles necessarily fall under the first and most universal principles by which we proceed in all instances. 9. For the principles of the sciences are not isolated from each other. 10. Nor are they foreign to each other. Rather, they are concordant and related. And the principles of being, insofar as they are of this order, encompass all the sciences. 11. He, however, who puts aside the principles of physics, discards in fact those of logic as well as those of physics. 12. Do you see what sort of absurdities follow hard upon these axioms of yours?

XIII 1 1. **The Philosopher.** Let us examine later, I said, whether or not these absurdities follow upon what I said. 2. I think, however, that propositions such as

34. Aristotle, *Posterior Analytics* 1.1.71a12–14: Διχῶς δ᾽ ἀναγκαῖον προγιγνώσκειν· τὰ μὲν γὰρ ὅτι ἔστι προϋπολαμβάνειν ἀναγκαῖον, τὰ δὲ τί τὸ λεγόμενόν ἐστι ξυνιέναι δεῖ, τὰ δ᾽ ἄμφω (trans. Tredennick: "There are two senses in which previous knowledge is necessary. Sometimes it is necessary to assume the *fact* beforehand, and sometimes one must understand the *meaning* of the term; sometimes both are necessary.").

θείου δόξῃ καὶ οἷς παντὸς μᾶλλον τίθεσθε προσήκειν. 3. πυνθάνομαι γὰρ ὑμᾶς ὅσα τε τοῖς προφήταις εἴρηται περὶ τοῦ θεοῦ | καὶ τῶν ἔργων αὐτοῦ πάντα ἀληθῆ 22v νομίζειν καὶ αὐτοὺς ἰδίᾳ πολλὰ τοιαῦτα δοξάζειν. 4. ταῦτα δὲ ἀδύνατον ἀπὸ τοῦ φυσικοῦ λόγου καὶ τῶν κοινῶν ἐννοιῶν δεικνύειν. 5. συμβαίνει τοίνυν τοὺς ἀπὸ τούτων μόνον ἀξιοῦντας τἀληθὲς κρίνειν ἐκεῖνα μὴ ἀληθῆ ἀποφαίνειν· ὅπερ οὐκ ἔστιν, οὐδ᾽ ἂν γένοιτο περὶ ὑμῶν ἀληθῶς ὑπολαβεῖν. 6. οὐδὲν οὖν μᾶλλον ὑμῶν ἐκεῖνα τὰ ἄτοπα ἀναιρετέον ἐστὶν ἐμοί. ἀλλὰ κοινὸς ὁ ἀγών.

XIV 1 1. **Ὁ Κρατῶν**. Καὶ τί τοιοῦτον ᾗ δ᾽ ὅς, οἱ προφῆταί φασι περὶ θεοῦ ὃ ταῖς κοιναῖς ἐννοίαις μάχεται, ἐπεὶ ὅσα γε ἡμεῖς νομίζομεν παντὸς μᾶλλον τοῖς κοινοῖς λογισμοῖς συνᾴδει; 2. ἦ καὶ | ὁ φιλόσοφος Ἀποαλῆς ἀπεφήνατο ὅτι μόνη 23r ἡ ἡμετέρα πίστις ταῖς κοιναῖς ἐννοίαις σύμφωνός ἐστι.

XV 1 1. **Ὁ Φιλοσόφος**. Πολλὰ ἔφην, ὦ βασιλεῦ, οἷον ὅτι χθιζός τε καὶ ἐκ μηδενὸς γέγονεν ὁ κόσμος, καὶ ὅτι τῆς τοῦ παντὸς προόδου οὐδεὶς γέγονε κοινωνός, ἀλλ᾽ αὐτουργὸς ὑπῆρξεν ἁπάντων ἡ πρώτη ἀρχή, μᾶλλον δὲ ἡ μόνη. 2. οὐ γὰρ ἐνδέχεται πρώτην ἔτι αὐτὴν εἰπεῖν ‹εἰ μὴ› μηδεμιᾶς ἄλλης εἰς τὴν

2 ὅσα τε] ὅσα τὲ T **5** ἀξιοῦντας] -ας super -ες scr. T[1] **8** Ὁ Κρατῶν] om. T, sed signo novum caput indicat **10** Ἀποαλῆς] in marg. sine linea superscripta iterat T[1] **12** Ὁ Φιλοσόφος] om. T, sed signo novum caput indicat || χθιζός] in marg. iterat T[1] **14** μόνη] in marg. annot. T[1]: λόγος τῆς ἐπανορθώσεως, ὅτι μᾶλλον μόνη ἢ πρώτη ἀρχὴ ὁ θεός **15** εἰ μὴ] supplevi

mine suit at the least our teaching concerning God and, above all, the teachings that you yourself assert. 3. For I hear that you hold to be all true whatever has been said by the prophets concerning God and his works, and that you yourselves glorify many such statements of the prophets that are peculiar to you. 4. These things are impossible to prove on the basis of physics and common notions. 5. The result is, therefore, that those who judge the truth on the basis of the sciences alone assert that these things are false, which is not something one assumes nor truly ought to assume about you. 6. It is then even more incumbent upon you than upon me to remove these absurdities. But the struggle is ours in common.

XIV 1 1. **The Conqueror.** What does such an argument amount to, he asked, namely, that prophets say things that conflict with common notions, when what we think accords in every way more with common reasoning? 2. Hence the philosopher Apoales asserted that only our faith is in harmony with common notions.[35]

XV 1 1. **The Philosopher.** I said many things, o king, for instance, yesterday,[36] that the world came from nothing and that there was no collaboration in the whole process of procession. Rather, the First Principle—or, more precisely, the Sole Principle—of all, working alone, began it. 2. For it is not possible still to call it the First Principle unless nothing else is admitted in the procession of

35. Mehmed unquestionably is speaking here about Avicenna. "Apoales," as one of the readers for the press pointed out, is simply the Greek form of Avicenna's name, Abu Ali Sina; see Monfasani, *George Amiroutzes the Philosopher*, 33–36. This is confirmed a little further on, at XV.5–7, when Amiroutzes attributes to "Apoales" a doctrine of creation that is distinctly characteristic of Avicenna and which Amiroutzes must have learned of from Thomas Aquinas's *Summa theologiae* in the Greek translation of Demetrius Cydones, as explained in Monfasani, ibid. The source of this assertion, that Avicenna considered Islam in harmony with common notions, seems to be his treatise *De Almahad*, in which he declared the laws delivered by Muhammad concerning life after death the best and most perfect possible (Avicenna, *De Almahad*, ff. 48r, 49v; *Epistola sulla vita futura*, 84, 92). The irony is that Avicenna also asserts here that the materialistic conception of paradise presented in the Koran is quite false, though perfectly suited to the mentality of the *vulgus*. Cf. also idem, *De philosophia prima* 2.546.36–37, ad notam; and *The Metaphysics of* The Healing, 373 ("that which the greatest of legislators commanded"). I thank Jules Janssens for his invaluable guidance on this reference.

36. This is the only indication in the text of the dialogue proper, as opposed to the introduction (I.4), that the conversation extended beyond a single day.

πρόοδον τῶν ὄντων εἰσαγομένης. 3. Καὶ ἄλλα τοιαῦτα. ὧν εἴ τις ἐκ τῶν κοινῶν ἐννοιῶν ἀπόδειξιν κομίσαι οἷός τε γένοιτο, θαῦμα ἂν εἴη. 4. τοὺς γοῦν φιλοσόφους σχεδὸν ἅπαντας ὧν τις καὶ λόγος ἔστι, τὰ | ἐναντία σαφῶς ἴσμεν νομίζοντας. 23v 5. αὐτόν τε Ἀποαλῆν ἀκούω τοῦ πλήθους τῶν ὄντων μὴ τὴν πρώτην ἀρχήν, ᾗπερ ὁ ἱερός φησι λόγος, αἰτίαν ἡγεῖσθαι, ἀλλὰ τὴν μὲν τὴν πρώτην μόνην παράγειν νόησιν. 6. οὐ γὰρ εἶναι πλείω ἐξ αὐτῆς προιέναι, ταύτην δὲ τῆς δευτέρας αἰτίαν ὑπάρξαι κἀκείνην ἄλλης μέχρι τῆς τοῦ οὐρανοῦ ψυχῆς. 7. ἐκείνην δὲ ἤδη τὸ πλῆθος τῶν ὄντων παραγαγεῖν. 8. καὶ μὴν καὶ τὰ θαύματα πάντα ὅσα κατὰ διαφόρους χρόνους τοὺς ἀνθρώπους ἐνάγων εἰς τὴν ἀλήθειαν πεποίηκεν ὁ θεὸς τοῦ αὐτοῦ γένους ἐστίν. οὐδὲν γὰρ αὐτῶν ταῖς κοιναῖς ἐννοίαις δεικνύειν ἐνδέχεται.

2 1. Ἐπεὶ τίσιν ἂν λόγοις ἀποδειχθείη ὅτι πέτρα ἐφ᾽ ἁμάξης κομιζομένη τοσοῦτον χρόνον | ἐπὶ τῆς ἐρήμου λαῷ τοσούτῳ ὅσον Μωϋσῆς ἦγεν ὕδωρ 24r αὐτοῖς τε καὶ θρέμμασιν ἔβλυζεν ἱκανόν; 2. εἴ γέ τις καὶ μεταβάλλειν κατὰ φύσιν οἷόν τε εἶναι τὰ τοιάδε εἰς ὕδωρ δώσειεν, ἀλλὰ τὸ πλῆθος ὑπερβάλλει πάντα φυσικὸν λόγον. 3. τὰ μὲν γὰρ πυκνότερα τῶν σωμάτων εἰς τὰ ἧττον τοιαῦτα μεταβάλλοντα μείζονα ἴσμεν γινόμενα, οὐ μὴν ἐν τοσαύτῃ ὑπεροχῇ. 4. οὐδὲ τὸ ὕδωρ εἰς ἀέρα μεταβάλλον ὁρῶμεν. καίτοι πολλαπλάσιον εἰκὸς ἐκ τοσοῦδε ὕδατος ἀέρα γενέσθαι ἢ ἐξ ἴσης γῆς ὕδωρ. 5. ἔοικε γὰρ τὴν μανότητα μὴ ὁμοίως προχωρεῖν ἐν ταῖς ἐφεξῆς μεταβολαῖς. 6. δηλοῖ δὲ ἡ σφαῖρα τοῦ ἀέρος. πολλῷ γὰρ | ὑπερβαίνει τὴν τοῦ ὕδατος πρὸς τὴν γῆν ἀναλογίαν. 7. πρόσεστι δὲ καὶ ὅτι 24v ἡ πέτρα οὐκ ἐμειοῦτο τοσοῦτον ὕδωρ ἑκάστοτε χορηγοῦσα. πόθεν δ᾽ ἄν τις κἀκεῖνο ἔχοι δεικνύειν, ὡς ἡ ῥάβδος ἀθρόον ἀληθῶς εἰς ὄφιν μεταβάλλοι καὶ αὖθις εἰς τὸ πρότερον εἶδος ὁμοίως ἐπανέλθοι; 8. καὶ τ᾽ ἄλλα ἃ μακρὸν ἂν εἴη διεξελθεῖν. τοῦ γὰρ αὐτοῦ λόγου εἰσὶ πάντα.

3 ἐναντία] ναυτία T **4** αὐτόν τε] αὐτὸν τὲ T **9–10** πεποίηκεν] in marg. scr. T **14** τε] τὲ T || θρέμμασιν] θρέμσιν corr. T/T[1] **15** τοιάδε] τοῖά δε T **21** καὶ] supra lin. scr. T **24** μακρὸν] μικρόν corr. T/T[1] **25** διεξελθεῖν] δι᾽ ἐξελθεῖν T

being. 3. And I said other such things. If someone were to appear who was capable of providing a scientific demonstration of these things on the basis of common notions, he would be a wonder. 4. Indeed, we clearly know that almost all philosophers about whom we have information held the opposite position. 5. I hear that this Apoales did not think that the First Principle was the cause of most beings in the way the holy word says. Instead, he thought that the First Principle produced only the First Mind. 6. For he did not think that the multiplicity of beings proceeds from it [the First Principle]. Rather, the First Principle is the cause of the second cause, and the latter of the next cause, up until the soul of the heavens. 7. That, then, became the producer of the multiplicity of beings.[37] 8. In point of fact, all the wonders that God has performed in different ages to lead men to the truth are of this sort. For one can prove none of them on the basis of common notions.

2 1. Indeed, by what arguments would you prove that the rock carried on a cart for such a long time by the horde of people whom Moses led in the desert bubbled forth enough water for them and their livestock?[38] 2. Even if someone were to concede that it is possible to transform these sorts of material into water, nonetheless the quantity exceeds the whole natural order. 3. For we know that denser bodies become transformed into larger, less dense bodies, but not to such an extraordinary degree. 4. Nor do we see the transforming of water into air. Indeed, one might suppose that a much larger amount of air is made from a given quantity of water or much more water from an equal amount of earth. 5. For it is reasonable to suppose that porousness does not continue to the same degree in successive transformations. 6. The sphere of the air, indeed, shows this. For it exceeds by far the proportion of water to earth. 7. There is an added factor here, however, namely, that the rock did not shrink each time it supplied a large quantity of water. Also, on what basis can someone demonstrate how a staff all at once truly turns into a snake and then similarly turns right back again into its former form?[39] 8. And there are other dilemmas which would be onerous to run through since they all reflect the same principle.

37. See n. 35.

38. Cf. Exod. 17:1–7.

39. Cf. Exod. 4:1–5; de la Cruz Palma, in *Diálogo de la Fe*, 46, refers to Exod. 7:12, but this is less apt since it concerns snakes in the plural and not a snake in the singular.

3 1. Ἐπεὶ εἰ ἐκ τῶν φυσικῶν ἀρχῶν καὶ ὅλως τῶν τοῦ λόγου τὰ τοιαῦτα ἐδείκνυτο ἦν ἂν καὶ αὐτὰ φυσικά. 2. δεῖ γὰρ ταῖς ἀρχαῖς πανταχοῦ συγγενῆ τὰ ἐξ αὐτῶν δεικνύμενα εἶναι. 3. τοιαῦτα δὲ ὄντα οὐκ ἂν ἦσαν θαύματα οὐδὲ πίστιν ἐποίουν ὧν οἱ | ταῦτα δεικνύοντες ἐβούλοντο. 4. οἱ δὲ φαίνονται τοὺς ἀνθρώ- 25r
πους ἐντεῦθεν εἰς ὧν ἔλεγον ἀλήθειαν ἄγοντες. 5. αὐτοί τε μᾶλλον οἱ ἄνθρωποι τούτοις ἐπίστευον ἢ τοῖς ἀπὸ τῆς φύσεως λογισμοῖς. 6. φανερὸν τοίνυν ὅτι τὰ θαύματα καὶ ὅλως τὰ κατὰ πρόνοιαν ἰδίως γινόμενα οἷς, ὁ θεὸς τοὺς ἀνθρώπους εἰς τὴν θείαν ἀλήθειαν ἕλκει. 7. ἥκιστα δείκνυται ἐκ τῶν φυσικῶν ἀρχῶν. 8. τὸ δὲ συνιέναι ἐκ τούτων τῶν λόγων οὐκ ἀναιρεῖται. συνετὰ γὰρ τὰ λεγόμενα ἐστὶ καὶ συνίασιν οἱ ἀκούοντες.

4 1. Εἰ οὖν τὸ συνιέναι τί τὸ λεγόμενόν ἐστιν, ἐν τῷ γένει τίθεται τῆς | ἀρχῆς. 25v
σῴζεται τὸ τοιοῦτον οὐδὲν ἧττον κἀνταῦθα. 2. ἀλλ᾽ οὐδὲ τὰς φυσικὰς ἀρχὰς ἁπλῶς ἀναιροῦσιν οἱ τὰ τοιαῦτα ἀξιοῦντες. εἰσὶ γὰρ ἀληθεῖς ἐν τῷ γένει τῷ οἰκείῳ καὶ τῷ ὑποκειμένῳ. 3. εἰς δὲ τὴν θείαν ἀλήθειαν αὐτὰς οὐ λαμβάνουσιν ὅτι μὴ ταύτης εἰσὶν ἀρχαί, ἀλλὰ τῆς φυσικῆς. 4. αὐτοὶ δέ, ὡς ἀρχὰς ὑποθέμενοι ἅπερ αὐτοῖς ὁ θεὸς ἀπεκάλυψε, τὰ τούτοις ἑπόμενα ἐξ ἀνάγκης τίθενται καὶ τοὺς λογικοὺς οὐδαμοῦ κινοῦσι κανόνας. 5. ἐπεὶ καὶ τὰ συμβαίνοντα πανταχοῦ τοῖς ὑποτεθειμένοις δέχονται.

XVI 1 1. **Ὁ Κρατῶν**. Ἀλλ᾽ εἰ μὴ ἐκ τῶν πᾶσιν ἐγνωσμένων ἀρχῶν | τὰ 26r
τοιαῦτα δείκνυται, ἔφη, ἀλλ᾽ ἐκ τῶν ἰδίων ὑποθέσεων ἕκαστα, πόθεν εἰσόμεθα τίνα μὲν ἐν τούτοις τὰ ἀληθῆ, τίνα δὲ τὰ πεπλασμένα; 2. ἃ γὰρ ἕκαστοι νομίζουσι καὶ Ἕλληνες καὶ Ἰουδαῖοι καὶ Χριστιανοὶ καὶ Ἄραβες ἐξ ὧν ὑποτίθενται δεικνύειν εἰσὶ δυνατοί, ὥστε οὕτω γε πάσας τὰς δόξας ἀληθεῖς εἶναι. 3. ἐπεὶ καὶ θαύματα τοῦ θείου νομίζουσιν ἕκαστοι, πολλὰ παραγαγεῖν ἔχουσι τὰ μὲν μνήμῃ σῳζόμενα ἐν αὐτοῖς, τὰ δὲ καὶ ἀναγεγραμμένα, καὶ θεοφανείας οὐκ ὀλίγοις ἅπαντες. 4. ἄλλα τε ὅμοια εἰπεῖν, οἷς αὐτὸς ἀξιοῖς τὰ δοκοῦντα ὑμῖν δεικνύειν, οἷς οὖν τὰ σαυτοῦ κύρια εἶναι καὶ ἀληθῆ νομίζεις. | 5. τούτοις δήπου 26v
καὶ τὰ τῶν ἄλλων συναποδείκνυται. θεία τε γὰρ εἶναι καὶ μὴ δεῖν αὐτὰ τοῖς

---

11 τὸ^1 . . . ἐστιν] sub linea scr. T^1 et in marg. annot.: ἀρχὴ τὸ συνιέναι τι ἐστὶ τὸ λεγόμενον **17** καὶ] super lin. scr. T^1 **19** Ὁ Κρατῶν] om. T, sed signo novum caput indicat || ἀρχῶν] in marg. iterat T^1 **24** θείου] οὖας (?) post scr. T/T^1 et in marg. scr. οὗ, γράφεται, deletis ante duobus verbis **28** αὐτὰ] in marg. scr. T

3 1. Next point. If such phenomena are demonstrated on the basis of physical principles and completely on logical principles, then they would be natural events. 2. For what is demonstrated on the basis of these principles is necessarily and completely akin to them. 3. As such, they would neither be miracles nor would they produce faith in the things those demonstrating them want to prove. 4. Rather, we see that it is these miracles that lead people to the truth of the things their proponents are asserting. 5. People more readily believe these miracles than they do proofs drawn from physics. 6. Clearly, then, the means by which God draws men to divine truth are miracles and, generally speaking, things that come to pass peculiarly by his providence. 7. Things proven on the basis of physical principles carry the least conviction. 8. We are not, however, eliminating understanding based on these arguments. For when stated, these arguments are intelligible and those who hear them grasp them.

4 1. If, then, what I have said makes sense, place it in the category of a basic principle. It should be maintained henceforth as nothing less than such. 2. But those who hold this view are absolutely not abolishing the principles of physics. For the latter remain true in their own genus and subject matter. 3. They do not accept such principles, however, into the realm of divine truth, since they are principles of physics and not of divinity. 4. On the other hand, having accepted as their basic principles what God has revealed to them, they posit as necessary what follows from these revelations, and in no way disturb the rules of logic. 5. Indeed, they completely accept the consequences of their assumptions.

XVI 1 1. **The Conqueror.** But, he said, if these things are not proved from universally recognized principles, and instead are based on their own peculiar assumptions, how shall we know in these matters what is the truth, what is fraudulent? 2. For pagans, Jews, Christians, and Arabs are capable of demonstrating the things each group believes on the basis of what they assume. The consequent would thus be that all their doctrines are true. 3. Since each group believes in miracles of the deity, they have much to place in evidence, namely, the miracles preserved in memory among themselves and those recorded in their written records, as well as all of God's appearances to no small number of persons. 4. One could mention other similar, worthy phenomena, on the basis of which you prove your beliefs and on the basis of which you consider your own doctrines to be authoritative and true. 5. Of course, on the basis of these things the doctrines of other religions are equally demonstrated. For they all similarly

κοινοῖς λογισμοῖς ἐξετάζειν ὁμοίως ἅπαντες ἀξιώσουσιν. 6. οὕτω δὲ μεγάλαι τοῖς πονηροῖς κατὰ τῆς ἀληθείας ἀναπετάννυνται πύλαι. ἅπαντα γὰρ ὁμοίως ἀληθῆ ταύτῃ ἔσται τὰ περὶ τοῦ θείου λεγόμενα, ὥσπερ Πρωταγόρας περὶ τῶν ὄντων ὑπέλαβεν. 7. ἀλλὰ τοῦτο ἀδύνατον. τὰ γὰρ ἀντικείμενα ἀληθῆ ἅμα ἔσται. 8. δεῖ τοίνυν τοὺς μὴ συγχωροῦντας τὰ θεῖα τοῖς κοινοῖς λογισμοῖς ἐξετάζειν, ἄλλην τινὰ πίστιν ἐπάγειν ὧν ἀξιοῦσι καὶ ἀπόδειξιν ὧν τίθενται.

XVII 1 1. **Ὁ Φιλόσοφος**. Χαλεπὸν μέν, ἔφην, ὦ βασιλεῦ, καθόλου | περὶ 27r
τούτου λόγον δοῦναι. 2. τίς μὲν ἡ θεία τῷ ὄντι ἀλήθεια, τίς δὲ ἡ πεπλασμένη ἐπεὶ αὕτη γε ἐκ μὲν τῶν κοινῶν ἐννοιῶν οὐ δείκνυται, ᾗ προείρηται; 3. οἷς δὲ δείκνυται, οὐκ ἔστι τοῖς ἀμφιβάλλουσιν ἀεὶ παραγαγεῖν. 4. οὐδ᾽ ἐπιδεῖξαι ὅτι αὐτὰ μὲν οὐκ ἔτι σῴζεται ὡς καὶ ταῖς ὄψεσιν ὑποκεῖσθαι. 5. οἷς δὲ σῴζεται μνήμη καὶ ξυγγραφή. ἀμφίβολα πεποιήκασι τὰ ψευδῆ πλασάμενοι, καὶ τοῖς ἔπειτα αὐτὰ παραδόντες. 6. πειρατέον δὲ ὅμως, ᾗπερ ἐνδέχεται, διορίσαι περὶ τούτου. 7. ἴσως γὰρ ὑπάρχει τι τῇ θείᾳ ἀληθείᾳ ὅπερ οὐκ ἔστιν οὐδὲ πλάσασθαι τῇ πεπλασμένῃ.
8. ὑποκρινομένη δὲ | ἐξελέγχεται αὐτίκα μικρὸν προϊοῦσα, ἅτε μὴ τὸ αὐτὸ 27v
προτιθεμένη. οὗ τὸν πάντα λόγον ἡ ἀληθὴς ἐποιεῖτο.

XVIII 1 1. **Ὁ Κρατῶν**. Καὶ πῶς ἂν εἴητε δίκαιοι τοῖς τῶν προφητῶν λόγοις χρῆσθαι, ἔφη, ὧν οὔτε τὸν νόμον οὔτε τὴν πίστιν δέχεσθε; 2. ἀλλ᾽ ἀντίκεισθε πάντῃ τοῖς ταῦτα δεχομένοις Ἑβραίοις. 3. Ὁ δὲ τὴν ἐκείνων μαρτυρίαν προτείνων δίκαιος ἂν εἴη καί τ᾽ ἄλλ᾽ ἅ φασιν ἐκεῖνοι δέχεσθαι, ἀλλ᾽ οὐ τὰ μὲν ἐγκρίνειν, τὰ δὲ ἀποβάλλεσθαι. 4. ὑμεῖς οὖν τὸν νόμον ὅλον τῶν Ἑβραίων ἀνῃρηκότες τοῖς αὐτῶν προφήταις πῶς ἂν δικαίως χρήσησθε;

XIX 1 1. **Ὁ Φιλόσοφος**. Οὐχ οὕτω νομίζειν δεῖ περὶ ἡμῶν, ἔφην ἐγώ, | ὅτι 28r
τοῖς προφήταις ἐν οἷς μὲν δεόμεθα χρώμεθα· ἐπὶ δὲ τῶν ἄλλων αὐτοὺς ἀποστρεφόμεθα. 2. καὶ γὰρ τὸν νόμον ὅλον τοῦ Μωϋσέως ἅγιον ἡγούμεθα καὶ τοὺς

2 ἀναπετάννυνται] ἀναπετάνυνται corr. T/T[1] **7** Ὁ Φιλόσοφος] om. T, sed signo novum caput indicat **12** ξυγγραφή] ξυν- corr. T, deinde ξυγγραφεῖν scr. T, sed ad ξυγγραφῆ [sic] corr. T/T[1] **17** Ὁ Κρατῶν] om. T, sed signo novum caput indicat **18** οὔτε[1]] ὄντε T **23** ἐγώ] sub linea add. T[1]

deem their doctrines to be divine and in no need of being examined on the basis of common reasoning. 6. Thus an enormous gateway is opened up for evildoers to assail the truth. For everything said about the deity would similarly be true, just as Protagoras postulated concerning the existence [of the gods].[40] 7. But that is impossible. For then contradictories would be true at the same time. 8. It is necessary, therefore, for those in disagreement to examine divine matters on the basis of common reasoning, to introduce some other proof for what they believe, and to demonstrate what they posit.

XVII 1 1. **The Philosopher.** O king, I said, it is hard to give a general rule concerning this. 2. What really is divine truth? What is fraudulent? This cannot be proven on the basis of common notions, in the way already stated, 3. and it is not always possible to present proofs by which faith is demonstrated to doubters. 4. The proofs have not been on display because they do not still survive, inasmuch as their existence depends upon visual observations. 5. What survives for believers are memory and written accounts. Confabulators have turned lies into ambiguities and passed them on to subsequent generations. 6. One should attempt, nonetheless, to the extent that it is possible, to make distinctions concerning this evidence. 7. For surely something remains of the divine truth that has not been falsified by fraud. 8. Once the fraud is enacted, it has to be immediately refuted so that it makes little headway, since it is not proposing the same thing [i.e., truth]. Truth created the whole logic of this procedure.

XVIII 1 1. **The Conqueror.** And how, he said, would you people be fair using the words of the prophets whose law and faith you do not accept? 2. You have, instead, completely set yourself against the Hebrews, who accept these things. 3. He would be putting forward fairly their witness who accepts those writings that the Hebrews themselves say that they accept and does not reject the others that they receive. 4. How then, having eliminated the whole law of the Hebrews, can you justly make use of their prophets?

XIX 1 1. **The Philosopher.** You must not think that way about us, I said, since we use the prophets in what we need them for. On other matters, however, we leave them aside. 2. For we consider sacred the whole law of Moses; we honor

40. Amiroutzes knew Protagoras's skepticism about the gods and dictum that man is the measure of all things from many sources, including Aristotle; see Diels, *Die Fragmente der Vorsokratiker*, 2:258–61 (§§12–14, 19, 21, 23), 265 (frag. 4).

προφήτας τῶν Ἑβραίων μᾶλλον τιμῶμεν ἑκάστοτε καὶ τοὺς λόγους αὐτῶν ἐπὶ τῆς ἐκκλησίας ἀναγινώσκομεν καὶ διδάσκομεν. 3. οὐδὲ γὰρ ἄλλην ἐκεῖνοι πίστιν ᾔδεσαν ἢ ἣν ἡμεῖς κηρύττομεν.

2 1. Ἑβραῖοι δέ εἰσιν οἱ τοὺς ἐκείνων διαστρέφοντες λόγους καὶ μὴ δεχόμενοι ἃ προηγόρευσαν. 2. τοῖς μέντοι νόμοις αὐτῶν οὐ χρώμεθα νῦν, ἀλλὰ τοῖς τοῦ Χριστοῦ. οἵπερ οὐδὲ ἐναντίοι εἰσίν, εἰ καὶ τοῖς πολλοῖς δοκεῖ. 3. ἀλλὰ πρὸς τὸ αὐτὸ βλέπει καὶ ὁ τοῦ Μωϋσέως νόμος, | 28v πρὸς ὃ καὶ ὁ τοῦ Χριστοῦ. ἑνὸς δὲ ἀντιποιούμενοι τέλους, οὐκ ἀντίκειται.

3 1. Τί δὲ τοῦτο ἐστί, σαφέστερον ἐρῶ. ὁ παλαιὸς νόμος τρία τινὰ γενικῶς περιέχει· 2. τὴν περὶ τοῦ θείου δόξαν, ὅτι δηλαδὴ θεός ἐστιν εἷς καὶ ὅτι αὐτός ἐστιν ἡ τοῦ εἶναι παντὸς ἀρχή, 3. καὶ ὅτι ἐν αὐτῷ ἵδρυται πάντα τὰ ὄντα καὶ αὐτὸς ταῦτα συνέχει καὶ κυβερνᾷ, καὶ τ᾽ ἄλλα τὰ τούτοις ὅμοια. 4. ἔτι τὸν τρόπον τῆς τοῦ θεοῦ λατρείας, ὅτι δεῖ τὰ σάββατα τηρεῖν καὶ μηδὲν ἐν αὐτοῖς ἐργάζεσθαι 5. ὅτι δεῖ ἐνδελεχῶς θυσιάζειν καὶ σπεύδειν ἤ τι προσφέρειν θεῷ, καὶ νηστεύειν καὶ τὰ παραπλήσια. 6. καὶ τρίτον τὴν τῶν ἀνθρώπων παιδείαν· | 29r πῶς δεῖ δηλαδὴ γονεῦσι προσφέρεσθαι, πῶς οἰκείοις, πῶς φίλοις, πῶς πολίταις, πῶς γυναικὶ χρῆσθαι, καὶ τ᾽ ἄλλα τὰ τούτοις ὅμοια.

4 1. Ὅσον μὲν οὖν περὶ τῆς θείας ἀληθείας διαλαμβάνει, αἰώνιόν τε ὀφείλει εἶναι καὶ ἀκίνητον καὶ ὑπὸ πάντων ἀεὶ πιστεύεσθαι τῶν ἀπὸ τοῦ θεοῦ τὸν νόμον ἐκεῖνον ἀφῖχθαι λεγόντων. 2. οὐ γὰρ ἐνδέχεται τὴν περὶ τοῦ θείου δόξαν μεταβάλλοντας, ἣν ὁ νόμος ἐκεῖνος κηρύττει, εὐσεβεῖν ἔτι, 3. ἐπείπερ ἀκίνητός ἐστι πᾶσα ἡ περὶ τὸ ἐξ ἀνάγκης ἀλήθεια, μάλιστα δὲ ἡ περὶ τοῦ θεοῦ, δι᾽ ὃν καὶ τ᾽ ἄλλα τυγχάνει, καὶ τοῦ εἶναι καὶ τοῦ ἀληθοῦς. 4. κινουμένης δὲ | 29v τῆς προτέρας δόξης καὶ ἄλλης εἰσαγομένης μὴ ἐν τῇ προτέρᾳ περιεχομένης, 5. ἀνάγκη τὴν μὲν εἶναι ψευδῆ, τὴν δὲ ἀληθῆ, ἄμφω δὲ μηδέποτε ἀληθεῖς μήδ᾽ ἐκ τοῦ θεοῦ. 6. διὰ ταῦτα ἡμεῖς ἐν τῇ περὶ τοῦ θεοῦ δόξῃ παντάπασιν ἑπόμεθα τοῖς προφήταις. οὐχ ἥπερ Ἰουδαῖοι φασὶ νῦν, ἀλλ᾽ ᾗπερ αἱ ἱεραὶ αὐτῶν διαλαμβάνουσιν βίβλοι.

5 1. Ἡ μὲν οὖν περὶ τοῦ θεοῦ δόξα, ἣν ὁ παλαιὸς νόμος κηρύττει, αἰώνιος, ὅπερ εἶπον, ὀφείλει εἶναι. 2. ὁ δὲ τῆς λατρείας τρόπος γενικῶς μὲν ἀκίνητός ἐστι.

---

3 κηρύττομεν] κ supra lin. iterat T^1 quoniam ambigua in textu est **12** ἔτι] in marg. add. T^1 **16** προσφέρεσθαι] προσφερέσθαι T **22** δι᾽ ὃν] δι᾽ οὗ in marg. ut alteram lectionem scr. T^1 **29** λατρείας] in marg. iterat T^1

the prophets of the Hebrews even more individually; and we read and teach their words concerning the church. 3. For they knew no other faith than that which we ourselves proclaim.

2 1. The Hebrews, however, are the ones who distort the words of the prophets and do not accept what they foretold. 2. We follow today not their law, but Christ's. These are not opposed to each other, even if it seems so to many. 3. Rather, the law of Moses aims at the same thing as does Christ's. Since they seek after one and the same end, they are not opposed.

3 1. What that end is, I shall make clear. The old law in general encompassed three things. 2. [First,] teaching concerning the deity, namely, that God is one and that he is the principle of everything, 3. that all beings have their foundation in him, that he holds them together and governs them, and other doctrines similar to these. 4. Second, the way to give worship to God, namely, that it is necessary to observe Sabbaths and not work on those days, 5. since it is necessary continually to offer sacrifice and be earnest in worship, that is to say, in offering something to God, and to fast, and such like things. 6. And, third, the instruction of the people,[41] namely, how to behave toward parents, toward neighbors, toward friends, toward fellow citizens, how to treat one's wife, and other things similar to these.

4 1. Given the great clarity with which the old law speaks concerning divine truth, it is right that it has always been believed to be eternal and inviolate by all who say that the law has come from God. 2. For it is not possible for people to remain pious who alter the doctrine proclaimed by that law concerning the deity, 3. in view of the fact that every truth concerning what is necessary is inviolate, and most of all the truth concerning God, on account of whom all else exists: that he is, and that he is the true God. 4. If, however, a prior teaching is altered and another introduced which is not encompassed in the prior teaching, 5. one must be false and one true, but both are not ever together true nor are they both from God. 6. Consequently, in our teaching about God, we follow in every respect the prophets, not in the way the Jews today say, but in the way their holy books distinctly state.

5 1. The teaching concerning God that the old law proclaims, then, is rightly eternal, as I said. 2. On the level of genus, its way of worship is also inviolate. For

41. Acciaiuoli translated this not unfairly as *ethica disciplina*.

καὶ γὰρ δεῖ λατρεύειν θεῷ καὶ προσκυνεῖν καὶ προσεύχεσθαι καὶ προσφέρειν. | 30r 3. κατ᾽ εἶδος δὲ οὐκ ἀνάγκη τοῦτον ἀεὶ τηρεῖν· 4. ἀλλ᾽ εἴ τις ἐπὶ τὸ ἄμεινον μεταβάλλοι, οὐκ ἐναντία πάντως ποιεῖ, οὐδ᾽ ἀναιρεῖ τὸν νόμον ἐκεῖνον, 5. ὥσπερ τὸ σαββατίζειν καὶ τὸ θυσιάζειν, ἃ προὔργου μάλιστα τῶν ἄλλων νομίμων ἦγον Ἑβραῖοι, τὸν σκοπὸν ἀγνοοῦντες τοῦ νόμου. 6. οὔτε γὰρ ἱερὰ καθ᾽ αὑτὴν ἡμέρα τυγχάνει τὸ σάββατον οὔτε ἀποφρὰς ὥστε μηδὲν ἐν αὐτῇ ἐξεῖναι ποιεῖν. 7. τοῦτο γὰρ ἐσχάτης ἐστὶ δεισιδαιμονίας οἴεσθαί τι καθ᾽ αὑτὴν τὴν ἑβδόμην ἡμέραν ἱερὸν ἢ ἀποτρόπαιον ἔχειν. 8. ἀλλ᾽ ὁ μὲν νόμος τῶν ἑπτὰ ἡμέραν μίαν ἡγεῖται δεῖν ἀφιεροῦν | 30v τῷ θεῷ ὥστε γενομένους ἀπὸ τῶν ἄλλων ἔργων σχολάζειν ἐν αὐτῇ τῇ τοῦ θεοῦ θεωρίᾳ. 9. οἱ δὲ αὐτὸ τοῦτο ἱερὸν ἐνόμισαν καθ᾽ αὑτὸ τὸ σάββατον καὶ ἅγιον ἢ ἀποτρόπαιον 10. ὥστε ἀνάγκην εἶναι λοιπὸν τοῦτο μετακινεῖν, ὥσπερ τὸ τιμᾶν τὸν πατέρα καὶ τὴν μητέρα, τὸ ἀγαπᾶν τὸν πλησίον, 11. τὸ μὴ φονεύειν καὶ μοιχεύειν, μὴ κλέπτειν, μὴ ψευδομαρτυρεῖν, καὶ εἴ τι τοιοῦτον ἄλλο τυγχάνει. 12. εἴ τις ἐπὶ τὸ ἄμεινον κινοίη, οὐκ ἀνατρέπει τὸν νόμον δι᾽ ὅτι ὁ νόμος ἄγει πρὸς τὸν θεὸν διά τε τῆς λατρείας καὶ τῆς παιδείας.

6 1. Ἔστι δὲ ἄγειν οὐχ ὡσαύτως ἀεί, ἀλλ᾽ ὡς ἂν ὁ καιρὸς | 31r ἑκάστοτε ἀπαιτῇ· 2. καὶ ἡ τῶν ἀνθρώπων ἕξις τὸ δὲ νομίζειν διὰ μόνης τῆς ὁδοῦ ταύτης τυγχάνειν τῆς ἀληθείας, δίχα δὲ ταύτης ἀναιρεῖσθαι τὴν πίστιν, οὐ μωρίας μόνον, ἀλλὰ καὶ δεισιδαιμονίας. 3. τὴν γὰρ πίστιν οὐ τὰ τοῦ νόμου ἔργα ποιεῖ, ἀλλ᾽ ἕστηκεν ἐκείνη προτέρα καθ᾽ αὑτήν. 4. τὰ δὲ τοῦ νόμου ἔργα δι᾽ ἐκείνην ἔστι καὶ πρὸς ἐκείνην φέρει πάντα. 5. καὶ ἔστιν εὑρεῖν ἃ μᾶλλον πρὸς ἐκείνην τὴν ἀλήθειαν ἄγει τοὺς ἀνθρώπους ἕως ἂν τοῦ τέλους ἐφικέσθαι γένηται. 6. τούτου δὲ περιγενομένου, κινεῖν οὐκ ἔτ᾽ ἔξεστι τά γε ὅπως ἀεὶ κρατῇ νενομοθετημένα. 7. ὃ δὴ καὶ πεποίηκεν τοῦ Χριστοῦ νόμος, | 31v οὐκ ἀνελὼν ἐκεῖνον ὡς οὐ καλόν, ἀλλὰ παύσας τελειοτέρᾳ νομοθεσίᾳ. 8. ταῦτα δὲ οὐ μάχονται, ἀλλὰ καὶ πρὸς ἓν ἄγουσι τέλος μάλιστα· καὶ ἑνὸς ἀντιποιοῦνται τῆς τῶν ἀνθρώπων πρὸς τὸν θεὸν ἐπιστροφῆς, 9. ὥσπερ ὁ διδάσκαλος οὐκ ἀντίκειται τῷ παιδαγωγῷ ἕτερα διδάσκων τὸν παῖδα καὶ ἐπ᾽ ἄλλα ἄγων ἢ ὁ παιδαγωγὸς ἦγεν, 10. ἀλλὰ τοῦτ᾽ ἐκεῖνο καὶ ὁ παιδαγω-

---

7 οἴεσθαί] οἲεσθαί corr. T/T[1] **13** μὴ[2]] καὶ ante supra lin. add. T[1] **14** τυγχάνει] post duo verba deleta sunt; in marg. tres verba scr. T[1] sed deinde del. **15** ἄγει] supra lineam scr. T **25** τελειοτέρᾳ] τελεωτέρᾳ T

it is necessary to worship God, to adore him, to pray to him, and to make offerings to him. 3. But at the level of species, it is not always necessary to observe this way of worship. 4. Rather, if one makes a change for the better, one is not doing something completely contradictory to that law, nor is one eliminating it. 5. For instance, take observing the Sabbath and offering sacrifice, things that the Hebrews, not understanding the purpose of the law, considered especially valuable in comparison to the other parts of the law. 6. In itself, the Sabbath is neither holy nor a consecrated day on which it is forbidden to work. 7. For it is the height of superstition to think that there is anything sacred about the seventh day or to treat it as something that wards off evil. 8. Rather, the law deemed it necessary to consecrate to God one day of the seven so that people would have leisure from other work on that day for the contemplation of God. 9. The Hebrews, however, thought that the Sabbath in itself was holy or possessed the power to ward off evil, 10. and thereby removed the necessity of the rest of the law, such as honoring one's father and mother, loving one's neighbor, 11. not killing or committing adultery, not stealing, not bearing false witness, and any other similar injunction you may encounter. 12. If someone progresses toward the better, he is not overturning the law, since the law leads to God through worship and instruction.

6 1. However, the law does not lead to God always in the same way, but always as the times demand. 2. The habit of people to think that truth is reached through a particular way alone and that faith perishes without that particular way is not only folly, but also superstition. 3. For the works of the law do not create faith. Rather, faith rises first by itself. 4. It is because of faith that the works of the law exist and all the works of the law bear upon faith, 5. and it is the task of faith to find the works that lead men more toward that truth until the time of its fulfillment has arrived. 6. Once the law has been superseded, however, it can no longer prompt these divinely legislated works as if they would always be the rule. 7. Christ's law has, in fact, created faith, but not by destroying the old law as if it were not admirable, but by bringing it to an end through more perfect legislation. 8. These laws, however, are not in conflict. Rather, they lead toward one paramount end, and the one end toward which they strive is the turning of men toward God, 9. just as the schoolteacher does not oppose the tutor by teaching the child something different and by leading him in a direction other than where the tutor was leading him. 10. Rather, the tutor wants to hand the

γὸς ἐβούλετο ῥυθμίζων τὸν παῖδα παραδοῦναι τῷ διδασκάλῳ. 11. πῶς οὖν
ἐναντίοι παιδαγωγὸς καὶ διδάσκαλος, εἰ ὁ ἕτερος τὸν παῖδα πρὸς τὸν ἕτερον
ἄγει, ὁ δὲ παραλαβὼν; οἷον ὁ παιδαγωγὸς εὔχεται, τοιοῦτον | αὐτὸν ἀποφαίνει. 32r
12. καὶ μὴν οὐδὲ τοῦ νόμου ἱσταμένου, εἴ τίς τι μεῖζον ἐποίει, ὑπεύθυνος ἦν. 13. ὁ
γοῦν Ἡλίας ὑπερέβη τὸν νόμον. γαμεῖν γὰρ ἐκείνου καὶ παιδοποιεῖσθαι κελεύον-
τος ὑπερεῖδεν, οὐ τοῦ νόμου καταφρονῶν ἀλλὰ τὸν σκοπὸν τοῦ νομοθέτου
εἰδώς.

7 1. Ἐξετάσατε τοίνυν πάντα τὸν τοῦ Χριστοῦ νόμον εἰ μὴ ἐπὶ τὸ τελειότερον
ἄγει τοὺς ἀνθρώπους καὶ ὅλως θειότερον, οὐκ ἀνάγκην ἐπιτιθείς, 2. οὐδ᾽
ἀπειλαῖς ἄγων ἐπὶ τὸν θεόν, ἀλλὰ νουθεσίᾳ καὶ τῇ τῆς ἀληθείας ἀποδείξῃ ἔτι δὲ
ἐλπίδι καὶ φόβῳ τοῦ μέλλοντος. 3. τὸ δὲ ἀνάγκῃ καὶ βίᾳ ἄγειν οὐ τοῦ θεοῦ. 4. τί
γὰρ βου|λόμενος προαίρεσιν ἐδίδου τὴν ἀρχὴν καὶ αὐτεξουσίους ἐποίει, ἀναιρεῖν 32v
μέλλων; 5. τίς δὲ καὶ μισθὸς ὀφείλεται τοῖς βίᾳ τὰ δέοντα ποιοῦσι; 6. καὶ πρὸς
τούτοις εἰ τοῦτο ἐβούλετο, σῴζειν μὴ βουλομένους, τίνος χάριν διδάσκει; διὰ τί
παρακαλεῖ καὶ συμβουλεύει; 7. δυνατὸς γάρ ἐστιν, εἰ μόνον βουληθείη, τὴν
προαίρεσιν ἀφελέσθαι καὶ μακαρίους μὴ βουλομένους ποιεῖν. 8. διὰ τοῦτο ὁ τοῦ
Χριστοῦ νόμος ἀνάγκην οὐδὲ μίαν ἐπάγει. μόνον δὲ διορίζει τὸ ποιητέον καὶ τὸ
μὴ τοιοῦτον.

8 1. Ὀλίγα γοῦν ὧν ὁ τοῦ Χριστοῦ νόμος διαλαμβάνει λέξω τὰ νῦν παραβάλ-
λων αὐτὰ πρὸς | ἅπερ ὁ τοῦ Μωϋσέως νόμος ἐν τούτοις κελεύει, 2. ἵνα γνώριμον 33r
γένηται τὸ διάφορον, ὅτι οὐκ ἐναντίον, ἀλλ᾽ ὑπέρτερον ἐστίν. 3. «οὐκ ἐπιορκή-

---

1 οὖν] supra lin. scr. T/T^{1}

child over to the schoolteacher because the tutor is teaching what the teacher is teaching. 11. How, then, are the schoolteacher and the tutor opposed to each other if one leads the child to the other and the latter receives the child from the former? The tutor prays for the sort of student that the teacher shows off. 12. Thus one is not guilty of frustrating the law if one has produced something greater. 13. Indeed, Elijah transgressed the law. For he ignored its command to marry and have children, not because he scorned the law, but because he understood the purpose of the lawgiver.[42]

7 1. Examine, then, if the whole law of Christ does not lead men to an end that is more perfect and wholly more divine. 2. It imposes no necessity and does not drive men to God by threats, but rather by admonition and the demonstration of truth. It does so also by hope in and fear of the life to come.[43] 3. To drive men by necessity and force is not the way of God. 4. For why would he grant men personal sovereignty by willing that they have free will when he planned to take these things away? 5. What reward, moreover, is owed to those who because of coercion fulfilled their duties? 6. Again, in respect to these duties, if this is what God wanted, to save people against their will, for what purpose did he teach these duties? Why does he preach and recommend them? 7. For he can, if he simply wants to, deprive us of the power of choice and to make us happy against our will. 8. Consequently, the law of Christ does not impose any necessity. It only distinguishes clearly what ought to be done and what ought not to be done.

8 1. I shall now speak of a few instance where the law of Christ differentiates itself by setting aside the injunctions of the law of Moses in these matters 2. in order to make clear the difference, namely, that the law of Christ is not opposed to that of Moses, but is an improvement upon it. 3. *Do not swear falsely*, the law

42. De la Cruz Palma (Amiroutzes, *Diálogo de la Fe*, 60) cites 1 Kings 17, but the chapter says nothing about Elijah not marrying and not having children, nor do any other passage concerning Elijah (1 Kings 18–19, 21:17–28; 2 Kings 1:8–2:14; 2 Chron. 21:12–15; Mal. 4:5–6). Amiroutzes is simply assuming that Elijah remained celibate, as was true of the prophet Jeremiah by the command of God (Jer. 16:2).

43. Amiroutzes introduces here for the first time one of the themes of the dialogue, namely, the necessity of human free will and liberty in matters of religion; see XXVII.1.1 and 4.3–5.

σης», φησὶν ἐκεῖνος, «ἀλλ᾽ ἀποδώσεις κυρίῳ τοὺς ὅρκους σου». 4. ὁ δὲ τοῦ Χριστοῦ «μὴ δὲ ὀμόσαι» τὴν ἀρχὴν συγχωρεῖ, ἀλλὰ τὸν «ναὶ» μόνον καὶ τὸ «οὒ» νομοθετεῖ. 5. «οὐ μοιχεύσης», ἐκεῖνος· ὁ δέ, οὐδὲ ἐμβλέψας «πρὸς τὸ ἐπιθυμῆσαι» ἢ μοιχὸς ἔσῃ ἀπηρτισμένος. 6. «ὀφθαλμὸν ἀντὶ ὀφθαλμοῦ καὶ ὀδόντα ἀντὶ ὀδόντος ἐξελεῖν» ἐκεῖνος· ὁ δὲ τοῦ Χριστοῦ «ἐάν τις σε ῥαπίσῃ εἰς τὴν δεξιὰν σιαγόνα, στρέψον αὐτῷ καὶ τὴν ἄλλην», 7. οὐκ ἄδειαν τῇ πονηρίᾳ διδούς, ἀλλὰ πρα|ότητι καὶ ἐπιεικείᾳ διορθούμενος. 8. οὐ γὰρ οὕτω μεταβάλλει τὴν κακίαν τὸ 33v ἀμύνεσθαι ὡς τὸ πράως φέρειν καὶ μηδὲν ἀντεπάγον προαιρεῖσθαι. 9. «ἀγαπήσεις τὸν πλησίον σου καὶ μισήσεις τὸν ἐχθρόν σου», ἐκεῖνος. 10. ὁ δὲ τοῦ Χριστοῦ «ἐὰν ἀγαπᾶτε τοὺς ἀγαπῶντας ὑμᾶς, τίνα μισθὸν ἔχετε;» «ἐγὼ δὲ λέγω ὑμῖν», φησίν, «ἀγαπᾶτε τοὺς ἐχθροὺς ὑμῶν. εὐλογεῖτε τοὺς καταρωμένους ὑμῖν».

9 1. Διὰ ταῦτα τοῦτον ἀνεῖλε τὸν νόμον ὁ Χριστὸς καὶ εἰς κρείττονα καὶ θειοτέραν ἤγαγε μοῖραν, 2. διὰ βίου σχολάζειν τοῖς τοῦ θεοῦ νομοθετήσας, καὶ τὸ ζωοθυτεῖν δὲ ἀνάξιον λοιπὸν ἐδόκει θεῷ. 3. αἵματι γὰρ ἐδόκει χαίρειν τὸ θεῖον καὶ | κνίσσῃ ὁλοκαυτουμένων τῶν ζῴων ἐν τῷ ναῷ. 4. ὁ δὲ σκοπὸς τοῦ νόμου οὐ 34r τοῦτο ἦν, ἀλλὰ προσφέρειν μέν τι τῷ θεῷ τοὺς ἀνθρώπους ἔκρινεν, 5. οὐ τοῦ θεοῦ δὲ χάριν ἧπερ ᾤοντο οἱ μὴ δὲ πλέον τοῦ γράμματος εἰδότες Ἑβραῖοι (τί γὰρ ἂν ὄναιτο ὁ θεὸς τῶν ἡμετέρων;), ἀλλ᾽ ἡμῶν αὐτῶν. 6. ἃ καλὰ νομίζομεν τούτοις τιμώντων τὸν θεῖον. 7. ἐπεὶ δὲ τότε τούτοις ἅπαντες τὸ θεῖον ἐτίμων, ὅπερ ἐνόμιζον, καὶ ταῦτα προσέφερον, τούτοις καὶ αὐτὸς τὸν ἀληθῆ θεὸν συγκαταβαίνων ἔκρινε τιμᾶν. 8. οὐδὲν οὖν ἐναντίον γέγονεν εἰ τοῦτον τὸν νόμον ἤργησεν ὁ θεός, ἐπεὶ καὶ τῶν ἐν αὐτῷ τῷ νόμῳ ὄντων πολλοὶ τοῦτο τὸ μέρος | περὶ 34v

7 ἐπιεικείᾳ] ἐπιεικιᾳ T || τὴν] supra lin. scr. T **13** διὰ] καὶ ante del. T **14** ζωοθυτεῖν] in marg. T[1] annot.: περὶ τοῦ ζωοθυτεῖν **15** κνίσσῃ] sic T **19** τιμώντων] τιμᾶν in marg. ut lectionem alternativam scr. T[1] **22** θεός] scripsi: Χριστός T, sed supra lin. θεὸς scr. T[1].

of Moses says, *but fulfill your oaths to the Lord.*[44] 4. The law of Christ agrees that we should *not swear*[45] in the first place; but it also legislates that we say only "yes" and "no."[46] 5. The law of Moses says *Do not commit adultery*; that of Christ, however, says, do not even look *with lust* or you will be a complete adulterer.[47] 6. The former tells us *to exact an eye for an eye and a tooth for a tooth.*[48] The law of Christ, however, says that *if someone strikes you on the right cheek, turn the other to him as well,*[49] 7. not to give license to wickedness, but to correct it with gentleness and clemency. 8. For avenging yourself does not alter evil while suffering it meekly and choosing not to retaliate does. 9. *You shall love your neighbor and hate your enemy,*[50] the former says. 10. The law of Christ, on the other hand, says, *If you love those who love you, what reward will you have?*[51] *I, however, tell you,* he says, *love your enemies. Praise those who curse you.*[52]

9 1. In these ways, Christ abolished that law and brought it to a superior and more divine destiny, 2. legislating that we give ourselves to the things of God throughout life and that henceforth the sacrificing of live victims would be seen as unworthy of God. 3. For it had been thought that the Divinity rejoiced in the blood and savor of the sacrifice of the burnt animals in the temple. 4. But that was not the purpose of the law. Rather, it enjoined men to offer something to God, 5. not for God's sake, as the Hebrews thought, not understanding more than the letter of the law—for what benefit would God derive from our possessions?—but for our own sake. 6. We consider the actions of those honoring the Deity by these means to be good. 7. Since everyone in those days used to honor the Deity by these means, as they understood the Deity, and offered these things to God, the law also enjoined the Hebrews in agreement with this practice to honor the true God thusly. 8. Nothing contrary occurred, then, if God vacated this particular law, especially when many of those who participated in the [old]

44. Matt. 5:33, which is said to be referring to Lev. 19:12, Num. 30:3, and Deut. 23:21.
45. Matt. 5:34.
46. Matt. 5:36.
47. Matt. 5:27.
48. Matt. 5:38.
49. Matt. 5:39.
50. Matt. 5:43.
51. Matt. 5:46.
52. Matt. 5:44.

πλείονος οὐκ ἐποιοῦντο. 9. Δαυὶδ γοῦν ὁ προφήτης ἐν τοῖς Ψαλμοῖς, «θῦσον τῷ θεῷ», φησί· «θυσίαν αἰνέσεως καὶ ἀπόδος τῷ ὑψίστῳ τὰς εὐχάς σου». 10. καὶ πάλιν ἄλλοθι· «ὅτι εἰ ἠθέλησας θυσίαν, ἔδωκα ἄν· ὁλοκαυτώματα οὐκ εὐδοκήσεις. θυσία τῷ θεῷ πνεῦμα συντετριμμένον». 11. καὶ ἄλλος δὲ προφήτης, «τί μοι τῶν θυσιῶν ὑμῶν; λέγει κύριος». 12. οὕτως οὐδ᾽ αὐτοὶ οἱ χρώμενοι ταῖς θυσίαις, ἔτι περὶ πλείονος φαίνονται τοῦτο μέρος ποιούμενοι. 13. οὐ μὴν οὐδ᾽ ὅσα περὶ τῆς τῶν ἀνθρώπων παιδείας ὁ παλαιὸς νόμος φησὶν αἰώνια πάντη καὶ ἀκίνητα ἐστὶ καθ᾽ ὃ τέθειται καὶ ἀμετάβλητα.

10 1. Ἃ δὲ καὶ ἐπὶ πλέον | διεξῆλθον ἵν᾽ εἰδῆτε ὅτι τὸν παλαιὸν νόμον ὁ 35r Χριστὸς οὐκ ἀνεῖλεν ὡς οὐ καλόν, ἀλλ᾽ ἐπὶ τὸ τελειότερον καὶ λυσιτελέστερον ἤγαγε. 2. τί δὴ λοιπὸν; οὐ δικαίως τὴν τῶν προφητῶν μαρτυρίαν προφέρομεν; ἢ διὰ τί ἢ πάντα δέχεσθαι καὶ ποιεῖν τε τοῦ νόμου χρὴ ἢ πάντων ὀλιγωρεῖν; 3. οὐ γὰρ δοκεῖ συμβαίνειν τοῦτο τοῖς τοῦ δικαίου λογισμοῖς. τὰ μὲν γὰρ ἀκίνητα τοῦ νόμου τοιαῦτα μένειν ἐῶμεν· 4. τὰ δὲ ἐπὶ τὸ ἄμεινον μεταβάλλοντες οὐκ ἐναντίον τι ποιοῦμεν. οὐδὲ διὰ τοῦτο ἡμᾶς εἴργεσθαι τῶν προφητῶν δίκαιον.

XX 1 1. **Ὁ Κρατῶν.** Καὶ ποῖον, ἔφη, βιβλίον προφητικὸν καταλελοίπατε | 35v ἀδιάφθορον, οἵ γε καὶ τὸ εὐαγγέλιον ἐπὶ τὸ δόξαν ὑμῖν διεφθείρατε, 2. τὰ μὲν προσθέντες ὅσα τὸν Ἰησοῦν προφήτην ὄντα θεὸν ἀγορεύει, τὰ δὲ ἀφελόντες ὅσα περὶ τοῦ ἡμετέρου προφήτου τῷ Ἰησοῦ προείρηται, 3. ὡς ἥξει παρὰ θεοῦ καὶ νόμον ἐκεῖθεν κομίσει, καὶ δεῖ τοῦτον τοὺς ἀνθρώπους εὐσεβεῖν βουλομένους δέχεσθαι; 4. ἃ πάντα ἐκεῖθεν ἐξείλετε. 5. ἔπειτα προφέρετε αὐτὸ εἰς ἀπόδειξιν ὧν

---

5 ταῖς θυσίαις] τὰς θυσίας corr. T[1] **6–8** οὐ . . . ἀμετάβλητα] signo in marg. (linea perpendicula) denotat T[1] **8** τέθειται] τέθηται T **12** τε] τὲ T **16** Ὁ Κρατῶν] om. T, sed signo novum caput indicat || καταλελοίπατε] -λοί- supra lin. scr. T **17** ἀδιάφθορον] ἢ ante del. T **19** Ἰησοῦ] ᾿Ιησῷ corr. T/T[1] et in marg. ᾿Ιησοῦ iterat

law made light of this particular part of it. 9. The prophet David in fact says in the Psalms, *Offer to God the sacrifice of praise and render to the Most High your prayers.*[53] 10. And again elsewhere, *If you wanted sacrifice, I would have given it. You do not delight in sacrifice; a sacrifice for God is a contrite spirit.*[54] 11. And another prophet says, *What value are your sacrifices to me? says the Lord.*[55] 12. Thus these prophets did not practice sacrifices, even when they seem to stress this part of the law. 13. And not even what the old law says concerning the [moral] instruction of mankind is totally eternal and inviolate in its enactments and unchangeable.

10 1. I explained these things at length in order that you might see that Christ did not abolish the old law on account of it not being good. Rather he brought it to a more perfect and beneficial state. 2. What is left? Are we not rightly bringing forward the witness of the prophets? Furthermore, why must it be the case that we either accept and do everything in the law or denigrate all of it? 3. For this choice would not seem to conform with the rationale of justice. Let us keep inviolable this aspect of the law [i.e., the principle of justice]. 4. When we revise the law toward the better, we are doing nothing contradictory. We have not thereby excluded the righteousness of the prophets.

XX 1 1. **The Conqueror.** And, he said, how much of the prophetic Book have you left uncorrupted? You in fact have corrupted the Gospel to suit your views,[56] 2. adding passages proclaiming the prophet Jesus to be God, while removing the passages where Jesus foretold the deeds of our prophet, 3. how he would come from God and receive from him the law, and how men who wish to be pious must embrace this law.[57] 4. All this you have expunged from the Gospel. 5. Next, you advanced it [the corrupted text] as proof of what you say concerning

53. Ps. 49:14.

54. Ps. 50:18–19.

55. Isa. 1:11.

56. ἐπὶ τὸ δόξαν ὑμῖν: a phrase found in Byzantine texts (the TLG reports Michael Psellus, *Epitaphius Funeral Oration on the Patriarch Michael Cerularius* 39 [f. 124]: ἐπὶ τὸ δόξαν ἑαυτοῖς; and John Eugenicus, *Consolation to Constantine Palaeologus* [ed. Lambros, p. 120]: ἐπὶ τὸ δόξαν τῷ κρείττονι), but not in any classical work.

57. I.e., the traditional accusation that Christians (and Jews) were guilty of *taḥrīf*; see Accad, "Corruption and/or Misinterpretation of the Bible"; and Toenies Keating, "Revisiting the Charge of *Taḥrīf*."

λέγετε περὶ τοῦ Ἰησοῦ, διαβάλλοντες αὐτόν, ὡς εἴποι θεὸς εἶναι, ὃ σαφῶς αὐτοὶ προστεθείκατε τῷ εὐαγγελίῳ. 6. ἐπεὶ τό γε ἀδιάφθορον, ἅγιόν τε εἶναι καὶ παρὰ θεοῦ ἥκειν καὶ αὐτοὶ πιστεύομεν, | τίς ἂν οὖν ἀπὸ τοιούτων βιβλίων μαρτυρίαν 36r δέξαιτο;

XXI 1 1. **Ὁ Φιλόσοφος**. Εἰ μὲν διεφθείραμεν ταῦτα τὰ βιβλία, ἔφην ἐγώ, αὐτοί τε ἀνόσια πεποιήκαμεν, καὶ ὑμεῖς δικαίως τὴν ἀπὸ τούτων οὐ προσίεσθε μαρτυρίαν. 2. πλὴν πόθεν τοῦτο δείκνυτε; τοῦτο γὰρ μὴ δεικνύντας διαβάλλειν ἄντικρυς δόξετε καὶ φεύγειν τὸν ἀπὸ τῶν βιβλίων ἐκείνων ἔλεγχον.

2 1. Πρὸς δὲ καὶ τὸ οὕτω περὶ τῶν ἄλλων ἀποφαίνεσθαι οὔτε δίκαιον ἔχει μεθ᾽ ἑαυτοῦ καὶ ἀντιστρέφει οὐκ ἀλόγως. ἀλλ᾽ ὑμεῖς γελάσετε, εὖ οἶδα, εἴ τις τοιόνδε τι πρὸς ὑμᾶς εἴποι. 2. οὐ μὴν ἀλλ᾽ εἰ καὶ μηδεμίαν ἀπόδειξιν τούτου παραγαγεῖν | ἀξιοῦτε, πρὸς ἣν ἀπολογεῖσθαι προσῆκεν ἡμῶν, οὐδὲν ἧττον αὐτοὶ 36v καὶ πρὸς τὴν τοιαύτην ἀξίωσιν ἀποκρινούμεθα.

3 1. Περὶ μὲν οὖν τῶν προφητικῶν βιβλίων ἐκεῖνο φαμέν, ὅτι ταῦτα οὐ παρ᾽ ἡμῖν σώζεται μόνον, ἀλλὰ πολλῷ πρότερον παρ᾽ Ἑβραίοις· 2. ἅτε τῇ ἐκείνων διαλέκτῳ γεγραμμένα ταῦτα λαβόντες ἐξετάσατε εἰ μὴ συμφωνεῖ τοῖς παρ᾽ ἡμῖν. 3. εἰ οὖν συμφωνεῖ, τίνες οἱ διαφθείροντες; ἀμφοτέρους γὰρ τοῦτο πεποιηκέναι, οὐκ ἐνδέχεται ὅτι καθάπαξ ἡμῖν ἐκεῖνοι ἀντίκεινται, 4. καὶ οὐκ ἂν ἐδέξαντο μεταβαλλόντων ἐπὶ τὸ ἡμῖν δοκοῦν. | ἀλλ᾽ οὐδ᾽ ἡμεῖς εἴ τι τοιοῦτον ἐτόλμων 37r ἐκεῖνοι. 5. εἰ δὲ καθ᾽ ἑαυτοὺς τοῦτ᾽ ἐποιοῦμεν, οὐκ ἂν σύμφωνα τοῖς ἑτέροις τὰ τῶν ἑτέρων ἦν. 6. οὐκ ἄρα διεφθείραμεν αὐτοὶ τὰ βιβλία τῶν προφητῶν· ἀλλὰ αὐτὰ τὰ παρ᾽ Ἑβραίοις ὄντα ὡς ἔχει δεχόμεθα. 7. κἀκεῖθεν δείκνυμεν ἃ περὶ τοῦ Ἰησοῦ δοξάζομεν καὶ οὐ δή πω γε Ἑβραῖοι ταῦτα διέφθειραν τῷ Χριστῷ χαριζόμενοι. 8. καὶ περὶ μὲν τῶν προφητικῶν βιβλίων τοσαῦτα.

4 1. Περὶ δὲ τοῦ εὐαγγελίου ἐκεῖνο λέγομεν, ὅτι τοῦτο οὐ γεγραμμένον ἡμῖν ἀφίκετο παρὰ θεοῦ, ἀλλ᾽ ὁ μὲν Ἰησοῦς ἐκεῖθεν ἀληθῶς ἥκει. 2. τοῦτο δὲ ἀπόστολοι ξυνέ|γραψαν ἐκείνου μαθηταὶ γεγονότες. ἃ μὲν παρ᾽ ἐκείνου ἤκουσαν καὶ 37v εἶδον, ταῦτα ξυνέγραψαν. 3. εἰ τοίνυν τοῦτο τὸ εὐαγγέλιον ἔφθαρται, ἀνάγκη ἢ

---

5 Ὁ Φιλόσοφος] om. T, sed signo novum caput indicat **6** αὐτοί τε] αὐτοὶ τὲ T **7** δείκνυτε] δείκνυται corr. T^1 || δεικνύντας] δεικνῦντες (-τες bis) corr. T **9** οὕτω] in marg. annot. T^1: οὑτὰ; [sic] αὔτως μάτην || δίκαιον] in marg. T^1 scr. δικαιολογεῖν || ἔχει] ἔχειν corr. T/T^1 **10** ἑαυτοῦ] ἐστὶ post scr. T^1 et in marg. iterat, sed deinde utrumque del. et scr. δῆλον ὅτι || ἀντιστρέφει] ἀντιστρέφειν corr. T/T^1 **11** τοιόνδε] δέ T **23** γε] supra lin. scr. T

Christ, falsely portraying him as saying that he is God. These things you yourselves have clearly inserted into the Gospel. 6. Since we ourselves believe that our law is uncorrupted, holy, and comes from God, who would therefore accept the witness of such books as yours?

XXI 1 1. **The Philosopher.** If we corrupted these books, I said, we ourselves have committed blasphemy, and you would be right not to accept the witness of these books. 2. Except where is your proof? For without having proved it, you seem to go straight to casting aspersions and avoiding any refutation drawn from these books.

2 1. Besides, to make assertions in this way about others has no fairness in it, and logically it is open to retorsion. But you would laugh, I well know, if anyone said any such thing against you. 2. But if you choose not to advance any proof against which we might fittingly mount a defense, we shall nonetheless make a response against such a position.

3 1. Therefore, concerning the prophetic books, this is what we say. These texts are not preserved by us alone, but also much earlier by the Hebrews. 2. Take them up as written by the Hebrews in their own language and examine if they do not agree with the texts we have. 3. If they agree, then who are the corrupters? For it is not possible both would have done this, inasmuch as the Hebrews are utterly opposed to us. 4. Nor, if we had changed things to our liking, would they have accepted it. But neither would we have accepted it if they were brazen enough to try any such thing. 5. If, however, we had made the changes in just the copies we keep for ourselves, neither of us would have texts that agree with each others'. 6. We have not, therefore, corrupted the books of the prophets. Rather, it is the case that we accept the very same texts as are accepted among the Hebrews. 7. Hence, we point to the passages that we think are about Jesus, and yet even the Hebrews have yielded to Christ and have not corrupted them. 8. This is what we have to say about the books of the prophets.[58]

4 1. Concerning the Gospel, we say as follows. The Gospel did not come to us from God in a written form. We say, rather, that Jesus truly came on earth, 2. and that the apostles, having become his disciples, wrote the Gospel. They wrote what they heard from him and what they saw. 3. If, then, this Gospel is corrupted,

58. Avicenna acknowledged the cogency of this argument; see *De Almahad*, f. 45r; *Epistola sulla vita futura*, 58.

αὐτοὺς τοὺς τοῦτο ξυγγραψαμένους οὕτως αὐτὸ πλάσασθαι 4. καὶ ἃ μὴ ἤκουσαν
παρὰ τοῦ Ἰησοῦ ταῦτα ὡς αὐτοῦ εἰρηκότος γράψαντας ἐκδοῦναι, 5. ἢ ἐκείνους
μὲν αὐτὸ ἀνόθευτον ἐκδοῦναι αὐτὰ τὰ ῥήματα ἐκθεμένους τοῦ Ἰησοῦ καὶ τὰ
θαύματα. 6. τοὺς δὲ μετὰ ταῦτα αὐτὸ δεξαμένους τοῦτο τολμῆσαι διότι δή; ἄλλο
γὰρ οὐκ ἐνδέχεται.

5 1. Ἐπεὶ τόν γε Ἰησοῦν οὐκ ἂν φαίητε τοσόνδε τι ἀλαζονεύσασθαι καὶ
προ|φήτην ὄντα θεὸν ἑαυτὸν εἰπεῖν, 2. ἐπεὶ δὲ οὐχ ὅλον τὸ εὐαγγέλιον διαβάλ- 38r
λετε, ἀλλὰ τὰ θαύματα καὶ τὴν διδασκαλείαν ἀποδεχόμενοι, 3. ἐκεῖνα μόνα
παραγράφεσθε ὅσα μὴ μόνον ἄνθρωπον ἀλλὰ καὶ θεὸν ὡς θεοῦ λόγον ἀναγο-
ρεύει τὸν Ἰησοῦν. 4. αὐτὸ τοῦτο μόνον ἐξετάσωμεν, εἰ πλάσαντες οἱ τὸ εὐαγγέ-
λιον συγγραψάμενοι ἐκδεδώκασι ἢ ὑπὸ τοῦ Ἰησοῦ εἰρημένον ἀπήγγειλαν. 5. ὅτι
μὲν οὖν οὐκ ἐξ αὐτῶν τοῦτο εἶπον μαρτυροῦσιν Ἑβραῖοι, οἱ τοῦτο μόνον
ἔγκλημα ἀπαγαγόντες θανάτου τῷ Ἰησοῦ ὅτι θεὸν ἐτόλμησεν αὐτὸν εἰπεῖν.
6. πολλὰ γὰρ ἐξετάζοντος Πιλάτου, | πρὸς ὃν αὐτὸν ἀποθανούμενον ἤγαγον, 38v
τίνος χάριν αὐτὸν θανάτου τιμῶνται μηδὲν ἀδικήσαντα, 7. ἔφασαν «ἡμεῖς νόμον
ἔχομεν καὶ κατὰ τὸν νόμον ἡμῶν ὀφείλει ἀποθανεῖν, ὅτι ἑαυτὸν θεοῦ υἱὸν
ἐποίησεν», ἴσον ἑαυτὸν ποιῶν τῷ θεῷ. 8. ταῦτα οἱ τότε Ἑβραῖοι. οἱ δὲ νῦν ἐκ
διαδοχῆς αὐτὸ λαβόντες οὐδὲν ἕτερον εἰς ἀπολογίαν φασὶν ὧν οἱ πατέρες αὐτῶν
ἐτόλμησαν εἰς Χριστὸν 9. ἢ ὅτι θεὸν ἑαυτὸν ἔλεγεν, οὐδὲ ἄνθρωπος ὢν ἀγαθός.

6 1. Ταῦτα γὰρ ἱκανὰ εἰς μαρτυρίαν ὅτι οὐκ οἴκοθεν οἱ ἀπόστολοι τοῦτο
ἐπλάσαντο, ἀλλ᾿ εἰρημένον ὑπὸ | τοῦ Ἰησοῦ συνέγραψαν. 2. εἰ τοίνυν ἐκεῖνος 39r
περὶ αὐτοῦ τοῦτο εἶπεν, οἱ ἀπόστολοι ἀνεύθυνοι ἃ ἤκουσαν ἀπαγγείλαντες καὶ
τὸ εὐαγγέλιον οὐ νόθον, οὐδὲ διεφθορὸς ὑπ᾿ οὐδενός. 3. ἀλλὰ μὴν εἰ ἐκεῖνος
περὶ αὐτοῦ τοῦτο εἶπεν, ἀνάγκη καὶ ἀληθὲς εἶναι. εἰ γὰρ μὴ ἦν ἀληθές, ἐψεύδετο
δηλαδή· μᾶλλον δὲ ἐβλασφήμει. 4. πῶς οὖν ἀνίστη λόγῳ μόνῳ νεκρούς; πῶς
ἰᾶτο τοὺς πεπηρωμένους; πῶς ἐθεράπευε τοὺς νοσοῦντας; πῶς ἐξήλαυνε τὰ
δαιμόνια; 5. ταῦτα γὰρ πάντα καὶ αὐτοὶ ὁμολογεῖτε ὅτι ἐποίει. οὔκουν πέπλασται
τὸ εὐαγγέλιον. | 6. οὐδὲ πονηρίᾳ τινὶ συντέθειται. ἔτι δὲ καὶ ὧδε δῆλον ὅτι οὐκ 39v
ἂν αὐτὸ εἶπον οἱ μαθηταὶ εἰ μὴ ἐκεῖνος εἰρήκει τοῦτο περὶ αὐτοῦ.

---

4 μετὰ ταῦτα] μεταταῦτα T || δεξαμένους] δεζαμένους corr. T[1] **7** ἑαυτὸν] ἑ- supra lin. scr. T **11** ὑπὸ] ἀ supra υ scr. T[1] **24** μὴ] in marg. scr. T

necessarily either the very authors of the Gospel thus falsified it 4. and published what they did not hear from Jesus, writing these things as if he had said them, 5. or they did publish the unadulterated Gospel itself, disseminating the very words and miracles of Jesus. 6. Why, moreover, would those who subsequently received the Gospel have dared to change it? For no other alternative is possible.

5 1. Since you would not say that Jesus himself feigned such an enormity and that as a prophet call himself God, 2. and since, moreover, you do not repudiate the whole Gospel, but accept his miracles and his teaching activity, 3. what you refuse to believe are only those texts that proclaim Jesus to be not only man but also God as the Word of God. 4. Let us examine just this one point, namely, whether the authors of the Gospel were guilty of fraud when they published this claim or whether they reported what Jesus said. 5. The Hebrews bear witness that in saying this the evangelists did not get this claim from themselves, inasmuch as the Hebrews themselves laid only this one capital charge against Jesus, namely, that he dared to say that he was God. 6. For when Pilate, to whom they brought him to be killed, closely examined them on the reason why they demanded his execution, though he had done no wrong, 7. they said: *We have a law, and according to our law he ought to die, because he made himself the Son of God,*[59] making himself equal to God. 8. This is what the Hebrews of that time said. Present-day Hebrews receiving this position from their tradition offer no other defense of what their fathers dared to do to Christ 9. other than that he said he was God and was therefore not a good man.

6 1. Let this suffice as proof that the apostles did not fabricate this assertion out of their own imagination, but wrote what Jesus himself said. 2. If, then, he said this about himself, the apostles innocently reported what they heard and the Gospel is not a counterfeit nor has it been corrupted by anyone. 3. But if in fact he said this concerning himself, it is also necessarily the truth. For if it were not the truth, he clearly lied; worse, he blasphemed. 4. How, then, did he raise the dead by his word alone? How did he heal the lame? How did he cure the sick? How did he expel the demons? 5. For you yourselves also acknowledge that he did all these things. The Gospel therefore is not falsified. 6. Nor was it put together with any evil intent. It is also consequently clear that his disciples would not have said this unless he had said it about himself.

59. John 19:7.

7 1. Ἄν τις τοίνυν ἀληθῶς ἐξετάζῃ, ἀρχὴν εὑρήσει τοῦ ἀγαθοῦ βίου, τὴν
ἀληθῆ περὶ θεοῦ δόξαν. 2. τοὺς δὲ ἐν τούτῳ ἢ ἑκόντας πονηροὺς γενομένους ἢ
ἀγνοοῦντας ἄλλως τὸ ἀληθὲς σφαλομένους οἰκείῳ καὶ ξυνῳδῷ τῇ δόξῃ καὶ βίῳ
χρωμένους.

8 1. Καὶ δηλοῦσιν οἱ πρότερον Ἕλληνες. ὅσοις γὰρ ἀρετῆς ἐμέλησεν, οὗτοι
καὶ δόγμασιν ἀληθεστέροις τῶν ὑπαρχόντων ἐχρήσαντο καὶ μύθους τὴν πρὶν
ὑπάρχουσαν σφίσιν περὶ τοῦ θείου δόξαν ἐνόμισαν. | 2. πῶς οὖν ἐπὶ τῶν ἀποστό- 40r
λων ἐνδέχεται τοῦτο εἰπεῖν, οἷς ἀρετῆς πλέον ἐμέλησιν ἢ τοῦ ζῆν, ὅτι ἐπλάσαντο
τοιαύτην ὑπόθεσιν 3. καὶ μὴ εἰρημένον παρὰ τοῦ Ἰησοῦ, ὅτι θεὸς εἴη, αὐτοὺς
οἴκοθεν ἡγεῖσθαι συνθεμένους κηρύξαι; 4. πρᾶγμα οὐ μόνον τῷ νόμῳ, ᾧ συνεβί-
ωσαν, δοκοῦν μάχεσθαι, ἀλλὰ καὶ ἀνθρώποις ἅπασι. καίτοι βίον μὲν ἐφθαρμένον
ἔστιν εὑρεῖν καὶ δόξης ἀληθοῦς ὑπαρχούσης περὶ τοῦ θείου. 5. τὸ γὰρ ἡδὺ
πολλάκις προτίθεμεν τοῦ ἀγαθοῦ, ὑπὸ φαύλου ἕξεως ἀγόμενοι, τοὺς δὲ ψευδῆ
καὶ πεπλασμένην περὶ τοῦ | θείου δόξαν εἰσάγοντας. 6. οὐκ ἄν τις εὕροι ἀρετῆς 40v
ἀληθοῦς ἐπιμελομένους. οὐκ ἔστι τοῦτο, οὐκ ἔστιν. 7. ἀλλὰ πρότερον ἂν κνίδη
σύκα ἐνέγκαι ἢ τοὺς τοιούτους λόγον ἀληθῆ τινα τῆς ἀρετῆς ἔχειν.

9 1. Καὶ μὴν κἀκεῖνο ἄξιον εἰπεῖν ὅτι οὐκ ἀνθρώπινος ὅδε ὁ νόμος ἐστίν, οὐδὲ
προαιρέσει τινὶ ξυντεθειμένος 2. ὅτι μὴ πρὸς τὸ τινῶν ἀγαθὸν ὁρᾷ, μὴ δὲ τὸ τινὶ
συνοῖσον ζητεῖ. 3. τοῦτο γὰρ ἐνίοτε ἄλλοις μάχεται. ἀλλὰ τὸ καθ᾽ αὑτὸ ἀγαθὸν
σκοπεῖ καὶ ὃ πᾶσιν ἐστὶ τὸ αὐτὸ καὶ ἀγαθὸν καὶ λυσιτελές. 4. οὗ περιγενομένου
ἀναιρεῖται λοιπὸν πᾶσα | διαφορὰ καὶ ἀντίθεσις, καὶ εἰρήνη σαφὴς ἐπιλάμπει τῷ 41r
βίῳ. 5. οὔκουν ἔστι τοὺς ψευδῆ πλασαμένους ὑπόθεσιν μᾶλλον δὲ ἐναντίον θεοῦ
τοιοῦτον νόμον εἰσάγειν τῷ βίῳ. 6. οὐ γὰρ ἔστι τὸν αὐτὸν ἀγαθόν τε καὶ
πονηρὸν εἶναι, οὐδὲ τῷ θεοῦ μαχόμενον ἃ μάλιστα ἐκείνῳ δοκεῖ νομοθετεῖν.
7. καὶ μὴν πάντας τοὺς τὰ ψευδῆ τοῦτον συνθεμένους τὸν τρόπον ἄν τις
ἀκριβῶς ἐξετάζῃ, εὑρήσει τινὸς αὐτοῖς συμφέροντος στοχαζομένους καὶ διὰ
τοῦτο τὸ ἀθέμιτον ἔργον ἐκεῖνο τολμῶντας. 8. τὸ γὰρ κακὸν οὐκ ἂν γέ|νοιτο δι᾽ 41v
ἑαυτὸ αἱρετόν, ἀλλὰ διάτι δοῦναι ἀγαθόν. ἔστι γὰρ τὸ κακὸν διὰ τὸ ἀγαθόν. καθ᾽
αὑτὸ δὲ οὐκ ἄν ποτε εἴη. 9. οἱ δὲ ἀπόστολοι οὐδὲν τοιοῦτον σκοποῦντες ἐν παντὶ

---

6 ὑπαρχόντων] ὑπάρχονσαν T **12** περὶ] τῷ βίῳ ante del. T/T^1 **15** ἐπιμελομένους] -ελλο- corr. T^1 **16** τοὺς] bis, sed corr. T/T^1 **20** περιγενομένου] περὶ γενομένου T **22** ἐναντίον] α supra ο scr.T^1 **23** βίῳ] αν supra ῳ scr. T^1 sed deinde del. **24** ἐκείνῳ] ἐκείνο corr. T^1

7 1. If, then, one honestly examines the Gospel, one would find the principle of the good life, namely, the true teaching concerning God. 2. One would find, however, that the evildoers in the Gospel, whether willfully or through ignorance of the truth, were overcome when they experienced the life proper to, and coherent with, this teaching.

8 1. The Greeks of yesteryear demonstrate this. For whosoever of them dedicated themselves to virtue came to rely upon teachings truer than what was then current, and came to view the opinion current among them about God as myths. 2. How, then, can one say about the apostles, for whom virtue mattered more than life, that they fabricated such a proposition, 3. and that colluding among themselves, they thought fit to proclaim on their own authority something he did not say, namely, that he was God? 4. This is an action that seems to run counter not only to the law by which the apostles lived in common, but also to the way all men act. This is in effect to enter into a life of wickedness at the very moment that the true teaching about God has arisen. 5. For driven by our evil ways, we often prefer the pleasurable over the good, preferring those who present a false and fabricated teaching about God. 6. But no one will find fraudsters who care deeply about true virtue [as did the apostles]. That is not the case. It just is not. 7. Rather, sooner would a nettle bear fruit than would such fraudsters have any share in true virtue.

9 1. It is also worth pointing out that this law [of the Gospel] is neither man-made nor a compact made to favor some particular party. 2. It does not look to the good of just some people, and it does not seek what is advantageous just to someone. 3. For a man-made law will at times be at odds with other man-made laws. Rather, the law of the Gospel intends the good itself and what is in itself good and beneficial for all people. 4. In addition, when it is fulfilled, all difference and enmity are destroyed, and a clear peace shines forth in people's lives. 5. So it is more the case that those who fabricate a mendacious proposition will institute in their own lives a form of law that contradicts God's law. 6. For the same law is not both good and evil, and it does not contradict God to legislate what he wants most. 7. Indeed, if anyone carefully studies all those who fabricate lies in this way, he will discover that they aimed for something that benefitted themselves, and that this was the reason why they undertook the crime. 8. Indeed, evil is not chosen for its own sake, but for the purpose of producing a good. For evil exists by virtue of the good; in itself, evil would never exist. 9. It is clear, however, that

τῷ βίῳ φαίνονται ἐξ οὗ συνεγένοντο τῷ Χριστῷ. 10. οὔτε γὰρ ἡδονῶν οὔτε
δόξης οὔτε δυνάμεως οὔτε χρημάτων λόγον ὁπωσοῦν ἐποιήσαντο.

10 1. Οὐκ ἄρα συνέθεντο αὐτοὶ τὰ ψευδῆ. οὐδὲ ἐπλάσαντο τοιαύτην ὑπόθε-
σιν. 2. εἰ δέ τις τὴν ἐλάττονα μὴ δέχεται, ἀλλὰ καὶ ταύτης ἀνάγκην ἀπαιτεῖ,
ἀναιρεῖται καὶ τοὺς τῆς διαλέξεως ὅρους, ἀναγκαίαν ἀπόδειξιν | ἀπαιτῶν τοῦ 42r
ἐνδεχομένου καὶ τοῦ καθέκαστα. 3. καίτοι καὶ τοῦτο δείκνυται ἐξ οὗ νομοθε-
τοῦσι. τὰ γὰρ ἄριστα καὶ τὰ θειότατα καὶ τῶν παρόντων ὑπεροψίαν ὁρίζουσι
πανταχοῦ. 4. ὧν οὐκ ἂν αὐτοὶ τοῖς ἐναντίοις χρώμενοι τοὺς ἀνθρώπους ἔπειθον,
οὐδὲ ἀπεκήρυττον οὕτως ἐλευθέρως τοὺς μὴ χρωμένους, εἴ τι συνῄδεσαν αὐτοῖς
πονηρὸν.

11 1. Εἰ δέ τις καὶ πρὸς ταῦτα ἐνσταίη, πεπαιδευμένος μὲν οὗτος οὐκ ἂν εἴη.
ἴστω δὲ πάντα τὰ ὁπωσοῦν περί τινων λεγόμενα τοῦτον τὸν τρόπον ἀναιρῶν.
2. τίς γὰρ ἂν ἀπόδειξις γένοιτο ὅτι Μωϋσῆς γέγονεν ἀνὴρ | ἀγαθὸς ἢ Δαυὶδ ἢ ὁ 42v
λοιπὸς τῶν προφητῶν χορός; 3. πόθεν δ᾽ ἄν τις πεισθείη ὅτι Σωκράτης τοιοῦτος
ἦν οἷον αὐτὸν ἡ κρατοῦσα δόξα φησίν; ὅλως γὰρ ἀπόδειξιν οὗτος ζητεῖ οὗ μὴ
ἔστιν ἀπόδειξις.

12 1. Ἔτι οὐδεὶς ἂν μὴ πεπεισμένος μέχρι θανάτου ἐνσταίη περὶ αὐτοῦ οὗ μὴ
πέπεισται. 2. ὅπου γὰρ καὶ οἱ σφόδρα πεπεισμένοι δέει θανάτου μεταβάλλονται,
σχολῇ γ᾽ ἂν οἱ μὴ τοιοῦτοι θανεῖν ἕλοιντο περὶ οὗ μὴ ἴσασιν ἢ τοὐναντίον
γινώσκουσιν. 3. ἀλλ᾽ οἱ ἀπόστολοι μέχρι θανάτου τὴν ἔνστασιν ἐποιήσαντο ὅτι
θεὸς εἴη ὁ παρ᾽ αὐτῶν κηρυττόμενος. | 4. πεπεισμένοι τοίνυν ἐτύγχανον ὅτι 43r
ἀληθῆ διδάσκουσιν. 5. ἀλλ᾽ οἱ τὰ ψευδῆ συντιθέντες ἐπὶ τῷ τοὺς ἄλλους ἐξαπα-
τᾶν οὐκ εἰσὶ πεπεισμένοι περὶ τούτου οὗ πλάττουσιν. 6. τὸν μὲν γὰρ ἐξηπατημέ-

4 ἐλάττονα] in marg. annot. T^1: σημείωσαι· ἐλάττονα Λατίνων δίκην **5** ἀναιρεῖται] ἀναιρεῖτο corr. T^1 || τοὺς] supra lin. scr. T^1 **7** τὰ^1] καὶ supra scr. T^1 **19** τοιοῦτοι] in marg. annot. T^1: καὶ σὺ τοιοῦτος γέγονας, ὦ ᾽γαθέ **21** εἴη] εἶ corr. T^1

for their whole lives, from the moment they became disciples of Christ, the apostles did not aim for such personal advantage. 10. For neither pleasure nor glory nor power nor wealth was the reason that made them do whatever they did.

10 1. They did not therefore devise lies. Neither did they fabricate such a proposition [that Jesus Christ was God]. 2. If, however, one does not accept the minor premise,[60] but rather denies its necessity, one destroys the rules of logic and is demanding the necessity of scientific demonstration from the contingent and particular. 3. That the apostles did not lie is also shown from what they legislated. For everywhere they prescribe the best and most divine things, as well as contempt for the present life. 4. If they themselves practiced the opposite of the principles which they were persuading men to practice, they would not have denounced so freely those who failed to follow these principles, especially if they themselves were to a degree complicit in the evildoing.

11 1. If anyone were to resist these inferences, he would be uneducated. Let him realize that by such a stance he would be rejecting everything that in any way has been said about anyone. 2. For what proof would there be that Moses was a good man, or that David was a good man, or that the rest of the prophets were? 3. How would someone make the case that Socrates was the person that prevailing opinion says he was? He would be looking for proof of something for which there is no proof.

12 1. Furthermore, no one who does not believe in something would stand firm unto death for what he does not believe in. 2. For when even those who intensely believe are made to change their mind by the fear of death,[61] those who are nonbelievers would hardly choose death for what they did not know or for what they believe to be the opposite of the truth. 3. But the apostles remained resolute unto death in the view that the one who preached among them was God. 4. They believed, then, that they were teaching the truth. 5. But those who devise lies in order to fool others are not themselves believers in what they fabricate. 6. For the person who is being fooled plausibly refuses to budge, thinking that he

60. The organizer of the Greek manuscript notes in the margin that Amiroutzes is following logical Latin usage here (see the apparatus criticus).

61. In a marginal note, the organizer of the Greek manuscript accuses Amiroutzes here of subsequently apostatizing (see the apparatus criticus).

νον ἔστιν ἴσως ἐνστῆναι οἰόμενον ὑπὲρ τοῦ ἀληθοῦς τοῦτο ποιεῖν. 7. τὸν δὲ αὐτὸν συντιθέντα οὔτ᾽ ἐξαπατηθῆναι ἐνδέχεται οὔτε πεπεῖσθαι, καὶ ἑπομένως οὐδὲ μέχρι θανάτου ἐνστῆναι. 8. οὐκ ἄρα συνέθεντο οἱ ἀπόστολοι τὸ καὶ θεὸν οὐκ ἄνθρωπον μόνον εἶναι τὸν Ἰησοῦν.

13 1. Ἔτι εἰ μὴ σφόδρα πεπεισμένοι ἦσαν καὶ ὑπὲρ αὐτῆς τῆς ἀληθείας τὸν ἀγῶνα τοῦτον εἰσήεσαν, 2. οὐκ ἂν ἐθάρ|ρησαν τοσούτῳ πράγματι ἐγχειρῆσαι τῇ 43v
τῆς οἰκουμένης πρός τε τἀγαθὸν καὶ τὴν ἀλήθειαν ἀπὸ τῆς πλάνης ἐπιστροφῇ, μηδὲν οἴκοθεν ἔχοντες πρὸς τοῦτο ἐφόδιον. 3. οὔτε γὰρ γένει περίβλεπτοι ἦσαν οὔτε ζηλωτοὶ πλούτῳ. οἷς εἰκὸς τὸ πλῆθος ἀγόμενον; οἷς ἂν αὐτοὶ γνοῖεν συντίθεσθαι; 4. ἀλλ᾽ οὐδὲ δύναμίν τινα περιβεβλημένοι ἦσαν, οὐδὲ σοφίαν, αἷς ἂν οὐκ ἀλόγως θαρρήσαντες τοιαῦτα διενοήθησαν. 5. τοὐναντία μὲν πάντα μετὰ περιουσίας αὐτοῖς προσῆν. καὶ γὰρ ἀγενεῖς ἦσαν καὶ πένητες καὶ ἰδιῶται. 6. ἔτι δὲ ἀμαθίᾳ συνέζων ἐσχάτῃ ἅτε περὶ ἁ|λείας ἀεὶ σχολάζοντες καὶ μηδὲν πλέον 44r
σαγήνης εἰδότες. 7. οὔκουν ἦν οὕτω τί μέγα καὶ χαλεπὸν ἔργον εἰς νοῦν ἐμβαλέσθαι μὴ σφόδρα πεπεισμένους περὶ ἧς ἐκήρυττον ἀληθείας. 8. οἱ δὲ φαίνονται τῷ ἔργῳ μετὰ τοσαύτης ἐλπίδος ἐπιθέμενοι μεθ᾽ ὅσης οὐδεὶς οὐδενὸς ἥψατο.

14 1. Πρῶτον μὲν γὰρ ἐμερίσαντο τὴν οἰκουμένην ἅπασαν. ἔπειτα κλήρῳ λαχόντες, εἰς τὴν λαχοῦσαν οὐδενὸς ἕκαστος οὐ πατρίδος, οὐ γένους, οὐκ οἴκου, οὐ τῆς ἄλλης περιουσίας ἐπιστρεφόμενος ἀπήει μετὰ σπουδῆς. 2. καίτοι προείρητο αὐτοῖς ὑπὸ τοῦ διδασκάλου μετὰ | κινδύνου καὶ θανάτου τὸ ἔργον 44v
σφίσι προβήσεσθαι καὶ πονηρᾶς αὐτίκα δόξης αἴτιον ἔσεσθαι. 3. ἀλλ᾽ οὐδὲν αὐτῶν τὴν ἔνστασιν ἤμβλυνεν, οὐδὲ τὴν ἐξ ἀρχῆς αἵρεσιν ἤμειψεν, ἀλλ᾽ ὥσπερ τι ὄφλημα ἀναγκαῖον ἐκπληροῦντες οὕτως ἐπεξῆλθον τῷ ἔργῳ. 4. καὶ οὐδ᾽ ἐν αὐτοῖς τοῖς κινδύνοις γενόμενοι μισούμενοι καὶ διωκόμενοι καὶ αἰκιζόμενοι καὶ ἀναιρούμενοι ἀλλοιότερον ἔσχον. 5. ἀλλ᾽ οὐδὲ ἧττον οἱ περιλελειμμένοι, καίπερ

---

6 ἐθάρρησαν] ἐταρ corr. T^1 et in marg. ἐθάρ- iterat **13** ἁλείας] ἀλείαν T **16** ὅσης] ὅσος corr. T^1 **22** ὥσπερ] ὥσπέρ T **25** ἀλλοιότερον] ἀλοιότερον corr. T^1 || περιλελειμμένοι] -λειμένοι corr. T^1

is doing this for the sake of the truth. 7. It is not possible, on the other hand, for the deviser of the deception himself to be fooled or to believe in the deception, and consequently he will not stand firm unto death. 8. Therefore the apostles did not fabricate the proposition that Jesus was God and not just man.

13 1. Furthermore, if they did not intensely believe this and were not entering the contest on behalf of truth itself, 2. they would not have dared to undertake such a grand enterprise, turning the whole world from error and toward goodness and truth itself, though they themselves had for the task no resources of their own. 3. For they were neither distinguished in lineage nor blessed with wealth. How is it likely that the masses would be led to them? How on their own would they know how to fabricate [the doctrine of Christ's divinity]? 4. On the contrary, they possessed neither power nor wisdom, that is, the means by which they might have reasonably dared to plan such great deeds. 5. What they had in abundance was the very opposite of all these resources. For they were of low birth, poor, and uneducated. 6. Furthermore, they lived together in extreme ignorance, continually occupied in fishing, and knew nothing more than what a dragnet is. 7. Such a massive and difficult task, therefore, would not have even entered into their heads if they did not intensely believe in the truth of what they preached. 8. But they seem to have set upon the work with a hope as great as anybody's who has set out on anything.

14 1. They first divided up the whole world into sections. Then, casting lots, each zealously went off to his own portion and not to another's, without even a backward glance to his homeland, his people, his native district, and the prosperity of the others.[62] 2. Indeed, it was foretold to them by their teacher [Christ] that their work would advance at their peril and through their deaths and would cause them to become instantaneously objects of contempt. 3. But nothing dulled their resolve nor did anything make them alter their original commitment. Rather, just as if they were paying off some unavoidable debt, they sallied forth to their work. 4. And in the course of these perils, though they suffered scorn, persecution, abuse, and executions, they had no change of heart. 5. Instead, those who survived, even though they knew full well that they would suffer death in

62. I.e., the legend of the *sortes apostolorum*; see Eusebius, *HE* 3.1; and Socrates, *HE* 1.19.

εἰδότες ὡς ταὐτὰ πάντως τοῖς ἄλλοις τελευτῶντες πείσονται τὸ προκείμενον ἔπραττον, | ὃ μὴ σφόδρα πεπεισμένοι ὄντες οὐκ ἐποίουν. 45r

15 1. Οὐκ ἄρα συνέθεντο αὐτοὶ τὰ ψευδῆ· οὐδὲ ἐπλάσαντο τοιαύτην ὑπόθεσιν. 2. ἔτι οὐδ᾽ ἔχει λόγον ἀνθρώπους τοιούτους τοιαύτην πλασαμένους ὑπόθεσιν εἰς τὴν οἰκουμένην ἐξελθεῖν τολμῆσαι 3. καὶ μετὰ παρρησίας κηρύξαι τοὺς ἀνθρώπους πάντας ἐπὶ τοῦτο παρακαλοῦντας καὶ ταῦτα μηδὲν ἐπαγγελομένους τοῖς πειθομένοις τῷ βίῳ τούτῳ χρηστόν. 4. οὐ δόξαν, οὐ πλοῦτον, οὐ δύναμιν, οὐχ ἡδονήν, οὐδὲ ῥαστώνην τινά, τοὐναντία μὲν οὖν νομοθετεῖν μέλλοντες, ἅτε εἰρημένον ὑπὸ τοῦ διδασκάλου, πενίαν | καὶ ἀδοξίαν καὶ πᾶσαν ἡδονῆς 45v ἀποστροφήν. 5. οὐ γὰρ οὕτως εὐήθεις ἦσαν ὡς ψεῦδος τοῦ βίου τοιούτου προστησαμένους ὑπόθεσιν καὶ μηδὲν ἀγαθὸν ἐπαγγελομένους ὧν ᾔδεσαν οἱ τότε ἄνθρωποι ἐλπίσαι τι δυνηθῆναι. 6. μᾶλλον δὲ ὅλως περιγενέσθαι καὶ μὴ διαφθαρῆναι οὕτως ἀλλοτρίᾳ τῇ τῶν πολλῶν δόξῃ καὶ διδάσκοντες καὶ νομοθετοῦντες. 7. ἀλλὰ δῆλον ὅτι οὗτοι πεπεισμένοι ἦσαν ὡς ἀληθῆ διδάσκουσι καὶ τὸ θεῖον αὐτοῖς ἄνωθεν συνέπραττεν τὴν τῶν ἀνθρώπων ἐπιστροφὴν ἐπιπνοίᾳ καὶ θαύμασιν. 8. οὐ γὰρ ἂν ἔπεισαν, οὐδὲ | τοσοῦτον ἠδυνήθησαν διὰ τῶν ἐναντίων 46r ἰόντες.

16 1. Τὰ γὰρ φίλτατα αὐτὰ καὶ ὧν ἄνευ οὐκ ἄν τις ἕλοιτο ζῆν, ἀρνεῖσθαι παρῄνουν. 2. ἔτι δὲ καὶ ἑαυτοὺς καὶ τὸν οἰκεῖον σταυρὸν ἀραμένους, ἑτοίμους εἰς θάνατον εἶναι ὑπὲρ τῆς ἀληθείας ἧς ἐκήρυττον. 3. καὶ τοιαῦτα διδάσκοντες ὅμως ἔπεισαν, οὐχ ἕνα καὶ δύο ἢ τρεῖς ἢ ὀλίγον τινὰ ἀριθμόν, ἀλλὰ τὴν οἰκουμένην, ὡς εἰπεῖν, ἅπασαν. 4. ἃ τίς ἂν σὺν τῷ δικαίῳ εἴποι μὴ οὐχὶ θείᾳ ῥοπῇ πεπράχθαι καὶ θαύμασι τὸν ἀνθρώπινον ὑπερβαίνουσι λόγον; 5. τίσι γὰρ ἄλλοις δῆμοι καὶ πόλεις | καὶ ἔθνη ὅλα πειθόμενοι τῆς μὲν οἰκείας θρησκείας ἀφίσταντο; 6. τῇ δὲ 46v εἰς Χριστὸν προσετίθεντο πίστει καὶ ἀρετὴν ἀντὶ τῆς κακίας ᾑροῦντο καὶ τὸν ἐπίπονον βίον ἀντὶ τοῦ ῥᾴστου καὶ τοῦ ἡδέος.

17 1. Καὶ τὸ δὴ μεῖζον ὅτι καὶ διωκόμενοι ὑπὲρ αὐτοῦ τούτου καὶ μισούμενοι καὶ μυρία δεινὰ πάσχοντες οὐδ᾽ ὑπὸ ἀλλοτρίων, ἀλλ᾽ ὑπὸ τῶν οἰκειοτάτων ἔνιοι. 2. πατέρες τε γὰρ παῖδας ἤλαυνον καὶ πατέρας παῖδες οὐδὲν ἧττον. 3. καὶ ᾑροῦντο τὸ κήρυγμα καὶ μέχρι θανάτου τῇ ἐνστάσει προσέμενον, θεὸν ἀληθῆ

1 ταὐτὰ] ταυτὰ T || πείσονται] -εί- supra lin. scr. T[1] (litterae ambiguae in textu) **6** μηδὲν] μὴδὲν T **7** πειθομένοις] ποιθο- corr. T[1] || τούτῳ] τοῦτο corr. T[1] **13–14** διδάσκοντες . . . νομοθετοῦντες] ad -κοντας και; -τοῦντας mut. T[1] **24** μὲν] supra lin. scr. T **26** ἡδέος] ἡδέως corr. T[1]

the same way as the others, did their duty, something those who do not intensely believe would not have done.

15 1. They therefore did not devise lies. Nor did they fabricate such a proposition. 2. Furthermore, it does not make sense for men of this sort to have dared to go out into the world and fabricate such a proposition, 3. openly preaching it to all men, exhorting them to it, and proclaiming that the things they preached to believers were of no value for earthly life. 4. Their concern, then, was not to prescribe glory, wealth, power, pleasure, or any comfort, but the very opposite, just as their teacher said, namely, poverty, ignominy, and the complete rejection of pleasure. 5. For they were not so simple-minded as to put forward as a lie their plan for life or to proclaim that it was not a good plan which men of that time knew they could put some hope in. 6. Rather, it was more the case that they taught and prescribed a good that in being so contrary to popular opinion was wholly superior and suffered no corruption. 7. Furthermore, they themselves were clearly convinced that they were teaching the truth, and that through inspiration and miracles the Deity was assisting them from on high to bring about the conversion of men. 8. For if they did not inspire belief, they would not have been able to achieve such a great work in the face of their opponents' attacks.

16 1. Indeed, they were exhorting people to renounce the very things they most sought after and without which no one would choose to live. 2. Furthermore, they themselves took up their own cross, prepared as they were to suffer death for the truth they preached. 3. And teaching such things, they inspired belief not in one or two or three persons, or in some small number, but, so to say, the whole world likewise. 4. Who would honestly say that they accomplished this without the aid of divine influence and miracles beyond human understanding? 5. For what else could have caused peoples, cities, and whole nations to believe and to repudiate their own religions? 6. Having given themselves over to faith in Christ, they chose virtue over evil and the arduous life over the easy and pleasant one.

17 1. What is even more amazing is that while being persecuted and hated because of him, some suffered a myriad of horrors not from foreigners but at the hands of their closest kinsmen. 2. For fathers were persecuting sons, and sons fathers to no less a degree. 3. And they embraced what they preached and maintained their commitment unto death, as they affirmed and in no way

μηδὲν ὑποστελλόμενοι τὸν ἐσταυρωμένον ἐκεῖνον ὁμολογοῦντες. | 4. εἰ τοίνυν 47r
θείᾳ δυνάμει ταῦτα πέπρακται, τό τε κήρυγμα ἀληθὲς εἶναι ἀνάγκη καὶ τὸ
εὐαγγέλιον οὐ νόθον οὐδὲ πονηρίᾳ τινὶ συντεθειμένον, θεὸν εὐαγγελιζόμενον,
οὐκ ἄνθρωπον μόνον τὸν Ἰησοῦν. 5. ἀλλὰ μὴν οὐδ᾽ ἐκεῖνο ἔστιν εἰπεῖν ὡς τῷ
διδασκάλῳ χαριζόμενοι τοιαῦτα ἐπλάσαντο. μετὰ γὰρ τὸν θάνατον αὐτοῦ καὶ
τὴν εἰς οὐρανοὺς ἄνοδον ταῦτα ἐκήρυττον. 6. καίτοι εἰ περιῆν, οὐκ ἂν μέχρι
θανάτου τὴν ἔνστασιν ἐποιήσαντο εἰ μὴ θεὸν αὐτὸν ἐνόμιζον ἀληθῆ. τίς γὰρ ἂν
ἕλοιτο ὑπὲρ τοῦ ψεύδους θανεῖν εἰδὼς ὅτι ψεῦδος ἐστί;

18 1. Οὐ μὴν οὐδὲ χαριζομένων | ἐστὶ τὸ τὰ ἐπονείδιστα δοκοῦντα μηδὲν 47v
ὑποκρυπτομένους ἀπαγγέλλειν. 2. μᾶλλον γὰρ ἂν ἕλοιτο ὁ χαριζόμενος τὰ
τοιαῦτα κρύπτειν ἢ μεῖζόν τι περὶ ἐκείνου εἰπεῖν ᾧ χαρίζεται. 3. ἀλλ᾽ οἱ τὸ
εὐαγγέλιον συγγραψάμενοι τὰ μὲν ἐπονείδιστα δοκοῦντα μετὰ πάσης ἀκριβείας
διεξέρχονται, οὐχ ὅσα μόνον Ἑβραῖοι παροινοῦντες ἀνέδην ἐτόλμησαν, 4. ἀλλὰ
καὶ ἃ τοὺς πολλοὺς μᾶλλον δὲ ἅπαντας πλὴν τῶν μαθητῶν ἐλελήθει, 5. τὴν
ἀναχώρησιν τοῦ Ἰησοῦ, τὸ ἐναγώνιον καὶ περιδεές, τὴν τοῦ θανάτου πρὸς τὸν
πατέρα παραίτησιν, τὴν τοῦ μαθητοῦ προδοσίαν, 6. καί, ὡς τῆς ἐφόδου | τῶν 48r
συλληψομένων ἡγήσατο, τὴν τῶν ἄλλων ἀπὸ τοῦ διδασκάλου φυγὴν καὶ
ἐγκατάλειψιν, 7. ὅτι δὲ θεὸς εἴη ἅπαξ ἢ δὶς εἰπόντες καὶ σφόδρα συνεσταλμένως,
8. ὥσπερ ὑπὸ τῶν πραγμάτων ἀναγκαζόμενοι, οὐδὲ προστιθέασι πλέον, οὐδὲ
συστῆσαι σπουδάζουσιν.

19 1. Οὐκ ἄρα πρὸς χάριν οἱ ἀπόστολοι τὸ εὐαγγέλιον συνέγραψαν, ἀλλ᾽ ὑπ᾽ ἐκείνου εἰρημένον ὡς εἴη θεὸς καὶ ἔργοις μυρίοις ἀποδεδειγμένον αὐτὸν ἐπαγγέλλουσιν.

20 1. Ὅτι μὲν οὖν οὐδὲν ἐκακούργησαν εἰς τὸ εὐαγγέλιον οἱ τοῦτο συγγρα-
ψάμενοι δῆλον τοῖς ἀπαθῶς τὰ τοιαῦτα κρίνειν ἐθελοῦσι. | 2. λοιπὸν δὲ δεῖξαι ὅτι 48v
οὐδὲ οἱ τοῦτο παρ᾽ αὐτῶν δεξάμενοι διέφθειραν. 3. τοῦτο τοίνυν τὸ εὐαγγέλιον οὐ χρόνοις ὕστερον, ἀλλ᾽ εὐθὺς εἰς πᾶσαν ἐξεδόθη τὴν οἰκουμένην. 4. ἡ γὰρ πίστις ἣν ἐκήρυττον οἱ ἀπόστολοι πανταχοῦ τοῦτο ἦν, θεόν, οὐκ ἄνθρωπον μόνον εἶναι τὸν Ἰησοῦν.

---

10 ἀπαγγέλλειν] ἀπαγγέλειν T; ad ἐπαγγ- mut. T[1] **23** ἐπαγγέλλουσιν] ἐπαγγέλουσιν T

minced words that the crucified one was truly God. 4. If they did these things by divine power, then what they preached necessarily was the truth and the Gospel was neither spurious nor tainted by some evil when it spread the good news that Jesus was not only a man but also God. 5. But we are not saying that they fabricated these things in order to please their teacher. For they preached these things after his death and ascension into heaven. 6. Indeed, if he had remained alive, or if they did not think that he was truly God, they would not have maintained their commitment unto death. For who would choose to die for a lie, knowing that it is a lie?

18 1. For it is not at all characteristic of those who enjoy the favor [of a patron] to proclaim and not to hide in the slightest what is seemingly disgraceful [about the patron]. 2. Rather, someone enjoying the favor [of a patron] would choose to hide such things or to say something more complimentary about the patron. 3. But the evangelists gave a thorough account down to the smallest detail of seemingly disgraceful things, not only of what the Hebrews dared to do in an unrestrained, violent rage, 4. but also of what escaped the attention of many, indeed, of everyone except the disciples, 5. such as Jesus's drawing back from the task, his anguish and fearfulness, his supplication to the Father for death, the betrayal of him by his disciple, 6. and, as can be gathered from the thrust of the combined texts, the desertion and abandonment of him, their teacher, by the other disciples, 7. and after saying once or twice that he was God, but very weakly, 8. driven, as it were, by events, they did not further assert it nor even try to stand firm about it.

19 1. The apostles therefore did not write the Gospel in order to curry favor, but in order to proclaim that he was God, as he himself said and proved by his innumerable works.

20 1. It should be obvious, then, to those who choose to judge the matter dispassionately, that the evangelists did not introduce anything fraudulent into the Gospel. 2. What is left to show is that those who received the Gospel from the apostles did not corrupt it. 3. This Gospel, then, was not published at some later date, but immediately to the whole world. 4. For it was the faith which the apostles preached everywhere, that Jesus was God and not merely man.

21 1. Ἐξεδόθη δὲ οὐ κατὰ μίαν διάλεκτον, ἀλλ᾽ οἱ μὲν αὐτὸ ξυγγεγραφότες ἐν τρισὶ διαλέκτοις ἐξέδωκαν. 2. οἱ δὲ λαβόντες ἅπαντες κατὰ τὴν οἰκείαν φωνὴν ἐξέλαβον. τίς οὖν ἴσχυσεν ἂν ἐξ ἁπάντων αὐτὸ συναγαγεῖν τῶν ἐθνῶν καὶ διαφθεῖραι; 3. πῶς δὲ διαφθείρας αὖθις ἐξέδωκεν; οὐ γὰρ ἂν ἐδέξαντο | οἱ πρὶν 49r
ἀνόθευτον αὐτὸ λαβόντες. 4. οὐδὲ θεὸν καὶ αὐτὸν τὸν Χριστὸν ὡμολόγουν, προφήτην ὑπὸ τῶν ἀποστόλων αὐτοῖς ἀνακεκηρύγμένον. 5. ἀλλὰ μὴν οὐδὲ πάντας εἰκὸς ἐκ συμφωνίας αὐτὸ νοθεῦσαι. ἕνα μὲν γὰρ ἢ δύο ἔστω πονηροὺς γεγονότας, διότι δὴ τοῦτο βουληθῆναι; 6. πάντας δὲ ἀνθρώπους εἰς τοιαύτην ἐπίνοιαν ἐλθεῖν οὐκ εἰκός. 7. τὸ δὴ κατὰ πᾶσαν διάλεκτον γεγραμμένον δίχα τῆς οἱασοῦν σώζεσθαι διαφορᾶς μαρτύριόν ἐστιν ἀληθὲς ὅτι ἀνόθετον διατελεῖ.

22 1. Ἔτι, πολλοὶ γεγόνασι παρ᾽ ἡμῖν οἱ μὲν εὐθὺς μετὰ τοὺς ἀποστόλους. | 49v
2. οἱ δὲ οὐ πολλοῖς χρόνοις ὕστερον οὐχ ἡγούμενοι δεῖν θεὸν ἀληθῆ λέγειν τὸν Χριστόν, ἀλλὰ κατά τινα χάριν, ὥς τινα θεῖον εἴ που εἴρηται, τοῦτο ῥηθῆναι. 3. εἶναι γὰρ ποίημα τὸν υἱὸν ἢ τὸν λόγον ἐκ μὴ ὄντων ὑπὸ τοῦ ἀληθινοῦ θεοῦ γεγενημένον Παῦλος τε ὁ Σαμονσατοὺς καὶ Ὡριγένης σοφώτατος γενόμενος καὶ

1 κατὰ μίαν] καταμίαν T **10** διαφορᾶς] διαφορὰς corr. T/T[1] **15** Ὡριγένης] ad ῾Ωρι- mut. T[1]

21 1. Also, it was not published in just one language. Rather, the evangelists published it in three languages.[63] 2. All those who accepted the Gospel received it in their own tongue. Who, therefore, would have had the power to have gathered up this text from all the nations and corrupted it? 3. Having corrupted the Gospel, how would this person then have published it? For those who had previously received in its uncounterfeited state would not have accepted [the counterfeit version]. 4. They would not have agreed that Christ was God after the apostles had proclaimed him far and wide to have been a prophet. 5. But it is not plausible that everyone would have worked in concert to counterfeit the Gospel. Even if there were one or two evil counterfeiters, why would they do even this? 6. It is not plausible, however, that all men would hit upon such a scheme. 7. The fact, then, that the Gospel survives written in every language without any such discrepancy is a true testimony that it has survived uncounterfeited.

22 1. Furthermore, after the apostles their successors immediately appeared among us Christians. 2. Since they were not much later than the apostles, they did not think it necessary to say that Christ was truly God; but by some grace—as something in any way divine is called—say it they did. 3. For Paul of Samosata,[64] the very learned Origen,[65] and lastly Arius[66] asserted that the Son

63. Greek and Hebrew (for Matthew, according to Eusebius, *HE* 3.24.6 and 3.39.16) are obvious, but the third language is not. It is dubious that Amiroutzes understood that Aramaic was the *lingua franca* of Palestine in Jesus's time. So, by a process of elimination, the third language would seem to be Latin. Amiroutzes must have thought that the Gospels were quickly translated into Latin after the apostles arrived in Rome and Christianity spread to the West. A reader for the press has pointed out to me that a Christian author would instinctively think of the *titulus* in the three languages over Christ on the cross (John 19:19–22); cf. Psellus, *On the Crucifixion*, in his *Hagiographical Orations*, 174.359–175.378; Augustine, *In Ioh.* 117.19.4; Isidore, *Etym.* 9.1.1.

64. In his *Ecclesiatical history* (7.27–30), Eusebius of Caesarea explains how a council at Antioch (in 269) deposed Paul of Samosata from the bishopric of the city for teaching that Jesus Christ was merely a man and not born the Son of God; for Paul's teachings and the relevant texts, see Navascués, *Pablo de Samosata y sus adversarios*; and Riedmatten, *Les actes du procès de Paul de Samosate.*

65. Rightly or wrongly, Origen (ca. 185–ca. 254) was mainly charged with believing in the preexistence of souls and other unacceptable conclusions stemming from his doctrine of universal salvation (*apokatastasis*) as well as the heresy of subordinationism in respect to the second person of the Trinity (the Son); see Clark, *Origenist Controversy*, 85–158; Henne, *Introduction à Origène*, 125–37; Ramelli, "Origen's Anti-Subordinationism."

Ἄρειος ὕστερον. 4. εἰ τοίνυν τίς ἐγεγόνει περὶ τὸ εὐαγγέλιον διαφθορὰ καὶ
μάλιστα ἐν οἷς ἡμῖν αὐτοὶ διεφέροντο, 5. οὐκ ἂν αὐτοὺς ἔλαθε, τοὺς μὲν ἔγγιστα
τῶν ἀποστόλων γεγενημένους, τοὺς δὲ ὀλίγῳ ὕστερον. 6. εἰδότες δὲ αὐτὸ | 50r
ἐνταῦθα διεφθαρμένον, οὐκ ἂν ἐσιώπησαν 7. ἀγχόμενοι καθ᾽ ἑκάστην ὑπὸ τῶν
θεὸν ἀληθῆ τὸν Χριστὸν λεγόντων τοῖς τοῦ εὐαγγελίου ῥητοῖς, καὶ ἐλεγχόμενοι
καὶ ἀποκηρυττόμενοι. 8. ἀλλ᾽ οὐδὲν τοιοῦτον αὐτῶν οὐδεὶς εἶπεν, οὐδὲ εἰς νοῦν
ἐβάλετο. 9. καὶ δηλοῦσιν οὓς συνέγραψαν περὶ τῆς σφῶν αἱρέσεως λόγους
σῳζόμενοι παρ᾽ ἡμῖν. 10. ῥητοῖς δὲ ἄλλοις τοῦ εὐαγγελίου δεικνύειν ἐπειρᾶτο
τὴν καινοτέραν αὐτοῦ δόξαν ἕκαστος. καίτοι πῶς ἂν ἀπέσχοντο εἰπεῖν εἴ γέ τι
τοιοῦτον ᾔδεσαν; 11. πῶς δ᾽ ἂν ἠγνόουν; ἢ λαθεῖν αὐτοὺς εἰκὸς | σοφούς τε 50v
γενομένους καὶ ὀλίγῳ ὕστερον τῷ βίῳ ἐπιπολάσαντας; 12. οὐκ ἔστι τοῦτο. οὐκ
ἔστι πολλοῦ γε καὶ δεῖ.

23 1. Ἀλλὰ ταῦτα πάντα σαφεῖς ἀποδείξεις ὅτι τὸ εὐαγγέλιον ἀδιάφθορον σώζεται, δηλοῖ δὲ οὐδὲν ἧττον καὶ τὸ πλῆθος τῶν ὑπὲρ τῆς πίστεως εἰρημένων.

24 1. Οἷς τοῦτο μόνον ἐπῆγον οἱ διώκοντες ἔγκλημα, ὅτι θεὸν ἔλεγον τὸν
Χριστόν. 2. διὰ τί γὰρ ἄλλο ἠλαύνοντο πανταχοῦ οἱ πιστεύοντες; διὰ τί δόγμα-
σιν ἀνῃροῦντο, τῶν τότε κρατούντων Ῥωμαίων; 3. ὁ γάρ τοι νόμος αὐτοῖς οὐ
προσίστατο. οἱ γοῦν Ἰουδαῖοι νόμοις | ἑτέροις χρώμενοι. διὰ ταῦτα οὐκ 51r
ἐδιώκοντο; 4. αὐτοί τε οὖν μαρτυροῦσιν ἡμῖν οἱ διώκοντες οἷς ἔπραξαν, οἷς
ἐψηφίσαντο. 5. καὶ οἱ τοὺς ἄθλους ἐκείνους τοὺς περιβοήτους ὑπομείναντες ἵνα
μηδὲν ἀλλοιότερον νομίσωσι περὶ τοῦ Ἰησοῦ. 6. καίτοι ὁ διωγμὸς οὐ χρόνοις
ὕστερον πολλοῖς γέγονεν, ἀλλ᾽ εὐθὺς ἡ ἡμετέρα πίστις ἀρξαμένη ἠλαύνετο, ἰδίᾳ
μὲν ὑπὸ τῶν ἐθνῶν ἑκάστων, κοινῇ δὲ δόγμασιν ὑπὸ τῶν Ῥωμαίων.

---

2 ἔγγιστα] ἔγκιστα T, ad ἔγιστα mut. T^{1} **7** ἐβάλετο] ἐβάλλετο T, ad ἐβουλετο mut. T^{1} **16** πιστεύοντες] in marg. T^{1}: γράφεται· οἱ πεπιστευκότες **17** ὁ . . . νόμος] in marg. signo denotat T^{1}

was a creature or the Word produced by the true God from non-being. 4. If, then, corruption had infested the Gospel, and especially if these heretics were arguing their different viewpoints among us Greeks, 5. the fact of the corruption would not have escaped them since they were very close in time to the apostles, coming only a little while later. 6. If at that moment they knew that the Gospel was corrupted, they would not have remained silent 7. when every day they were hard pressed, refuted, and publicly denounced by those who asserted on the basis of the very words of the Gospel that Christ was truly God. 8. But none of them made any such assertion. It did not even enter their minds; 9. and their very words, which they wrote concerning their own heresies and which we still have, show this. 10. Each tried to demonstrate his own new doctrine through different passages of the Gospel. And yet, how would they have refrained from speaking of the corruption if in fact they knew of any such thing? 11. How would they not have known? Is it plausible that these learned men would have missed it, even though they flourished only a little after the apostles? 12. This cannot be. Most certainly, it cannot be!

23 1. All these arguments are obvious proof that the Gospel is preserved uncorrupted, but there exists a large number of arguments propounded on behalf of the faith that no less obviously prove the same.

24 1. Against these arguments persecutors used to advance only this one complaint, namely, that Christians asserted Christ to be God. 2. For what other reason have the faithful been persecuted everywhere? Why were they killed for their doctrines when the Romans of yesteryear reigned? 3. For no adjustment in law was made for them. The Jews in fact conducted themselves according to a different set of laws. Why were they not for this reason persecuted? 4. Our Roman persecutors are witnesses for us by their very actions, by their very decrees. 5. At the time, while persisting in those notorious gladiatorial contests of theirs, they in no way changed in their opinion of Jesus. 6. And indeed, the persecution did not begin after a long delay. Rather immediately after our faith began, it was attacked for its doctrines. Individual nations did so privately; the Romans, however, did so publicly.

66. Arius reduced the second person of the Trinity to the status of the first creature, see Böhm, *Die Christologie des Arius*; Hanson, *Search for the Christian Doctrine*, 3–178; and two revisionist works: Gwynn, *Eusebians*; and Pietras, *Council of Nicaea*.

25 1. Πῶς οὖν ὑφ᾽ ἡμῶν ἐφθάρη τὸ εὐαγγέλιον θεὸν ἀναγορεῦσαι τὸν Ἰησοῦν, ὁπότε οἱ τοῦτο | παρὰ τῶν ἀποστόλων δεξάμενοι φαίνονται ὑπὲρ αὐτοῦ 51v τούτου ὑπὸ τῶν ἑκάστοτε διωκόντων ἀποθανόντες;

XXII 1 1. **Ὁ Κρατῶν**. Ταῦτα εἰ μὲν ἀποδείξεις, ἔφη, νομίζεις ὅ τί ποτέ ἐστιν ἀπόδειξις, ἔοικας ἀγνοεῖν. 2. εἰ δὲ προσποιῇ ἀπαντᾶν ἐπιχειρῶν, κακουργεῖς. 3. εἰ δὲ εἰκότα νομίζεις, ἔπειτα τούτοις πειθόμενος θεὸν ὁμολογεῖς τὸν Ἰησοῦν, εὐήθης λοιπὸν εἶ. 4. μᾶλλον δὲ πονηρὸς ἑκὼν τοιούτοις λόγοις τοσαύτην ἀπονέμων πίστιν.

2 1. Ἀλλὰ ταῦτα μὲν ἐατέον. ἐκεῖνο δὲ λοιπόν· μαθεῖν βούλομαι παρά σου τίνος χάριν οὕτως ἄτοπον ἔργον ὑπέστη θεός. 2. καὶ εἰ ἀδύ|νατον ἦν ἄλλως αὐτὸ 52r διαπράξασθαι ἢ ἄνθρωπον γεγονότα, καίτοι τοῦτο ἀδυναμίας ἂν εἴη. καὶ πῶς ἀδύνατος ὁ πάντα δυνάμενος; 3. καὶ εἰ μὴ ἄλλως ἦν αὐτὸ γενέσθαι, τί δήποτε οὐ παρῆκον διὰ τὸ τοῦ τρόπου ἀνάξιον ἢ βίᾳ; 4. καὶ ἐδέξατο τὴν ἀρχὴν καὶ ἤνυσε;

XXIII 1 1. **Ὁ Φιλόσοφος**. Τὴν μὲν φύσιν, ἔφην ἐγώ, τῶν παρόντων λόγων οὐκ ἀγνοῶ. τὸ μέντοι ὑποκείμενον οἶδα περὶ οὗ οἱ λόγοι γίνονται οὐκ ἄλλους λόγους πρὸς ὑμᾶς ἐπιδεχόμενον. 2. πεπαιδευμένου δὲ εἶναι νομίζω τὸ τοὺς λόγους ἑκάστου κατὰ τὸ ὑποκείμενον κρίνειν, καὶ τὸ ἐνδεχόμενον ἀποδεχόμενον, μὴ παν|ταχοῦ τὴν ἀκρίβειαν ζητεῖν τὴν γεωμετρικήν. 3. πρὸς δέ, οὐδ᾽ αὐτοὶ 52v τούτους εἰσάγομεν. ἀλλ᾽ ὑμεῖς τοιούτοις ἀνατρέπειν πειρώμενοι τὴν πίστιν, εἰς ἀνάγκην ἄγετε αὐτοῖς κεχρῆσθαι. 4. οὔκουν ἔστι τὸ ἐνδεχόμενον ἀναγκαίως ἀποδεικνύναι. ἀλλὰ τὰ ἐπαγόμενα ὁποῖα ποτ᾽ ἂν ᾖ, λύειν ὁμοίως ἐπιχειροῦμεν. 5. ἡ δὲ αἰτία δι᾽ ἣν ὁ θεὸς ἄνθρωπος γενέσθαι οὐκ ἀπηξίωσε τοιάδε τις τυγχάνει.

---

1 ἐφθάρη] η supra lin. scr. T[1] (non liquet in textu) **16** ἐπιδεχόμενον] ὑποδεχέται supra lin. scr. T[1] **19** πειρώμενοι] -ρόμ- corr. T[1] **20** ἀναγκαίως] -γ- supra lin. iterat T[1] **21** ἀποδεικνύναι] ἀποδεικνῦναι T **22** τοιάδε] τοῖα δέ T

25 1. How, then, was the Gospel falsified by us to make it proclaim that Jesus is God, when those who received this doctrine from the apostles appear to have been killed by their then persecutors precisely because of this doctrine?

XXII 1 1. **The Conqueror.** If you think, he said, that these arguments constitute scientific demonstration, you seem to be ignorant as to what in the world a scientific demonstration is. 2. And if you are just trying to put up a front, you are a knave. 3. On the other hand, if you consider your arguments to be plausible and, because you are persuaded by them, you confess that Christ is God, then you are, well, a simpleton. 4. More to the point, he who assigns so much faith to such arguments is willingly an evil man.

2 1. But let us grant that you are right. This, however, is left: I want to know from you why would God have consented to such an absurd deed. 2. And if it was impossible for him to have accomplished it[67] in any other way than by becoming a man, this would reflect impotence.[68] But how is the omnipotent impotent? 3. And, if this could not have happened otherwise, why was it not at some point just dropped, either because of the unworthiness of its manner or because force was applied? 4. And why did he accept its beginning and see it through to the end?

XXIII 1 1. **The Philosopher.** I am aware, I said, of the nature of the arguments I am presently making. I know, however, that the subject about which these arguments revolve does not admit other arguments as far as you are concerned. 2. Also, I believe that it takes an educated person to judge arguments in each case in relation to their subject and to seek acceptable plausibility instead of geometric exactness everywhere. 3. Besides, we are not the ones who are introducing this issue. Rather, you are the one who did so, seeking to refute the Christian faith in this way. You demand that we use arguments that reach necessary conclusions. 4. It is not possible to prove these matters with scientific necessity. But let us try to resolve whatever sort of subjects may be adduced in a manner appropriate to them. 5. The reason why God became man has not

67. It is not clear what "it" means here; probably the conversion of the world.

68. Cf. Gregory of Nazianzus, *De Filio* (*Or.* 30) 11.3: τοῦτο γάρ ἀδυναμίας ἂν εἴη μᾶλλον θεοῦ; and, earlier, Plutarch, *Moralia*, Tyrwhitt 6.17 (Εἰ μέρος τὸ παθητικὸν τῆς ἀνθρώπου ψυχῆς ἢ δύναμις): τὸ γὰρ μὴ ἐνεργεῖν ἀδυναμίας ἄν εἴη.

2 1. Τὸν ἄνθρωπον αὐτοὶ νομίζομεν τιμιώτερον ἔργον εἶναι θεοῦ πάντων τῶν
αἰσθητῶν καὶ δι᾽ αὐτὸν πάντα παρῆχθαι, 2. ἐπεὶ τόν γε θεὸν μηδὲν αὐτῶν
δεῖσθαι, ὄντα τῇ φύσει ἀνενδεῆ. 3. ταῦτα εἰ μὲν | δίδως, τὰ ἐφεξῆς ἐρῶ. εἰ δὲ μὴ 53r
δίδως, ἀποδεῖξαι περάσομαι.

XXIV 1 1. **Ὁ Κρατῶν**. Συγχωρῶ, ἔφη, καὶ γὰρ οὕτω περί γε τούτου δοξάζομεν καὶ αὐτοί.

XXV 1 1. **Ὁ Φιλόσοφος**. Οὗτος τοίνυν, ἔφην ἐγώ, ἅπαξ ἀποστὰς τοῦ θείου
θελήματος καὶ παραβὰς τὸν νόμον ὃν ἔλαβεν, εἰς πᾶσαν ἦλθεν κακίας ὑπερβολήν. 2. διττὸς γὰρ ὢν ἅτε ξύνθετος διττὸν καὶ τὸ ἀντικείμενον εἶχε, τὸ μὲν κατὰ
τὸν νοῦν, τὸ δὲ κατὰ τὸ συναμφότερον. 3. ὧν ἀποπίπτων ἄθλιος ἐξ ἀνάγκης ἦν.
καὶ τοῦ σκοποῦ δι᾽ ὃν γέγονεν ἀποτυχής. 4. τὸ μὲν οὖν τοῦ νοῦ τέλος, πρὸς ὃ
φέρεται, τυγχάνει ἀλήθεια· τὸ δὲ τοῦ | ξυναμφοτέρου τὸ ἀγαθόν. 5. τούτων 53v
ἀμφοτέρων καθάπαξ ὁ ἄνθρωπος ἐξεπεπτώκει, περὶ μὲν τὴν ἀλήθειαν τυφλώττων, τὴν πρώτην καὶ θεὸν ἀγνοῶν, 6. ἄλλοις τισὶν ἀπονέμων τὸ σέβας, οὐδὲ
τιμίοις κτίσμασιν, τὸ δὲ ἀγαθὸν τῇ αἰσθήσει ζητῶν, καὶ οὐδὲ τοῦτο κατὰ φύσιν
δρῶν, ὡς γοῦν τὰ ἄλογα, 7. ἀλλὰ καὶ αὐτὸ ἐπὶ τὸ χεῖρον ἀμείβων, ἀνόσιος καὶ
ἀσεβὴς καὶ ἄδικος καὶ ὅλως πονηρὸς ἀποτελεσθείς, 8. ὥστε τὴν μὲν ἀρετὴν καὶ
τὴν τῆς ἀληθείας γνῶσιν ἐκποδὼν οἴχεσθαι, τὸν ἀνθρώπειον καθάπαξ ἀπολελοιπότα βίον, τὴν δὲ κακίαν καὶ τὴν πλάνην κρατεῖν ἐν | ἅπασι. 9. καὶ συμβαίνειν 54r
μάτην λοιπὸν τὸ τοιοῦτον ἔργον τὸν ἄνθρωπον εἶναι ἐκπεπτωκότα τοῦ τέλους
δι᾽ ὃ γέγονεν. 10. οὐ γὰρ ὁ μέν, ὁ δ᾽ οὔ, τοιοῦτος ἦν, ἀλλ᾽ ὁμοίως ἅπαντες,
πλεῖστον ἤδη χρόνον, ἐσχάτῃ πονηρίᾳ καὶ ἀγνοίᾳ συνέζων.

2 1. Καὶ γὰρ εἴ τινες ἐδέξαντο τὸν νόμον, ὀψὲ καὶ μόλις καὶ ὀλίγοι τινὲς ἐν τῇ
Παλαιστίνῃ, οὐδὲν μέρος, ὡς εἰπεῖν, ὄντες τοῦ παντὸς ἀριθμοῦ τῶν ἀνθρώπων
τοῦτον ἐδέξαντο. 2. καὶ οὐδὲ αὐτὸν καλῶς ἐφύλαττον, ἀλλ᾽ ἀφίσταντο καὶ
ὠλιγώρουν. καὶ εἰς τὴν ἐπὶ τὸ χεῖρον αὐτονομίαν ηὐτομόλουν. 3. καὶ ταῦτα οὐ
φορτικὸν ὄντα, οὐδὲ τοῦ προσήκοντος παντὸς ἐφικνούμενον. | 4. προφήτας 54v
γοῦν ὁ θεὸς ἑκάστοτε πέμπων καὶ μυρίοις αὐτοὺς ἐπαγόμενος οὐδὲν ἤνυεν, ὡς

---

2 πάντα] ταῦτα in marg. scr. T^1 **3** ἀνενδεῆ] ἀνουδεῆ corr. T^1 et in marg. ἀνανδεῆ iterat || δὲ] supra lin. scr. T **7** Φιλόσοφος] in marg. scr. T^1 **8** ἦλθεν] -εν supra lin. iterat T^1 **21** ὁ^2] ὅ T **23** τὸν] τὸ T

rendered unworthy the sort of arguments one might come up with for this happening.

2 1. We ourselves consider man a work of God that is nobler than all sensible things and the reason why he produced everything, 2. since God did not need any of his creatures, being by nature in need of nothing. 3. If you grant me this point, I shall tell you what follows from it. If you do not grant it, I shall try to prove it.

XXIV 1 1. **The Conqueror.** I concede it, he said. For we ourselves think likewise in this matter.

XXV 1 1. **The Philosopher.** Man, then, I said, having completely revolted against the will of God and having violated the law that he received [from God], perpetrated every excess of evil. 2. Because he is twofold, in that he is a composite, man was conflicted twice over, that is, in respect to his mind and in respect to his composite nature. 3. Since he had failed in respect to both, man was of necessity wretched. He had failed in the purpose for which he was made. 4. The goal to which the mind is borne is truth; the goal of the composite man is goodness. 5. Man has utterly fallen away from both goals by being blind to the first truth and not knowing God, 6. by allotting his reverence to some other things (and not even to worthy creatures!), by seeking goodness through sensuality, and by not even acting according to nature, as at least irrational animals do, 7. but changing his nature into something worse, man has made himself impious, godless, unjust, and totally depraved. 8. The result is that he has left virtue and knowledge of the truth far behind and appropriated in every which way evil, error, and a completely dissolute human life. 9. And so it happens that this grand work, man, has fallen from the purpose for which he was made and is left purposeless. 10. For it is not the case that one man is in this state and another is not, but rather that all men are like this, living today for the most part in utter evil and ignorance.

2 1. For even if some accepted the law, they accepted it late and just barely, and they were few in number, living in Palestine and counting, so to speak, for nothing in the totality of mankind. 2. Nor did they keep the law especially well. Rather they strayed from it and treated it cavalierly. They even deserted it for the freedom to do evil things. 3. The law, to be sure, did not treat mundane matters, and it did not cover every duty. 4. Indeed, God sent prophets at every opportunity and supplied them with countless [evidences], but he accomplished nothing,

αὐτοὶ μαρτυροῦσιν οἱ πεμφθέντες προφῆται. 5. τί τοίνυν ἔδει ποιεῖν τὸν θεόν; καταλιπεῖν τὸν ἄνθρωπον οὕτως ἀθλίως ἔχοντα, μὴ ἐπιστρέφειν ἐνόν, μὴ δὲ ἐπὶ τὸ ἄμεινον ὁδηγεῖν; 6. ἀλλ᾽ ἐᾶν οὕτω φερόμενον ἀτυχῶς. εἰ μὲν γὰρ πάντα ἐποίει, ὁ δ᾽ ἔμενε πονηρός, καταλιπεῖν ἐχρῆν, ἅτε ἀνίατα, ἤδη νοσοῦντα. 7. εἰ δ᾽ ἦν, τίς τρόπος δι᾽ οὗ ἂν ἐπὶ τὸ προσῆκον ἐπανήει; 8. οὐ τῆς ἀγαθότητος ἐκεῖνον παραλιπεῖν. ὃν γὰρ μὴ ὄντα, ἀγαθότητι μόνῃ παρήγαγε. | 9. πῶς ἂν ὑπερεῖδε 55r
διορθωθῆναι δυνάμενον;

3 1. Διὰ ταῦτα ὁ τοῦ θεοῦ λόγος γέγονεν ἄνθρωπος ὅπως ἀρετὴν καὶ ὀρθὴν γνῶσιν ἐμφυτεύσῃ τῷ βίῳ. 2. οἷν μόνοιν ἀμφότερα ἐκεῖνα ὧν τελέως ὁ ἄνθρωπος ἐξεπεπτώκει, ἀγαθὸν καὶ ἀλήθεια, περιγίνεται, 3. ἀπὸ μὲν τῆς πλάνης ἐπιστρέφων πρὸς τὸν ἕνα θεόν, ἀπὸ δὲ τῆς κακίας, δι᾽ ἣν ἐκεῖνα τὰ δεινὰ ἐτολμᾶτο, ἐπανάγων ἐπὶ τὸν ἀμείνω βίον. 4. οὗτος ὁ τοῦ θεοῦ σκοπός. τὸ μὲν οὖν βούλημα οὐδεὶς ἔχει μέμψασθαι, ὡς οὐ προσῆκον αὐτῷ.

4 1. Λοιπὸν δὲ ἐκεῖνο ἐξετάσαι εἰ μὴ ἀνάξιος ὁ τρόπος δι᾽ οὗ τοῦτό φαμεν τὸν θεὸν ἐκτελέσαι. 2. τούτου γὰρ | δεδειγμένου, οὐκ ἔτι λείπεται ἀπορία εἰ μὴ 55v
ἐνδέχεται αὐτὸ διαπράξασθαι ἄλλως. 3. ἐπὶ πάσης γὰρ πράξεως δύο τινὰ ἐξ ἀνάγκης ζητεῖται, τὸ προκείμενον τέλος εἴ ἐστιν ἀληθῶς ἀγαθὸν καὶ συμβαῖνον τῇ φύσει τοῦ πράττοντος, καὶ τὰ μεταξὺ δι᾽ ὧν ἐπὶ τοῦτο ἔρχεται εἰ προσήκει τῷ τέλει. 4. οὐ γὰρ τὰ καλὰ δεῖ πράττειν μόνον, ἀλλὰ καὶ καλῶς ἴσως. 5. καὶ ὥσπερ ἐπὶ τῆς ἀποδείξεως ἔστι μὲν τὸ συμπέρασμα δι᾽ ἀληθῶν δεικνύειν, ἔστι δὲ καὶ μὴ διὰ τοιούτων, 6. τὸν αὐτὸν τρόπον καὶ ἐπὶ τῆς πράξεως ἔχει· ἐνδέχεται τἀγαθόν, μή, ὡς δεῖ, | πραχθῆναι. 7. ὅταν οὖν οὐκ ἀνάξιος ὁ τρόπος δι᾽ οὗ ἡ τῶν ἀνθρώ- 56r

---

1 τί . . . ἔδει] ἴσθι in marg. scr. et deinde del. T^1 **2** ἐνόν] αὐτὸν in marg. scr. et deinde del. T^1 **4** ὁ] ὅ T **5** τίς τρόπος] in marg. iterat T^1 (in textu non plene liquent) **14** ἐξετάσαι] in marg. iterat T^1

a fact to which the prophets he sent themselves bear testimony. 5. What, then, was God supposed to do? Abandon man because he was such a moral wretch, incapable of reform or of embarking on a better path? 6. But let us suppose that man is in this state just through some bad luck. For if God had done everything and man still remained wicked, God would necessarily have had to abandon him as incorrigible in his sickness. 7. But if that was the case, what way would there be for man to return to the right? 8. It is not the nature of God's goodness to abandon man. For when man did not yet exist, God created him out of his goodness alone. 9. If man can correct his ways, how would God show disdain for him?

3 1. This is the reason why the Word of God became man, in order that virtue and right knowledge might be grafted to human life.[69] 2. Only through acquiring virtue and right knowledge would man gain both goodness and truth, that is, the ends from which he had totally fallen, 3. and turn back from error to the one God, returning to the better life from the evil which had caused him to commit atrocities so defiantly. 4. This was God's purpose. No one, then, can criticize this plan as not befitting him.

4 1. What we have left to examine is the question of whether it was not unworthy. We mean the method by which God accomplished this. 2. For once it is shown to have been not unworthy, then, if no other method of accomplishing the task was possible, the last of the difficulties disappears. 3. For in every action there are roughly two things that are necessary to ask: first, whether the proposed goal is truly good and suits the nature of the actor; and second, whether the means by which the goal is reached befit the goal. 4. For one must not simply do good things; one must also do them by means that are equally good. 5. And just as in a demonstration one may seek to prove the conclusion through true premises and through premises that are not so true, 6. in the case of an action, one may act in the same way: an action may have the good as its end, but it may not be performed, as it ought to be, in a good way. 7. Whenever,

69. For an attempt to answer the same question but with a different explanation, see Anselm of Canterbury, *Cur Deus Homo*, which explained the Incarnation in terms of satisfaction for sin and which had been translated into Greek by Manuel Calecas before the end of the fourteenth century; see Demetracopoulos, "Latin Philosophical Works," 823; and Pertusi, "Gli studi latini di Manuele Caleca," 290–91.

πων πρός τε τἀληθὲς καὶ τἀγαθὸν ἐπιστροφὴ γέγονεν ἀποδειχθῇ, οὐδὲν ἔτι πλέον ζητεῖν δεῖ, ἀλλὰ μὴν ὅτι μὴ ἀνάξιος εἴρηται μὲν καὶ πρότερον.

5 1. Εἰρήσεται δὲ καὶ νῦν. 2. εἰ μὲν γὰρ γεγονέναι περὶ τὴν θείαν φύσιν ἐλέγομεν ἢ πάθος ἢ ἀλλοίωσιν ἢ ὅλως μεταβολὴν ἢ οἷς λέγομεν συνέβαινεν ὅ τε τρόπος ἀνάξιος ἂν θεοῦ, 3. καὶ ὑμεῖς καίτοι τὸ τέλος προσῆκον ἡγούμενοι, τὴν τῶν ἀνθρώπων ἀπὸ τοῦ κακοῦ καὶ τοῦ ψεύδους ἐπιστροφήν, 4. δικαίως αὐτὰ οὐκ ἐνδέχεσθε, ὥσπερ ἀληθὲς συμπέ|ρασμα ἐκ ψευδῶν προτάσεων συναγόμενον. 56v
5. εἰ δὲ τοῦτο καὶ αὐτοὶ καθάπαξ ἀρνούμεθα καὶ οἷς τιθέμεθα οὐχ ἕπεται, τί ἐγκαλεῖτε; 6. τί δὲ περιάπτετε ψευδῆ δόξαν ἡμῖν τὴν τῆς θείας φύσεως μεταβολήν; 7. δίχα πάθους, δίχα μεταβολῆς τῆς θείας οὐσίας φαμὲν γεγονέναι τὴν εἰς μίαν ὑπόστασιν τοῦ Χριστοῦ σύνοδον τοῦ θεοῦ λόγου καὶ τῆς ἀνθρωπείας φύσεως. 8. οἵ γε καὶ μετὰ τὴν ἕνωσιν, ὡς ἂν μηδέν τι τοιοῦτον ὑπονοηθῇ, δύο τὰς ἐν Χριστῷ φύσεις λέγομεν ἀσυγχήτους καὶ ἀμεταβλήτους· 9. καὶ τοὺς ἄλλως λέγοντας ἀποκηρύττομεν αὐ|τὸ τοῦτο ἐγκαλοῦντες, ὅτι πάθος οἷς λέγουσι τῇ 57r
θείᾳ περιάπτουσι φύσει.

6 1. Ἐκ μὲν τῶν εἰρημένων οὐκ ἔτι λείπεται ἀπορία, εἰ μὴ ἐνεδέχετο αὐτὸ διαπράξασθαι ἄλλως. 2. ὅπου γὰρ τὸ μὲν τέλος οὕτω προσήκει θεῷ, ὁ δὲ τρόπος οὐκ ἀνάξιος αὐτοῦ, τί δεῖ λοιπὸν ζητεῖν, εἰ ἐνῆν αὐτὸ ἄλλως ποιεῖν; 3. εἰ γὰρ τούτων ἀποδιδομένων, ἔτι ζητεῖν ἐστιν περὶ ὁτουοῦν, 4. περὶ πάντων ἔσται τῶν γινομένων οὐχ ὑπὸ τῆς πρώτης ἀρχῆς μόνον, ἀλλὰ καὶ τῆς φύσεως ἀπορεῖν, 5. καὶ μηδὲν εἰδέναι, ἀλλ᾽ εἰς ἀεὶ ζητουμένης αἰτίας ἢ τρόπου.

7 1. Ἐκ περιουσίας δὲ ὅμως | καὶ ὅτι ἀδύνατον ἦν, τοῦ αὐτεξουσίου φυλαττο- 57v
μένου — καὶ γὰρ ἔδει πειθοῖ καὶ λόγοις, μὴ βίᾳ, μὴ δὲ φόβῳ τοὺς ἀνθρώπους ἐπὶ τἀγαθὸν καὶ τὴν ἀλήθειαν ἄγειν — ἄλλως γενέσθαι δείξομεν. 2. εἰ γὰρ ἦν δυνατὸν ἄλλως γενέσθαι τὴν τῶν ἀνθρώπων ἐπιστροφήν, κἂν ἐγεγόνει πρὶν τὸν Ἰησοῦν ἥκειν ἐπεὶ οὐκ ἂν παρέλιπεν αὐτὸ ὁ θεός, 3. ὃς ἀεὶ θέλει πάντας ἀνθρώπους σωθῆναι καὶ εἰς ἐπίγνωσιν ἀληθείας ἐλθεῖν. 4. ἀλλ᾽ ὥσπερ ἄλλα μυρία ὑπὲρ

---

4 οἷς] ἐκείνοις ἅ in marg. scr. T[1] **13** ἀσυγχήτους] ἀσύγχήτους T **19** ὁτουοῦν] οὑτουοῦν T; ινος supra -του- scr. T[1]

therefore, the method through which men are turned back toward truth and goodness proves to be not unworthy, we should not seek anything more, but rather stipulate beforehand that it is not unworthy.

5 1. Let us now stipulate this. 2. For if we had said that the divine nature was acted upon, or that it was affected, altered, or experienced change in any way, or that things came about through the method we have stated and that this method was unworthy of God, 3. then even if you considered the goal proper, namely, the turning of men from evil and falsehood, 4. you would rightly not accept these things, just as you would not accept as true a conclusion reached on the basis of false premises. 5. If, however, we absolutely deny that such is the case or that it follows from what we posit, why do you hurl accusations? 6. Why, moreover, do you attribute to us the false doctrine of change in the divine nature? 7. We say that the union of Christ into one hypostasis of the Word of God and of human nature took place without the divine nature being acted upon or experiencing change. 8. We further say that after the union, which exceeds anything we can imagine, the two natures in Christ remained uncombined and unmixed; 9. and we denounce those who say otherwise, hurling against them this very same accusation, namely, that in what they themselves are saying, they are attributing to the divine nature the capacity of being acted upon.

6 1. On the basis of these stipulations, and if it is not possible to accomplish the task otherwise, no difficulty is left. 2. When the goal thus befits God and the method of achieving it also is not unworthy of him, what is left to seek, even if it were possible to do it in some other way? 3. For if there was anything whatsoever still left to seek out after our stipulations have been conceded, 4. then we would be at a loss concerning everything that has come about not only through the First Principle, but also through nature, 5. and we would be in a position of not knowing, and would instead be always seeking out the cause or the method of the cause.

7 1. Nonetheless, we shall abundantly show that it was impossible for this to happen otherwise if free will were to be preserved. For it was necessary to bring men to goodness and truth by persuasion and argument, not by force and fear. 2. If it were possible to have the reform of men come about in another way, it would have happened before Jesus came, since God would not have neglected it. 3. God always wishes all men to be saved and to come to the full knowledge of the truth. 4. But just like the countless other things he did to this end, he urged

αὐτοῦ τούτου πεποίηκε, δι᾽ ἑαυτοῦ τε γὰρ παρῄνεσε τὰ δέοντα καὶ ἠπείλησε καὶ δι᾽ ἀγγέλων καὶ προφητῶν, 5. τοὺς μὲν πονηροὺς κολάζων, | τοὺς δὲ ἀγαθοὺς 58r
στεφανῶν καὶ ἀνακηρύττων.

8 1. Τὸν αὐτὸν τρόπον οὐδ᾽ ἐκεῖνο παρῆκεν ᾧ τοῦτ᾽ ἂν ἐξετέλεσεν. 2. οὐ γὰρ ἔστι θέλειν μὲν τοῖς ἀνθρώποις τὰ ἀγαθά, ὃ δείκνυται οἷς ἐποίησεν, ἔπειτα ἐνὸν μὴ ποιεῖν. 3. ἐπεὶ δὲ οὐ γέγονεν, οὐ δυνατὸν ἦν. ὅτι δὲ οὐ γέγονε, δῆλον. 4. Μῶσης γὰρ καὶ οἱ τοσοῦτοι προφῆται τοῖς γε πολλοῖς ἐκείνοις οἷς εἶπον καὶ οἷς ἔπραξαν οὐδὲν ἤνυσαν, ἢ ὅσον τοὺς Ἰουδαίους παιδαγωγῆσαι καὶ ἀνθρώπους εὐαριθμήτους. 5. ἡ γὰρ Παλαιστίνη καίτοι εἶχον οὐ πᾶσαν, οὐδὲν μέρος, ὡς εἰπεῖν, τῆς οἰκουμένης ἦν. 6. καὶ οὐδὲ τούτους ἴσχυσαν, | ἐπὶ τὸ τέλειον ἀγαγεῖν, 58v
καὶ ὅσον ἀνήκει τῷ τῶν ἀνθρώπων γένει, ἀλλὰ καθαπερεὶ στοιχεῖα τοῦ ὀφειλομένου παντὸς αὐτοὺς ἐδίδαξαν. 7. ἡ δὲ οἰκουμένη, ὡς εἰπεῖν, πᾶσα περὶ ἄμφω τὰ προκείμενα ἐπλανᾶτο.

9 1. Ἐπεὶ δὲ ὁ τοῦ θεοῦ λόγος γέγονεν ἄνθρωπος, οὐχ ὃ ἦν ἀποβαλών, ἀλλὰ τὴν ἡμέτεραν φύσιν δίχα τροπῆς προσλαβών, 2. πᾶσα ἡ οἰκουμένη τῆς πλάνης εὐθὺς ἀποστᾶσα προσέδραμε τῷ ἑνὶ θεῷ καὶ τὴν κακίαν ἀποστραφέντες καὶ βδελυξάμενοι εἵλοντο τὴν ἀρετήν. 3. ἀμφοτέρωθεν οὖν δείκνυται ὅτι δυνατὸν ἄλλως οὐκ ἦν· ἔκ τε τοῦ μηδὲν ἀνύσαι | τοὺς προφήτας καὶ ἐκ τοῦ τὸν λόγον 59r
παραγενόμενον ἐπιθεῖναι τὸ τέλος. 4. ἐπεὶ τί δήποτε μὴ γέγονεν ὅπερ ὑπῆρξεν, ἀφιγμένου τοῦ Ἰησοῦ; 5. οὐ γὰρ διὰ τὸ μὴ βούλεσθαι τὸν θεόν, ὃς ἀεὶ θέλει τὴν τῶν ἀνθρώπων σωτηρίαν καὶ τὴν ἐπιστροφὴν πρὸς αὐτόν, καὶ διὰ τοῦτο τοὺς τοσούτους προφήτας ἀπέστελεν. 6. ἀλλ᾽ ὅτι ἦν ἀδύνατον ἄλλως γενέσθαι τὸ μέγα ἐκεῖνο ἔργον ἢ ὡς γέγονεν.

10 1. Ἔτι οὐδὲν ἄτοπον εἰ γέγονεν αὐτουργὸς ὁ τοῦ θεοῦ λόγος τοσούτου πράγματος, τῆς τῶν ἀνθρώπων πρὸς τἀγαθὸν καὶ τὴν ἀλήθειαν ἐπιστροφῆς 2. ἐπεὶ καὶ τῆς αὐτοῦ προόδου αὐτουργὸν αὐτὸν γενέσθαι φασὶ τὰ λόγια. | 59v
3. ἔστι δὲ μεῖζον εἰς τέλος δι᾽ ὃ γέγονεν αὐτὸν ἐπαναγαγεῖν ἢ ἐκ μὴ ὄντος

1 πεποίηκε] πέπεοίηκε T || τε] τὲ T **5** οἷς] ἐκείνοις ἅ in marg. scr. T^1 **10** ἐπὶ τὸ] bis T, sed corr. T^1 **17** ἀμφοτέρωθεν] -φωτ- corr. T/T^1

and threatened people to do what they should, intervening personally as well as through angels and prophets, 5. while punishing malefactors on the one hand and honoring and glorifying the good on the other.

8 1. Likewise, God would not have ignored a way by which he could have achieved this goal. 2. For it is not the case that he wished good things for men, which is proven by the things he did, and then did not have a way of doing it. 3. If the reform did not happen [before Christ], it was because it was not possible. That it did not happen is obvious. 4. For Moses and those great prophets of yore, despite the many things they said and did, accomplished nothing save to educate the Jews, a distinctly small segment of mankind. 5. For Palestine was in fact not the whole world, nor, so to speak, was it even a part of it. 6. And the prophets were not able to lead even the Jews to complete education, and, inasmuch as this education appertains to the human race, the prophets taught the Jews exactly as if they, the Jews, were elements of the whole debt.[70] 7. The whole world, so to speak, was deluded about both [goodness and the truth] that were proposed to it.

9 1. When the Word of God became man, however, he did so not by abandoning what he was, but by assuming our nature without any change. 2. The whole world immediately revolted against its delusion and rushed toward the one God, and those who had turned away from evil and had once been abominable sinners chose virtue. 3. That this reform was not possible in any other way is therefore shown both by the fact that the prophets achieved nothing and from the fact that the Word, once it arrived, set out upon this goal. 4. How could it be that what had not happened before began after Jesus came? 5. For it was not because God did not wish it. God always wants the salvation of men and the turning back of men toward him. That is why he sent the great prophets of yore. 6. Rather it was because it was impossible for that great work to have happened in any other way than the way it did happen.

10 1. Furthermore, there is nothing absurd about the Word of God himself being the executor of such a grand enterprise as the turning of men toward goodness and truth, 2. since the oracles say that he himself would become executor of his own procession. 3. It was a greater feat, moreover, for God to have drawn man back to the end for which he was born than for him to have created

70. Cf. Matt. 18:34: ἕως οὗ ἀποδῷ πᾶν τὸ ὀφειλόμενον ("until he has paid the whole debt"). Amiroutzes seems to be echoing Anselm of Canterbury here; see n. 69.

παραγαγεῖν (δι᾽ ἐκεῖνο γὰρ καὶ ἡ πρόοδος γέγονεν) τὴν ἀρχήν. 4. εἰ τοίνυν τοῦ ἐλάττονος οὐκ ἀπηξίωσεν αὐτουργὸς γενέσθαι, πολλῷ μᾶλλον τοῦ μείζονος. 5. εἰ δὲ γενόμενος ἄνθρωπος, οὐδὲν ξένον. ἡ γὰρ συγκατάβασις, τὸν μὲν ἄνθρωπον εἰς τὸ προσῆκον τέλος ἐπέστρεψεν, τὸ ἀγαθόν τε καὶ ἀληθές, ἓν καὶ ταὐτὸ ὑπάρχον ἐν τῷ θεῷ. 6. τῇ δὲ θείᾳ φύσει μεταβολὴν οὐδὲ μίαν ἐπήγαγεν, καὶ ἅμα ἡ ποικίλη οἰκονομία καὶ συγκατάβασις ὑπὲρ τῆς τῶν ἀνθρώπων ἐπιστροφῆς οἰκεία θεῷ. 7. ἢ τοίνυν πᾶσαν ἀναιρεῖν δεῖ | τὴν τοῦ θεοῦ ὑπὲρ ἀνθρώπων οἰκονομίαν 60r καὶ μὴ δὲ μίαν δέχεσθαι, καθάπερ οἱ πάλαι Ἕλληνες, 8. ἢ τοῦτο δεχόμενοι τὸ γένος καὶ τὴν τοσαύτην πρόνοιαν, οὐκ ἂν δικαίως ἐκεῖνο ἀποδοκιμάζετε, ὃ πλέον τῶν ἄλλων ἤνυσε καὶ δι᾽ οὗ ἅπαν τὸ τέλος περιγέγονε μόνον.

XXVI 1 1. **Ὁ Κρατῶν.** Καὶ μήν, ἔφη, οὐ πάνυ τι μέγα ἤνυσε διὰ τῆς τοσαύτης καινοτομίας καθάπερ κομπάζεις αὐτός. 2. οὐδὲ τὴν οἰκουμένην πᾶσαν ἐπέστρεψεν ᾗπερ ἀλαζονεύῃ. Ἰνδοί τε γὰρ ἔτι μέγιστον ἔθνος καὶ Λιβύων καὶ Αἰθιόπων πολλοὶ τῇ πλάνῃ προσμένουσιν, ἀγνοοῦντες τὸν ἕνα θεόν. 3. οἵ τε τῷ | 60v ἡμετέρῳ προφήτῃ τιθέμενοι πλείους ὑμῶν εἰσὶ τῶν Χριστιανῶν. ἤδη οἱ τὸν ἕνα θεὸν ἔγνωσαν οὐκ ἀπὸ τοῦ Ἰησοῦ, ἀλλ᾽ ἀπὸ τοῦ ἡμετέρου προφήτου. 4. τί γοῦν μέγα πεποίηκεν ὁ θεὸς δι᾽ ἑαυτοῦ; ἢ τί μεῖζον ἄνθρωπος γενόμενος ἢ διὰ τοῦ ἡμετέρου προφήτου πεποίηκεν;

2 1. Καὶ προσέτι τοῦτο δείκνυσι μὴ ὄντα θεὸν τὸν Ἰησοῦν, ὅτι ὃ προέθετο οὐκ ἴσχυσεν ἀνύσαι. 2. οὐ γὰρ πάντας ἐπέστρεψε. τὸ δὲ ἀποτυγχάνειν τοῦ προκειμένου ἢ καθόλου ἢ ἐν μέρει οὐ τοῦ θεοῦ. 3. τὰ γὰρ ἐκείνου ἀνελλειπῆ. οὐκ ἄρα θεὸς ἦν προθέμενος ἐπιστρέψαι πάντας εἶτα μὴ δυνηθείς.

---

7 τὴν] bis T, sed corr. T[1] **9** καὶ] supra lin. scr. T **15** ἤδη] εἰσιν ante del. T **16–21** τί . . . θεοῦ] signo in marg. denotat T[1] **20** πάντας] in marg. scr. T || ἀποτυγχάνειν] -ειν ad ον mut. T[1]

ex nihilo (for that end was the reason why the procession [of creation] happened).[71] 4. If he did not think it unworthy of himself to become the executor of the lesser deed, much more so would he deem the greater deed worthy. 5. Nor was there anything alien in his becoming man. For this condescension in becoming man he turned to a fitting purpose, goodness and truth, which are one and the same thing in God. 6. He did not, however, introduce a single change into the divine nature. At the same time the complex economy[72] and condescension proper to God took place for the conversion of men. 7. Therefore it is necessary either that you annul all of God's plan for man and not accept that there was a single plan, just like the Greeks of old believed, 8. or that, having accepted the general proposition and God's providence, you unjustly reject this solution as unworthy even though it achieved more than the other solutions and even though through it alone did his goal became a reality.

XXVI 1 1. **The Conqueror.** The fact is, he said, that through this monstrous novelty he did not achieve anything like the grand deed you brag about. 2. He did not reform the whole world in the way you pretend. The fact is, the Indians, the largest nation of all, and many of the Libyans and Ethiopians still cling to their error, ignorant of the one God. 3. Moreover, the adherents of our prophet are more numerous than you Christians. They already knew of the one God not from Jesus, but from our prophet. 4. Indeed, what great thing did God accomplish through himself? What is greater: to have accomplished his goal by becoming man or to accomplish it through our prophet?

2 1. In addition, the fact that Jesus could not achieve what he proposed to do proves that he was not God. 2. For he did not bring about a conversion. Failing in one's purpose either totally or in part is not a characteristic of God. 3. For God would not have failed in his goal. Therefore Jesus was not God, in that he proposed to convert everyone and was not able to do it.

71. That the Incarnation is a greater feat than creation is a notable thesis of Gregory of Nazianzus; see his *Or.* 45.9 ("Second Oration on Easter"; PG 36:636A): Τοῦτο τοῦ προτέρου θεοειδέστερον· τοῦτο τοῖς νοῦν ἔχουσιν ὑψηλότερον ("This [the Incarnation] is more godlike than the former action [creation of man]; this is loftier in the eyes of all men of understanding"; trans. Browne and Swallow, 426).

72. Cf. Photius, *Bibl.* 222 (PG 103:748D): διὰ τοῦτο πολυτρόπου τε καὶ ποικίλης οἰκονομίας; and George Scholarius, *Tractatus de primo servitu dei* 28, in *Oeuvres complètes*, 4:257.28–29: τῆς δὲ ποικίλης οἰκονομίας τοῦ θεοῦ.

XXVII 1 1. **Ὁ Φιλόσοφος.** Οὐ πᾶσαν μὲν ἅμα | 61r τὴν οἰκουμένην, ἔφην ἐγώ, οὐδὲ αὐτίκα πρὸς τὴν ἀλήθειαν ἀπὸ τῆς πλάνης ἐπέστρεψεν. οὐ γὰρ ἦν οἷόν τε, σωζομένου τοῦ ἐφ᾽ ἡμῖν. 2. τὸ μέν τι πλέον αὐτῆς μέρος αὐτίκα εἰς τοῦτο ἤγαγεν, οὐ κατ᾽ ἀριθμόν, ἴσως τῶν καθ᾽ ἕκαστον, ἀλλὰ κατὰ ἔθνη, μετὰ δὲ ταῦτα καὶ κατὰ τὸ καθ᾽ ἕκαστον. 3. καὶ τοῦτο μέχρι τοῦ νῦν μαρτυροῦσιν οἱ κάλλει καὶ μεγέθει διαφέροντες πανταχοῦ τῆς οἰκουμένης ναοί, οὓς τοσούτοις ἔτεσιν αὐτοὶ κατασκάπτοντες ἐξανύσαι οὐκ ἰσχύσατε. 4. εἰ μὴ γὰρ ἐν παντὶ τῷ κόσμῳ ἐξετάθη τὸ κήρυγμα καὶ οἱ προσελθόντες τῇ πίστει τὸ κράτος εἶχον κατ᾽ ἀριθμόν, οὐκ ἂν ταῦτα πανταχοῦ ἐποίουν, | 61v οὐδὲ μίαν ἀπολείποντες ὑπερβολήν. 5. εἰ δέ τινες ἔτι προσμένουσι τῇ πλάνῃ, θαυμαστὸν οὐδέν.

2 1. Πρῶτον μὲν γὰρ οὐ πολλοὶ τινές εἰσιν, ἀλλ᾽ ἔν τε Ἰνδοῖς οἱ τὸν ἕνα θεὸν ἐπεγνωκότες καὶ τὴν ἀρετὴν ᾑρημένοι μέρος εἰσὶν οὐ φαῦλον, 2. καὶ ἐν Αἰθιοπίᾳ αὖ καὶ Λιβύῃ ἐλάχιστοί τινες πρὶν ὑπῆρχον οἱ τὸ κήρυγμα μὴ δεδεγμένοι. 3. οὐκ ἔδει τοίνυν διὰ τὴν τῶν ὀλίγων πονηρίαν τὴν τῆς οἰκουμένης διόρθωσιν παραλιπεῖν 4. ἔπειτα οὐδὲ δυνατὸν ἦν πάντας ἁπλῶς πρὸς τἀγαθὸν καὶ τὴν ἀλήθειαν ἐπιστρέφειν, ἀλλά τινα εἶναι ἔδει καὶ τοὺς τῇ πονηρίᾳ προσμένοντας. 5. τὸ οὖν | 62r Ἰησοῦ ἔργον, εἰ θεῖον, οὐκ ἀπὸ τούτου κρίνειν προσήκει ὅτι τινὲς τὴν ἀλήθειαν οὐκ ἐδέξαντο.

3 1. Καὶ γὰρ νῦν ὄντος θεοῦ καὶ πρόνοιαν πολλὴν εἰς ἡμᾶς ἐπιδεικνυμένου, ὅμως ἔστι τὸ κακόν, καὶ οὐ δήπω διατοῦτο ἐροῦμεν μὴ εἶναι θεὸν ἢ πρόνοιαν. 2. ἀλλ᾽ εἰ μὴ πᾶσα οἰκουμένη κατέγνω τῆς πλάνης, εἰ μὴ ἐπέγνω τὸ ἀληθές, εἰ μὴ ἐβδελύξατο τὴν κακίαν, 3. εἰ μὴ εἵλετο τὴν ἀρετήν, εἰ μὴ ἐπὶ τὸ ἄμεινον καὶ θειότατον ὅλως μετέβαλεν, ἔν τε τοῖς πρὸς θεὸν καὶ τοῖς πρὸς ἀλλήλους. 4. ἐκ τούτων δεῖ κρίνειν τὸ τοῦ Χριστοῦ ἔργον εἰ θεῖον.

---

1 Ὁ Φιλόσοφος] in marg. scr. T **5** κάλλει] κάλει corr. T[1] **14** τῶν] supra lin. scr. T

XXVII 1 1. **The Philosopher.** I responded: God did not convert the world from error to the truth straight away and all at once. For that was not possible if our free will was to be preserved.[73] 2. He brought the somewhat larger part of the world right away to the truth, not numerically, in terms of individuals, but in terms of nations, but subsequently he did so also in terms of individuals. 3. Church buildings all over the world witness to this up to today, however much they differ in beauty and size. Over the course of many years you have been destroying these churches, but without being able to complete their eradication. 4. For if the preaching of the Gospel had not extended to every part of the world and if individual rulers were not themselves adherents to the faith, they would not have built these churches everywhere and without stinting on a single extravagance. 5. If, however, some people remain who cling to error, that itself is no surprise.

2 1. For first of all, on the one hand, those who cling to error do not constitute some large number, and on the other, those among the Indians who have acknowledged the one God and who have chosen virtue are not a paltry portion; 2. and in Ethiopia and Libya, moreover, there have been before now very few people who have not accepted the preaching of the Gospel. 3. It was not necessary, then, to put aside the correction of the world on account of the evil of a few. 4. And afterward it was not possible simply to convert everyone to goodness and truth. Rather, some time was needed to convert those still committed to evil. 5. It is not right, therefore, to judge whether or not the work of Jesus was divine from the fact that some people did not accept the truth.

3 1. For let it be granted that God exists and that he demonstrates abundant providential care over us. Nonetheless, evil also exists. Yet, we would not, I think, say that therefore neither God nor providence exists. 2. Rather, even if the whole world has not condemned error, even if it has not acknowledged the truth, even if it has not despised evil, 3. even if it has not chosen virtue, even if it has not completely changed toward the better and what is most divine, in the case of some there still was a conversion toward God and for some a change of attitude toward each other. 4. It is on the basis of these latter points that we must judge whether the work of Christ was divine.

73. On the theme of free will, see XIX.7.2.

4 1. Ἐκεῖνο δὲ ἁπλῶς ἐστι ζητεῖν· τί δήποτε θεοῦ τοῖς οὖσιν ἐφεστηκότος καὶ
προνοίας | οὔσης, ὅλως ἔστι τὸ κακόν; 2. ἀλλ᾽ οὐχ οὕτως αὐτὸ ζητεῖτε. ἀλλὰ 62v
κοινὸν ὂν ἰδίως αὐτῷ κέχρησθε κατὰ τοῦ Ἰησοῦ. 3. περὶ δὲ τοῦ ὑμετέρου προφήτου ἐκεῖνο φαμέν, ὅτι οἱ τούτῳ προσθέμενοι οὐκ ἀπὸ τῆς πλάνης οὐδὲ ἑκόντες εἰς τοῦτο ἦλθον, 4. ἀλλ᾽ ἀπὸ τῆς ὑμετέρας θρησκείας βιασθέντες, οἱ μὲν θανάτου δέει, οἱ δὲ χαλεπῷ δουλείας ζυγῷ. 5. ὅ τε οὖν τρόπος τῆς μεταβολῆς πλεῖστον διαφέρει καὶ ὅθεν μετέβαλον. εἰ δὲ καὶ μὴ εἰς ὅ, χαλεπὸν ἦν.

5 1. Ὃ δέ, φατέ, ὡς τῆς προθέσεως ἁμαρτεῖν, οὐ θεοῦ ἀληθές τέ ἐστι. 2. καὶ ἡμῖν, εἴπερ τι ἄλλο δοκοῦν, οὐ μὴν ἀληθὲς ὅτι τῆς προθέσεως ἥμαρτεν Ἰησοῦς.
3. οὐ γὰρ ἁπλῶς προέ|θετο πάντας πρὸς τὴν ἀλήθειαν ἐπιστρέψαι, ἀλλὰ τοὺς 63r
αἱρησομένους. 4. εἰ δὲ τοῦτο φῂς ἀτυχίαν ὅτι μὴ πάντας, καὶ ἐπὶ τοῦ θεοῦ ἁπλῶς τοῦτο ἐρεῖς. 5. τί γὰρ δήποτε οὐ πάντας ἕλκει νῦν πρὸς τἀγαθόν; εἰ μὲν γὰρ βουλόμενος οὐκ ἰσχύει, ἀτυχεῖ τῆς προθέσεως. καὶ πῶς θεὸς κατὰ σέ; 6. εἰ δὲ μὴ βούλεται, ἀνεύθυνοι μὲν οἱ τἀγαθοῦ ἀπολειπόμενοι, τῶν δὲ κακῶν δὲ αἴτιος ὁ θεός. 7. καίτοι εἰ μὴ μόνον τῶν οὐσιῶν καὶ τῶν καταφύσιν γινομένων, ἀλλὰ καὶ τοῦ αἱρεῖσθαι καὶ πράττειν αἴτιός ἐστιν ὁ θεός, 8. οὐχ ᾗ μόνον ἀρχή ἐστιν τοῦ ἐν
ἡμῖν αὐτὰ εἶναι, καὶ ᾗ τἀγαθὸν ὑποτίθησι καὶ ὁδηγεῖ, ᾑρημένους ἐπὶ τὸ | τέλος 63v
ἄγει. 9. ἀλλ᾽ ὅτι καὶ ἐπὶ τὸ αἱρεῖσθαι ὅλως αὐτὸς ἐφ᾽ ἑκάτερα κινεῖ καὶ οὐδέν ἐστιν ἐφ᾽ ἡμῖν, τί δεῖ νόμων; 10. οὐ γὰρ ἐφ᾽ ἡμῖν ἔστι τὸ ποιητέον καὶ μή. μάταιον οὖν τὸ ταῦτα διορίζειν. οὐ γὰρ ἔσται τι πλέον ἐντεῦθεν οὐδέν. 11. μάταιον δὲ καὶ τὸ βουλεύεσθαι ὅτι μηδὲν ἄμεινον ἐκ τούτων συμβαίνει. 12. πάντων ἐξ ἀνάγκης ἄνωθεν γινομένων, τί δὲ καὶ τοὺς πονηροὺς εὐθάνομεν; 13. τί δὲ τοὺς ἀγαθοὺς στεφανοῦμεν; τίς δὲ ἀρετῆς αἵρεσις; τίς δὲ κακίας φυγή; 14. πάντα γὰρ ταῦτα μάτην ἔσται εἰ μὴ τὸ κῦρος τῶν πράξεων ἔστιν ἐφ᾽ ἡμῖν. 15. ἀλλ᾽ ἀπείη τοιαῦτα
νομίζειν | τινάς, ἐπεὶ ἀναιρεῖται καθάπαξ ὁ τῶν ἀνθρώπων βίος. 64r

7 μὴ] supra lin. scr. T; in marg. scr. T[1]: μὴ διενηχέναι δῆλον ὅτι **9** εἴπερ] εἴπέρ T || ἥμαρτεν] -εν supra lin. iterat T[1] **14** κακῶν] in marg. scr. T[1] || δὲ[2]] bis T, sed corr. T[1] **18** ἐφ᾽ ἑκάτερα] ἐφεκάτερα T **21** μηδὲν] μὴδὲν T || τούτων] in marg. annot. T[1]: γράφεται· τούτου **22** εὐθάνομεν] non in *TLG*; cf. Sophocles, *Greek Lexicon*: εὔθνητος, "subject to death"

4 1. The question, however, that absolutely has to be asked is: Why is there any evil at all, if God has paid attention to his creation and if providence exists? 2. But this is not how you put the question. Rather, what is an issue in general you have cast against Jesus in particular. 3. We, on the other hand, say the following concerning your prophet: his followers did not willingly desert error for belief in one God, 4. but were coerced into doing so by your religion, some by fear of death, some by the harsh yoke of slavery.[74] 5. The mode of change here, then, is extremely different, as is the religion from which people changed. If, in fact, they did not change to your religion, things would have gone harshly for them.

5 1. You say that failing in his mission is not something that is true of God. 2. Yet, even if it might seem otherwise, we do not think it true that Jesus failed in his mission. 3. For he set out to convert not absolutely everyone to the truth, but those who would choose it. 4. If, however, you say that it is a failure not to have converted everyone, you are in an absolute sense accusing God. 5. For why has he not by now, at some previous point in time, drawn everyone to the truth? For if he wishes it, but cannot do it, he fails of his purpose. So how can you call him God? 6. If, however, he does not wish to convert everyone, those who fall short of the truth are blameless while God, conversely, is the cause of evils. 7. Indeed, if God is the cause not only of [higher] beings and of things in nature, but also of our choices and of our actions, 8. he is not only the cause of these powers being in us, but also wholly responsible for presenting what is good to the elect and leading them to that goal. 9. But since he completely controls how we choose among things and since we have no free will, what need is there for laws? 10. For what must be done or not done is not up to us. It is pointless, therefore, to make careful determinations in these matters. For something more will not be coming out of these determinations. 11. It is pointless, moreover, even to deliberate, since nothing better will result from these deliberations. 12. If everything happens of necessity as it is ordained from on high, why do we execute the wicked? 13. Why do we honor what is good? What choice of virtue is there, really? What escape from evil is there, really? 14. For all these things are in vain if control over our actions does not reside with us. 15. But perish the thought that such is the case! This kind of thinking will absolutely destroy the life of men.

74. On coercion in religion, see XIX.7.2

6 1. Εἰ τοίνυν ἔστι τὸ ἐφ᾽ ἡμῖν, πᾶσι μὲν ὁ θεὸς ἁπλῶς βούλεται τἀγαθά. οὐ
μὴν ἄκοντας, ἀλλὰ βουλομένους ἄγει, καίτοι πάντας ἐπὶ τἀγαθὸν παρακαλῶν.
2. ἀλλὰ τῶν ἀπολειπομένων οὐχ ὁ θεὸς αἴτιος, ἀλλ᾽ αὐτοὶ μὴ ἑλόμενοι τἀγαθὸν.
3. ταὐτὸ τοίνυν ἔστιν εἰπεῖν καὶ ἐπὶ τοῦ Χριστοῦ, ὅτι πάντας μὲν ἐβούλετο
ἐπιστρέψαι, βουλομένους μέντοι καὶ θέλοντας. 4. εἰ δὲ μὴ βούλοιντο, τοὺς
βουλομένους μόνον. οὐ τοίνυν ἀτυχεῖ τῆς προθέσεως, οὐδ᾽ ἐλλιπὲς τῶν αὐτοῦ
ἔργων οὐδέν. 5. ἀλλὰ τὸ μὲν οὕτως ἄγειν φυλάττοντός ἐστι τὴν | προαίρεσιν. τὸ 64v
δὲ ἄλλως οὐ πρὸς θεοῦ. 6. οὐδεὶς γὰρ ἄκων γένοιτ᾽ ἂν ἀγαθός, οὐδὲ μακάριος.
οὐδ᾽ ἔστιν ἀρετὴ τὸ βεβιασμέμον.

XXVIII 1 1. **Ὁ Κρατῶν**. Ἔοικας οἰομένῳ λέγειν τι πρὸς τὴν ἡμετέραν
ἀντίθεσιν, ἔφη. τῇ δὲ ἀληθείᾳ λέγεις, οὐδὲν ἀλλὰ παῖς ἂν ἄμεινον πρὸς ταῦτα
εἴποι. 2. οὐκ οἶδα γοῦν εἴ τινα πείθεις τούτοις τοῖς λόγοις λίαν οὖσι παιδικοῖς καὶ
οὐδὲ ἀπολογίας λοιπὸν δεομένοις, ἀλλ᾽ αἰσχύνης ἢ κολάσεως. 3. ἀλλὰ ταῦτα
μὲν ἐατέον. ἐπεὶ δὲ τοὺς προφήτας ἡμῖν ἀνατείνεις ἀεὶ ὡς ὑπ᾽ ἐκείνων ὅλον τοῦθ᾽
ὃ φατὲ προειραμένον, 4. βούλομαι μαθεῖν τίνες οἱ τοῦτο εἰπόντες | ὅτι ὁ θεὸς 65r
γενήσεται ἄνθρωπος καὶ ποῦ. 5. καὶ γὰρ εἰ μὴ πάνυ πιστεύομεν αἷς νῦν ἔχετε
βίβλοις τῶν προφητῶν, ἀλλ᾽ ὅμως μαθεῖν βούλομαι τίνας πότε φατὲ τὸ παράδο-
ξον εἰρηκέναι τοῦτο. 6. τάχα γὰρ καὶ τοῦτο νῦν πλάττετε, οὐδὲ γεγραμμένον ὄν,
ἐπεὶ τί δήποτε Ἑβραῖοι μὴ ὁμολογοῦσιν αὐτοὶ πρῶτοι τὰς βίβλους ἔχοντες τῶν
προφητῶν; 7. διὰ τοῦτο μαθεῖν βούλομαι τίνες οἱ τοῦτο εἰπόντες καὶ ποῦ. καὶ
ὅρα μηδὲν ἀπὸ σαυτοῦ προσθεῖς. 8. καὶ γὰρ Ἰακὼβ ὅδε πάρ᾽ ἐστὶν Ἑβραῖος
πρότερον ὤν, καὶ ἅμα ταῖς βίβλοις ἔστιν αὐταῖς | ἐν τυχεῖν. 9. ἔστι γὰρ καὶ παρ᾽ 65v
ἡμῖν Ἀραβικῶς.

XXIX 1 1. **Ὁ Φιλόσοφος**. Τὸ μὲν τοὺς εἰπόντας προφήτας προφέρειν οὐ
χαλεπόν. 2. δέδοικα δὲ μή τι μοι χαλεπὸν ἐντεῦθεν ξυμβῇ. καὶ γὰρ αἰσθάνομαι
τοῦ ὁριζομένου. 3. εἰ μὲν οὖν πράως ἐπακούσῃ τῶν λεγομένων, ἐρῶ. εἰ δὲ μή,

---

4 ταὐτὸ] ταυτὸ T **7** φυλάττοντός] -οντα corr. T[1] **10** Ὁ Κρατῶν] in marg. scr. T **13** αἰσχύνης] αισθήσεως T; in marg. annot. T[1]: γράφεται· κίσεως [sc. αἰκίσεως] **17** πότε] ποτε T **20–22** καὶ[1] . . . αὐταῖς] signo [linea perpendicula] in marg. denotat T[1] **21** μηδὲν] μὴδὲν T **26** τοῦ] ad σοῦ mut. T[1]

6 1. If we have free will then, God absolutely wills what is good for us. But he leads not the unwilling, but the willing, while in fact calling everyone to what is good. 2. But God is not the cause of those forsaking what is good to act so. Rather, they themselves chose not to do what is good. 3. The same thing can be said about Christ, namely, that he wished to convert everyone, assuming that everyone is willing and chooses to do so. 4. If, however, not everyone is willing, he then would convert only the willing. He therefore did not fail in his purpose, nor did he in any way fall short in what he achieved. 5. Rather, to lead men to the good in this fashion is the action of a God who is preserving the power of free choice. To act otherwise would not be proper to God. 6. For no one becomes good or happy against his will. Nor is virtue anything that is compelled.

XXVIII 1 1. **The Conqueror.** He said: You seem to believe that you have said something worthwhile in response to my criticism. But the truth is that you have said nothing better than a child would say in the matter. 2. Indeed, I do not see how you are in any way persuasive with these overly childish arguments of yours, which require in any case not rebuttal, but rather shaming or chastisement. 3. But I shall let this go. Since you are always holding up the prophets to us, as if the entirety of what you talk about was predicted by them, 4. I wish to know which of them said that God would become man and where they said this. 5. For even if we do not entirely believe in the books of the prophets that you possess today, we nonetheless want to learn which ones you say once pronounced this paradox. 6. Perhaps this is something you are fabricating right now and it was not really written down. For why is it that the Hebrews, who first had the books of the prophets, do not agree with you? 7. Consequently, we want to learn who are the ones who say this and where they say it. And mind you, do not insert anything of your own making. 8. For we have Jacob here, who was once a Hebrew and who can read these books on the spot.[75] 9. He will also be able to read them to us in Arabic.[76]

XXIX 1 1. **The Philosopher.** Adducing the prophets who say this is no problem. 2. I fear, however, some sort of difficulty befalling me from this. For I understand the task that has been set for me. 3. If, then, you listen patiently to

75. On Iacopo da Gaeta (Jaʿqūb-Pasha), see pp. 8 (n. 34), 24.

76. As a long-time intimate of Mehmed II, it is implausible to suppose that Iacopo did not speak to Mehmed in Turkish—so Amiroutzes is guilty of not distinguishing Turkish from Arabic.

παύσομαι. οὐ γὰρ αἱροῦμαι «πρὸς κέντρα λακτίζειν».

XXX 1 1. **Ὁ Κρατῶν**. Μὴ δέδιθι, ἔφη. πράως γάρ σου ἀκούσομαι καὶ ὀργῆς
χωρίς, ἐπεὶ καὶ εἴ τι μὴ προσῆκον εἴρηται, οὐκ ἐμὸν ἦν, ἀλλὰ τοῦ ἑρμηνέως. 2. καὶ
ἅμα οἴκοι διαλεγομένοις ἐν οὐ πολλοῖς, οὐδὲ ἐν θεά|τρῳ ἔξεστι καὶ τοιαῦτα δίχα 66r
κατηγορίας εἰπεῖν. λέγε τοίνυν θαρρῶν. οὐδὲν γὰρ ἔτι φαῦλον ἐρῶ.

XXXI 1 1. **Ὁ Φιλόσοφος**. Πάντες μὲν οἱ προφῆται περὶ τοῦ Χριστοῦ
προεφήτευσαν, ἔφην ἐγώ, οὐ μὴν περὶ πάντων τῶν κατ᾽ αὐτὸν ἅπαντες, 2. ἀλλ᾽
ὁ μὲν ὅτι ἥξει προεῖπεν μηδὲν προσθείς, ὁ δὲ περὶ τῆς γεννήσεως αὐτοῦ προαγο-
ρεύει, 3. ὁ δὲ περὶ ὧν ἔπαθεν, ὁ δὲ περὶ τῆς ἀναστάσεως, ὁ δὲ περὶ τῆς θεότητος,
καὶ ἄλλος ἄλλο τι. 4. τὰ μὲν οὖν ἄλλα παρήσειν μοι δοκεῖ, ὅσα δὲ δεικνύει θεὸν
αὐτὸν τὸν ἐλπιζόμενον αὐτοῖς Χριστόν, τούτων ὅσα εἰς μνήμην ἥκει, ἐκθήσομαι.

2 1. Δοκεῖ δέ μοι πρῶτον | ἐκεῖνο προθεῖναι ὅτι προηγορευμένον ἦν τοῖς 66v
Ἑβραίοις τὸν Χριστὸν ἥξειν, καὶ δόξα τοῦτο κοινὴ τοῦ γένους παντὸς ἦν. 2. καὶ
νῦν δὲ καίτοι λοιπὸν ἐληλεγμένοι τῷ χρόνῳ, ἥξειν ὅμως αὐτὸν ἑκάστοτε
προσδοκῶσι. 3. τούτου μὲν οὖν οὐκ ἂν γένοιτο κρείττων ἀπόδειξις τῆς κοινῆς
ἐλπίδος αὐτῶν. 4. ἀλλὰ καὶ ἀπὸ τοῦ νομοθέτου Μωσέως οὐδὲν ἧττον δείκνυται.
5. φησὶ γὰρ ἐκεῖνος τὸν Ἰακὼβ μέλλοντα τελευτᾶν προσκαλέσασθαι τοὺς
οἰκείους παῖδας καὶ παρελθόντας εὐλογῆσαί τε κατάταξιν καὶ προειπεῖν ἅπερ
ἔμελλεν ἑκάστῳ | συμβήσεσθαι. 6. τὰ μὲν οὖν ἄλλα περίημι. ἐπεὶ δὲ ἐπὶ τὸν 67r
Ἰούδαν ἔλθοι τάδε φάναι «Ἰοῦδα, σὲ αἰνέσουσιν οἱ ἀδελφοί σου ‹...› σκύμνος
λέοντος Ἰούδα. 7. ἐκ βλαστοῦ, υἱέ μου, ἀνέβης. ἀναπεσὼν ἐκοιμήθη. ‹...› τίς
ἐγερεῖ αὐτόν; οὐκ ἐκλείψει ἄρχων ἐξ Ἰούδα καὶ ἡγούμενος ἐκ τῶν μηρῶν αὐτοῦ
ἕως οὗ ἔλθοι ὃ ἀπόκειται, καὶ αὐτὸς προσδοκεία ἐθνῶν». 8. ταῦτα σαφῶς περὶ

---

2 δέδιθι] in marg. iterat T[1] || ἀκούσομαι] ἀκού- in rasura scr. T/T[1] **3** μὴ] μοὶ corr. T[1] **6** Ὁ Φιλόσοφος] in marg. scr. T **10** ἄλλο] ἄλο corr. T[1]; in marg. scr. et deinde del. T[1] τῶν ἐκ τῶν Σιβυλλίων ἐπῶν καὶ ὅσα **15** κρείττων] -ω-supra lin. iterat T[1] **16** αὐτῶν] οὐ μὲν post in marg. scr. T[1] **18** κατάταξιν] κατατάξιν T **20** Ἰούδαν] Ἰοῦδαν T, et similiter nonnumquam postea **21** Ἰούδα] in marg. scr. T || μου] ante υἱέ del. et post rescr. T

what is said, I shall speak. If not, I shall remain silent. For I do not choose *to kick against the goads.*[77]

XXX 1 1. **The Conqueror.** He said: Fear not. For I shall patiently listen to you without anger, especially since if anything was rudely said, it was the translator's doing, not mine. 2. At the same time, since we are just a small group having a discussion at home and not in a theater, we can speak about these matters free of accusations. Speak boldly then. For hereafter I shall not say anything harsh.

XXXI 1 1. **The Philosopher.** I said: All the prophets prophesized about Christ, not all of them, to be sure, about everything concerning him, 2. but one predicted that he would come without giving any details; another prophesized concerning his birth; 3. yet another concerning his sufferings; another concerning his resurrection; another concerning his divinity; and some other about some other thing. 4. I think I should set aside these other prophecies, from among those that have come down to us, in order to expound upon the prophecies that show that Christ was the God hoped for by the prophets.

2 1. The first one I would like to cite is the prophecy made to the Hebrews that the Christ would come. This was the common opinion of the whole nation. 2. Now, however, even though they have indeed been proven otherwise wrong as to the time, they nonetheless at every opportunity continue to look forward to his coming. 3. We can have no greater proof of this prophecy than this common hope of theirs. 4. But we can demonstrate the same no less easily by quoting the lawgiver Moses. 5. For he says that when Jacob was about to die, he summoned his sons, and once they had come, he praised each in sequence and prophesized what would happen to them. 6. But I shall pass over what he said about the others and quote what he said when he came to Judah: *Judah, your brothers will praise you. . . . Judah is the lion's cub. 7. From the prey you have returned, my son. Having lain down, he rested. . . . Who will rouse him? The scepter will not depart from Judah, and the ruler will come from his thighs until he who is in reserve comes, and he will be the expectation of the nations.*[78] 8. God was clearly speaking

77. Acts 26:14.

78. Gen. 49:8–10 (with variations and omissions). The Greek Septuagint text differs here from the Hebrew, and how exactly one should translate what Amiroutzes understood the words καὶ ἡγούμενος ἐκ τῶν μηρῶν αὐτοῦ ἕως οὗ ἔλθοι ὃ ἀπόκειται to mean is not clear to me.

τοῦ Μεσία ἔχρησεν ὁ θεός. ἅπερ οὐχ ὅτι ἥξει μόνον προαγορεύει, ἀλλὰ καὶ τὸν χρόνον δείκνυσιν ὅτε βασιλεύσει μὲν γὰρ τὴν τοῦ Ἰούδα φυλὴν προλέγει. 9. ἥξειν δὲ ὃ ἀπόκειται, | παυομένης λοιπὸν αὐτῆς. ἔτι δὲ τὸ γένος ὅθεν ἔσται. 67v 10. αἰνίττεται δὲ αὐτὴν τὴν τοῦ Ἰοῦδα φυλήν. οὐ γὰρ ἂν πρὸς αὐτὸν εἴρητο. σαφέστερον δὲ αὐτό φασιν οἱ μετὰ ταῦτα προφῆται, 11. καὶ μὴν καὶ ὅτι οὐκ Ἰουδαίων μόνον, ἀλλὰ καὶ ἐθνῶν ἔσται προσδοκία. τὰ μὲν οὖν εἰρημένα τῷ Μωϋσῇ περὶ τοῦ Χριστοῦ ταῦτα ἐστί.

3 1. Ἐξετάσωμεν τοίνυν εἰ μὴ ἐνδέχεται ἄλλῳ τινὶ ἐφαρμόζειν ἢ τῷ Ἰησοῦ. 2. πρῶτον μὲν τοίνυν παυομένης τῆς τοῦ Ἰούδα βασιλείας, οὐδεὶς ἧκεν εἰ μὴ Ἰησοῦς. 3. ἐπὶ γὰρ Ἡρώδου γέγονε τοῦ πρώτου, ὃς μετὰ τὴν Ἰούδα φυλὴν εὐθὺς ἐβα|σίλευσε. μεθ᾽ ὃν οὐκ ἔτι βασιλεὺς ἐξ αὐτῆς γένετο. 4. εἰ γὰρ ἧκέ τις ἄλλος, 68r οὐκ ἂν ἔλαθεν. ἀλλὰ μὴν οὐδὲ πλάσασθαί τις αὐτὸ μέχρι τοῦ νῦν ἐτόλμησεν. 5. ἔτι ἀριδηλότατα φαίνεται διὰ τοῦ Δανιήλ. καὶ γὰρ καὶ οὗτος τὸν χρόνον σημαίνει μεθ᾽ ὃν ἥξει ὁ Χριστὸς ἡγούμενος ὅτι μετὰ τὰ πάθη μέν, ἃ πείσονται ἐπὶ τῆς τρίτης βασιλείας Ἑβραῖοι, ἃ γέγονεν ἐπὶ Ἀντιόχου. 6. ταῦτα δὲ πάντα γέγονεν ἐπὶ τοῦ Ἰησοῦ, τῆς τετάρτης βασιλείας κρατούσης. 7. ἐπὶ γὰρ Αὐγούστου γέγονε τοῦ πρώτου βασιλέως Ῥωμαίων τὸ μυστήριον.

4 1. Τὸ αὐτὸ δὲ δείκνυται καὶ | ἀπὸ τοῦ γένους. καὶ γὰρ ἐκ τῆς τοῦ Ἰούδα 68v φυλῆς ἐτύγχανεν ἡ μήτηρ αὐτοῦ Μαριάμ, ὡς φαίνεται ἀπὸ τοῦ γένους τοῦ Ἰωσήφ, τοῦ ἀνδρὸς δῆθεν αὐτῆς. 2. οὐ γὰρ ἐξῆν ἑτέρωθι γαμεῖν ἢ ἐκ τῆς φυλῆς

---

1 Μεσία] sic, et similiter postea **3** παυομένης] παπαυομένης T **6** μόνον] μόνων corr. T/T^1 **14** ἃ πείσονται] ἀπερίσονται T; in marg. annot. T^1: ἴσθι· γράφεται· ἃ πείσονται ἢ ἅπερ οἴωνται **15** Ἀντιόχου] post unam lineam del. T **16** τῆς . . . κρατούσης] in marg. scr. T^1

of the Messiah in these words. They not only predict that he will come, but also indicate the time when. For they foretell that he will rule the tribe of Judah. 9. He who has been in reserve will come and thereafter the tribe will come to an end. The family whence came the Messiah, however, will still continue to exist. 10. The passage speaks enigmatically of the tribe of Judah. For it was not said apropos of the [Messiah's] family. The prophets who come after are much clearer, however, on this point, 11. and they say that the Messiah will be the expectation not only of the Jews, but also of the nations. These words of Moses, then, refer to Christ.

3 1. Let us examine, therefore, if it is not possible to adapt the passage to someone other than Jesus. 2. First then, when the kingdom of Judah ended, no one came except Jesus. 3. For he lived in the reign of Herod I, who was king immediately after the tribe of Judah.[79] After him there was never again a king from the tribe of Judah. 4. For if someone else had come, he would not have escaped notice. But up to this day no one has dared to fabricate such an alternative. 5. Furthermore, we can see the prophecy most clearly from Daniel. For he announced the time after which would come Christ, the ruler: it would happen after the suffering which the Hebrews endured under the third empire, which happened under Antiochus.[80] 6. All these things occurred under Jesus, when the fourth empire held power. 7. For the mystery took place under Augustus, the first Roman emperor.

4 1. The same, moreover, can be shown on the basis of his family. For his mother Mary came from the tribe of Judah.[81] This is also clear on the basis of Joseph's, that is to say, of her husband's family.[82] 2. For it was not permissible for

79. I.e., the first king after the Romans in 37 BCE ended the Hasmonean dynasty that had begun with Simon Maccabeus (r. 142–135 BCE) as rulers of Judaea.

80. I.e., Antiochus IV Epiphanes (ca. 215–164 BCE), king of the Seleucid Empire, whose suppression of Jewish rites and desecration of the Temple provoked the revolt of the Maccabees. On the prophecies in the Book of Daniel, see Collins, *Apocalyptic Imagination*, 85–115.

81. The genealogy at the start of the Matthew and in Luke 3:23–28 traces the line of Joseph back through Judah, but the Protoevangelium of James (10) assigns Mary to the family of David and therefore of the tribe of Judah. The "lion of the tribe of Judah" of Rev. 5:5 was commonly taken as a reference to Jesus.

82. See n. 81.

τῆς οἰκείας ἕκαστον καὶ τῆς πατριᾶς, οὐχ ἥκιστα δὲ καὶ ὅτι προσδοκία ὑπῆρξεν ἐθνῶν. 3. ταῦτα γὰρ ἐκ τῆς πλάνης ἐπέστρεψεν εἰς τὴν ἀλήθειαν καὶ ἐκ τῆς κακίας εἰς ἀρετήν.

5 1. Οὕτω μὲν οὖν ἀπὸ τοῦ παρήκοντος χρόνου εἰς αὐτὸν ἥκειν τὸν Ἰησοῦν ὁ χρησμός, 2. οὐδὲν δὲ ἧττον ἐνδείκνυται καὶ ἀπὸ τοῦ μέλλοντος ὅτι μὴ ἐνδέχεται ἔτι τὸν Μεσίαν ἐλθεῖν. | 3. εἰ γὰρ μηκέτι ἐνδέχεται, δῆλον ὅτι ἧκεν, καὶ οὐκ 69r
ἀποπίπτει ὁ τοῦ θεοῦ χρησμός. 4. ὅτι δὲ οὐκ ἐνδέχεται, δῆλον ἔσται σκοπουμένοις ὧδε ἀπὸ τῆς Ἰούδα φυλῆς αὐτὸν ἐλθεῖν δεῖ. καὶ τοῦτο γνώριμον εἶναι μὴ ἄδηλον. 5. αἱ δὲ φυλαὶ νῦν πᾶσαι συγκέχυνται καὶ οὐδεὶς οἶδε τίς μὲν ἡ τοῦ Ἰούδα, τίς δὲ ἡ τοῦ Ρουβήν. τίνες δὲ αἱ λοιπαί; 6. ἔτι δὲ εἰς προσεχέστερον οἱ προφῆται τὸ γένος αὐτοῦ κατάγοντες ἐκ τοῦ Δαυὶδ ἥκειν προσαγορεύουσιν. 7. ἡ δὲ καθόλου ἐξέλιπεν, καὶ οὐκ ἔστιν εὑρεῖν ἐξ αὐτῆς οὐδένα βεβαίως. 8. πόθεν | 69v
οὖν ἥξει; οὐ γὰρ οὐθενοῦν. ἀλλὰ δεῖ δῆλον εἶναι ὅθεν ἥξει. 9. ἔτι παυομένης τῆς ‹τρίτης› βασιλείας, ἡ τοῦ Ἰούδα φυλή. 10. «οὐκ ἐκλείψει», γάρ φησίν, «ἄρχων ἐξ Ἰούδα καὶ ἡγούμενος ἐκ τῶν μηρῶν αὐτοῦ ἕως οὗ ἔλθῃ ὃ ἀπόκειται». 11. δεῖ τοίνυν αὐτοῦ ἥκοντος παύσασθαι. τῇ δὲ πλείω ἢ χίλια πεντακόσια ἔτη παρῆλθεν ἀφ᾽ οὗπερ ἔληξεν. 12. καὶ μὴν ἐπὶ τῆς τετάρτης βασιλείας Δανιὴλ φησί. ταύτην

---

4 ἥκειν] ad ἥκει perperam corr. T^1 **6** μηκέτι] μὴ κἒτι corr. T^1 **7** ἀποπίπτει] ἀπὸ τίπει corr. T/T^1 **8** ὧδε] ᾧδε T; ad ᾧδε mut. T^1 **11** προσαγορεύουσιν] in marg. annot. T^1: γρᾶφεται· προαγορεύουσιν **14** τρίτης] supplevi || βασιλείας] post in marg. add. T^1: ἣν εἶχεν **15** ἔλθῃ] cf. ἔλθοι in XXXI.2.7 supra

either to marry outside of their own tribe and lineage,[83] and not the least because Jesus was *the expectation of the nations*.[84] 3. For he would convert them from error to the truth and from evil to virtue.

5 1. Thus, therefore, from what has happened from the past up to the present, the oracular pronouncement shows that Jesus has come. 2. This can just as easily be shown from the perspective of the future, namely, that it is not possible that the Messiah is yet to come. 3. For if it is in no way possible that he is yet to come, then clearly he has come, and God's oracular pronouncement is not a failure. 4. That it is not possible that he is yet to come will be obvious to those who observe how he necessarily had to come from the tribe of Judah. And that this was common knowledge is hardly a secret. 5. All the tribes nowadays are mixed together, and no one knows which is the tribe of Judah, which the tribe of Ruben. Which ones are left? 6. Still more to the point, the prophets, when tracing his lineage, proclaim that he will come from David.[85] 7. But David's tribe has completely ceased to exist, and it is impossible to find anyone from it with confidence. 8. From where, then, would the Messiah come? For he would not come just out of nowhere. Rather, it is clearly necessary that he came out of some lineage. 9. Yet, when the third empire ceased to exist, so did the tribe of Judah. 10. For Jacob said: *The scepter will not depart from Judah and the ruler will come from his thighs until he who is in reserve comes*.[86] 11. Therefore, with his coming, the tribe of Judah necessarily ceased to exist. Up to now more than fifteen hundred years have elapsed since it ceased to exist. 12. And, in fact, Daniel said that this would happen in the fourth empire.[87] The fourth empire happens to be

83. Amiroutzes must be thinking of Num. 36:6–9, where marriage outside the tribe is forbidden; cf. Milgrom, *Numbers*, 512.

84. Gen. 49:10. Christians early on claimed this phrase for Jesus Christ. The TLG reports numerous church fathers making this argument, including Justin Martyr eight times, Eusebius of Caesaria twelve times in just the *Demonstratio Evangelica* alone, Athanasius of Alexandria eight times, and so on.

85. Lineage from David was the point of the genealogy at the start of Matthew and of Luke 3:23–28; see also Romans 1:1–3.

86. See n. 78.

87. Christian commentators had traditionally counted the four monarchies of Daniel 2, 7, and 8 as the Babylonian, Persian, Greek, and Roman, but Daniel says nothing about the line of Judah. Rev. 5:5 predicts that "the lion of the tribe of Judah, the root of David" will open the scroll and the seven seals.

δὲ συμβαίνει τὴν Ῥωμαίων εἶναι. ἡ δὲ καθόλου ἐξέλιπεν. 13. ὅτε οὖν χρόνος
ἐξήκει, καὶ τὸ γένος τό τε προσεχὲς ἀνῄρηται καὶ τὸ πόρρω. καὶ ἄδηλον | εἴ τις 70r
ἐκεῖσε σώζεται. 14. καὶ μὴν ἐκ Βηθλεὲμ ἕξειν φασὶ τὰ λόγια. ἐνταῦθα δὲ νῦν οὐχ
ὅτι Ἰουδαῖοι. 15. ἢ τῶν ἀπὸ τοῦ Ἰεσσαί, ἀλλ᾽ οὐδὲ Ἑβραῖον ἔστιν εὑρεῖν.

6 1. Φανερὸν ἄρα ὅτι ὁ Ἰησοῦς, ὁ τῆς Μαριὰμ τῆς παρθένου παῖς, οὐκ ἄλλος
ἐστὶν ἢ ὁ Χριστός, περὶ οὗ καὶ Μωσῆς καὶ οἱ ἄλλοι προφῆται ἀνεῖλον. 2. ὃν
Ἑβραῖοι σὺν οὐδενὶ δικαίῳ παρωσάμενοι ἄλλον ἥξειν ἐκδέχονται. 3. ὅστις δὲ
αὐτοῖς ἥξει καὶ ὃν δέξονται, αὐτοί τε σὺν ἡμῖν ἴστε, καὶ ὁ Ἰησοῦς εἴρηκε, καὶ
ἀνάγκη γενέσθαι.

7 1. Ἃ μὲν οὖν ἔδει προυποτιθέναι καὶ εἴρηται, οἶμαι, καὶ δέδεικται ἱκανῶς.
2. λείπεται δὲ δεῖξαι καὶ | ὅτι θεὸν προφῆταί φασι τὸν Χριστόν, ὃ προέκειτο. 70v
3. Δαυὶδ οὖν ὁ προφήτης ἐν μδʹ ψαλμῷ, ὃν «εἰς τὸν ἀγαπητὸν» ἐπιγράφει, τάδε
φησί· «περίζωσαι τὴν ῥομφαίαν σου ἐπὶ τὸν μηρόν σου, δυνατέ, τῇ ὡραιότητί
σου καὶ τῷ κάλλει σου. 4. καὶ ἔντεινε καὶ κατευοδοῦ καὶ βασίλευε ἕνεκα
ἀληθείας καὶ πραότητος καὶ δικαιοσύνης. καὶ ὁδηγήσει σε θαυμαστῶς ἡ δεξιά
σου. 5. τὰ βέλη σου ἠκονημένα, δυνατέ. λαοὶ ὑποκάτω σου πεσοῦνται. 6. ἐν
καρδίᾳ τῶν ἐχθρῶν τοῦ βασιλέως ὁ θρόνος σου, ὁ θεός, εἰς τὸν αἰῶνα τοῦ
αἰῶνος. ῥάβδος εὐθύτητος, ἡ ῥάβδος | τῆς βασιλείας σου. 7. ἠγάπησας δικαιοσύ- 71r
νην καὶ ἐμίσησας ἀνομίαν. διὰ τοῦτο ἔχρισέ σε ὁ θεός, ὁ θεός σου, ἔλαιον
ἀγαλλιάσεως παρὰ τοὺς μετόχους σου». 8. ταῦτα εἰ μὴ ἐπὶ τὸν Μεσίαν ἤρηται,
λεγέτω ὁ βουλόμενος περὶ τίνος ἄλλου λοιπόν. 9. οὐ γὰρ δὴ μάτην εἴρηται τῷ
προφήτῃ. οὐδὲ εἰκῇ τὸν χρησμὸν ὅλον ᾖδε. 10. οὐδὲ φενακίζων κατ᾽ οὐδενὸς

---

6 ἢ] supra lin. scr. T^1 **8** εἴρηκε] in marg. annot T^1: ἤγουν τὸν ᾿Αντιχριστον **14** κάλλει] κάλει corr. T^1 **15** ὁδηγήσει] -γήση corr. T^1 || δεξιά] δεξιᾶ corr. T^1 **18** ῥάβδος^1] ῥαύδος T (v. XXXI.7.14 infra) || ῥάβδος^2] ῥαύδος T (v. XXXI.7.14 infra) **21** εἴρηται] ἤρηται corr. T/T^1 **22** ᾖδε] ᾖσε in marg. scr. T^1 || φενακίζων] αι supra φε- scr. T^1

that of the Romans.[88] It, however, has completely expired. 13. When, therefore, its time had run out, then the lineage of Judah was the next thing also to disappear and to remain so into the future. It is not even clear whether anyone of that lineage survives. 14. And the oracles also say that he will come from Bethlehem.[89] Today, however, Jews do not live there. 15. Alternatively, there is the prophecy that he will come from the root of Jesse; but there is no Hebrew from that line around to be found.

6 1. It is clear, therefore, that Jesus, the son of the Virgin Mary, and no other, is the Christ, concerning whom Moses and the other prophets made their oracles. 2. He is the one whom the Hebrews unjustly rejected while still expecting another to come. 3. Whoever this is will come to them and be accepted by them; this you yourself acknowledge along with us, and it is what Jesus himself said, and it is what must happen.[90]

7 1. These things, then, must be laid down as axiomatic, and, I think, affirmed. They are sufficiently proved. 2. What we have left to show, however, is the proposition that the prophets say that the Christ is God. 3. The prophet David, then, in the forty-fourth psalm, to which he gave the title "On the Beloved," says as follows: *Gird your sword upon your thigh, mighty one, in the bloom of your youth and in beauty. 4. And draw [your bow] and succeed and rule for the sake of truth, gentleness, and justice. And your right hand will lead you in wondrous ways. 5. Your arrows are sharpened, mighty one. The peoples fall down beneath you. 6. In the heart of the king of your enemies is your throne, God, forever and ever. The scepter of righteousness is the scepter of your kingdom. 7. You have loved justice and hated lawlessness. This is the reason why God, your God, has anointed you with the oil of gladness for the benefit of your companions.*[91] 8. If these things were not said in regard to the Messiah, then let whoever wishes to tell us whom else was meant. 9. For this was not said in vain by the prophet. He is not singing the whole oracle aimlessly. 10. Nor did he announce such things

88. See n. 87.

89. See Matt. 2:5–6, where the chief priests quote Mic. 5:2.

90. T[1] takes this to be a reference to the Antichrist (see the *apparatus criticus*). De la Cruz Palma implausibly believes the reference is to the Holy Spirit and cites passages from John. For Jesus claiming that he is the Messiah, see John 4:25–26, 10:25–30, 38, and 5:36; cf. John 1:41–42.

91. Ps. 44:4–8.

ὑποκειμένου τοσαῦτα ἔχρησεν. οὐ γὰρ ἔχει λόγον τοῦτό γε. 11. ὃν τοίνυν «ἀγαπητὸν» ἐπιγράφει καὶ ὡραῖον κάλλει παρὰ τοὺς υἱοὺς καλεῖ τῶν ἀνθρώπων, 12. καὶ ὃν περιζωσάμενον τὴν ῥομφαίαν καὶ τὸ τόξον ἐντείναντα | βασιλεύειν 71v ἕνεκεν ἀληθείας καὶ πραότητος καὶ δικαιοσύνης ἐπικελεύεται. 13. τοῦτον θεὸν ὑποκατιὼν φανερῶς ἀναγορεύει. «ὁ θρόνος», γάρ φησιν, «ὁ θεὸς εἰς τὸν αἰῶνα τοῦ αἰῶνος». 14. «ῥάβδος εὐθύτητος ἡ ῥάβδος τῆς βασιλείας σου. ἠγάπησας δικαιοσύνην καὶ ἐμίσησας ἀνομίαν». 15. καὶ ἵνα μὴ δόξῃ περὶ τοῦ ἁπλῶς θεοῦ τοῦτο εἰπεῖν, ἐπιφέρει· 16. «διὰ τοῦτο ἔχρισέ σε ὁ θεός, ὁ θεός σου, ἔλαιον ἀγαλλιάσεως παρὰ τοὺς μετόχους σου». 17. ὃν πρῶτον θεὸν εἶπε τοῦτον νῦν κεχρίσθαί φησιν ὑπὸ τοῦ θεοῦ «ἔλαιον ἀγαλλιάσεως παρὰ τοὺς | μετόχους» 72r αὐτοῦ. 18. ἐξ οὗ κἀκεῖνο ἀριδηλοτάτου δείκνυται ὅτι τε ἐπὶ τὸν Χριστὸν ὅλος ὁ ψαλμὸς ᾔσθη καὶ ὅτι οὐ κατὰ τοὺς ἄλλους χριστοὺς ἡ χρίσις ἔσται, ἀλλ᾽ ὑπέρτερόν τινα τρόπον.

8 1. Ἔτι αὐτὸς Δαυὶδ ἐν ἑβδομηκοστῷ ψαλμῷ, ὃν «εἰς Σολομῶντα» ἐπιγράφει, δηλαδή, τὸν εἰρηνικόν, οὕτω φησίν· 2. «ὁ θεός, τὸ κρίμα σου τῷ βασιλεῖ δὸς καὶ τὴν δικαιοσύνην σου τῷ υἱῷ τοῦ βασιλέως κρίνειν τὸν λαόν σου ἐν δικαιοσύνῃ, καὶ τοὺς πτωχούς σου ἐν κρίσει. 3. ἀναλαβέτω τὰ ὄρη εἰρήνην τῷ λαῷ, καὶ οἱ βουνοὶ δικαιοσύνην. κρινεῖ τοὺς πτωχοὺς τοῦ λαοῦ καὶ σώσει τοὺς υἱοὺς τῶν πενήτων | καὶ ταπεινώσει συκοφάντην. 4. καὶ συμπαραμενεῖ τῷ ἡλίῳ καὶ πρὸ τῆς 72v σελήνης γενεὰς γενεῶν. καταβήσεται ὡς ὑετὸς ἐπὶ πόκον καὶ ὡσεὶ σταγὼν ἡ στάζουσα ἐπὶ τὴν γῆν. 5. ‹...› καὶ μετ᾽ ὀλίγα ἔσται τὸ ὄνομα αὐτοῦ εὐλογημένον εἰς τοὺς αἰῶνας. πρὸ τοῦ ἡλίου διαμένει τὸ ὄνομα αὐτοῦ καὶ εὐλογηθήσονται ἐν αὐτῷ πᾶσαι αἱ φυλαὶ τῆς γῆς». 6. καὶ ἐπευχόμενὸς ἐπιφέρει· «γένοιτο. γένοιτο». 7. ὅτι μὲν οὖν καὶ οὗτος ὁ ψαλμὸς ὅλος ἐπὶ τὸν Χριστὸν γέγραπται καὶ ὡς ἐκ τοῦ γένους αὐτός φησι τοῦ Δαυὶδ ἥξειν (ὁ δὲ ἦν ἐκ τῆς Ἰούδα φυλῆς, ὅθεν ἀνεῖ|λε 73r πρῶτον ὁ Μωϋσῆς τὸν Χριστὸν ἥξειν), 8. καὶ ὡς πάντα ἐκβέβηκεν ἐπὶ τοῦ Ἰησοῦ ὅσα περὶ αὐτοῦ ἐνταῦθά φησιν ὁ Δαυίδ, δῆλον ὄν, περίεργον ἀποδεικνύναι πειρᾶσθαι.

9 1. Ἃ δὲ αὐτοῦ τὸν Χριστὸν θεὸν ἀναγορεύειν αὐτοὶ νομίζομεν, δεῖ λοιπὸν

3 ὃν] supra lin. scr. T[1]; ᾧ T **6** ῥάβδος[1]] ῥαύδος T (v. XXXI.7.6 supra) **22** εὐλογηθήσονται] ἐν ante delevi **27** ἀποδεικνύναι] ἀποδεικνῦναι T

deceptively with no one particular in mind, for that makes no sense. 11. The one he entitles "beloved," he also describes as in the bloom of his youth, beyond the sons of men in beauty. 12. And he called on the beloved to rule as king for the sake of truth, gentleness, and justice after he had girded his sword and drawn his bow. 13. The beloved is the one whom further on in the text he clearly calls God, for he says *the throne, God, is forever and ever.* 14. *The scepter of righteousness is the scepter of your kingdom. You have loved justice and hated lawlessness.* 15. And lest he seemed to be saying this simply about God, he added: 16. *This is the reason why God, your God, has anointed you with the oil of gladness for the benefit of your companions.* 17. The one whom he first called God is the one he now says is anointed by God with *the oil of gladness for the benefit of his companions.* 18. This passage makes it crystal clear that the whole psalm was singing about the Christ and that his anointing will not have same meaning it does for other anointed persons, but is meant in some higher respect.

8 1. Again, in the seventieth psalm, which he entitles "On Solomon," that is, on the peaceful, the same David says the following: 2. *God, give your judgment to the king and your justice to the son of the king to judge your people in justice, and your lowly ones with discretion.* 3. *Let the mountains bring peace to the people and the hills justice. He will judge the lowly ones of the people and save the sons of the poor and humble the slanderer.* 4. *And he will endure as long as the sun and will exist for generations upon generations before the moon. He will descend like the rain upon wool, and just like a shower falling upon the earth.* 5. . . . *And in a little while his name will be blessed down through the ages. His name will continue on before the sun and all the tribes of the earth will be blessed in him.*[92] 6. Then in prayer he adds: *Let it be! Let it be!*[93] 7. Since it is clear, then, that this whole psalm was written about the Christ, inasmuch as the psalm says that the Christ will come from the line of David (and he from the tribe of Judah, whence, Moses was the first to prophesy, the Christ would come), 8. and inasmuch as all the things which David says here about him have been fulfilled in Jesus, it is superfluous to try to prove it.

9 1. Since we ourselves believe that these passages proclaim that the Christ is God, what we must next do is examine whether they accord with what we hold.

92. Ps. 71: 2–17.
93. Ps. 71: 19.

ἐξετάζειν εἰ συμβαίνει οἷς ὑπειλήφαμεν. 2. φησὶ τοίνυν «αὐτὸν συμπαραμενεῖν τῷ
ἡλίῳ καὶ πρὸ τῆς σελήνης εἶναι γενεὰς γενεῶν ὅτι πρὸ τοῦ ἡλίου διαμένει τὸ
ὄνομα αὐτοῦ». 3. ταῦτα δὲ σαφῶς ἀΐδιον ἀναγορεύει. ἀΐδιον δὲ οὐδὲν ἄλλον
πλὴν τὸν θεὸν ὑπειλήφαμεν ἡμεῖς. | οἶμαι δέ, οὐδὲ αὐτοί. 4. ἔτι οὐδ᾽ ἔστιν ἔργον. 73v
οὐδὲν τοῦ θεοῦ, εἰ πάντα μὴ ὄντα γέγονεν ὑπ᾽ αὐτοῦ, ὃ πρὸ τοῦ ἡλίου καὶ πρὸ
τῆς σελήνης ἦν γενεὰς γενεῶν; 5. τὸν δὲ Χριστὸν τοιοῦτον εἶναί φησιν ὁ Δαυίδ.
οὐκ ἄρα ἔργον ἐστὶ τοῦ θεοῦ ἢ λόγος ἐστὶν αὐτοῦ. λείπεται δὴ θεόν. ἅπαν γὰρ ὂν
ἢ ἔργον θεοῦ ἢ θεός.

XXXII 1 1. **Ὁ Κρατῶν.** Τὰ μὲν ἄλλα συγχωρῆσαι μ᾽ ἄν, ἔφη, ὅτι ὃν εἶπον
ἔσεσθαι Χριστὸν οἱ προφῆται, ὁ Ἰησοῦς εἴη, ὁ τῆς Μαριὰμ τῆς παρθένου παῖς,
2. καὶ ὡς ἐκ τῆς φυλῆς γένοιτο τοῦ Ἰούδα καὶ προσεχέστερον τοῦ Δαυίδ, ὅτι δὲ
θεὸν αὐτὸν ὁ Δαυίδ οἶδεν, ὃ τὸ ζητούμενον ἦν, ἥκιστα. | 3. οὐ γὰρ ἔκ γε τοῦ 74r
ψαλμοῦ τούτου δείκνυται, ὃν «εἰς τὸν Σολομῶντα» φῂς ἐπιγράφειν, ἀλλ᾽ οὐδ᾽
οἷς αὐτὸς οἴει συμβαίνει. 4. «τὸ γὰρ συμπαραμενεῖν τῷ ἡλίῳ» καὶ «πρὸ τῆς
σελήνης εἶναι γενεὰς γενεῶν» καὶ «πρὸ τοῦ ἡλίου» εἶναι τὸ ὄνομα αὐτοῦ οὐδὲν
τοιοῦτον ἐξ ἀνάγκης δείκνυσι. ταῦτα γὰρ πάντα καὶ τοῖς δικαίοις ὑπάρχει.

2 1. Εἴπερ ἀθάνατος αὐτῶν ἡ ἑκάστου ψυχή, καὶ μετὰ θεοῦ τὸν ἅπαντα αἰῶνα
διατελεῖ. 2. ὅτι μὲν οὖν ἀθάνατος οὖσα ψυχὴ τὸν ἅπαντα αἰῶνα διατελεῖ καὶ ὅτι
ταύτῃ οὐ μόνον ἐσμὲν εἶδός γε οὔσῃ καὶ χωριστῇ, 3. ἀλλ᾽ οὐδὲν ἧττον ἕκαστος
λεγόμεθα, δεικνύνειν οὐ δεῖ. | πᾶσι γὰρ ἀνωμολόγηται. 74v

3 1. Λοιπὸν δὲ δεικνύειν καὶ ὅτι πρὸ τῆς σελήνης ἦν καὶ τοῦ ἡλίου, ὅθεν
αὐτὸς τὸ ἀΐδιον ᾤου συμβαίνειν. 2. τοῦτο γὰρ διχῶς ἐνδέχεται ταῖς ψυχαῖς
ὑπάρχειν, ἕνα μὲν τρόπον ὅτι ψυχὴ λογικὴ πᾶσα πρὸ τοῦ αἰσθητοῦ παντὸς
κόσμου παρήχθη, οὐ πρὸ τῆς σελήνης, οὐδὲ πρὸ τοῦ ἡλίου μόνον. 3. ἀνάγκῃ γὰρ
τὰς χωριστὰς οὐσίας ἅμα παρῆχθαι ὁμογενεῖς οὔσας καὶ ὕλης οὐδεμιᾶς ὑφεστά-
ναι δεόμεναι. 4. οἱ δὲ ἄγγελοι πρὸ τοῦ οὐρανοῦ τοῦ εἶναι μετέσχον. οὐ γὰρ εἰκὸς
οὔθ᾽ ὕστερον αὐτοὺς παρῆχθαι, οὔθ᾽ ἅμα ἀΰλους | ὄντας καὶ ἀσωμάτους καὶ τὴν 75r
ὑπεροχὴν ἀπὸ τῆς φύσεως ἔχοντας. 5. καὶ ἄλλως δὲ ἀνάγκη τὴν πρώτην ἀρχὴν
ἀπὸ τῶν οἰκειοτάτων ἄρξασθαι, καὶ ἐγγυτάτω οὐκ ἀπὸ τῶν πορρωτάτω. 6. ἐφ᾽

---

1 φησὶ] signum (†) in marg. scr. T¹ || συμπαραμενεῖν] ν finalem supra lin scr. T/T¹ **4** ἡμεῖς] in marg. annot T¹: οἱ Χριστιανοί || οἶμαι . . . αὐτοί] bis scr. T (in marg. infer. f. 73r et prima lin. f. 73v) **7** ἐστὶ] post spatium quattuor litterarum in T **9** Ὁ Κρατῶν] in marg. scr. T **11** τοῦ¹] τοὺ corr. T/T¹ **12** οἶδεν] in marg. iterat T¹ et deinde annot.: ἴσθι· ᾔδεν **13** τὸν] supra lin. scr. T **16** τοῖς] τῆς T **19** γε] signo (:) supra lin. denotat T¹ et in marg. annot.: ἴσως, νοητῇ γε οὔσῃ

2. The psalm then says that *he will endure as long as the sun and will exist for generations upon generations before the moon*, since *his name will continue on before the sun*. 3. These statements clearly proclaim that he will be eternal. We hold nothing as eternal, however, except God. Neither do you, I think. 4. Furthermore, he is not a product. If everything that does not exist comes into existence from God, does he who existed before the sun and before the moon through generations upon generations have nothing of God? 5. The Christ is such, says David. Therefore he is not a product of God insofar as he is the Word of God. What is left, then, is that he is God. For everything that exists is either a product of God or is God.

XXXII 1 1. **The Conqueror.** I would agree, he said, that the one whom the prophets say would be the Christ is Jesus, the son of the Virgin Mary, 2. and also that he would come from the tribe of Judah and, more specifically, of the line of David. That, however, David knows him as God, which is the point in question, I do not agree in the slightest. 3. For that is not shown from this psalm, which you say is entitled "On Solomon." Rather it does not agree with what you suppose. 4. For *to endure as long as the sun*, and *to exist through generations upon generations before the moon*, and that his name is *before the sun* do not necessarily prove any such thing. For all such phrases befit righteous men.

2 1. If in fact the soul of each of them is immortal, it abides with God for all ages. 2. Therefore, since the soul is immortal, it is not necessary to prove that the soul abides for all ages and that in this way not only are we forms, since our souls are separable, 3. but also everyone of us no less so is said to be such. For we concede all these points.

3 1. What you still have to demonstrate, however, is that he [the Christ] existed before the moon and the sun, which is the reason why you thought eternity befitted him. 2. For this phrase can be applied to souls in two senses. In one sense, every rational soul pre-existed the whole sensible universe, and not just the moon or the sun. 3. For inasmuch as they are of the same genus, separable beings necessarily exist at one and the same time without need of any single bit of matter as a substrate. 4. The angels partook of being before the heavens did. For it is not plausible either that they were the last to come into existence, or that being immaterial and without bodies, they received their preeminence from nature. 5. Otherwise the First Principle would have necessarily begun with the most particular of things and what is closest to them, not what is the most

ὧν μὲν γὰρ οὐκ ἔστιν ἐπὶ τὸ τέλειον προϊέναι εἰ μὴ διὰ τῶν ἀτελῶν. 7. ἐνταῦθα
ἀνάγκη τὰ ἀτελέστερα προηγεῖσθαι χρόνῳ, ἅτε ἐκ τούτων τῆς προόδου τῶν
τελεωτέρων γινομένης. 8. ἐν οἷς δὲ τοιοῦτον οὐδὲ ἐστίν. οὐκ εἰκὸς τὰ χείρω
προηγεῖσθαι ὅτι μὴ ἐκ τούτων ἐκεῖνα γίνεται ᾗπερ ἐπὶ τῆς προόδου συμβαίνει
τῆς φυσικῆς. 9. αἴτιον δὲ ὅτι ἐν τούτοις | ὕλης χρεία. ἡ δὲ ἀπὸ τοῦ ἀτελοῦς 75v
ἄρχεται καὶ πρόεισι χρόνῳ ἐπὶ τὸ τέλειον. 10. ἐν οἷς δὲ μὴ ἔστιν ὕλη, οὐδ᾽ ὃ τῆς
ὕλης ἐστὶν ἀνάγκη παρεῖναι.

4 1. Ἀνάγκη τοίνυν τοὺς ἀγγέλους καὶ νοητὸν πάντα διάκοσμον πρὸ τοῦ
αἰσθητοῦ παντὸς ὑποστῆναι. 2. ἐν οἷς συμβαίνει καὶ τὰς ἡμετέρας ψυχὰς εἶναι
συγγενεῖς ἐκείνοις οὔσας κατὰ τὸ χωριστὸν καὶ ὕλης οὐδὲ μιᾶς ὑφεστάναι δεομέ-
νας. 3. οὐδὲν οὖν μέγα οὐδὲ θεῖον εἶναί τινας λέγεσθαι ταύτῃ «πρὸ τῆς σελήνης
καὶ πρὸ τοῦ ἡλίου».

5 1. Ἄλλον δὲ τρόπον κατὰ τὸν θεῖον προορισμὸν | ἐνδέχεταί τι ἀΐδιον 76r
λέγεσθαι. 2. ἐν γὰρ τῷ θεῷ πάντα μὲν ἀϊδίως ἔστι καὶ πρὸ τοῦ ἐν αὐτοῖς ὑποστῆ-
ναι, μάλιστα δὲ οἱ προωρισμένοι ἐπί τι θεῖον ἔργον ἢ τὴν αἰώνιον ζωήν, 3. καθά-
περ ὁ ἡμέτερος περὶ αὑτοῦ εἶπε προφήτης, ὅτι «πρὸ τοῦ τὸν κόσμον εἶναι
προφήτης ἤμην ἐγώ».

XXXIII 1 1. **Ὁ Φιλόσοφος**. Γενναίως μέν, ἔφην, ᾗπερ εἰκός, καὶ ὡς οὐκ ἂν
ἄμεινον ἐπεξῆλθες τῷ λόγῳ. 2. ἐγὼ δὲ ὅτι μὲν ὅμως χρὴ πρὸς ταῦτα εἰπεῖν οὐκ
ἀπορῶν ὀκνῶ καὶ ἀναβάλλομαι μεγάλου προβλήματος προτεθέντος. 3. εἰ πᾶσαι
ἅμα γεγόνασιν αἱ λογικαὶ ψυχαὶ μετὰ | τῶν χωριστῶν οὐσιῶν καὶ εἰ ταῦτα πάντα 76v
προήχθη πρὸ τοῦ οὐρανοῦ τοῦδε καὶ τοῦ κόσμου παντὸς 4. (ταῦτα γὰρ χαλεπὸν
μὲν ὅπως ἀληθείας ἔχει δεῖξαι), καταλιπεῖν δὲ ὅμως οὐκ ἔνι τοιαύτης ἐφόδου

---

13 κατὰ] καὶ corr. T[1] et in marg. scr. κατὰ τὸν **16** αὑτοῦ] αὐτοῦ corr. T/T[1] **18** Ὁ Φιλόσοφος] in marg. scr. T

distant from them. 6. For in that case it would only be possible to proceed to the perfection of the whole through the imperfect. 7. Hence the imperfect would have had to come first in time, inasmuch as the procession of the more perfect would come from the imperfect. 8. In the imperfect, however, such a procession is not possible. It is not plausible that inferior things came first, since the more perfect things did not come from them in the same way that happens in a physical procession. 9. The reason is that in the imperfect there is need of matter. Matter, however, takes its start from the imperfect and processes in time toward the perfect. 10. In the more perfect things, however, there is no matter nor is it necessary that any matter be present.

4 1. The angels and every member of the noetic order necessarily therefore existed before anything sensible. 2. It so happens that among the former are our souls, since they are cognate with noetic forms,[94] inasmuch as they are separable and not in need of a single bit of matter in order to exist. 3. It is therefore nothing special nor divine for some things to be said thus to be *before the moon and before the sun.*

5 1. There is another way, however, which allows something to be said to be eternal by divine predestination. 2. For everything eternally is in God, even in fact before it possesses existence, and especially those who have been preordained for some divine task or for eternal life, 3. just as our prophet says about himself: "Before the world was, I was a prophet."[95]

XXXIII 1 1. **The Philosopher.** I said: Nobly put, as I would expect. You could not have made your argument more cogently. 2. I think, however, that I nonetheless have to say in this regard that I am not about to shrink from the substantial difficulty you have raised as if I were at a loss, nor am I one to put off responding to it. 3. If all rational souls came to be along with separable beings at the same time, and if all of them came into existence before these very heavens above and the whole world 4. (for it would be difficult to show how this is true), nonetheless it is not possible to admit such a line of argumentation contrived

94. For Amiroutzes speaking specifically of "noetic forms" (νοητὰ εἴδη), see XXXIII.1.5, XXXV.2. 3, XXXVII.1.1, and XXXVII.6.1.

95. Apparently a rendition of the hadith canonized by al-Tirmidhī (d. 892 CE), "I was a prophet when Adam was between the water and the mud." See Holmes Katz, *Birth of the Prophet*, 13–15.

κατὰ τῆς ἀληθείας ἐντεῦθεν συνισταμένης. 5. ἰτέον οὖν, ἔφην ἐγώ, κοινῇ τῆς σκέψεως. πρῶτον δὲ ἐρέσθαι βούλομαι πότερον καὶ ἀΐδιον οἴεσθε τὴν ψυχὴν καὶ τὰ νοητὰ εἴδη πάντα ἢ μή.

XXXIV 1 1. **Ὁ Κρατῶν**. Οὐδαμῶς γε, ἔφη, ὑπολαβών, ἀλλ᾽ ἀΐδιον μόνην τὴν πρώτην ἴσμεν ἀρχήν, τὰ δ᾽ ἄλλα πάντα μὴ ὄντα πρότερον ὑπὸ ταύτης παρῆχθαι. 2. ἀδύνατον οὖν ἐπιγίνεται ἀΐδια | εἶναι τά γε τοῦ εἶναι αἰτίαν ἔχοντα. 77r

XXXV 1 1. **Ὁ Φιλόσοφος**. Εἰ μὲν ἀδύνατον, ἔφην, ἢ μή, οὐ καιρὸς σκοπεῖν πλὴν ὅτι Ἀριστοτέλης τοῦτο οὐκ ἀδύνατον οἴεται. 2. οὐ γὰρ ταὐτὸν τὸ ἀΐδιον καὶ τὸ ἀναίτιον ὑπείληφεν. ἀλλὰ ἀΐδιον μὲν ὃ μὴ ἐνδέχεταί ποτε μὴ εἶναι. 3. ἀναίτιον δὲ οὗ μηδεμία τοῦ εἶναι αἰτία ἐστίν. τὸ μὲν οὖν αἰτίαν οὐδεμίαν ἔχον τοῦ εἶναι ὄν γε αὐτὸ καὶ ἀΐδιον. 4. τὸ δὲ ἀΐδιον οὐ πάντως τοιοῦτον. ἐνδέχεταται γάρ τι ἀΐδιον μὲν εἶναι αἰτίαν δὲ ὅμως ἔχειν τοῦ εἶναι, 5. καθάπερ τὸ τὰς τρεῖς γωνίας δυσὶν ὀρθαῖς ἴσας ἔχειν ὑπάρχον τῷ τριγώνῳ. 6. τοῦτο γὰρ ἀΐδιον μέν, ἀλλ᾽ ὅ|μως 77v ἔστιν αὐτοῦ ἕτερον αἴτιον. ἀλλὰ τοῦτο μὲν ἐατέον.

2 1. Αὐτοὶ δὲ περὶ ὧν διαφερώμεθα σκεψώμεθα. 2. δοκεῖ δέ μοι πρῶτον τὰ κοινῇ ὁμολογούμενα ὑποθέσθαι. 3. φαμὲν τοίνυν τὴν ψυχὴν καὶ τὰ νοητὰ εἴδη πάντα γεγονέναι μὴ ὄντα πρότερον, ἔτι ταῦτα ἀθάνατα μὲν καὶ ἀνώλεθρα γεγονότα λοιπὸν ἔσεσθαι τὸν ἅπαντα χρόνον. 4. ἀΐδια δὲ μηδαμῶς εἶναι μὴ ἀεὶ πρότερον ὄντα. οὐ ταῦτα κοινῇ δοκεῖ.

XXXVI 1 1. **Ὁ Κρατῶν**. Πάνυ γε, ἔφη.

XXXVII 1 1. **Ὁ Φιλόσοφος**. Τούτοις τοίνυν οὐ ξυνᾴδει, ἐγὼ ἔφην, τὸ τὰς ψυχὰς καὶ τὰ νοητὰ εἴδη πρὸ τοῦ οὐρανοῦ, τοῦ δὲ καὶ τοῦ κόσμου προῆχθαι παντός. 2. ἀλλὰ | «παντὸς» μᾶλλον ἀπᾴδει. ὧδε σκοποῦ μέν. 3. πρῶτον μὲν 78r

1 ἐγώ κοινῇ] ἐγκνῇ corr. T/T^1 **2** ἐρέσθαι] ad ἔρεσθαι mut. T^1 **4** Ὁ Κρατῶν] in marg. scr. T **7** Ὁ Φιλόσοφος] in marg. scr. T **18** ἀΐδια] in marg. annot. T^1: γράφεται· αἰῶνα **20** Ὁ Κρατῶν] in marg. scr. T **21** Ὁ Φιλόσοφος] in marg. scr. T **23** ἀπᾴδει] ἐπᾴδει T; in marg. ἀπᾴδει scr. T^1 || ὧδε] ad ὧ δὲ mut. T^1 || σκοποῦ] σκόπου corr. T^1

from this against the truth. 5. Let us investigate the issue together, I said. I would like first to ask whether you think the soul and all the noetic forms are eternal or not.

XXXIV 1 1. **The Conqueror.** In no way have I supposed that, he said. Rather, I think that only the First Principle is eternal, while all other beings are not prior to it, but created by it. 2. Consequently, it is impossible for things that owe their existence to a cause to be eternal.

XXXV 1 1. **The Philosopher.** It would not be profitable, I said, to look into whether this is impossible or not except that Aristotle thinks that it is possible. 2. For he did not assume that the eternal was also uncaused.[96] Rather, the eternal is that which cannot ever not be. 3. The uncaused, on the other hand, is that for which there is no cause of its existence. That, therefore, which has no single thing as the cause of its existence is being itself and eternal. 4. What is eternal is not always such. For something can be eternal while nonetheless having a cause of its existence, 5. just as in the case of a triangle, it happens that the three angles are equal to two right angles. 6. For while the relationship is eternal, nonetheless something else is its cause. But let us pass over this.

2 1. And let us take into consideration that we disagree on these matters. 2. It seems best to me, though, first to stipulate what we mutually agree upon. 3. We both affirm, then, that the soul and all the noetic forms came to be and did not exist before then, and furthermore, that having been made immortal and indestructible, they will exist for all time thereafter. 4. On the other hand, they are in no way eternal, since they did not always exist before coming into existence. It is on this last point that we seem not to be in agreement.

XXXVI 1 1. **The Conqueror.** Quite so, he said.

XXXVII 1 1. **The Philosopher.** It is on these points then, I said, that we disagree, namely, whether souls and noetic forms preceded heaven and whether they preceded the whole cosmos. 2. But the disagreement concerns mainly the word "whole." Look at it this way. 3. I affirm as a general proposition that

96. Although this assertion allows Aristotle to be compatible with the Christian belief in the eternity of angels and human souls, he never explicitly stated this assumption, and, indeed, he seems to suggest the contrary when criticizing Plato and the Pythagoreans at *Metaphysics* 14.3.1091a12–13 (trans. Tredennick): "It is absurd also, or rather it is one of the impossibilities of this theory, to introduce generation of things that are eternal."

τοίνυν ἐκεῖνο καθόλου φημί, ὅτι γενητῶν ἁπάντων ὑποτιθεμένων ἐκ τοῦ μὴ ὄντος, καὶ τῶν νοητῶν καὶ τῶν αἰσθητῶν, 4. οὐκ ἐνδέχεται τὴν πρόοδον τῶν νοητῶν προτέραν γενέσθαι. 5. τὰ μὲν γὰρ ἀεὶ ὄντα ἔστι πρότερα τῶν ἐν χρόνῳ ὄντων ἢ γενομένων εἰπεῖν. 6. ἐπεὶ ὁ αἰὼν περιέχει τὸν χρόνον ἐν ᾧ τὰ ἀεὶ ὄντα τυγχάνει, τὰ δὲ μὴ ἀεὶ ὄντα πῶς ἐνδέχεται πρότερα τοῦ χρόνου παντὸς εἶναι; 7. καὶ γὰρ ὥρισται τούτῳ πρότερον ἢ μή. εἰ μὲν οὖν μὴ ὥρισται ἀλλὰ παντὸς τοῦ ληφθέντος ὑπερέχει, ἀεὶ ἂν εἴη καὶ ἀΐδια. | 8. ὧν γὰρ οὐκ ἔστιν ὅρον τοῦ εἶναι 78v εὑρεῖν, ἀνάγκη τοιαῦτα εἶναι. 9. ἀλλὰ τὸ μὴ ἀεὶ ὂν οὐκ ἀΐδιον, ᾗπερ ὡμολογήσαμεν. εἰ δὲ ὥρισται, ἀΐδια μὲν ἔτι οὐκ ἂν εἴη. 10. τὸν δὲ χρόνον ἀνάγκη περιέχειν τὸν ὁρίζοντα τὸ τοῦ προτέρου ποσόν. 11. ἐν οἷς ἄρα τὸ πρότερον ὥρισται. ἀδύνατον μὴ περιέχεσθαι ὑπὸ τοῦ χρόνου. 12. ἀλλὰ μὴν εἰ περιέχεται ὑπὸ τοῦ χρόνου, πῶς ἂν πρὸ τοῦ οὐρανοῦ τοῦδε καὶ τοῦ κόσμου προήχθη παντός; 13. ἅμα γὰρ τῷ οὐρανῷ ὁ χρόνος ἐστίν. διότι ὁ χρόνος οὐδὲν ἄλλο τυγχάνει ἢ τὸ μέτρον τῆς κινήσεως τοῦ οὐρανοῦ κατὰ τὸ πρότερον καὶ ὕστερον. 14. οὐκ ἄρα προτέρα γέγονεν ἡ τῶν | νοητῶν πρόοδος τοῦ οὐρανοῦ τοῦδε καὶ τοῦ κόσμου 79r παντός.

2 1. Ἔτι τὸ πρότερον και τὸ ὕστερον οὐκ ἔστιν εἰ μὴ ἐν χρόνῳ. ταῦτα γὰρ λέγεται ἐπί τε τοῦ παρελθόντος καὶ τοῦ μέλλοντος μόνου. 2. ἐπὶ μὲν τοῦ παρελθόντος πρότερον μὲν τὸ πορρώτερον τοῦ παρόντος νῦν, ὕστερον δὲ τὸ ἐγγύτερον. 3. ἐπὶ δὲ τοῦ μέλλοντος τὸ ἀνάπαλιν, τὸ δὲ παρελθόν, καὶ τὸ μέλλον οὐκ ἔστιν εἰ μὴ ἐν χρόνῳ. 4. ἐν οἷς ἄρα τὸ πρότερον καὶ τὸ ὕστερον ἔστιν. ἀνάγκη ταῦτα ἐν χρόνῳ εἶναι. 5. διότι ὁ χρόνος ἅμα τυγχάνει τῷ οὐρανῷ μέτρον ὢν τῆς κινήσεως αὐτοῦ. 6. ἐπειδὴ τὰ | ἐν χρόνῳ ὄντα οὐκ ἐνδέχεται πρὸ τοῦ οὐρανοῦ 79v εἶναι, ἔτι εἰ πρὸ τοῦ χρόνου γέγονεν ἡ τῶν νοητῶν πρόοδος, ἀνάγκη ἐν τῷ αἰῶνι εἶναι. 7. ἀλλὰ τὰ ἐν τῷ αἰῶνι ὄντα ἀνάγκη ἀΐδια εἶναι. αἱ δὲ ψυχαὶ οὐκ ἀΐδιοι. οὐκ ἄρα ἐν τῷ αἰῶνι γεγόνασιν. 8. ὅτι δὲ τὰ ἐν τῷ αἰῶνι ὄντα ἀνάγκη ἀΐδια εἶναι δείκνυται ὧδε, ἐν τῷ αἰῶνι οὐδὲν ἔστι πεπερασμένον ἢ ὡρισμένον. 9. οὔτε γὰρ

6 τούτῳ] τοῦτῳ corr. T^1 et in marg. iterat τούτῳ **12** προήχθη] παρήχθη in marg. scr. T^1 **19** τοῦ . . . νῦν] ad νῦν τοῦ παρόντος mut. T^1 **19–20** ἐγγύτερον] ἐγγυήτερον corr. T/T^1 **26** τῷ^2] supra του non deleto scr. T

inasmuch as all generated beings, both the noetic and the sensible, are instituted from non-being, 4. it is not possible for a prior procession of the noetic forms to have taken place. 5. For beings that always exist are prior to beings that exist in time or, one might say, that become. 6. Since that which is eternal encompasses the time in which are the things that always exist, how can beings that do not always exist be prior to all time? 7. For beings limited by time are prior to time or they are not. If, then, they are not limited by time, but rather transcend everything fixed in time, they would always exist and would be eternal. 8. For if you cannot find a limit to their existence, they are necessarily eternal. 9. On the other hand, what does not always exist is not eternal, just as we have agreed. If, however these things are limited by time, they would still not be eternal. 10. Rather, since time necessarily encompasses them, it also defines the amount of their "before." 11. In these beings, therefore, their "before" is defined. It is impossible that they not be encompassed by time. 12. But if in fact they are encompassed by time, how would they have come before heaven and the whole cosmos? 13. For time exists together with heaven. This is why time is nothing other than the measure of the motion of heaven in respect to "before" and "after."[97] 14. Therefore, the procession of the noetic forms did not occur before the heaven above and the whole world.

2 1. Furthermore, there is no before and after except in time. For these terms are applied only to the past and the future. 2. In respect to the past, what is before a past event is further from the present now; what is next after a past event, however, is closer. 3. In respect to the future, what happens again, what happens in the past, and what happens in the future do not exist save in time. 4. Hence, in these things there is a before and an after. They necessarily are in time. 5. This is why time exists in conjunction with the heavens, being the measure of its movement. 6. Since things that exist in time cannot be before the heavens, and if, furthermore, the procession of the noetic forms did occur before time, then noetic forms would of necessity be in eternity. 7. But things that are in eternity are necessarily eternal. Souls, however, are not eternal. Therefore they are not in eternity. 8. Since it has thus been shown that things that exist in eternity are necessarily eternal, nothing delimited or defined exists in eternity. 9. For there

97. Standard Aristotelian doctrine, established in Aristotle, *Physics* 4.12 (221b8: "time is the measure of a motion"); see also 4.14, especially 223b13–16.

διάστημα οὔτε μέγεθος οὔτε κίνησις ἐν τούτῳ εἶναι ἐνδέχεται. 10. οὗ δὲ μὴ ἔστι
ὅρος ἢ πέρας, ἀνάγκη ἄπειρον εἶναι. ἀνάγκη ἄρα τὰ ἐν τῷ αἰῶνι ὄντα ἄπειρον
ἔχειν τὸ εἶναι. 11. τὸ δὲ τοιοῦτον ἀΐδιον. | τὰ ἐν τῷ αἰῶνι ὄντα ἄρα ἀνάγκῃ ἀΐδια 80r
εἶναι. εἰ γὰρ ἐν αἰῶνι προελθόντα, μὴ εἶεν ἀΐδια. 12. ἀνάγκη πρότερον μὴ εἶναι.
ἐν δὲ αἰῶνι οὐκ ἔστι τὸ πρότερον καὶ ὕστερον. ἀνάγκη ἄρα ἀΐδια εἶναι.

3 1. Φανερὸν τοίνυν ὅτι τὸ γενητὸν ἅπαν ἢ ἐν χρόνῳ γενέσθαι ἢ ἅμα τῷ
χρόνῳ. 2. γενητὸν δὲ ὂν πρὸ τοῦ χρόνου παντὸς εἶναι ἀδύνατον. τὸ μὲν οὖν
συμπέρασμα οὕτως ἀδύνατον δέδεικται. 3. τὰς δὲ προτάσεις λύειν οὐ χαλεπόν.
οὐ γὰρ ἀνάγκη, εἰ κρείττω τὴν φύσιν τὰ νοητὰ καὶ τὴν πρόοδον τούτων προτέ-
ραν γενέσθαι. 4. διότι τὸ κρεῖττον ἐν | αὐτοῖς οὐ κατὰ τὸ πρεσβύτερον, οὐ δὲ τῷ 80v
χρόνῳ ἧκον θεωρεῖται, ἀλλὰ κατὰ τὴν πρὸς τὸ ἔσχατον τέλος τάξιν. 5. ὅθεν
αὐτοῖς καὶ τὸ προτέροις εἶναι περιγίνεται. ἅμα δὲ οὐδὲ γίνεται. 6. τὸ ἀδύνατον τὸ
δὲ γενητόν τι ὄν. πρὸ τοῦ χρόνου εἶναι δέδεικται ἀδύνατον ὄν. οὔκουν ἦν αὐτὰ
πρότερα τοῦτον προϊέναι τὸν τρόπον.

4 1. Ἔτι τὰ ἔργα τῆς πρώτης ἀρχῆς ἐν τῇ προόδῳ οὐ καθ᾽ αὐτὰ δεῖ θεωρεῖν,
ἀλλ᾽ ᾗ ἐξ αὐτῆς πρόεισι. 2. πρόεισι δὲ οὐ καθ᾽ αὐτὰ ἕκαστον, οὐδ᾽ ὥς τι πλῆθος
εἰκαῖον, ἀλλὰ κατὰ τὴν πρὸς ὅλον ἀναφοράν. 3. εἰ γὰρ καθ᾽ αὐτὰ προήει,
οὐκ | ἂν ἦν τάξις πρὸς ἄλληλα, ἴσως δὲ οὐδὲ πρὸς τὸ ἔσχατον τέλος. 4. ἀλλ᾽ ἦν 81r
ἂν ἐπεισοδιῶδες τὸ πᾶν καὶ κατὰ συμβεβηκὸς ὅλον, ὅπερ ἄτοπον.

5 1. Τὰ γὰρ ὄντα πάντα τέτακται καὶ πρὸς ἄλληλα καὶ πρὸς τὸ ἔσχατον
ἀγαθὸν ὡς φαίνεται ἐν τῷ ιβ´ τῶν Μετὰ Τὰ Φυσικά. 2. ἐν οἷς δὲ θεωρεῖται τάξις
ἀνάγκη, καὶ ὅλον τι θεωρεῖσθαι ἐκ τῶν τεταγμένων ἐκείνων ἀποτελούμενον.

---

10 γενέσθαι] in marg. annot. T[1]: σημείωσαι· ταῦτα κατὰ τοὺς Λατίνους καὶ κατὰ τοῦ Μεγάλου Βασιλείου καὶ κατὰ τοῦ Θεολόγου Γρηγορίου **11** χρόνῳ] signum (..) supra ῳ scr. T[1] et in marg. .. προ scr., (forte = πρὸ χρόνου quoniam signum ["] supra πρὸ τοῦ χρόνου in XXXVII.3.6 infra scr.) **13** τοῦ] signum (") supra scr. T **15** θεωρεῖν] in marg. iterat T[1] **19** ἐπεισοδιῶδες . . . πᾶν] in marg. iterat T[1] cum annotatione praefata σημείωσαι

cannot be extension, magnitude, or motion in this sort of existence. 10. What has no definition or limit, necessarily is infinite. Necessarily therefore things existing in eternity have an infinite existence. 11. Such a thing, however, is eternal. Consequently, things existing in eternity must be eternal. For if things were to have processed [into being] in eternity, they would not be eternal, 12. since necessarily they had not existed beforehand. In eternity, however, there is no before and after. Therefore it is necessary that things existing in eternity be eternal.

3 1. Clearly, then, every engendered thing is engendered in time or is engendered together with time. 2. It is impossible, however, for something to be engendered before all of time. Your conclusion, therefore, has thus been shown to be impossible. 3. Its premises were not difficult to dismantle. For they are not necessary premises, even if noetic forms are superior by nature and their procession was before [that of the sun and the moon].[98] 4. The reason is that they are superior not by virtue of their seniority, nor by virtue of being seen as entering time, but by virtue of where they are positioned in the order [of things] in respect to the final end. 5. This is the source of their having the advantage of being prior. But they did not come to be simultaneously with time. 6. That is impossible for anything that is engendered. We have shown that they cannot be before time. It is therefore not the case that they precede time in some way.

4 1. Furthermore, we have to observe the products of the First Principle in their procession not as they are in themselves, but rather in the way by which they process from the First Principle. 2. They do not, however, each process individually, nor as some random multitude, but in reference to the whole. 3. For if each processed individually, they would have no ordered relationship with each other, and likewise they would not have one with the final end. 4. Instead, everything would be hit-or-miss and the whole accidental. This is absurd.

5 1. For all things are ordered toward each other and toward the final good, as is clear in book 12 of the *Metaphysics*. 2. You can see there that there is a necessary order.[99] You can also see that a certain completed whole is achieved

98. In a marginal comment the organizer of the manuscript attributes this view to the Latins, Basil the Great, and Gregory of Nazianzus.

99. Amiroutzes makes a similar argument concerning order and randomness in his tractates; see Monfasani, *George Amiroutzes the Philosopher*, 94–95, 104–5.

3. οὐ γὰρ ἔστι τάττεσθαι πρὸς ἄλληλα μὴ πρὸς ὅλον τι ἀναφερόμενα. 4. ἐν δὲ τῷ
ὅλῳ τὰ μέρη οὐχ ὑστερεῖ εἰ μὴ ἐν οἷς ἡ πρόοδός ἐστι χρονική. διότι ἐν τῇ
τοιαύτῃ | προόδῳ ἀνάγκη καὶ ὑποκείμενον παρεῖναι. 5. ἄν τε ἐν αὐτοῖς ᾖ τοῖς 81v
προϊοῦσιν ἡ ἀρχή, ἄν τε ἔξωθεν, καθάπερ ἥ τε φύσις ποιεῖ καὶ ἡ τέχνη. 6. τὴν δὲ
ὕλην οὐκ ἔστιν ἄγειν ἐπὶ τὸ εἶδος δίχα κινήσεως. κίνησιν δὲ εἶναι ἄνευ χρόνου
οὐχ οἷόν τε. 7. τὰ δὲ τοῦ χρόνου μέρη οὐκ εἰσὶν ἅμα. οὔκουν δὲ τῶν ἐν αὐτῷ
γινομένων τὰ μέρη ἅμα οἷόν τε προιέναι. ἐν γὰρ τῷ νῦν οὐδὲν γίνεται. 8. διὰ
τοῦτο τὰ ἐν χρόνῳ γινόμενα, τόδε γίνεται μετὰ τόδε. ἡ δὲ πρόοδος τῶν ὄντων
ἀπὸ τῆς πρώτης ἀρχῆς οὐκ ἐν χρόνῳ γίνεται. 9. οὐ γὰρ ἐξ ὑποκειμένου προάγει | 82r
τὸ πρῶτον αἴτιον. οὐδὲ τὴν ὕλην ἄγει ἐπὶ τὸ εἶδος. 10. ἀλλ᾽ ἅμα τό τε ὑποκείμενον καὶ τὸ εἶδος ἐξ αὐτῆς δίχα κινήσεως πρόεισιν. 11. ἐπεὶ τοίνυν ἡ τοιαύτη πρόοδος οὐ δεῖται χρόνου, ἀνάγκη πᾶν ὡς ἕν τι καὶ ὅλον ἅμα προϊέναι, τὰ μὲν κατὰ τὰ εἴδη, 12. τὰ δὲ κατὰ τὸ καθ᾽ ἕκαστον, ὡς εἴη τέλειον ὑπὸ τοῦ τελεωτάτου γεγενημένον. 13. καθόλου μὲν οὖν περὶ τῆς προόδου τῶν χωριστῶν οὐσιῶν ὅτι μὴ πρὸ τοῦ χρόνου εἴη τοσαῦτα.

6 1. Περὶ δὲ τῆς ψυχῆς ἰδίως πρῶτον μὲν ἐκεῖνο φαμέν, ὅτι ταύτην οὐ χρὴ
συντάττειν τοῖς νοητοῖς εἴδεσι, σώματος ἐντελέ|χειαν, καὶ νοερὰν οὖσαν, οὐ 82v
νοητήν. 2. ὑπερτέραν γὰρ ἐκεῖνα φύσιν εἴληχε καὶ θειοτέραν, καθάπαξ τοῦ σώματος καὶ ὅλως τῆς ὕλης ἀπῳκισμένη. 3. ἡ δὲ τοιοῦδε σώματος εἶδος ἐστί, καὶ θανάτῳ αὐτοῦ ἀπαλλαττομένη, αὖθις ἀϊδίως, ᾗπερ ἀμφότεροι νομίζομεν, συνάπτεται. 4. οὔκουν προσήκει τοῖς τοσοῦτον διεστηκόσιν αὐτὴν συντάττειν. δεύτερον δὲ ὅτι τοὺς ἅμα πάσας εἴτε πρὸ χρόνου εἴτε ἐν χρόνῳ παράγοντας.

---

6 οὔκουν] ad οὔκ οὐ (= ?) mut. T[1] **12** πρόοδος] πρόδος T **14** προόδου] in marg. scr. T
19 ἀπῳκισμένη] -νη ad -νην mut. T[1]

out of arranged parts. 3. For parts cannot be ordered relative to each other without them being also ordered in reference to some whole. 4. In the [cosmic] whole, however, the parts are not inferior unless their procession happens in time. For that reason, in such a procession, there must be a substrate. 5. The cause [of their procession] would be in them as they proceed, even if it comes from the outside, just the way nature and art function. 6. It is not possible, however, for matter to pass into form without motion. Motion, on the other hand, is not possible without time, 7. and the parts of time are not at the same instant. Therefore, it is not possible for the parts of things that take place in time to proceed at the same instant. For nothing happens in an [indivisible] now.[100] 8. Hence, for things that occur in time, one particular thing happens after another particular thing. The procession of being from the First Principle, however, did not happen in time. 9. For the First Principle does not work from a substrate. Nor does it apply matter to a form. 10. Rather, the substrate and the form process together without motion from the First Principle. 11. Since such a procession, then, has no need of time, all of it must process as both a single something and as a whole, some things [in it] as forms 12. and some as particulars, so that a perfect product is produced by the most perfect [principle]. 13. Concerning the procession of separable beings then, it is a general principle that there cannot be any such entities before time.

6 1. Concerning the soul in particular, first we say this, that one does not have to group it with the noetic forms, since it is the actualization of the body, being intellectual but not noetic. 2. For noetic forms possess a higher and more divine nature, which is absolutely and completely removed from body and matter. 3. The intellectual, on the other hand, is the form of a material body and is released by its death, after which it continues on eternally, as both of us believe. 4. Therefore, it is not right to group the soul with forms that are so different from it. My second point is that all these things were created either before time or in time.

100. Cf. Aristotle, *Physics* 6.3.233b33–10.241b20, e.g., 6.3.234a24: οὐδὲν ἐν τῷ νῦν κινεῖται ("nothing can move in the 'present now'" [trans. Wicksteed]); 6.10.241a15: εἰ ἅπαν ἐν χρόνῳ κινεῖται, ἐν δὲ τῷ νῦν μηθέν ("a thing must occupy a certain period of time in moving (and cannot move in a 'now')" [trans. Wicksteed]).

7 1. Χαλεπόν, μᾶλλον δὲ ἴσως ἀδύνατον, λόγον δοῦναι δι᾽ ὃν ἐπὶ τὴν γένησιν
ἔρχονται. ἣν μὲν γὰρ οἴεται Πλάτων αἰτίαν. 2. οὔθ᾽ ὑμῖν | οἶμαι δοκεῖν, καὶ ἅμα 83r
πολλὰ τὰ ἄτοπα ταύτῃ ἀκολουθεῖ. 3. φησὶ γὰρ ἐκεῖνος εἰς γένησιν αὐτὰς ὑπὸ θεοῦ πέμπεσθαι, ὡς δίκην δοῖεν ὅτι τῷ ἀγαθῷ συνοῦσαι, παρεῖναι τοῦ τε τῆς ὕλης ἵμερον ἔσχον. 4. τούτῳ τοίνυν, ἐγὼ φημί, πολλὰ μὲν καὶ ἄλλα ἄτοπα ἀκολουθεῖν. 5. ὃ δὲ μεῖζον ὅτι τῆς τῶν ἀνθρώπων γενέσεως οὐ καθ᾽ αὑτό τι αἴτιον τίθεται, ἀλλά τι συμβεβηκὸς καὶ παρὰ τὸν σκοπὸν τοῦ τῶν ὅλων δημιουργοῦ. 6. τὸ γὰρ τοῦ μὲν ἀγαθοῦ τὴν ψυχὴν ὀλιγωρεῖν, πόθον δὲ τῆς ὕλης λαβεῖν, συμβεβηκὸς καὶ οὐδὲ δοκοῦν τῷ θεῷ. 7. οὐ γὰρ ἂν ἐπὶ τῷ δίκην δοῦναι εἰς
γένησιν | ἔπεμπε. τὸ δὲ κατὰ συμβεβηκὸς ὂν ἢ γινόμενον ἐνδέχεταί ποτε μὴ 83v
εἶναι. τοιοῦτον γὰρ τὸ συμβεβηκός. 8. ἄλλως τε καὶ διὰ βουλῆς ὂν τῷ θεῷ καὶ αὐταῖς ταῖς ψυχαῖς ἄμεινον. ἀλλὰ τοῦτο ἄτοπον. 9. τὸ γὰρ ἄριστον τῶν ζῴων καὶ δι᾽ ὃ τἄλλα ζῷα γέγονε κατὰ συμβεβηκὸς ἐν τοῖς οὖσιν ἔσται. καὶ παρὰ τὸν σκοπὸν τῆς πρώτης ἀρχῆς.

8 1. Ἄλλως τε καὶ τὸ συμβεβηκὸς πρότερον ἔσται τοῦ καθ᾽ αὑτό. ὁ μὲν γὰρ ἄνθρωπος καθ᾽ αὑτὸ καὶ οὐσία τις, τὸ δὲ τοιοῦτον αἴτιον συμβεβηκός. 2. ἀλλὰ τοῦτο ἀδύνατον. καὶ μὴν οὐδ᾽ οἷς αὐτοὶ περὶ γενέσεως νομίζετε τὴν τοιαύτην,
| οἶμαι, δόξαν συμβαίνειν. 84r

9 1. Τὴν γάρ τοι τῶν ἀνθρώπων γένεσιν οὐκ ἀΐδιον οἴεσθε, ἀλλὰ τέλος αὐτῆς καὶ πάσης κινήσεως τίθεσθε μεθ᾽ ἡμῶν. 2. πότερον οὖν παυομένης τῆς γενέσεως παύσονται καὶ αἱ ψυχαὶ τοῦ τῆς ὕλης ἱμέρου ἢ πόθον αὐτῆς πάλιν ἕξουσιν; 3. εἰ μὲν γὰρ παύσονται, τίς ὁ λόγος τοῦ ποτὲ μὲν ἐρᾶν, ποτὲ δὲ μή; 4. οὐ γὰρ ἵνα γένησις ᾖ. τοῦ γὰρ εἴδους αὕτη χάριν, οὐ τῆς ὕλης. 5. τοῦτο δὲ ὁ λόγος ὅδε, προϋποτίθησιν. 6. εἰ δὲ μὴ παύσονται, δεῖ πάλιν γένεσιν εἶναι ἢ τρόπον ἕτερον τὰς
ψυχὰς εὐθύνεσθαι. 7. ἀλλὰ ταῦτα καὶ παρὰ τὴν κατέχουσαν | δόξαν καὶ ἄτοπα. 84v

1 γένησιν] ad γέννησιν corr. T^1 sed not similiter postea (e.g., XXXVII.7.2, 7.7, 8.2) **4** τοῦ τε] ad τό δε mut. T^1 **11–14** ἄλλως . . . ἀρχῆς] signo (linea perpendicula) in marg. denotat T^1 **16** τοιοῦτον] ad τοιούτου mut. T^1 **17** περὶ γενέσεως] περιγενέσεως T

7 1. It is difficult—no, rather, it is quite impossible—to make a rational case for souls reaching a point of being born. For that is what Plato thinks was their cause. 2. Nor do you agree, I think, since Plato's position at once brings in its train a host of absurdities.[101] 3. For he says that souls were consigned to birth by God in order that by suffering punishment they might be able to cleave to the good and shed their craving for matter. 4. As I say, many and various absurdities follow from this position. 5. One greater one is that it supposes the generation of men not to have some cause in itself, but to be accidental and contrary to the purpose of the maker of all. 6. For disregarding the good or yearning for matter would be accidental and not becoming of God. 7. For he did not send souls to be born in order to suffer punishment. Also, that which exists or comes to be accidentally can at some moment not be. For that is the nature of an accident. 8. Otherwise, being accidental by design would be better for God and the souls themselves. But that is absurd. 9. For the best of living things, and that through which all other living things come to be, would be among beings accidentally. This is contrary to the purpose of the First Principle.

8 1. Otherwise the accidental would be prior to the essential [or what is *per se*]. For man is an essence [or something *per se*] and a certain substance, but such a cause would be an accident. 2. But that is absurd. Nor indeed, I believe, do you yourself think that such a doctrine concerning their generation reflects what happens to souls.

9 1. For you do not think that the generation of men is eternal. Rather, you posit its end and the end of every motion, just as we do. 2. Can it be, then, that when their generation ceases, souls also cease to crave matter, or will they yearn for it again? 3. For if they cease to crave matter, what is the logic of their loving it at one time and not loving it at another? 4. For this is not the purpose of generation. Generation is for the sake of form, not of matter. 5. That is the argument which they [the Platonists] take as a premise. 6. But if souls do not cease to yearn for matter, then necessarily souls are born over again or are chastised in another fashion. 7. Yet these alternatives are contrary to received doctrine and are absurd.

101. Criticism of Plato's psychology was a major aspect of Amiroutzes' tractates, some arguments of which are repeated here; see Monfasani, *George Amiroutzes the Philosopher*, 43–49, 90–107, 133–35, 164–73. See also XXXVII.5.

10 1. Ταύτην μὲν οὖν τὴν αἰτίαν οὐκ ἔστιν εἰπεῖν δι᾽ ἣν ἂν οὖσαι πρότερον αἱ
ψυχαὶ εἰς γένεσιν ἔλθοιεν, ἄλλην δὲ γενναιοτέραν εὑρεῖν ἀμήχανον. 2. τί γὰρ δεῖ
γένεσις εἰ τὰ εἴδη ταῦτα προϋφιστᾶσιν; οὐ γὰρ διὰ τὴν ὕλην τὸ εἶδος ἐστίν, ἀλλ᾽
ἐκείνη διὰ τὸ εἶδος. 3. ἐπεὶ τὸ μὲν οὗ ἕνεκα ἐπὶ τῆς γενέσεως τὸ εἶδος ἐστίν, ἡ δὲ
ὕλη τὸ ἕνεκά του, περιττὴ τοίνυν ἡ γένεσις γίνεται, παρόντος τοῦ τέλους. 4. ἔτι
εἰ μὲν ἐπὶ τῷ ἀμείνονι τῆς ψυχῆς ἐγίνετο ἡ τοῦ σώματος ἕνωσις, ἦν ἂν οὐκ
ἀπεικὸς | εἰς γένεσιν ἐλθεῖν καθ᾽ αὑτὰς οὔσας πρότερον. 5. εἰ δὲ τοῦτο τῷ καλῷ 85r
τῆς ψυχῆς λυμαίνεται, τί δεῖ γενέσεως; 6. τοῦτο δὲ τοῖς ἅμα τῷ σώματι τὴν
ψυχὴν τιθεμένοις οὐκ ἀντίκειται. 7. οὐ γὰρ τὸν ἄνθρωπον τίθενται, ἀλλὰ τὸ
συμφότερον. οὐδ᾽ εἶναι ταύτην πρὸ τοῦ σώματος λέγουσιν, ἀλλὰ μετὰ τοῦ
σώματος εἰς τὸ εἶναι προάγεσθαι. 8. δεῖ τοίνυν γενέσεως ἵνα ἄνθρωπος γένηται
καὶ ἵνα μετὰ ταῦτα τὸ εἶδος ᾖ. 9. οὐχ ὅπως οὖν αὐτοῖς ἡ γένεσις περιττή, ἀλλὰ
καὶ ἀναγκαῖα τὰ μάλιστα. εἶεν.

11 1. Τὴν μὲν οὖν ἀπὸ τῆς ψυχῆς ἔφοδον οὕτως ἀπεκρουσάμεθα.

12 1. Λοιπὸν δὲ τὴν ἀπὸ | τοῦ προορισμοῦ καὶ τῆς θείας προγνώσεως ἀντίθε- 85v
σιν ἰδεῖν. 2. καίτοι χαλεπὸν πρὸς ταύτην ἵστασθαι, οὐχ ὅτι γενναία τις καὶ
ἀναντήρριτός ἐστιν πόθεν, 3. ἀλλ᾽ ὅτι ἀπὸ τοῦ εἰκότος εἴληπται καὶ ἀξίωσις
μᾶλλον ἐστὶν ἀπὸ τοῦ βούλεσθαι προϊοῦσαι ἢ ἀπόδειξις. 4. ὅτι μὲν γὰρ ὁ θεὸς
ἀϊδίως πάντα προοῖδε καὶ προορίζει κατὰ τὴν πρόγνωσιν, ἀνάγκη τε λέγειν καὶ
ἀδύνατον ἄλλως ἔχειν. 5. ἃ δὲ αὐτοὶ περὶ τοῦ Χριστοῦ τῷ Δαυὶδ εἰρημένα
παρηγίγομεν, τοῦτον εἰρῆσθαι φάναι τὸν τρόπον οὐχ ὅπως ἀναγκαῖον, ἀλλ᾽
οὐδὲ τὸ εἰκὸς ἔχει μεθ᾽ ἑαυτοῦ πάνυ τι;

13 1. «Βοᾷ γοῦν ὡς | ἑλκόμενα» ὑπὸ τοῦ βούλεσθαι. 2. τοῦτο τοίνυν χαλεπὸν 86r
μεταβαλεῖν ὅταν μὴ μετὰ λόγου, ἀλλὰ κατὰ κοινὴν ἀξίωσιν ἰσχύῃ. 3. ἀνάγκη δὲ

---

2 ἔλθοιεν] -εν in marg. iterat T[1] **10** συμφότερον] ad συν ἀμφότερον mut. T[1] **12** περιττή] οὐ ante supra lin. scr. T[1] **16** γενναία] ad γενναῖα mut. T[1] **17** ἀναντήρριτός] -τήριτος corr. T[1]

10 1. It is therefore not possible to give this as the reason why souls exist before they are born, and it is quite impossible to find one that works better. 2. For why is generation necessary if these forms preexist? For form does not exist on account of matter, but matter on account of form. 3. Since form is the purpose in generation and since matter is what is for the purpose of something else, generation becomes superfluous when the end is [already] present. 4. Furthermore, if union with the matter takes place for the betterment of the soul, it would not make sense for souls to be born when they exist independently beforehand. 5. If, on the other hand, being born ruins the splendor of the soul, what good is generation? 6. Being born, however, does not pose a problem for those who posit the soul being generated at the same moment as the body. 7. For it is not man that is posited, but the individual who combines both natures. They do not say that the soul existed before the body, but rather that the soul proceeds into existence with the body. 8. Generation is therefore necessary in order for a man to come to be and in order subsequently for his form to exist. 9. For those who hold this view generation is in no way superfluous. Rather, it is totally necessary. Let us assume that this is the case.

11 1. We have thus refuted, then, the argument from the soul.

12 1. We still have to look into the contrary argument posed by predestination and divine foreknowledge. 2. Indeed, it is difficult to resist this line of criticism, not because it is somehow valid and in any way irrefutable, 3. but because it is based on plausibility, and, by proceeding from wishful thinking, is more axiomatic in nature than a scientific demonstration. 4. For one must affirm—and it is impossible to hold otherwise—that God eternally foreknows all things and foreordains them in accordance with his foreknowledge. 5. The passages we ourselves have adduced as said by David about the Christ seem to have been said in a way that does not impose some sort of necessary interpretation. But does not the way they were said bring with it a high degree of plausibility?

13 1. Indeed, these passages "protest at being dragged in"[102] by wishful thinking. 2. It is difficult to change this, then, when these passages have their force not from logic but from their accord with a common assumption. 3. One

102. Cf. Aristotle, *Metaphysics* 14.3.1091a11: βοᾶν ὡς ἑλκόμενα.

ὅμως τὰ δοκοῦντα εἰπεῖν. ἄλλως τε καὶ ὅπου μᾶλλον τὸν λόγον ἢ τὸ ἔθος ἴσμεν
ἰσχύον;

14 1. Πρῶτον δὲ περὶ τοῦ προορισμοῦ καθ᾽ αὑτὸ ῥητέον. ἀκούω γὰρ μὴ
συνᾴδειν ἐν τούτῳ τὴν ὑμετέραν δόξαν οἷς αὐτοὶ πιστεύομεν. 2. ἡμεῖς τοίνυν τὸν
προορισμὸν οὐδὲν ἄλλο τυγχάνειν ἢ τὴν θείαν πρόγνωσιν ἐν τοῖς λογικοῖς
νομίζομεν, καὶ θέλησιν ἑπομένην οἷς ἂν ἕλοιντο οἱ προοριζόμενοι. 3. οὐ γὰρ
ἀποκληρωτικῶς ὁ θεὸς οὐδὲ θελήματι ἀλόγῳ τοὺς μὲν προώρισεν | εἰς τὴν 86v
αἰώνιον ζωήν, τοὺς δὲ εἰς τοὐναντίον, 4. ἀλλ᾽ ἐκείνους ἀϊδίως προώρισεν ἐφ᾽
ἑκάτερον, οὓς προοῖδε τόδε ἢ τοὐναντίον αἱρησομένους, 5. ὥστε τοὺς μὲν
τἀγαθὸν ἑλομένους εἰς τὴν αἰώνιον ζωὴν προορίζειν, τοὺς δὲ τοὐναντίον εἰς τὸ
ἐναντίον.

15 1. Εἰ δέ τις ἄλλο νομίζει, πρῶτον μὲν ἀναιρεῖ τὸ ἐφ᾽ ἡμῖν. 2. τούτῳ δὲ ὅσα
ἄτοπα ἀκολουθεῖ πρότερον εἴρηται, ἔπειτα οὐ τῶν ἀγαθῶν μόνων αἴτιον τὸν
θεόν, ἀλλὰ καὶ τῶν κακῶν ἀποφαίνει. 3. πρὸς δὲ οὐδὲ τὸ δίκαιον ἔχει μεθ᾽
ἑαυτῆς ἡ τοῦ θεοῦ δίκη ἣν ἐπάγει τοῖς πονηροῖς. 4. τί | γὰρ δή ποτε κολάζει οὓς 87r
αὐτὸς συνέταξε τῷ πονηρῷ καὶ βίᾳ; οὐ γὰρ ἦν ἐκφυγεῖν εἰ εἰς τοῦτο ἤγαγεν;
5. οὐκ ἄρα ἐστὶν ὁ προορισμὸς ἡγουμένη τοῦ θεοῦ θέλησις κατὰ ἀποκλήρωσιν,
ἀλλ᾽ ἑπομένη οἷς ἂν ὁ προοριζόμενος ἕλοιτο, 6. οὐχ ὅτι μετὰ τὸ ἑλέσθαι
γινώσκει ἢ ὁρίζει, ἀλλ᾽ ὅτι ἀϊδίως προοῖδεν ὁπότερον ἄν τις ἕλοιτο ἢ τἀγαθὸν ἢ
τοὐναντίον καὶ οὕτω προορίζει, 7. ὥστε τοῦ προορισμοῦ αἰτίαν εἶναι τὴν ὑπὸ
τοῦ θεοῦ γινωσκομένην αἵρεσιν τοῦ προοριζομένου. 8. οὐδὲν οὖν μέγα φαίνεται
τὸ προωρίσθαι. πάντα γὰρ οἶδεν ὁ τοῦ θεοῦ ὀφθαλμὸς καὶ πρὸ | τοῦ ἐν αὐτοῖς 87v
εἶναι καὶ τὸ προσῆκον ἑπομένως ὁρίζει. 9. κοινὸν ἄρα τυγχάνει τὸ προεγνῶσθαι
καὶ τοῖς ἀγαθοῖς καὶ τοῖς πονηροῖς, καὶ ἡ ἑπομένη τούτῳ τοῦ θεοῦ θέλησις.
10. τὸ δὴ τοιοῦτον οὐκ ἄν τις δικαίως ὡς ἴδιον ἀποδοίη οὐδ᾽ ὡς μέγα, οὐδ᾽ ὡς
σεμνόν.

16 1. Ἀλλὰ «τὸ συμπαραμενεῖν τῷ ἡλίῳ» καὶ «πρὸ τῆς σελήνης εἶναι γενεὰς
γενεῶν» καὶ «πρὸ τοῦ ἡλίου διαμένειν τὸ ὄνομα αὐτοῦ καὶ ἔσεσθαι αὐτὸ εὐλογη-

---

12 τούτῳ] τοῦτῳ corr. T^1 et in marg. iterat **16** πονηρῷ . . . βίᾳ] in marg. annot. T^1: γράφεται· κακια (sic) / ἴσθι || εἰ] supra lin. scr. T/T^1 **20** ὑπὸ] supra lin. scr. T/T^1

must state, however, what seems plausible. Put differently, where do we see logic having more force than habit?

14 1. The first thing we need to talk about is predestination in and of itself. For I hear that on this issue your doctrine is not in accord with what we believe. 2. We consider predestination, then, to be nothing else than divine foreknowledge in rational creatures, and the divine will to be consequent of what the predestined themselves chose. 3. For God does not predestine some to eternal life and others to the opposite by way of a lottery or through an irrational will. 4. Rather, he eternally predestined them to their separate destinies as he foresaw how they themselves would choose the good or the opposite, 5. so that he foreordained to eternal life those who chose the good and to the opposite life those who chose the opposite.[103]

15 1. If, however, anyone thinks differently, the first thing he does is take away our free will. 2. We have already noted the absurdities that follow from this position, since in that case God is revealed as the cause not only of good acts, but also of the bad. 3. Besides, God's punishment of evildoers would have nothing of justice in it. 4. For why should he punish those whom he has abetted in their evil and violence? Should he not acquit them if he led them to do these things? 5. Predestination therefore is not God's will conducted along the lines of a lottery, but in consequence of what the predestined has chosen, 6. not because he knows or ordains after the person has chosen, but because he eternally foreknows whether someone will choose good or its opposite, and he foreordains accordingly. 7. Hence, the cause of predestination is the choice known to God made by the predestined. 8. Predestination, then, is no great wonder. For the eye of God sees all actions even before they take place, and in consequence of them he determines what they deserve. 9. Good acts as well as bad fall beneath a common foreknowledge, and God's will is in consequence of this foreknowledge. 10. No one would judge such a consequence as arbitrary, or as a wonder, or as inspiring dread.

16 1. But David refers to the Christ as follows: *to endure as long as the sun*, and *to exist for generations upon generations before the moon*, and *his name will*

103. Amiroutzes' explanation of divine providence is the same as Boethius's in the *Consolation of Philosophy*, translated into Greek by Maximus Planudes in the late thirteenth century; see Demetracopoulos, "Latin Philosophical Works," 824.

μένον εἰς τοὺς αἰῶνας», τοῦτον τὸν τρόπον ἀνατίθησιν ὁ Δαυὶδ τῷ Χριστῷ. 2. οὐκ ἄρα διὰ τὸν θεῖον προορισμὸν εἴρηται. ἔτι τὸ ἁπλῶς εἰρημένον οὐκ ἔστι καλῶς | 88r ἀντὶ τοῦ πῶς ἐκλαβεῖν. 3. τὸ δὲ «συμπαραμενεῖν τῷ ἡλίῳ» οὐκ ἔστι δήπου κατὰ τὸν προορισμόν, ἀλλ᾽ ᾖ ἐν αὐτῷ ἀϊδίως ἔσται. 4. καὶ τὸ «πρὸ τῆς σελήνης οὖν εἶναι συνημμένως ἐπαγόμενον» ἐπιπνοίᾳ θείᾳ οὕτω προσήκει νοεῖν. 5. εἰ δέ τις ἄνευ διορισμοῦ λέγει τὰ τούτου δεόμενα, οὐκ καλῶς ἐρεῖ, ἀλλὰ σοφιστικῶς, ὅθεν ἄγνοια καὶ ἀπάτη συμβαίνει.

17 1. Ἔτι τοῦ δυνάμει ὄντος, οὐκ ἔστι ἐνεργείᾳ· τὸ δὲ ἐν τῷ θεῷ ὂν ἐνεργείᾳ οὐ καθ᾽ αὐτό ἐστι, δυνάμει πρὶν ἂν εἰς οἰκείαν ὕπαρξιν ἔλθῃ καὶ οὐσίαν. 2. τοῦ κατὰ τὴν πρόγνωσιν ἄρα ὄντος, οὐκ ἔστιν ἐνεργείᾳ. δυνάμει γὰρ ἔστι καθ᾽ αὐτό. | 88v 3. ἀλλὰ τοῦ Χριστοῦ ἀεὶ εἶναι τὰς ἐνεργείας ὁ προφήτης Δαυὶδ φησί. 4. γέγραπται γάρ· «καὶ σὺ Βηθλεέμ, γῆ Ἰούδα, οὐδαμῶς ἐλαχίστη εἶ ἐν τοῖς ἡγεμόσιν Ἰούδα. 5. ἐκ σοῦ γάρ μοι ἐξελεύσεται ἡγούμενος, ὅστις ποιμανεῖ τὸν λαόν μου τὸν Ἰσραήλ. καὶ αἱ ἔξοδοι αὐτοῦ ἀπ᾽ ἀρχῆς ἐξ ἡμερῶν αἰῶνος». 6. ἀνάγκη ἄρα καθ᾽ αὐτὸν ἀεὶ εἶναι ἐνεργείᾳ, οὐ κατὰ τὸν προορισμὸν μόνον. 7. τὸ δὲ ἀεὶ εἶναι θεοῦ. θεὸν ἄρα τὸν Χριστὸν ἴσασιν οἱ προφῆται. 8. εἰ δέ τις εἴποι οὐ τὴν ἐνέργειαν εἶναι καθάπερ καὶ τὴν οὐσίαν ἐν τῷ θεῷ τερατεύεται καὶ οὐδὲν εἰκὸς ἐρεῖ. 9. τίς | 89r γὰρ νοῦν ἔχων τοῦ μὴ ὄντος, μόνον δὲ ἐγνωσμένου τὰς ἐνεργείας εἴποι «ἐξ ἡμερῶν εἶναι αἰῶνος»;

18 1. Πολλοὺς ἔχω καὶ ἄλλους προφήτας παραγαγεῖν ὅτι τὸν Χριστὸν θεὸν ἴσασιν, ἀλλὰ περισσὸν εἶναι νομίζω. 2. τὸ γὰρ ἀξίωμα ἓν καὶ τοῦ ἑνὸς καὶ τῶν πλειόνων. εἰ οὖν τούτοις ἀπιστεῖ τις, οὐδὲ ἐκείνοις πιστεύσει. 3. δέδεικται δὲ ὅτι ὁ Χριστὸς θεός ἐστιν ἀληθὴς καὶ θεοῦ λόγος, οὐχ ᾗ ἄνθρωπος ἐγεγόνει, ἀλλὰ καθ᾽ ὃ ἦν ἐν ἀρχῇ τοῦ θεοῦ λόγος.

XXXVIII 1 1. **Ὁ Κρατῶν**. Ταῦτα, ἔφη, πολλὰς καὶ δικαίας ἐνστάσεις ἔχει καὶ ἀντιρρήσεις· 2. ἀλλ᾽ ἵνα μὴ πολὺν χρόνον ἐν τούτοις ἀναλύσαντες, | 89v ῥάθυμοι γενώμεθα πρὸς τὰ ἐφεξῆς, ἃ παντὸς μᾶλλον βούλομαι μαθεῖν παρὰ σοῦ. 3. τὰ

2 ἔστι] ἔτι supra lin. scr. T[1] sed deinde del. **3** ἐκλαβεῖν] δεῖ post del. T **5** συνημμένως] συνημένως corr. T[1] **8** ἐνεργείᾳ[1]] ἐνέργειᾳ T **10** αὐτό] αὐτὸν corr. T[1] **11** Δαυὶδ] in spatio vacuo scr. T[1] **14** ἀπ᾽ ἀρχῆς] ἀπαρχῆς T **16** οὐ] supra lin. scr. T[1], καὶ in textu deleto, et sententiam signo (†) in marg. denotat **18–19** τίς . . . αἰῶνος] signo (†) denotat T[1] **25** Ὁ Κρατῶν] in marg. scr. T **26** πολὺν] πολλὺν corr. T/T[1]

continue on before the sun and shall be blessed down through the ages. 2. These things therefore were not said as reflective of divine predestination. Yet, to suppose that they were said merely as words is to misinterpret instead of to interpret them. 3. Of course, *to endure as long as the sun* is not reflective of predestination, but insofar as he [Christ] is referred to in the passage, he will exist eternally. 4. Thus it is right to think that *before the moon* was said with divine inspiration. 5. If, however, someone were to say without any making any distinctions that these statements lack divine inspiration, he would be speaking not rightly but sophistically, whence spring ignorance and deceit.

17 1. Another point. What exists potentially does not actually exist, and what is in God actually does not exist in itself, but exists only potentially before it comes into its own existence and essence. 2. Therefore, if something exists by foreknowledge, it does not exist in actuality. For it is only potentially existing in itself. 3. But the prophet David says that the actions of the Christ exist eternally. 4. For it is written, *And you Bethlehem, land of Judah, are by no means the least among the leaders of Judah.* 5. *For from you shall come forth for me a leader who will rule my people, Israel. And his goings forth are from the beginning out of the days of eternity.*[104] 6. Necessarily, therefore, in himself Christ always existed in actuality and not only as reflecting predestination. 7. To exist always, however, is a characteristic of God. The prophets, therefore, knew the Christ to be God. 8. If, however, someone says that activity is not like essence in God, he is speaking fantasy and saying nothing plausible. 9. For who in their right mind would speak of the actions of someone who does not exist but is only known about as being *out of the days of eternity*?

18 1. I can cite many other prophets who knew the Christ was God, but I think that it would be excessive to do so. 2. For one axiom and many axioms have the same force as one axiom. Certainly, if someone does not believe these quotations, he will not believe those others. 3. It has been shown, however, that the Christ is truly God and the Word of God, not insofar as he became man, but insofar as he was thus the Word of God from the beginning.

XXXVIII 1 1. **The Conqueror.** These things, he said, have many valid ways of being opposed and refuted. 2. But lest we lose a great deal of time analyzing them, let us not worry ourselves about their consequences, though I very much

104. Mic. 5:1; cf. Matt. 2:6.

μὲν τοιαῦτα τό γε νῦν ἔχον, χαίρειν ἐῶμεν· τόδε δέ μοι ἀπόκριναι· πότερον ἕνα
θεὸν νομίζετε ἢ πολλούς; 4. εἰ μὲν γὰρ πολλούς, ἐκπεπτώκατε τῆς ἀληθείας
σαφῶς καὶ πλανᾶσθε πλάνην ἀνύποιστον. 5. εἰ δὲ ἕνα, τίνα ποτέ ἐστιν ἃ πατέρα
καὶ υἱὸν καὶ πνεῦμα ἅγιον ὀνομάζετε; καὶ τίς ἡ εἰς τριάδα πίστις; 6. τὰ γὰρ τρία
οὐκ ἄν ποτε ἓν εἴη, πῶς οὖν εἷς θεός; ταῦτα γὰρ ἀμήχανον συνελθεῖν. 7. περὶ
τούτων οὖν ὅ τι δοξάζετε καὶ διατί | πάνυ μαθεῖν ἐφίεμαι. 90r

XXXIX 1 1. **Ὁ Φιλόσοφος.** Ἡ ἡμετέρα πίστις, ἔφην ἐγώ, ἕνα θεὸν ἀληθῶς
οἶδεν ἁπλοῦν, μᾶλλον δὲ καὶ ὑπὲρ ἁπλότητα, 2. ὅτι μηδεμία σύνθεσις ἐν αὐτῷ
ἐνδέχεται εἶναι, οὐκ οὐσίας καὶ τοῦ εἶναι, οὐ γένους καὶ διαφορᾶς, οὐχ ὕλης καὶ
εἴδους, οὐκ οὐσίας καὶ συμβεβηκότος, οὐκ ἄλλου τινὸς οὐδενός. 3. ἔστι γὰρ ἕν,
μᾶλλον δὲ αὐτοὲν ἅτε μὴ δὲ τὸ εἶναι διάφορον τῆς οὐσίας ἔχων. 4. καὶ εἴ τις μὴ
ἕνα θεὸν ἀνακηρύττει, τοῦτον ἀποκηρύττομεν αὐτοὶ καὶ ἐς Χριστιανοὺς τελεῖν
οὐ συγχωροῦμεν. ἕνα μὲν οὖν θεὸν ὁμολογοῦμεν. 5. διάκρισιν μέν τοι τινὰ
εὑρίσκομεν αὐτῷ, | οὐ τὴν οὐσίαν αὐτοῦ διακρίνουσαν, μὴ γένοιτο, 6. (τοῦτο γὰρ 90v
ἀρνεῖσθαι τὸν ἕνα τυγχάνει θεόν), ἀλλ᾽ ἰδιότητες ὑφεστῶσαν. 7. τοῦτο δὲ οὐκ
ἀπὸ τοῦ λόγου εὑρόντες πιστεύομεν, ἀλλὰ διαρρήδην μὲν ἐν τῷ εὐαγγελίῳ,
συνεπτυγμένως δὲ καὶ ἐν τοῖς προφήταις. 8. ἐπεὶ δὲ ἡμῖν ταῦτα διαβέβληται,
ἀνάγκη λοιπὸν ἀπὸ τοῦ φυσικοῦ λόγου ἐπιχειρεῖν. 9. κοινὰς γὰρ ἄλλας ἀρχὰς
οὐκ ἔχομεν. καίτοι ὅ γε φυσικὸς λόγος ἐν τούτοις παντὸς τοῦ προσήκοντος οὐκ
ἐφικνεῖται. 10. ἥ τε γὰρ φύσις κάτω καὶ πορρωτάτω τυγχάνει τῆς θείας οὐσίας.
11. ὅ τε ἀπ᾽ αὐτῆς λόγος ἀδυνατεῖ πρὸς τοσοῦτον ὕψος ἐλθεῖν. ὁ μὲν γὰρ ἄνευ | 91r
ὑποκειμένου οὐδεμίαν ἀλήθειαν θεωρεῖ. 12. ἐπεὶ κἂν τῷ τί ἔστιν ὅπου δοκεῖ
μάλιστα τὴν σύνθεσιν ὑπερβαίνειν, οὐκ ἄνευ ὑποκειμένου πρόεισιν. 13. ἀλλὰ τὸ
μέν, γένος οἶδε, τὸ δέ, διαφοράν, οἷον ἀνάγκη τὸ μὲν ὑποκεῖσθαι, τὸ δὲ ἐν αὐτῷ
εἶναι. 14. ἐν δὲ τῷ θεῷ οὐδὲν ἔστιν ὑποκείμενον. ἀλλὰ καὶ εἴ τι τοιοῦτον ἐν αὐτῷ
λέγομεν, ἀπὸ τοῦ φυσικοῦ λόγου συμβαίνει, καὶ τοῦτο οὐδ᾽ αὐτὸς ἀγνοεῖ.
15. «ἀλήθειαν» γοῦν οὐκ ἀληθῆ μόνον τὸν θεὸν ὀνομάζει, καὶ «ἀγαθότητα» καὶ

---

1 ἔχον] ἔχων corr. T/T[1] **7** Ὁ Φιλόσοφος] in marg. scr. T **12** ἀνακηρύττει] οι supra -ει scr. T[1] || ἀποκηρύττομεν] ἀπο in rasura scr. T **15** ἰδιότητες ὑφεστῶσαν] ad ἰδιότητας ὑφιστῶσαν mut. T[1] **26** ἀγνοεῖ] in marg. annot. T[1]: ὁ φυσικὸς λόγος δῆλος ἔστι

want to hear them from you. 3. For the time being, however, let us set them aside. But answer me this: Do you think God is one or many? 4. For if you answer "many," you have manifestly deserted the truth and have strayed into intolerable error. 5. If, on the other hand, you answer "one," what then is that which you name the "Father," the "Son," and the "Holy Spirit"? And what is the faith in a triune? 6. For three would never be one. How is it one God? These things are impossible to reconcile. 7. I am quite eager to hear, then, what you teach concerning these things and why.

XXXIX 1 1. **The Philosopher.** Our faith, I said, sees God as truly and simply one, indeed, as in fact transcending the simplest things, 2. since there cannot be any combination whatsoever in him, not of essence and being, not of genus and *differentia*, not of matter and form, not of essence and accident, not of anything else whatsoever. 3. For he is one. Indeed, he is oneness in itself inasmuch as he has no difference between his being and his essence. 4. And if anyone proclaims that God is not one, we denounce him and refuse to account him a Christian. We agree, then, that God is one. 5. We find also that there is some division in him. It is not the case that his essence has any division. Perish the thought. 6. For that would amount to denying that God is one. Rather, God's essence is the substratum of God's properties. 7. We believe this not because we arrived at it logically, but because it is stated expressly in the Gospel and in veiled fashion in the prophets. 8. Since these properties of God's essence have caused us considerable abuse, we must next try to argue for them on the basis of physics. 9. For we do not have other principles in common. Indeed, in these matters, physics also fails to be completely satisfactory. 10. For physics is beneath and very distant from the divine essence. 11. An argument based on it cannot reach such heights. For without there being a substrate, it does not have a single truth to contemplate. 12. Since by its very definition the divine essence would emphatically seem to transcend in every way the composite, physics has no substrate so as to proceed [concerning God]. 13. But when a substrate is present, physics knows its genus; when the substrate is present, physics also knows its *differentia*, inasmuch as the genus must have a substrate and the *differentia* must be in the substrate. 14. In God, however, there is no substrate. Yet, if we say some such thing is in him, that statement derives from an argument based on physics; and physics would not be aware of this. 15. To be sure, physics not only names the

«ζωήν», 16. καὶ προστίθησι «τὸ αὐτό» ἵνα μηδὲν ἕτερον ὑπονοηθῇ. 17. οὔκουν
ἀγνοεῖ τὴν αὐτοῦ ἀδυναμίαν, ἀλλὰ ἀφαιρεῖ μὲν τὰ ἐντεῦθεν συμβαίνοντα παντα- 91v
χοῦ. 18. οὐδὲν μέντοι ἧττον ἀγνοεῖ ὅ τί ποτέ ἐστι ὁ θεός. 19. οὐ γὰρ ἔχει ὅθεν τοῦτο θηρεύσει, μηδενὸς ὄντος κοινοῦ αὐτῷ τε καὶ τοῖς ἄλλοις. 20. οὔκουν ἔστιν ἐντεῦθεν ὁρμωμένους τοῦ ὀφειλομένου παντὸς τυχεῖν, ἀλλ᾽ ὅμως, ᾗπερ ἐνδέχεται, ἐκ τούτου πειρασόμεθα προβαίνειν.

2 1. Φαμὲν τοίνυν τὸν θεὸν νοῦν τε τυγχάνειν καὶ νοητόν. 2. ὅ τε γὰρ Ἀριστοτέλης νοῦν τὸν ἄριστον αὐτὸν ὀνομάζει, καὶ ὁ λόγος εἰς τοῦτο ἄνεισι.
3. καίτοι πολλοὺς οἶδα τοῦτο μὴ δεχομένους. 4. οἱ γὰρ ἀπὸ τοῦ | Πλάτωνος 92r
ἀντιφθέγγονται καὶ ὑπὲρ τὸν νοῦν καὶ ὑπὲρ τἀγαθὸν καὶ ὑπὲρ τ᾽ ἄλλα αὐτὸν νομίζοντες. 5. μόνον γὰρ τὸ αὐτοὲν αὐτοῦ κατηγοροῦσι, τὸν δὲ νοῦν κάτω που εἶναι καὶ μεθεκτόν. 6. ἐκεῖνον δὲ τυγχάνειν ἀμέθεκτον, καὶ τῷ μὲν νῷ πολλὰ ἥκειν ἑτέρωθεν. τὸ ὄν, τὸ ἀγαθόν, τὸ καλὸν τῷ δὲ ἑνὶ μηδαμόθεν ἥκειν μηδέν. 7. μὴ γὰρ ἂν ἔτι ἀρχὴν εἶναι, ἐπεὶ εἴ τῳ τι ὑπάρχει, μὴ ὅπερ αὐτὸ ὄν, ἀνάγκη τοῦτο ἑτέρωθεν αὐτῷ ἥκειν. 8. ὅπερ ἀνάγκη πρότερον εἶναι καὶ ἀρχὴν τοῦ
μετέχοντος. 9. τοιοῦτον δὲ συμβαίνει μόνον τὸ ἓν εἶναι. | οὐδὲν γὰρ ἕτερον ἐξ 92v
ἀνάγκης αὐτῷ ὑπάρχει.

3 1. Αἴτιον δὲ ὅτι πάντα τὰ καθόλου καὶ ὑφεστάναι ἁπλῶς ἐνόμιζον καὶ καθ᾽ αὑτὰ εἶναι. 2. οὐ γὰρ ἂν μὴ ὄντα τὸν νοῦν νοεῖν. 3. ἐπεὶ ἐν τούτοις ἔστι τὰ μὲν πρότερα, τὰ δὲ ὕστερα ὥστε τὰ μὲν ἀναιρούμενα, τ᾽ ἄλλα συναναιρεῖν, τῶν δὲ

---

1 ὑπονοηθῇ] in marg. annot. T^1: ᾗ αὐτό ἐστι **2** ἀγνοεῖ] in marg. annot. T^1: ὁ φυσικὸς λόγος **18** ὑφεστάναι] ὑφεστᾶναι corr. T/T^1

true God as "truth," but also as "the best of things" and "a living being."[105] 16. It also adds that God is "the same," lest he be conjectured to be something else [in each of these predicates].[106] 17. Therefore physics is not ignorant of its own incapacity, but quite completely eliminates from consideration subjects that stem from this incapacity. 18. Nevertheless, it certainly does not know what God is. 19. For it lacks the means to hunt this down, since there is nothing in common between God and other things. 20. Therefore, if we start out on the basis of physics, we shall fail in what we are obligated to prove. Nonetheless, insofar as possible, let us try to make headway on the basis of physics.

2 1. We say, then, that God is both Mind and noetic being. 2. For Aristotle calls him "the best mind,"[107] and reason arrives at the same conclusion. 3. Nonetheless, I know many do not accept this conclusion. 4. For the Platonists criticize it and think that God is beyond mind, beyond good, and beyond all other things.[108] 5. For they characterize him only as the One in itself. Conversely, they characterize Mind as in some way below him and as mixed. 6. God, on the other hand, is unmixed, while many things affect Mind from outside it. "Being," "good," and "beautiful," however, in no way apply to the One. 7. For it would not still be the [First] Principle, since if something that is not it itself befalls it, necessarily the former comes to the latter from the outside. 8. The former is necessarily prior and the principle of what is participating in it. 9. Only the One, however, is this way. For of necessity there is no "other" that befalls it.

3 1. The reason is because they believe that the One gives existence to all the universals and is the universals in themselves. 2. For Mind would not think of things that do not exist. 3. Inasmuch as among things some are prior and some are later, so that when some [i.e., the prior] are destroyed they co-destroy others

105. Cf. Aristotle, *Metaphysics* 12.7.1072b29–30: ἐνέργεια δὲ ἡ καθ' αὑτὴν ἐκείνου ζωὴ ἀρίστη καὶ ἀΐδιος. φαμὲν δὴ τὸν θεὸν εἶναι ζῷον ἀΐδιον ἄριστον.

106. Cf. ibid., 12.9.1074b23: εἰ ἕτερόν τι, ἢ τὸ αὐτὸ ἀεὶ ἢ ἄλλο [νοεῖ] and 12.10.1075a4–5: οὐχ ἑτέρου οὖν ὄντος τοῦ νοουμένου καὶ τοῦ νοῦ . . . τὸ αὐτὸ ἔσται.

107. See nn. 105–6.

108. For Amiroutzes' criticism of the Neoplatonic divine hierarchy of the One, Mind, and Soul, see Monfasani, *George Amiroutzes the Philosopher*, 78–89, 102–5.

ἀναιρουμένων ἐκεῖνα μηδὲν ἧττον εἶναι, 4. τὰ πρότερα ταῦτα καὶ ἀρχὰς ἐτίθεντο τῶν ὑστέρων καὶ αἴτια.

4 1. Οὔκουν ἦν ἔτι τι τῆς πρώτης ἀρχῆς κατηγορεῖν. 2. συμβαίνει γὰρ ἐκεῖνο πρότερον εἶναι. οὔτε νοῦν τοίνυν οὔτε ἀγαθὸν οὔτε ὂν πρώτην ἀρχὴν ἔλεγον, | 93r
3. ἀγνοῦντες τὴν τοῦ λόγου διάκρισιν ὅτι ἐν τῳ` θεῷ πράγματος διαφορὰν οὐ ποιεῖ ἥ γε οὐδ᾽ ἐν τοῖς ἄλλοις ἐξ ἀνάγκης τοῦτο ποιεῖ. 4. σίτος γοῦν καὶ σπέρμα καὶ καρπὸς τῷ μὲν λόγῳ διαφέρουσι, πράγματι δὲ οὐδαμῶς.

5 1. Ἀλλὰ τὴν ἄγνοιαν ἐκείνων ἐλέγχειν οὐ χαλεπόν. καθ᾽ ἣν νομίζουσι τὰ ὁπωσοῦν πρότερα καὶ ἁπλῶς πρότερα εἶναι. 2. οὐ γὰρ ὅσα τῷ λόγῳ πρότερα καὶ τῇ οὐσίᾳ ἀνάγκη τοιαῦτα εἶναι. ἡ γοῦν λευκότης προτέρα τοῦ λευκοῦ τῷ λόγῳ, 3. ἀλλὰ τῇ οὐσίᾳ τὸ λευκὸν πρότερον. οὐ γὰρ ὑφέστηκεν ἐκείνη. 4. οὐδ᾽ ἔτι καθόλου εἴη, | καὶ οὐχ ὑφεστάναι ἁπλῶς ἀνάγκη. 5. ἢ καὶ τὰ συμβεβηκότα πάντα 93v
ὑποστήσεται καὶ ἔσται οὐσία; 6. ἀλλὰ ταῦτα καὶ ἄτοπα καὶ ἀδύνατα.

6 1. Καὶ τὴν πρώτην αἰτίαν νοῦν ἀνάγκη τὸν ἄριστον καὶ νοητὸν εἶναι, 2. ἐπεὶ κἀκεῖνοι αὐτὴν εἰδέναι ἑαυτήν τε καὶ τὰ ὄντα, οὐκ ἂν ἀρνήσαιντο. ἢ μυρίοις ἀτόποις περιπεσοῦνται. 3. πόθεν γὰρ ἡ τῶν ὄντων διάκρισις καὶ τὸ πλῆθος; ἢ πόθεν ἡ πρὸς τὸ ἓν ἐκεῖνο τάξις αὐτῶν καὶ ἐπιστροφή; 4. εἰ γὰρ μὴ παρὰ τῆς πρώτης ἀρχῆς εἴη, ἀνάγκη ἤτοι τοῦτο τοῖς πράγμασιν ὑπάρχειν κατὰ | συμβεβη- 94r
κός, 5. ἢ ἀπό τινος ἑτέρας ἀρχῆς ἢ ἀπὸ τῆς ὅλης, ὥσπερ Ἐμπεδοκλῆς ὑπέλαβε

3 τι] supra lin. scr. T **12** οὐχ] supra lin. scr. T **14** εἶναι] = finis §5 in ed. de la Cruz Palma || ἐπεὶ] initium §6 in ed. de la Cruiz Palma **19** ὅλης] υ supra ο scr. T^1

[i.e., the latter],[109] and if the latter are destroyed the former no less continue in existence, 4. the Platonists make the prior into principles and the causes of the later.

4 1. Furthermore, it is not possible, then, to predicate anything of the First Principle. 2. For that predicate would be prior. In fact, the Platonists predicate of the First Principle neither mind, nor good, nor being, 3. because they are ignorant of logical division, namely, that logical division causes no real differentiation in God, nor, of necessity, does it do so it in other things. 4. Certainly grain, seed, and fruit differ in terms of definition; but in terms of their reality, they differ not in the least.

5 1. But it is easy to rebut their ignorance. Because of it they think that things which are prior in any way whatsoever are prior in an absolute sense. 2. For it is not necessarily the case that what is prior in terms of definition is also prior in terms of substance, that is to say, whiteness is prior to a white thing in terms of definition, 3. but in terms of substance the white thing is prior. For whiteness does not exist substantively. 4. And, even if it exists as a universal, it still is not necessarily the case that it absolutely exists. 5. Or do all accidents exist substantively and act as substances? 6. This is nonsense and impossible.

6 1. Of necessity, the First Principle is the best Mind and a noetic being, 2. since even the Platonists would not deny that the First Principle knows itself and the things that exist. Otherwise they would be entangled in a myriad of absurdities. 3. For whence would come the division and multiplicity of things? Or whence would come their relationship to the One and their return back to it? 4. For if they do not come from the First Principle, then either they must have substance to their reality accidentally, 5. or they must come from some other

109. Cf. Porphyry, *Introduction* 16.16–18: ἔτι τὰ μὲν ἴδια ἀναιρούμενα οὐ συναναιρεῖ τὰ γένη, τὰ δὲ γένη ἀναιρούμενα συναναιρεῖ τὰ εἴδη, ὧν ἐστιν ἴδια ὥστε καὶ ὧν ἐστιν ἴδια ἀναιρουμένων καὶ αὐτὰ συνανεῖται (trans. Barnes: “Again, if properties are removed, they do not co-remove the genera; but if genera are removed, they co-remove the species to which the properties belong, so that, that of which they are the properties being removed, the properties themselves are also co-removed.”).

καὶ Λεύκιππος καὶ Δημόκριτος. 6. εἰ μὲν οὖν κατὰ συμβεβηκὸς εἴη, τῆς οὐσίας ἔσται ἀρχὴ τὸ συμβεβηκός. 7. τὴν μὲν γὰρ τοιαύτην διάκρισιν ἀνάγκη γίνεσθαι κατὰ τὰ εἴδη. ταῦτα δὲ ἡ ἑκάστου οὐσία τυγχάνει. 8. τὸ τοίνυν αἴτιον τῆς τοιαύτης διακρίσεως καὶ τῆς οὐσίας αἴτιον ἔσται. ἀλλὰ τοῦτο ἀδύνατον.

7 1. Ἔτι οὐδὲν τῶν κατὰ συμβεβηκὸς ὄντων, τέτακται πρός τι τέλος. 2. τὰ δὲ ὄντα πάντα τέτακται πρὸς ἕν τι τὸ ἔσχατον τέλος. οὐκ ἄρα κατὰ συμβεβηκὸς εἰσίν. 3. ἀλλ᾽ εἰ κατὰ συμβεβηκὸς | 94v αὐτοῖς ἡ τοιαύτη τυγχάνειν διάκρισις, ἀνάγκη κατὰ συμβεβηκὸς εἶναι. 4. διότι ἡ τοιαύτη διάκρισις τὰ εἴδη παράγει οἷς τὰ ὄντα πάντα ὑφίσαται. οὐκ ἄρα κατὰ συμβεβηκός ἐστιν. 5. εἰ δὲ ἀπό τινος ἑτέρας ἀρχῆς, εἰ μὲν ὑπὸ τὴν πρώτην ταττομένης, ἐκείνη καὶ τῆς διακρίσεως αἰτία ἔσται, 6. ἐπεὶ τὰ ἔργα τῆς δευτέρας αἰτίας μᾶλλον ἀνήκει τῇ πρώτῃ. 7. εἰ δὲ μὴ ταττομένης ὑπὸ τὴν πρώτην, οὐκ ἔσται μία ἀρχή, ἀλλὰ πλείους. 8. καίτοι περιττὴ λοιπὸν ἡ ἑτέρα γίνεται. τὸ γὰρ αἴτιον τῆς διακρίσεως αὐτὸ καὶ τοῦ εἶναι τὰ ὄντα αἴτιον ἔσται. 9. τί οὖν δεῖ τῆς λοιπῆς | 95r ἀρχῆς, εἰ μή τις τὸ μὲν ὡς τέλος εἴποι ἀρχήν, τὸ δὲ ὡς παράγον; ἀλλὰ τοῦτο ἀδύνατον.

8 1. Ἓν γὰρ ἀνάγκη εἶναι, τό τε τοῦ εἶναι τὰ ὄντα αἴτιον καὶ τὸ τέλος. 2. διὰ τί γὰρ ἐκεῖνο τὰ ἑαυτοῦ ἔργα πρὸς τόδε τάττοι εἰ μὴ ἐκεῖθεν εἴη; 3. ἀλλὰ μὴν οὐδὲ τὴν ὕλην τῆς τοιαύτης διακρίσεως ἐνδέχεται αἰτίαν εἶναι. 4. πρῶτον μὲν γὰρ περιττὴ ἡ κατὰ τὸ εἶδος ἀρχὴ γίνεται, τῆς ὕλης οἴκοθεν τὰ εἴδη γεννώσης. 5. μαρτυροῦσι δὲ οἱ ἀρχαῖοι ἔργῳ καὶ ὅσοι τὴν ὕλην αἰτίαν τοῦ πλήθους

1–2 τῆς . . . συμβεβηκός] signo (†) in marg. denotat T[1] **4** ἀλλὰ τοῦτο] in marg. scr. T **12** πρώτην] πρώτου T **19** γεννώσης] γενώσης corr. T[1]

principle or from the whole, just as Empedocles maintained,[110] and Leucippos and Democritus as well.[111] 6. If, then, they exist accidentally, the [first] principle of substance would be an accident. 7. For such a division [of things] must occur at the level of forms, but the forms constitute the substance of each thing, 8. and accident, then, would be the cause of such a division and also the cause of substance. But that is impossible.

7 1. Furthermore, insofar as things do not have existence accidentally, they are ordered toward some end. 2. And all things are ordered toward some single thing as their final end. They therefore do not have existence accidentally. 3. But if such a division of things occurs accidentally, they necessarily exist accidentally, 4. because such a division creates the forms through which all beings have substantial existence. Therefore, this division is not accidental. 5. If, however, things came from another principle, and if this other principle was ordered under the First Principle, the First Principle would still be the cause of the division, 6. since the product of the second cause would belong more to the first cause. 7. If, however, this other principle was not ordered under the First Principle, there would not be one principle, but a plurality of principles. 8. But having another principle is superfluous. For the cause of division will itself be the cause of the existence of things. 9. What need, then, is there for a further principle, unless one says that one principle functions as the end, the other as the creator? But that is impossible.

8 1. The One necessarily exists, was the cause of the existence of things, and is their end. 2. For why would it order its own products toward a point other than their origin? 3. And matter is not capable of being the cause of such a division. 4. First of all, the principle in relation to the form would itself become superfluous, since matter would be generating form out of itself. 5. The ancients are in fact evidence for this view, since they thought matter was the cause of multiplic-

110. Amiroutzes must be thinking of Simplicius's commentary on *Physics* 2.8.199b7 (Simplicius, *On Aristotle's Physics* 381.22–382.21 [= Diels, *Fragmente der Vorsokratiker*, 1:335, frag. 62]), where Empedocles is identified as the author of the notion of the primal οὐλοφυὲς that Aristotle is criticizing.

111. Leucippos and his disciple Democritus (see Aristotle, *Metaphysics* 1.4.985b.5) were the famous founders, known from many sources, of the theory that the world is composed of eternally existent atoms.

ἐνόμισαν. 6. ἀρχὴν γὰρ ἑτέραν εἰς τὴν τῶν ὄντων πρόοδον οὐκ εἰσάγουσιν. | 95v ἀλλὰ τοῦτο ἀδύνατον.

9 1. Ὁρῶμεν γὰρ πανταχοῦ τὴν ὕλην κινουμένην ὑπὸ τοῦ εἴδους καὶ διατιθεμένην, καὶ πάσχουσαν δεχομένην τὸ εἶδος. 2. οὐ γὰρ ἀνακύπτει ἀπ᾽ αὐτῆς τὸ εἶδος ἐνόν. οὐδὲ ἀνίσχει, ὥς τινες ἔφασαν, ἀλλ᾽ ἐγγίνεται ὑπὸ τοῦ κινοῦντος τὸ δυνάμει ταύτης εἰς ἐνέργειαν ἄγοντος. 3. διὰ τοῦτο οὐχ ἅπαν, οὐδὲ τὸ τυχὸν κινεῖ, ἀλλὰ τόδε μέν, τόδε κινεῖ, ἄλλο δὲ ἄλλο. 4. εἰ δὲ κινήσεως ἔδει μόνον, ὥστε τὸ δυνάμει εἰς ἐνέργειαν προελθεῖν, ἓν ἂν εἶδος ἅπαντα τὰ λοιπὰ παρῆγε κινοῦν ὁπωσοῦν. 5. νῦν δὲ τοῦτο οὐχ ὁρῶμεν. | ἀλλ᾽ εἰ μὲν ἄνθρωπον δεῖ γενέσθαι, 96r ἄνθρωπον δεῖ τὸ κινοῦν εἶναι. 6. εἰ δὲ ἵππον, ἵππον, καὶ ἐπὶ τῶν ἄλλων ὡσαύτως. οὐκ ἄρα ἀπὸ τῆς ὕλης ἀναθρώσκει τὸ εἶδος ἐνόν. 7. οὐ μὴν ἀλλ᾽ οὐδὲ καθ᾽ αὑτὸ γινόμενον εἰς τὴν ὕλην εἰσάγεται ἅπαν. ἀλλ᾽ ἐν αὐτῇ γίνεται ὑπὸ τοῦ κινοῦντος. 8. ἔτι εἰ ἦν ἡ ὕλη τῆς διακρίσεως αἰτία, ἐκεῖνα ἂν μόνα διεκρίνετο ὅσα ὕλην εἶχε. 9. ἀλλὰ τὰ νοητὰ εἴδη οὐδαμῇ ταύτης μετέχοντα οὐδὲν ἧττον ἀλλήλων διακρίνεται.

10 1. Φανερὸν τοίνυν ὅτι οὔθ᾽ ὕλη οὔτ᾽ ἄλλη τις ἀρχὴ παρὰ τὴν πρώτην αἰτία τῆς διακρίσεως | τῶν ὄντων ἐστίν. 2. ἀλλ᾽ οὐδὲ κατὰ συμβεβηκὸς τοῦτο 96v τοῖς οὖσιν ὑπάρχει. 3. λείπεται ἄρα τὴν πρώτην ἀρχὴν τοῦ τε πλήθους τῶν ὄντων καὶ τῆς διακρίσεως αἰτίαν εἶναι. 4. ἀλλὰ μὴν εἰ τῆς διακρίσεως καὶ τῆς πρὸς τὸ τέλος τάξεως, ἐπεὶ ἡ τάξις ἐκείνης τῆς αἰτίας ἐστὶν ἧς ἐστὶ καὶ τὸ εἶναι τῶν ταττομένων, 5. διχῶς δέ τι καὶ διακρίνει κατ᾽ εἶδος τὰ ἔργα καὶ πρὸς τὸ τέλος τάττει. 6. ἕνα μὲν τρόπον ὡς ἡ φύσις. καὶ γὰρ αὕτη καὶ διακρίνει τὰ εἴδη καὶ τάττει. 7. ἄλλον δὲ ὡς τὰ μετὰ λόγου ποιοῦντα. διαφέρει δὲ ὅτι τῇ μὲν φύσει τὸ τάττειν ἑτέρωθεν ἥκει. | 8. ἐπεὶ κινεῖ κινουμένη, συμβαίνει τοίνυν τὰ ταύτης 97r ἔργα τάττεσθαι μὲν πρὸς τὸ τέλος. 9. ἀλλ᾽ οὐχ ὑπ᾽ αὐτῆς πρώτης οὐδὲ εἰδυίας,

---

4 γὰρ] μὴν supra lin scr. T^1 **7** ἄλλο[1]] ἄλλη corr. T/T^1 **18** ἄρα] supra lin. scr. T

ity. 6. For they do not introduce an alternative cause for the procession of beings. But this is impossible.

9 1. For we see in all instances that matter is moved and organized by form and is the passive recipient of form. 2. For the imparted form cannot emerge from matter. Nor does form just arise, as some have said, but rather it comes to be through the agency of a mover bringing the potency of matter into act. 3. Consequently, the mover does not move everything or anything haphazardly, but this specific thing and that specific thing, a different mover for a different thing. 4. If, however, only the form of motion is needed for what is in potency to come into act, then there would be a single form that causes everything else to move in some way or the other. 5. That, however, is not what we see today. Rather, if a man has to come to be, a man has to be the mover. 6. If, however, a horse has to come to be, then a horse is necessarily the mover, and likewise for other things. Therefore, form cannot spring up from matter. 7. But it is also not the case that everything is self-generated and self-introduced into matter. Rather, a thing comes about in matter through the agency of the mover. 8. Furthermore, if matter is the cause of division, only those things which possess matter would be divided. 9. But noetic forms, though they do not participate in matter, nonetheless are divided from each other.

10 1. Clearly, then, neither matter nor some principle other than the First Principle is the cause of the division of beings. 2. But that division does not accidentally occur to beings. 3. We are left, therefore, to conclude that the First Principle is the cause of the multiplicity of beings and of their division. 4. But if in fact the First Principle is the cause of the division of beings and of their relationship with their end, because the relationship is from that cause whose existence is also the cause of the beings ordered [under it],[112] 5. then there are two ways by which to any extent this cause divides its products by form and orders them toward their end. 6. One way is as nature. For nature divides forms and orders them. 7. The other way is that this cause acts just like things that create with a purpose. This last way differs from the former in that the ordering to the end enters nature from outside of nature. 8. Since the moved [in its turn] causes motion, it is the case that its products too are ordered to their end, 9. but

112. A difficult sentence. Acciaiuoli translates it *quandoquidem dispositio* [*dipositio* De la Cruz] *ab ea est causa a qua et illa sunt quae disponuntur.*

ἀλλ᾽ ὑφ᾽ ἑτέρου ἀφ᾽ οὗπερ αὐτῇ τὸ κινεῖν ὑπάρχει. 10. ἐν δὲ τοῖς ἀπὸ τοῦ λόγου
γινομένοις ἡ τάξις ἀπὸ τοῦ ποιοῦντος ἐστὶ πρώτου. 11. οὔκουν ἐνδέχεται τὴν
πρώτην αἰτίαν οὔτε πράττειν οὔτε διακρίνειν ὥσπερ ἡ φύσις. 12. διότι ἐξ αὐτῆς
πρώτης ἐστὶν ἑκάτερον. ἀνάγκη ἄρα μετὰ λόγου καὶ τὴν διάκρισιν τῶν ὄντων καὶ
τὴν τάξιν ἐξ αὐτῆς εἶναι. 13. οἶδεν ἄρα ἡ πρώτη ἀρχὴ καὶ τὸ πλῆθος τῶν ὄντων
καὶ τὴν διάκρισιν | καὶ τὴν τάξιν. εἴτε ἀμέσως αὐτὰ παράγει εἴτε δι᾽ ἑτέρου. 97v
14. οὐδὲν γὰρ διαφέρει πρός γε ὃ νῦν βουλόμεθα. εἰ δὲ οἶδε καὶ οὐκ ἐν ἀγνοίᾳ
τούτων τυγχάνει, νοεῖν ἀνάγκη. 15. ἢ ὅπως ἄν τις καλεῖν βούλοιτο τοῦτο τὸ
εἰδέναι; καίτοι νοεῖ οὐκ ἄλλο ἢ ἑαυτὸν ὁ θεός. 16. ἀλλ᾽ ἐπείπερ αὐτός ἐστιν ἡ
τοῦ εἶναι παντὸς ἀρχή, νοῶν ἑαυτὸν ᾗ τοιοῦτός ἐστι τὰ ὄντα πάντα νοεῖ. 17. οὐ
γάρ ἐστι τὴν αἰτίαν εἰδότα, ᾗ αἰτία ἐστίν, ἀγνοεῖν τὰ αἰτιατά. ἕπεται τοίνυν τὸν
θεὸν καὶ νοῦν τὸν ἄριστον εἶναι καὶ νοεῖν.

11 1. Φημὶ δὲ ὅτι καὶ θέλει. οὐ γὰρ ὁπωσοῦν ἔχει πρός τε ἑαυτὸν καὶ τὰ ἄλλα.
| 2. οὐδ᾽ ἀδιάφορον αὐτῷ τυγχάνει εἶναί τε αὐτὰ ἢ μὴ εἶναι. 3. εἰ γὰρ ὁπωσοῦν 98r
εἶχε πρὸς τὴν ἀντίφασιν, οὐδὲν μᾶλλον ἐξ αὐτοῦ θάτερον ἦν ἢ θάτερον. 4. οὕτω
δὲ συμβαίνει μηδὲν μᾶλλον ἐξ αὐτοῦ τὰ ὄντα εἶναι ἢ μὴ εἶναι ὥστε ἐνδέχεται
μηδὲν εἶναι τῶν ὄντων, ὅπερ ἀδύνατον.

12 1. Οὐκ ἄρα ὁμοίως ἔχει πρὸς τὴν ἀντίφασιν. ῥέπειν ἄρα ἀνάγκη πρὸς
θάτερον. 2. τοῦτο δέ ἐστι θέλειν. ἡ γὰρ πρός τι ῥοπή (τοῦ λόγον ἔχοντος ᾗ
τοιοῦτον) θέλησις ἐστίν. 3. ἔτι ὅπερ ἥδεται ἢ χαίρει τινί, οὐχ ὁμοίως ἔχει πρὸς
τὴν ἐκείνου ἀντίφασιν. 4. ὁ δὲ θεὸς ἥδεται τῇ ἑαυτοῦ θεωρίᾳ, | καὶ τοῦτο διαρρή- 98v
δην φησὶν Ἀριστοτέλης ἐν τῷ λ´ τῶν Μετὰ τὰ Φυσικά, ἐν οἷς διδάσκει τίς ἐστιν ἡ
ζωὴ τῆς πρώτης ἀρχῆς. 5. «διαγωγὴ δὲ ἔστιν αὐτῷ», φησίν, ‹οἵα› ἡ ἀρίστη μικρὸν
χρόνον ἡμῖν. οὕτω γὰρ ἀεὶ ἐκεῖνο. ‹. . .› 6. ἡ γὰρ θεωρία τὸ ἥδιστον καὶ ἄριστον.

3 πράττειν] ad ταττειν mut. T^1 **9** νοεῖ] νοειν corr. T/T^1 **19** λόγον] λόγου corr. T^1 **21–22** ὁ . . . διδάσκει] in marg. annot. T^1: σημείωσαι **21** τοῦτο] supra lin. scr. T^1 **22** λ´] $λ^ω$ T, in marg. rescr. T^1 **23** οἵα] supplevi; spatium relinq. T **24** ἐκεῖνο] ad ἐκείνῳ mut. T^1

not by the First Principle, nor by a mind that cognizes them, but by something else, namely, that which was the source of the moved having motion. 10. In the case of things whose generation was purposeful, their organization is from their first maker. 11. Therefore the First Principle must act and divide just like nature does. 12. This is the reason why the moved and its product are each from the First Principle. Logically, therefore, the division of beings and their organization must be from the First Principle as well. 13. Hence, the First Principle is cognizant of the multitude of beings, their division, and their organization. It either creates them directly or through another; 14. either way, it does not affect the point we want to make here. If, however, the First Principle is cognizant of the multitude of beings and is not ignorant of them, the First Principle necessarily thinks of these beings.[113] 15. What name, then, would someone want to give this cognition? Indeed, it is nothing other than God knowing himself. 16. But precisely because he is the cause of every existence, thinking himself is equivalent to him thinking all beings. 17. For, insofar as it is the cause, a cause that is cognizant cannot but think of what it has caused. It follows, then, that God is the supreme mind and supreme act of thinking.

11 1. I say, however, that God also wills. For he does not have just any sort of relationship with himself and with other things. 2. It is not a matter of indifference to him whether they exist or not. 3. For if he could have any sort of contrary relationships, it would not matter whether one alternative or another came from him. 4. It would thus not matter whether beings had existence from him or not. Consequently, it could happen that no beings exist, which is impossible.

12 1. He therefore does not view opposites in a similar way. Necessarily, therefore, he is inclined to this alternative or to that one. 2. That, however, is to will. For the inclination toward something (provided that an such inclination is the act of a rational entity) is willing. 3. Furthermore, when one takes delight or enjoys something, one does not view its contrary in a similar way. 4. God, however, takes pleasure in contemplating himself. And that is what Aristotle expressly says in book 12 of the *Metaphysics*, in which he teaches what the life of the First Principle is. 5. "Its existence," he says, "is like the best we enjoy only briefly. For it is always thus. . . . 6. For contemplation is the most enjoyable and

113. That God cognizes particulars is a theme of Thomas Aquinas: see *Summa contra gentiles* 1.55 and 1.67.

εἰ οὖν οὕτως εὖ ἔχει. ὡς ἡμεῖς ποτέ, ὁ θεὸς ἀεί, θαυμαστόν. 7. εἰ δὲ καὶ μᾶλλον, ἔτι θαυμασιώτερον. ἔχει δὲ ὧδε». 8. οὐκ ἄρα ὁμοίως ἔχει πρὸς τὸ νοεῖν ἢ μή, ἀλλὰ τῷ μὲν χαίρει. ἔστι γὰρ ἡ αὐτοῦ ζωή. τῷ δὲ οὔ. 9. τοῦτο δέ ἐστι θέλειν. ὁ θεὸς ἄρα καὶ νοεῖ καὶ θέλει.

13 1. Ἔτι οὐδ᾽ ἔχει λόγον, νοοῦντα μὴ θέλειν. ἀλλὰ παρὰ | 99r τὰς κοινὰς ἐννοίας ἐστὶ καὶ παρὰ τὴν ἐνέργειαν αὐτήν. 2. τὰ γὰρ νοῦ μετέχοντα πάντως καὶ θέλοντα ἴσμεν. δεῖ δὴ λόγον ἀποδοῦναι δι᾽ ὃν οὐχ οὕτως ἐπὶ τῆς πρώτης ἀρχῆς ἔχει. 3. καὶ μὴ οὕτως ἀξίωμα ἄλογον ἀξιοῦν. νοῦς τοίνυν ὁ ἄριστος ὢν ὁ θεὸς καὶ νοεῖ καὶ θέλει.

14 1. Φαίνεται οὖν ἐνταῦθα διάκρισις οὐκ ἀπὸ τοῦ λόγου τοῦ ἡμετέρου ἀνίσχουσα, ἀλλ᾽ ἀπ᾽ αὐτοῦ τοῦ πράγματος. 2. ὁ μὲν γὰρ νοῦς ἀρχή ἐστι καὶ αἰτία καὶ τοῦ νοεῖν καὶ τοῦ θέλειν, ἤγουν τῆς νοήσεως καὶ τῆς θελήσεως. 3. τὰ δὲ πρόεισι ἐξ αὐτοῦ διαφόρως, ὅτι τὸ μὲν αὐτόθεν, οὐδενὸς ἐπινοουμένου μέσου, | 99v ἡ δὲ θέλησις διὰ τῆς νοήσεως. 4. οὐ γάρ ἐστι θέλειν μὴν νοοῦντα πρότερον, καὶ τοῦτό ἐστιν ὅ φησιν ὁ φιλόσοφος· 5. «ὀρεγόμεθα δὲ ὅτι δοκεῖ μᾶλλον ἢ δοκεῖ διότι ὀρεγόμεθα. ἀρχὴ γὰρ ἡ νόησις». 6. καὶ διὰ τοῦτο προηγεῖται καὶ προεπινοεῖται ὅτι ἀρχή ἐστιν.

15 1. Οὕτως οὖν διακρίνονται, τοῦ μὲν νοῦ ὅτι ἐξ αὐτοῦ ἄμφω προΐασιν, ἀλλήλων δέ, ᾗ τὸ μὲν αὐτόθεν ἀπὸ τοῦ νοῦ, τὸ δὲ δι᾽ ἐκείνου καὶ ᾗ αὐτοῦ τυγχάνει ἄρχή. 2. ἡ δὲ ἀρχὴ καὶ τὰ ἐξ αὐτῆς οὐκ ἄν ποτε εἴη καθ᾽ ὃ τοιαῦτα. τρία τοίνυν γίνεται, νοῦς καὶ νόησις καὶ θέλησις. 3. τὸν μὲν νοῦν αὐτὸν καὶ πατέρα | 100r ὀνομάζομεν. διότι ἃ πρόεισιν ἐξ αὐτοῦ, τῆς αὐτῆς οὐσίας ἐστὶ τῷ ἀριθμῷ. 4. ὁ γὰρ πατὴρ κἂν τῇ φύσει τῆς αὐτῆς οὐσίας αὐτῷ προάγει ἅττ᾽ ἂν ὡς πατὴρ

6 ἐνέργειαν] -έρ- in marg. rescr. T^{1} **23** προάγει] ad -γη mut. T^{1} || ἅττ᾽] ἅ τ᾽ corr. T^{1}

best thing. If, then, God is always happy in a way that we are sporadically, that is a wonder. 7. If, however, he is more happy, that is still more wondrous. But this is how he is."[114] 8. Therefore he does not view thinking or not thinking in a similar way. Rather, he takes pleasure in the former. For this is his life. On the other hand, he does not take pleasure in the latter. 9. That, however, is to will. God therefore both thinks and wills.

13 1. Furthermore, it does not make sense that while thinking, he does not will. Rather, that is contrary to common notions and contrary to the action itself. 2. For we know that what fully participates in mind also wills. Indeed, one must come up with a reason for why the same is not also true for the First Principle. 3. In arguing thus we are not positing an irrational axiom. Accordingly, since he is the best mind, God both thinks and wills.

14 1. It is apparent from the foregoing, then, that division does not arise from our reasoning, but from the object itself. 2. For the mind is the principle and cause of thinking and of willing, that is to say, of thought and will. 3. Thought and will, however, proceed from the mind differently, since thinking starts from itself with no mediating thinking agent, while willing works through thought.[115] 4. For there is no willing without prior thought, exactly as the philosopher says: 5. "Desire is the result of opinion rather than opinion that of desire. It is the act of thinking that is the principle."[116] 6. And for that reason thought precedes and thinking is first, since that is what a principle is.

15 1. Thus, then, thought and will are to be distinguished. While both proceed from mind, they are distinguished from each other in that one of them, thought, starts from itself, while the other, will, works through the other and in this way has mind as its principle. 2. The principle, however, and the things that proceed from it thus will never be the same. They are therefore three things: mind, thought, and will. 3. Mind we also call the Father. The reason is because thought and will proceed from it. Numerically, however, they are of the one same substance. 4. For a father would produce by nature whatever he would produce

114. Aristotle, *Metaphysics* 12.7.1072b14–16, 24–26.

115. Amiroutzes seems to be consciously taking the side of Aquinas in the Latin scholastic debate on the priority of the mind vs. the will; for a capsule description of the debate, see Hoffmann, "Intellectualism and Voluntarism."

116. Aristotle, *Metaphysics* 12.7.1072a29–30 (translation adapted from Tredennick).

προάγει, 5. οὐ μέντοι τῷ ἀριθμῷ, ἀλλὰ τῷ εἴδει μόνον. αἴτιον δὲ ὅτι αὐτός τε ὕλῃ σύνεστι καὶ τὰ προαγόμενα τοιαῦτα παράγει. 6. ἐν τούτοις δὲ δύο τινὰ ἢ πλείω ἀδύνατον, ἑνὸς ἀριθμοῦ εἶναι. 7. ἔνθα δὲ μὴ ἔστι μὲν ὁπωσοῦν ὕλη. πρόοδος δὲ γίνεται κατὰ τὴν οὐσίαν. 8. ἀνάγκη ἐκεῖ τὰ προϊόντα καὶ μιᾶς οὐσίας τῷ ἀριθμῷ εἶναι. τί γὰρ ἂν αὐτῶν καὶ διακρινεῖ τὴν οὐσίαν εἰ μιᾶς εἶεν τῷ εἴδει; 9. ὕλη δηλαδή, ἐπεὶ διὰ μόνην | τὴν ὕλην τοῦτο ἴσμεν συμβαῖνον. 10. καὶ τοῦτο φησὶν 100v Ἀριστοτέλης ἐν τῷ ιβʹ τῶν Μετὰ τὰ Φυσικὰ ὅτι «ὅσα ἀριθμῷ πολλὰ ὕλην ἔχει. ‹. . .› ἀλλὰ τὸ πρῶτον εἶδος ὕλην οὐκ ἔχει».

16 1. Μία ἄρα τῷ ἀριθμῷ ἡ τῶν τριῶν ἐκείνων οὐσία. καὶ διὰ τοῦτο εἷς θεός, οὐ πολλοί. 2. ὅπερ οὖν εἶπον τοὶ μὲν νοῦν καὶ πατέρα φαμὲν ὅτι μὴ διάφορα τῇ φύσει προάγει τὴν νόησιν καὶ τὴν θέλησιν. 3. τὴν δὲ νόησιν καὶ λόγον καὶ υἱόν, ἀλλὰ λόγον μὲν ᾗ ἐκ τοῦ νοῦ πρόεισιν. 4. λόγος γὰρ καὶ παρὰ τοῖς φιλοσόφοις τὸ ἐκ τοῦ νοῦ προϊὸν αὐτόθεν λέγεται. | 5. υἱὸν δέ, ᾗ τῆς αὐτῆς οὐσίας τυγχάνει 101r τῷ νῷ ὅθεν πρόεισι. 6. τὴν δὲ θέλησιν πνεῦμα ἅγιον ὀνομάζομεν ὅτι οὕτως αὐτὸ καὶ οἱ προφῆται ἐκάλεσαν. 7. καὶ αὐτὸς ὁ λόγος ὡς ἑπόμενον ἴσως τῷ λόγῳ διότι καὶ τῷ κατὰ προφορὰν λόγῳ ἕπεται. 8. καὶ πνεῦμα ὁριζόμενον ὑπʼ αὐτοῦ καὶ εἰδοποιούμενον.

17 1. Αὕτη δέ ἐστιν ἡ τριὰς εἰς ἣν αὐτοὶ πιστεύομεν. ταῦτα δὲ τὰ τρία εἷς ἐστὶ θεὸς ὅτι μία τῷ ἀριθμῷ ἡ τούτων οὐσία. 2. ἐκεῖνα δὲ τὰ τρία ἰδιότητάς φαμεν, οὐκ ἐκ τοῦ λόγου, ἀλλʼ ἐκ τῆς τοῦ πράγματος ἀνίσχουσας φύσεως. 3. οὐ δεῖ δὲ θαυμάζειν | εἰ καὶ ἀπὸ τοῦ φυσικοῦ ταῦτα δείκνυται λόγου. 4. ἐν πᾶσι γὰρ τοῖς 101v οὖσιν ἔνεισιν εἰκόνες τῆς μιᾶς ἀρχῆς, αἱ μὲν μείζους, αἱ δὲ ἥττους. 5. καὶ οὐδέν ἐστιν ἐν αὐτοῖς ᾧ μηδὲ μία τις ἐμφέρεια θεωρεῖται. 6. ἐπεὶ δὲ ὁ νοῦς τυγχάνει τῶν ὄντων τὸ ἄριστον καὶ θειότατον, οὐδὲν ἀπεικὸς ἐν αὐτῷ, καὶ τὴν ἀρίστην εἰκόνα τοῦ θεοῦ θεωρεῖσθαι. 7. ἀλλʼ ἡμεῖς οὐκ ἐντεῦθεν ἐπὶ τὴν θείαν ἐκείνην διάκρισιν ἤλθομεν. 8. ἀλλʼ ὑπʼ αὐτοῦ τοῦ θεοῦ διὰ τῶν προφητῶν πρῶτον, ἔπειτα τοῦ λόγου τοῦτο μεμαθηκότες, συνᾴδοντα τὸν φυσικὸν λόγον εὑρόντες ἀποδεχόμεθα. | 102r

---

5–6 ὕλη δηλαδή] in marg. scr. T[1] **6** διὰ μόνην] διαμόνην T; ad διαμήνην mut. T[1] || τὴν] del. T/T[1] **7** Ἀριστοτέλης] ʼΑριστοτέλος corr. T[1] **16** τῷ] τὸ corr. T/T[1] **18** δέ] supra lin. scr. T[1] **20** τῆς] supra lin. scr. T[1] || ἀνίσχουσας] -χουσα corr. T[1]

as a father, that is, things that are of the same substance as his own, 5. not the same numerically, to be sure, but only in form. The reason for this is that a father is tied to matter and generates offspring that are such of the same nature. 6. In the products of the mind, however, any sort of number two or higher is impossible, since numerically they are one. 7. There is here no way whatsoever that matter is present. Rather, procession [from the mind] occurs by substance. 8. Of necessity, in this case, the things that proceed forth are numerically of one substance. For if they are one in form, what divides their substance? 9. The answer obviously is matter, since we know that this happens only through matter, 10. just as Aristotle says in book 12 of the *Metaphysics*: "Whichever things are many in number, have matter. . . . But the first form has no matter."[117]

16 1. The substance of these three things is therefore numerically one. And for that reason God is one, not many. 2. He, then, is what I call Mind. And we say "the Father" because he does not send forth his thought and will as different in nature. 3. We call his thought the Word and the Son. He is the Word in that he proceeds from the Mind. 4. For "word" is said by philosophers to be that which issues spontaneously from the mind. 5. He is "the Son," on the other hand, in that he is of the same substance as the Mind whence he comes. 6. The Will, on the other hand, we call "the Holy Spirit," because that is what the prophets called him, just as the Word itself called him. 7. And he is subsequent to the Word because in terms of going forth he follows the Word. 8. And he is defined and characterized as spirit by the Word.

17 1. This is the Trinity in which we believe. These three, however, are the one God because their substance is numerically one. 2. On the other hand, we say that the three are properties, arising not from their definition but from the nature of their reality. 3. But there is no need for surprise if these things are shown on the basis of physics. 4. For in all things there are images of a single principle, in some to a larger extent, in others to a lesser. 5. And there is nothing in them in which some likeness is not observed. 6. Since, however, Mind is the best and most divine of beings, it is not unreasonable to see in it the best image of God. 7. But this is not why we have come to this divine division. 8. Rather, we received this doctrine from God himself, first through the prophets, then through the Word, and discovered that physics agreed with it.

117. Aristotle, *Metaphysics* 12.8.1074a33–34, 36–37.

18 1. Οὕτως ἡμεῖς καὶ εἰς ἕνα θεὸν ἀληθῶς πιστεύομεν, ὡς ἐκ τῆς κοινῆς ἡμῶν ὁμολογίας φαίνεται, 2. καὶ τὰς τρεῖς ἰδιότητας ὁμολογοῦμεν φυσικὰς οὔσας ἐν τῷ θεῷ, μᾶλλον δὲ αὐτὰ τὸν θεὸν ὄντα.

XL 1 1. **Ὁ Κρατῶν**. Εἰ ταῦτα διακρίσεις ἐπὶ τοῦ ἑνὸς οἴεσθε θεοῦ, ἔφη, τί δήποτε μὴ καὶ τ᾽ ἄλλα τὰ ἐν αὐτῷ θεωρούμενα συναριθμεῖτε; 2. οὐ γὰρ λόγος μόνον ἔστιν ἐν αὐτῷ καὶ θέλησις (αὐτὸς δέ ἐστι νοῦς), ἀλλὰ καὶ οὐσία καὶ ἀγαθότης καὶ ἀλήθεια καὶ ζωὴ καὶ ἕτερα πλείω. 3. τί δὴ οὖν οὐ πάντα ταῦτα συναριθμεῖτε; καίτοι οὐδὲν ἧττον ταῦτα ἐκείνων | 102v εἰσὶν ἐν τῷ θεῷ. 4. ἔνια δὲ καὶ μᾶλλον αὐτῷ ἀποδοτέα, τὸ εἶναι καὶ τὴν ἀγαθότητα καὶ τὴν ἀλήθειαν. 5. εἰ οὖν καὶ ταῦτά τις κατὰ τὸ εἰκὸς ἀριθμοίη, οὐκ εἰς τριάδα, 6. ἀλλ᾽ εἰς δεκάδα ἴσως ἔσεσθε πιστεύοντες. ἀλλὰ πολὺς λῆρος ἐκ τοιούτων πεπεῖσθαι.

2 1. Πρὸς δέ, οὐδὲ ἀληθές ἐστι τὸ τὸν θεὸν νοῦν τυγχάνει. 2. ἄρρητον γὰρ καὶ ἀκατωνόμαστον τὸ θεῖον ὅτι μόνον ἔστι γινωσκόμενον. τί δέ ἐστι, καθάπαξ ἀγνοούμενον. 3. οὔτε νοῦν τοίνυν οὔτε ἀγαθὸν οὔτ᾽ ἄλλο τῶν ὄντων οὐδὲν ἔστιν ἀληθῶς εἰπεῖν τὸν θεόν. 4. ἀλλὰ ταῦτα πάντα λέγεται ὑφ᾽ ἡμῶν ἀπὸ τῶν | 103r ἐνεργειῶν αὐτοῦ. 5. οὔκουν ἔστιν αὐτὰ καὶ ἐπὶ τῆς θείας οὐσίας τιθέναι ἢ καθ᾽ αὐτὰ προσόντα τῷ ζώῳ τῆς θείας οὐσίας κατηγορήσομεν ὅτι καὶ ζωὴ λέγεται εἶναι ἐν τῷ θεῷ. 6. καίτοι καὶ εἰ νοῦς ἦν, ἥ γε νόησις αὐτοῦ τῆς αὐτῆς οὐσίας οὐκ ἂν ἦν. 7. ἀλλ᾽ εἰ μὲν ὑφίστατο, ἔργον ἂν αὐτοῦ ἦν, καθάπερ τὰ λοιπὰ ὄντα. οὐ γὰρ ἐνδέχεται ταὐτὸν εἶναι τό τε δι᾽ αὐτὸ ὂν καὶ τὸ δι᾽ ἕτερον. 8. εἰ δὲ μὴ ὑφίστατο, συμβεβηκός. τοῦτο δὲ ταὐτὸν εἶναι τῇ οὐσίᾳ, καθάπαξ ἀμήχανον. 9. τὸ αὐτὸ δέ ἐστι καὶ περὶ τῆς θελήσεως εἰπεῖν.

3 1. Πολλὰ οὖν μωρία τοιαῦτα πιστεύειν. ἄμεινον δὲ καὶ ἀληθέστερον | 103v ἄρρητον τὸ θεῖον εἰδότες καὶ ἀνενόητον ὅτι ἔστι μόνον τιθέναι. 2. καὶ ὅσα αὐτὸν ἐνεργοῦντα δείκνυσι, περὶ δὲ τῆς οὐσίας αὐτοῦ μὴ δ᾽ ἐπιχειρεῖν τί, μήτε εἰπεῖν, μήτε λογίσασθαι. 3. ὑμεῖς δ᾽ ἐοίκατε καὶ τὴν οὐσίαν αὐτὴν οἰομένοις εἰδέναι καὶ τὸν θεὸν αὐτόν, 4. ὃ τίς ἂν ἀνάσχοιτο λεγόντων ἀκούειν βουλόμενος εὐσεβεῖν;

XLI 1 1. **Ὁ Φιλόσοφος**. Τὸν θεόν, ἔφην ἐγώ, νοῦν τε εἶναι καὶ λόγον ἔχειν καὶ θέλησιν ἐξ ἀνάγκης φαμέν. 2. οὐδὲν δὲ ἧττον ἐν αὐτῷ καὶ ἀγαθότητα εἶναι

---

11 ἔσεσθε] ἔσεσθαι corr. T^1 **13** ἀκατωνόμαστον] sic T **21** ταὐτὸν] ταυτὸν T
24 εἰδότες] ad εἰδότας mut. T^1 **28** Ὁ Φιλόσοφος] in marg. scr. T

18 1. Thus we truly believe in the one God, which, it would seem, is a belief we share in common, 2. and we affirm that there are three natural properties in God, and still further that they are each God.

XL 1 1. **The Conqueror.** If you think, he said, that these are divisions in the one God, why in fact do you not count similarly the other things that are seen in him? 2. For not only are word and will in him (he is, after all, Mind), but he is also substance, goodness, truth, life, and many other things. 3. Why do you not similarly count all these things? Indeed, they are no less in God than your three. 4. Some should be ascribed even more so to God, namely, being, goodness, and truth. 5. If one counts these, as is reasonable, then you will by the same measure believe not in a trinity, 6. but in a decady. But such talk produces belief in a heap of nonsense.

2 1. Furthermore, it is not true that God is Mind. 2. For the divine is ineffable and nameless. This is the only thing we know. What the divine is, however, is utterly unknown. 3. God, in fact, is not truly said to be either Mind, goodness, or any other thing. 4. We instead say all these things on the basis of his actions. 5. They should therefore not be attributed to the divine substance, nor should we predicate of the divine substance things that in themselves are appropriate to a living being just because life is said to be in God. 6. Indeed, if God were Mind, his thought would not be of the same substance [as God]. 7. Rather, if his thought were to exist as a substance, it would be his product, just like everything else. For the same thing can never be both self-caused and caused by another. 8. If, however, it does not exist as a substance, it is an accident. But it is [supposed to be] the same thing as substance. This is a completely indefensible position. 9. The same point holds concerning will.

3 1. You believe many such imbecilities, then. Better and truer, on the other hand, is the position of those who know that the deity is ineffable and inconceivable, since that is the only thing that should be posited. 2. And whatever actions they point to as his, they do not attempt to offer any explanation about his substance, speak about it, or make logical inferences about it. 3. You, on the other hand, seem to be like those people who think they know his very substance and even know God himself. 4. Would anyone wishing to be pious be able to bear to listen to people who claim this?

XLI 1 1. **The Philosopher.** We affirm, I said, that God necessarily is Mind and has word and will. 2. We further affirm that to no less a degree there is in

καὶ ἀλήθειαν καὶ ζωὴν καὶ τὰ ἄλλα ὅσα ἁπλῶς αὐτοῦ καὶ ἀπολελυμένως κατηγο-
ροῦμεν. 3. ἀλλὰ διαφορὰν ἐν | τούτοις ὁρῶμεν οὐ μικράν, οὐδ᾽ οἵαν ὑπεριδεῖν 104r
ἀκίνδυνον. 4. τὰ μὲν γὰρ αὐτὸν ἀληθῶς ἐν αὑτῷ διακρίνει· ὅ τε λόγος καὶ ἡ
θέλησις. 5. οὐ γάρ ἐστιν ὁ νοῦς παντάπασιν ὁ λόγος αὐτοῦ, οὐδὲ ἡ θέλησις, ἀλλ᾽
οὐδὲ ταῦτα, ᾗ τοιαῦτα ἐνδέχεται, εἶναι τὸν νοῦν. 6. διακέκριται δὲ ἀπ᾽ ἀλλήλων
καὶ οὐκ ἂν συνέλθοιεν, ᾗ τοιαῦτα ἤδη ἐστί. 7. τὰ δὲ οὔτε τὸν θεὸν ἐν ἑαυτῷ
διακρίνει οὔτε αὐτοῦ διακρίνεται. 8. ἡ γὰρ ἀγαθότης πῶς ἂν αὐτὸν διακρίνοι ἢ ἡ
ἀλήθεια ἢ ἡ ζωή; 9. οὐκ ἔστιν ἐπινοῆσαι ὅτι αὐτὸς ‹οὔκ› ἐστιν ἡ ἀγαθότης αὐτοῦ
καὶ ἡ ἀλήθεια καὶ ἡ ζωὴ καὶ ὅσα τοῦτον τρόπον αὐτοῦ κατηγοροῦμεν. | 10. καὶ 104v
οὔκ ἐστιν ἐν αὐτῷ ἕτερον μὲν τὸ οἷον συγκεκριμένον, ἕτερον δὲ τὸ οἷον ἀφαιρε-
ματικόν, 11. ἀλλὰ «τὸ αὐτὸ ἀγαθόν τε καὶ ἀγαθῷ εἶναι καὶ ‹. . .› ὂν καὶ ὄντι εἶναι»
καὶ ἐπὶ τῶν ἄλλων ὡσαύτως, ὥς φησιν ὁ φιλόσοφος ἐν τῷ ζ´ Μετὰ τὰ Φυσικά·
12. εἰ γὰρ ἦν ἄλλο τι, οὔτ᾽ ἂν ἁπλοῦς ἦν οὔτ᾽ ἂν τὸ ὑποκείμενον καθ᾽ αὐτὸ ἦν,
ὅπερ ἐκεῖνα. 13. ἀλλ᾽ ἦν ἂν ἡ τοῦ θεοῦ σοφία καθ᾽ αὑτήν, οὐκ ἀγαθή· καὶ ἦν ἂν
ἐν αὐτῷ ὃ οὐκ ἦν. †ἀλήθεια καὶ ἀληθές† 14. ἀλλὰ τοιαῦτα οὐ θέμις εἰπεῖν ἐπὶ
θεοῦ.

3 γὰρ] supra lin. scr. T **13** ἄλλο τι] ἀλλότι T **14** ἐκεῖνα] signum supra scr. sed deinde del. T^{1} || ἀλλ᾽ . . . ἀγαθή] lineam sub scr. T^{1}; in marg. scr.: γράφεται· οὐσία, deinde signum (†), et in infima pagina annot.: γράφεται· ἀλλ᾽ ἦνἂν ἡ τοῦ θεοῦ οὐσία καθ᾽ αὑτήν, οὐκ ἀγαθὴ οὔτε σοφή (sc. substituendo οὐσία pro σοφία et addendo οὔτε σοφή post ἀγαθὴ) || σοφία] in marg. scr. T^{1} et annot.: γράφεται· οὐσία

him goodness, truth, life and the other things that we predicate of him absolutely and unconditionally. 3. But between these [two categories of] things we see no small difference, which we ignore at our peril. 4. For there are in him things that truly divide him. These things are word and mind. 5. For his mind is not altogether his word nor his will; neither of them, insofar as such things are possible, is his mind. 6. They are distinct from each other and could not unite insofar as they are already what they are. 7. The other things, on the other hand, do not divide God in himself nor are they distinct from him. 8. For how would goodness divide him, or how would truth or life? 9. It is not possible to think that he is <not> his goodness and his truth and his life and whatever else we similarly predicate of him. 10. And there is in him not one thing that can be combined and another that can be separated out. 11. Rather there is "goodness itself and being good, and existence itself and being existent," and similarly for the other things, as the philosopher says in book 7 of the *Metaphysics*.[118] 12. For if they were something other [than he], then he would not be simple; nor would he have his own separate substantive existence, which is what these things would have. 13. Rather, if God's wisdom existed in itself, it would not be good; and there would be in him what he is not. †This is neither the truth nor truthful†.[119] 14. But it is impious to say such things about God.

118. Aristotle, *Metaphysics* 7.6.1031a31–b1. Tredennick translates the whole passage as "For if the Ideal Good is to be different from the essence of good, and the Ideal Animal and Being from the essence of animal and being. . . ." Ross translates the passage as "If the essence of good is to be different from good-itself, and the essence of animal from animal-itself, and the essence of being from being-itself . . ."

119. The text seems corrupt here. In T, the corrector T^1 tried to emend the corruption by changing the preceding clauses to read (I retain the punctuation of T^1): "[which is what these things would have], but that would be the substance of God, in itself being neither good nor wise," which does not make much sense. Acciaiuoli's Latin translation agrees with the text of T^1 and tries to make sense of it (*sed divina substantia nec bona per seipsam esset nec sapiens essetque in Deo quippiam quod nec veritas esset nec verum*), but at the price of completely omitting the sentence "and there would be in him what he is not" (καὶ ἦν ἂν ἐν αὐτῷ ὃ οὐκ ἦν) between "would not be good" (οὐκ ἀγαθή) and "This is neither the truth or truthful" (ἀλήθεια καὶ ἀληθές).

2 1. Ἔτι τὸ συγκεκριμένον οὐκ ἔστιν εἰπεῖν ὅπερ τὸ ἀφαιρεματικὸν εἰ μὴ ταὐτὸν ἐκείνῳ | καθάπαξ εἴη. 2. ἀλλ᾿ ὁ θεὸς οὐ μόνον ἀγαθὸς λέγεται, ὅπέρ 105r ἐστιν οἷον συγκεκριμένον, ἀλλὰ καὶ ἀγαθότης· 3. καὶ ὅπερ ἀγαθότης ἢ αὐτὴ ἀγαθότης ἢ αὐτοαγαθότης, ὅπερ ἐστὶν οἷον ἀφαιρεματικόν. 4. ταὐτὸν ἄρά ἐστιν ὁ θεὸς καὶ ἡ ἀγαθότης αὐτοῦ καὶ ἡ ἀλήθεια καὶ ἡ ζωή. φανερὸν τοίνυν ὅτι τὰ μὲν τοιαῦτα οὐ διακρίνεται τοῦ θεοῦ, ἀλλ᾿ ἔστιν αὐτὰ ὁ θεός.

3 1. Ἡ δὲ κατηγορία καὶ τὸ συγκεκριμένον ἀπὸ τοῦ ἡμετέρου λόγου συμβαίνει, ὃ δεῖ μὴ ἀγνοεῖν. 2. ὁ δὲ λόγος καὶ ἡ θέλησις καὶ τοῦ νοῦ διακρίνεται καὶ ἀλλήλων. 3. ἔτι ὁ μὲν λόγος καὶ ἡ θέλησις προΐασιν ἀπὸ τοῦ νοῦ καὶ ἔστιν αὐτὸς | 105v ἐκείνων ἀρχή. 4. ἡ δὲ ἀγαθότης καὶ τὰ τοιαῦτα ἃ τοῦ θεοῦ κατηγοροῦμεν οὐδαμῶς. 5. ἀλλ᾿ ἔστιν αὐτός. ἕτερα ἄρα ἐκεῖνα τούτων ἐστὶ καὶ οὐ ταὐτά. 6. διὰ ταῦτα οὐ πολλὰς ἰδιότητας ἐν τῷ θεῷ φαμέν, ἀλλὰ τρεῖς μόνον, αἳ ἀληθῶς εἰσιν ἐν αὐτῷ καί εἰσι ταῦτα καὶ ταὐτὰ καὶ ἕτερα. 7. ταὐτὰ μὲν ὅτι οὐ διαφέρουσι κατὰ τὴν οὐσίαν. ὁ γὰρ νοῦς καὶ ὁ λόγος αὐτοῦ καὶ ἡ θέλησις μιᾶς οὐσίας εἰσὶν. 8. ἕτερα δὲ ᾗ τὸ μὲν προΐησι, τὰ δὲ πρόεισιν ἐξ αὐτοῦ. καὶ τοῦτό ἐστιν ἡμῖν ὁ εἷς

3 ὅπερ] in marg. annot. T[1]: σημείωσαι· ὅπερ || αὐτὴ] αὐτή corr. T/T[1] **4** αὐτοαγαθότης] αὐτοἀγαθότης T; signum coniunctionis sub αὐτο et ἀγαθότης scr. T[1] || ταὐτὸν] ταυτὸν T **5** ὁ θεὸς] ἡ θ... (rasura) corr. T[1] **7** συγκεκριμένον] συκεγριμένον corr. T[1] **11** ταὐτά] ταυτά T **12** ταῦτα] ταυτὰ T **15** πρόεισιν] ad προίασιν mut. T[1]

2 1. Moreover, a concrete entity[120] cannot be said to be what is abstracted unless the latter is completely identical with the concrete entity.[121] 2. But God is said not only to be good, which any concrete entity can be, but also goodness. 3. And what is goodness is either pure goodness or goodness in itself, both of which can be abstracted. 4. God, therefore, is the same thing as his goodness, his truth, and his life. Clearly, then, these things are not divided from God, but rather God is them.

3 1. The [concepts of] category and concrete entity are products of our reason, which is something we need to recognize. 2. Word and will, on the other hand, are distinct from the mind and from each other. 3. Furthermore, word and will proceed from the mind, and the mind is their principle. 4. Goodness and other such things which we predicate of God are in no way principles. 5. Rather, he is their principle. Therefore, the former [sc., mind, word, and will] are different from these latter, and not the same as they. 6. Hence we say that there are not many properties in God, but only three, which truly are in him, and these are the same and different [from each other]. 7. They are the same because they do not differ in substance. For his mind, word, and will belong to a sole substance. 8. They are different, on the other hand, insofar as mind sends forth

120. The use of the perfect middle participle συγκεκριμένον to mean "concrete entity" seems to have emerged in late Byzantium, probably because of the need Demetrius Cydones had in translating the numerous forms of *concretum* in Thomas Aquinas's *Summa theologiae, Summa contra gentiles*, and *Quaestiones de potentia* (see n. 121). According to the TLG, συγκεκριμένον is not found in this sense in antiquity; the earliest attested examples in the TLG are the writings of George Scholarius, who uses this word frequently; see *Oeuvres complètes*, vol. 6, s.v. συγκεκριμένον, -μένα, -μέναι, -μένη, μένην, and -μένως. For instance, he translated Thomas Aquinas, *De ente et essentia* 6.39, *ideo in substantiis nomina concreta quae compositum significant*, as (George Scholarius, *Oeuvres complètes*, 6:175.32–33) διὰ τοῦτο ἐν ταῖς ὀσίαις τὰ συγκεκριμένα ὀνόματα, ἅπερ εἰσί; and *Unde nomina accidentalia concretive dicta non ponuntur in praedicamento sicut species vel genera* as (ibid., 176.3–4) Ὅθεν τὰ τοῦ συμβεβηκότος ὀνόματα συγκεριμένως οὐ τίθενται ἐν κατηγορίᾳ ὡς εἴδη ἢ ὡς γένη.

121. Cf. Thomas Aquinas, *Summa theologiae*, 1.31.1: *in omnibus quae dicuntur de deo, concretum praedicatur de abstracto. Deitas enim est deus*; ibid., 1.40.1: *in divinis idem est abstractum et concretum, ut deitas et deus*; ibid., 1.40.2: *in divinis non differt abstractum et concretum*; *De potentia*, 8.3: *abstractum et concretum in divinis non differunt* (cf. also 2.7). Cf. also *Scriptum super libros Sententiarum* 1.33.1.2, 3.4.2.2; *Sententia super Metaphysicam* 7.5.25; and *Contra errores Graecorum* 1.4

θεὸς καὶ αὖθις αἱ τρεῖς ἰδιότητες.

4 1. Ἀλλ᾽ ἐπὶ τὸ λοιπὸν τῆς ἀντιθέσεως ἰτέον. ἔφης γὰρ μὴ δεῖν | τὸν θεὸν 106r
ὀνομάζειν ἀνενόητον ὄντα καὶ ἀκατάληπτον, μηδὲ κατηγορεῖν αὐτοῦ μηδέν, 2. ἀλλὰ τὰ κατηγορούμενα δὴ ταῦτα τὴν ἐνέργειαν αὐτοῦ μόνον σημαίνειν. 3. αὐτῆς δὲ τῆς οὐσίας οὐ θέμις τι κατηγορεῖν ὥστε μὴ δὲ νοῦν αὐτὸν ἀληθῶς εἶναι, μὴ δὲ νόησιν ἔχειν ἢ θέλησιν. 4. ὅτι μὲν οὖν ἡ τοῦ θεοῦ οὐσία, ᾗ ἔστι καθ᾽ αὑτήν, ἄρρητος τυγχάνει καὶ ἀνενόητος καὶ ἀκατάληπτος, οὐδεὶς ἀντερεῖ. θεὸν γὰρ οὐδεὶς ἑώρακε πώποτε. 5. καὶ ὅτι μὴ δ᾽ ὑπάρχειν τι τῇ θείᾳ οὐσίᾳ ἐνδέχεται. 6. οὐ γάρ ἐστιν ὑποκείμενον οὐδενὸς πράγματος ὅτι μὴ ἔστιν ἐν αὐτῷ | ἄλλο τι 106v
παρὰ τὴν οἰκείαν οὐσίαν. 7. ἀλλ᾽ ἔστι καθάπαξ ἁπλοῦς καὶ ἀσύνθετος. καὶ ἓν αὐτὸ ὅ τι ποτε ὄν. 8. ὅτι δὲ αὖθις αὐτός ἐστι τὸ κυρίως ἀγαθόν, καὶ ὂν καὶ ἀληθὲς καὶ ζωή, ἔτι δὲ μᾶλλον ἀγαθότης καὶ οὐσία καὶ ἀλήθεια καὶ ζωὴ αὐτή. 9. τὰ δ᾽ ἄλλα οὐ κυρίως, ἀλλὰ κατὰ μετοχὴν ἢ ἀναλογικῶς οὔτ᾽ ἀγνοεῖν οὔτε μὴ δοξάζειν προσήκει. 10. ἥ τε γὰρ ἱερὰ ἀλήθεια ταῦτα φησὶ περὶ αὐτοῦ καὶ ἡ φιλοσοφία συνᾴδει καὶ αἱ κοιναὶ περὶ τοῦ θείου ἔννοιαι, οἷς ἀπιστεῖν οὐ θέμις. 11. ἐπεὶ τοίνυν καὶ ἄμφω περὶ τοῦ θεοῦ λέγεται ὑπό τε ἱερῶν ἀνδρῶν καὶ τῆς σε|μνοτάτης φιλοσοφίας, διαιτητοῦ δεῖ, ἀλλ᾽ οὐκ ἀντιδίκου, ᾗ ταῦτα συμβαίνει 107r
πειρωμένου εὑρεῖν, καὶ μὴ τὰ μὲν ἐγκρίνειν, τὰ δὲ ὡς ἀλλότρια ἐλαύνειν. 12. οἱ γὰρ αὐτὰ καὶ ἄμφω εἰρήκασιν. οὔκουν ἔστι τὰ μὲν αὐτῶν ἀποδοκιμάζειν, τὰ δὲ προσίεσθαι. 13. οὐ γὰρ ἔστι συμφωνεῖν τῇ ἀληθείᾳ τοὺς αἱρουμένους θάτερα· ἀλλ᾽ ὁπότερα ἄν τις ἕλοιτο, ἐκπίπτειν ἀνάγκη ταύτης.

5 1. Φαμὲν ὅτι τὸ θεῖον ὃ μέν ἐστι καθ᾽ αὑτὸ καὶ ᾗ ποτε ὂν τυγχάνει ἀνενόητον ἐστὶ καὶ ἄρρητον ἀληθῶς. 2. μόνον δὲ αὐτὸ αὑτὸ οἶδε ὅ τι ποτ᾽ ἐστὶ καθ᾽ αὑτό. 3. ὃ δὲ ἔστιν ἡμῖν | ᾗ αἰτία καὶ ἀρχὴ τῶν ὄντων ἐστὶν καὶ ἴσμεν καὶ ὀνομά- 107v
ζομεν, 4. καὶ ὅπως εἰδῶμεν τὰ πολλὰ ταῦτα καὶ διάφορα εἴδη παραγαγεῖν τὸν θεόν. 5. οὐ γὰρ χρείας ἕνεκα τὰ πολλὰ ταῦτα παρήχθη, οὐδὲ διὰ τὸ τὴν ὕλην ταῦτα δυνάμει πάντα εἶναι, ὥς τινες ἐνόμισαν, 6. ἀλλ᾽ ἵνα τέλειον ὡς ἐνδέχεται

---

6 ὅτι] signum paragraphi ante scr. T[1] **13** κυρίως] in marg. annot. T[1]: παρὰ τὸν θεὸν || κατὰ μετοχὴν] καταμετοχὴν T **24** αὐτό] finis translationis Acciaiuoli in edd. de la Cruz Palma et Argyriou-Lagarrigue et initium in ed. Monfasani

and the other two proceed from it. And this is for us the one God and, in turn, his three properties.

4 1. But let us turn to the rest of the counterargument. For you said that we ought not name God since he is unnamable and ungraspable, nor should we predicate anything of him; 2. instead, the things that we have predicated of him only signify his action. 3. You say it is impious, moreover, to predicate anything of his substance, and so he really is not mind and does not have thought or will. 4. No one will deny that God's substance, as it is in itself, is ineffable, unthinkable, and ungraspable. For no one has ever seen God. 5. And no one will deny that it is impossible for anything to happen to the divine substance. 6. For God is not the subject of anything,[122] since there is not in him anything other than his own substance. 7. Rather, he is absolutely simple and uncombined. And he is One itself, whatever that exactly is. 8. Since, however, he is in turn eminently the good, he is also both truth and life; still more, he is goodness, substance, truth, and life itself. 9. But it is wrong not to know or to teach that he is not the other things in an eminent way, but is them by participation or analogy. 10. For sacred truth make these assertions about him, and philosophy agrees, as do also common notions concerning divinity, which to disbelieve would be impious. 11. Since both things[123] then are said about God by the saints and by the noblest philosophy, we need not an opponent, but an arbiter who seeks to discover how these two positions agree and does not endorse one while rejecting the other. 12. For sacred truth and philosophy have stated both. Therefore, we should not repudiate one and accept the other. 13. For they who choose one side or the other do not agree with truth. Rather, if one opts for one or the other, one will necessarily mistake the truth.

5 1. We affirm that the divine is what is in itself and that it is truly unthinkable and ineffable, whatever it may be. 2. Only it itself knows whatever it is in itself. 3. It is, however, accessible to us insofar as we recognize and name it the cause and principle of things, 4. so that we understand that God created the multitude of things and their different forms. 5. For this multitude was created not out of need nor because matter is potentially all things, as some think, 6. but in order that the world might have as perfect a definition as possible of its archetypal

122. I.e., the subject of any predicate.

123. I.e., that he is one and that he is these other things.

τὸν τῆς εἰκόνος λόγον ὁ κόσμος ἔχῃ καὶ ὁ τούτου θεωρὸς ἄνθρωπος εἰκόνων μὴ
ἀπορῇ, ἀλλ᾽ ἔχῃ δαψιλῆ ὅθεν ἂν ἐπὶ τὴν θείαν ἀρχὴν ἀνίοι. 7. ἐπεὶ τοίνυν ὁ θεὸς
αἰτία καὶ ἀρχὴ τῶν ὄντων ἐστίν, ἀνάγκη τὰ ὄντα πάντα ἐοικέναι πῃ αὐτῷ καὶ
εἶναι αὐτοῦ εἰκόνας. 8. πᾶν γὰρ τὸ παράγον | παράγει ἐοικὸς ὁπωσοῦν ἑαυτῷ εἰ 108r
μὴ κατὰ συμβεβηκὸς αἴτιον εἴη. 9. ὃ δὲ ἐν τοῖς αἰτιατοῖς εὑρίσκεται, τελειότης
αὐτῶν ὄν, ἀνάγκη τοῦτο αὐτοῖς ἀπὸ τῆς αἰτίας ἥκειν, 10. διότι τὸ εἶναι τούτων
ὅλον ἐστὶν ἐκεῖθεν. ἡ δὲ τελειότης ἐστὶν ἀπὸ τοῦ εἶναι. ἀνάγκη τοίνυν τὴν
τελειότητα αὐτοῖς ἀπὸ τῆς αἰτίας ἥκειν. 11. ἔτι ταύτην αὐτοῖς οὔτε ἐξ αὐτομάτου
ἐνδέχεται εἶναι οὔτε οἴκοθεν, οὖσί γε ἀφ᾽ ἑτέρου. λείπεται δὴ ἀπὸ τῆς αἰτίας.
12. ὃ δὲ ἐν τοῖς αἰτιατοῖς ἀπὸ τῆς αἰτίας ἥκει, ἀνάγκη πρῶτον τῇ αἰτίᾳ ὑπάρχειν.
13. ἀλλ᾽ εἰ μὴ συνώνυμα εἴη, οὐ τὸν αὐτὸν τρόπον, ἀλλὰ τῇ μὲν αἰτίᾳ ἀρχικῶς ἢ
παραδειγματικῶς, τοῖς δὲ ἐξ αὐτῆς οὖσι ἀναλογικῶς καὶ ὑφειμένως. | 14. ἐπεὶ 108v
τοίνυν πάντων τῶν ὄντων ἀρχὴ καὶ αἰτία ἐστὶν ὁ θεός, ἀνάγκη τὰς τούτων
τελειότητας ἐκεῖθέν τε εἶναι. 15. καὶ αὐτὴ πρῶτον καθ᾽ αὑτὸ ὑπάρχειν καὶ ἐν
αὐτῇ μὲν ἰδέας εἶναι καὶ παραδείγματα. 16. ἐν δὲ τοῖς οὖσιν εἰκόνας καὶ ὁμοιώ-
ματα· καὶ ἐν μὲν τοῖς αἰτιατοῖς διῃρημένως, ἐν δὲ τῇ πρώτῃ ἀρχῇ ἑνιαίως. 17. οὐ
γάρ εἰσιν ἐκεῖ πολλά, ἀλλ᾽ ἐκεῖνο τὸ ἓν ὅ τί ποτέ ἐστιν ἡ θεία οὐσία. 18. πάντα
τυγχάνει ἑνοειδῶς, τὸ δὲ πλῆθος ἐξ ἡμῶν αὐτῇ πρόσεστιν. 19. ἃ γὰρ αὐτοὶ
διῃρημένως νοοῦμεν, ἴδιον ἑκάστου λόγον ἀποδιδόντες, ἅτε μὴ δυνάμενοι τὰ
πολλὰ ἑνικῶς θεωρεῖν. 20. ταῦτα τῆς | θείας οὐσίας κατηγοροῦμεν. ἴσμεν δὲ 109r
ὅμως ὅτι τὰ πολλὰ ταῦτα ἐκεῖ ἑνικῶς ἔστιν. 21. εἰ καὶ ἀγνοοῦμεν πῶς τοῦτο
ἐνδέχεται, μὴ δὲ μίαν ἐν τοῖς οὖσιν ὅθεν ἐπὶ τὴν κατάληψιν ἀφικνούμεθα τοῦ
θείου τοιαύτην εὑρεῖν εἰκόνα δυνάμενοι. 22. οὐ γὰρ ἦν κτίσμά τι τὰς τελειότητας
ἁπάσας χωρεῖν. καὶ εἰ ἐνῆν δέ, οὐκ ἂν ἑνοειδῶς αὐτῇ ταῦτα προσῆν, ὅτι τὸ εἶναι
τούτων διαφέρειν ἦν ἀνάγκη τῆς οὐσίας καὶ μὴ ταὐτὸν εἶναι. 23. ἐκ δὴ τῶν
εἰρημένων ἁπάντων τ᾽ ἐκεῖνο φαίνεται, ὅτι πᾶν ὅπέρ ἐστι τελειότητος ἐν τοῖς
οὖσιν ἀρχικῶς ἔστιν ἐν τῷ θεῷ. 24. διὰ ταῦτα τοίνυν αὐτὸν | καὶ ὀνομάζομεν καὶ 109v

---

4 εἰκόνας] εἰκόνες corr. T[1] **9** ἐνδέχεται . . . οἴκοθεν] in marg. scr. T **25** ταὐτὸν] ταὐτῶν corr. T/T[1]

image, and in order that when man contemplates the world, he will not want for archetypal images, but will have an abundance of them whence he might proceed upward to the divine principle. 7. Since God, then, is the cause and principle of beings, all beings must resemble him in some way and be images of him. 8. For every creator creates a thing in some way similar to itself, if it is not the cause accidentally. 9. This resemblance, however, which is found in creatures, because it is a perfection of theirs, necessarily reaches them from their cause, 10. because their whole being comes from this source. And their perfection comes from their being. Necessarily, therefore, their perfection comes from their cause. 11. Furthermore, this perfection can neither spontaneously happen to them nor arise from their own resources, since they themselves derive from another. We are left to conclude that it comes from their cause. 12. But what comes to creatures from their cause necessarily first exists in the cause. 13. But if they are not just synonyms, those things that are in both do not exist in the same way, but rather principally and paradigmatically in the cause while analogously and secondarily in its creatures. 14. Since, therefore, God is the first principle and cause of all beings, the perfections in things necessarily derive from him. 15. What is primary is that the first principle exists by its own essence and that the ideas and the paradigms are in it. 16. In creatures, on the other hand, images and likenesses are found. In creatures, things exist discretely; in the First Principle, however, they exist as a unity. 17. For in the First Principle there are no multiple things, but just that one thing which is whatever the divine substance is. 18. In it everything exists as a radical unity. Multiplicity, on the other hand, is present in it from our perspective. 19. For we think of things discretely, in that we take into account the peculiar definition of each thing and are not capable of conceptualizing the many as unity. 20. It is these things that we predicate of the divine substance. We know, nonetheless, that these many things are there [in the First Principle] as a unity. 21. And if we do not understand how this is possible, it is because we are incapable of catching in creatures a glimpse of that one great image of God through which we could arrive at this understanding. 22. For a creature cannot possess all the perfections. And if it were possible, the perfections would not be present in a radical unity, since their existence is necessarily other than their essence, not the same. 23. For all the aforesaid reasons it is clear, then, that whatever perfection exists in creatures exists principally in God. 24. This, then, is why we name him as good and call him being, what is true, and

ἀγαθὸν καὶ ὂν καλοῦμεν καὶ ἀληθὲς καὶ πάντα τὰ τοιαῦτα, καὶ τούτων ἕκαστον ἁπλῶς ὅπερ αὐτὸ τυγχάνει, οὐχ ὅπερ αὐτὸ τί.

6 1. Νοῦν ἄρα τὸν ἄριστον λέγοντες τὸν θεὸν εἰκότως οὕτω καλοῦμεν. καὶ λόγος ἔστιν ἐν αὐτῷ καὶ θέλησις. 2. ἡ μὲν οὖν κατηγορία οὕτως ἀποδίδοται τῷ θεῷ καὶ οὕτως ἐστὶν ἐν αὐτῷ. 3. ἡ δὲ ἀπόφασις ταύτην οὐκ ἀναιρεῖ ᾗ ἔστιν ἐν τῷ θεῷ, ἀλλ᾽ ᾗ γινώσκεται ὑφ᾽ ἡμῶν. 4. ἃ γὰρ αὐτοὶ ἐννοοῦμεν ᾗ τοιαῦτα οὐχ ἁρμόζει τῇ θείᾳ οὐσίᾳ. διότι ὁ ἡμέτερος νοῦς ἀπὸ τῶν αἰσθητῶν αὐτὰ ἀφαιρεῖται.
5. | οἷον οὖν ἐν τοῖς κτίσμασιν ἕκαστον νοοῦμεν τοιοῦτον τῇ θείᾳ περιάπτομεν 110r
φύσει. 6. καὶ διὰ τοῦτο ἄρρητον λέγεται καὶ ἀνενόητον καὶ ἀκατάληπτον. 7. ὧν μέντοι ταῦτα εἰκόνες ἀνάγκη τὸν θεὸν ἀληθῶς εἶναι, ὥστε ἡ μὲν κατάφασις αὐτῷ ἁρμόζει ᾗ ἐν αὐτῷ ἐστι τὸ κατηγορούμενον, 8. ἡ δὲ ἀπόφασις ᾗ νοεῖται ὑφ᾽ ἡμῶν καὶ ᾗ εἴληπται ἀπὸ τῶν αἰσθητῶν. 9. ἡ μέντοι σύνθεσις τοῦ ὑποκειμένου καὶ κατηγορουμένου τοῦ ἡμετέρου λόγου ἐστὶ μόνου. οὗπερ ἐστὶ καὶ τὸ πλῆθος.
10. ἐκεῖ δὲ τὸ ὑποκείμενον, ὅπερ τὸ κατηγορούμενον | ἐστί, καὶ τὸ πλῆθος 110v
συνῄρηται εἰς τὸ ἕν. καὶ περὶ μὲν τούτων τοσαῦτα.

7 1. Τὸ δὲ ἀπὸ τῶν ἐνεργειῶν μόνον τὸν θεὸν ὀνομάζεσθαι ἀληθὲς μέν ἐστιν. οὐ μὴν ἀναιρεῖ τὸν θεὸν ἀληθῶς ταῦτα ἃ λέγεται εἶναι. 2. ἃ γὰρ τῆς θείας οὐσίας κατηγοροῦμεν ἡμεῖς ἀπὸ τῶν ἔργων αὐτῆς εἴληπται. 3. ἀνάγκη μέντοι τούτοις ἀνταποκρίνασθαί τι καθ᾽ αὐτὸ προσὸν τῷ θεῷ. 4. τούτων δὲ τὸ μὲν ἰδέα τυγχάνει καὶ παράδειγμα, καὶ τοῦτο αὐτὸ ὃ λέγεται εἶναι· τὸ δὲ εἰκὼν ἢ εἴδωλον ἐκείνου, πλεῖστον ἀπέχον τοῦ ὃ λέγεται εἶναι. 5. καὶ μὴν οὐδὲ τὴν νόησιν τῆς
πρώτης ἀρχῆς ἐνδέχεται ἢ ἑτέρας οὐσίας | ἢ συμβεβηκὸς εἶναι. 6. διότι ὁ νοῦς 111r
ἐκεῖνος οὐδὲν ἄλλο νοεῖ ἢ ἑαυτόν. δεῖ μὲν γὰρ τὸ ἄριστον καὶ θειότατον νοεῖν καὶ μὴ μεταβάλλειν. 7. τοιοῦτον δὲ μόνος ἐστὶν αὐτός. αὑτὸν ἄρα νοεῖ καὶ μόνον. εἴπερ μὴ μεταβάλλει, ὥστε ταὐτὸν νοῦς καὶ νοητόν, 8. ἀλλ᾽ ἡ νόησίς ἐστιν ὅπερ τὸ νοητόν, ὥσπερ ἡ αἴσθησις ὅπερ τὸ αἰσθητόν. ταὐτὸν ἄρα ἥ τε νόησις καὶ τὸ νοητόν. 9. ἔτι δὲ νοῦς καὶ ταῦτα πάντα διαρρήδην φησὶν Ἀριστοτέλης ἐν τῷ ιβʹ

5 ἔστιν] ἐν ante del. T **8** οὖν] supra lin. scr. T **9** ὧν] οὗ in marg. scr. T^1 **21** εἶναι] in marg. scr. T/T^1 **24** μὴ] supra lin. scr. T^1 **25** ταὐτὸν] ταυτὸν T **26** ταὐτὸν] ταυτὸν T

all other such things, and mean each of them in an absolute sense, as each is in itself, and not as is some particular thing.

6 1. Therefore, when we say that God is the best mind, we have good reason to call him so. In him are also word and will. 2. A category is thus ascribed to God and is thus in him. 3. Denial, however, does not remove the category insofar as it is in God, but insofar as he is known by us. 4. For we ourselves conceive of categories in a way inappropriate to the divine essence. The reason is because our mind abstracts them from sensible things. 5. We then ascribe each of the categories to the divine nature in the same way that we think of them in creatures. 6. This is why God is said to be ineffable, unthinkable, and ungraspable. 7. Necessarily, then, those categories of which things here below are images are truly God. Consequently, their affirmation is appropriate to him insofar as what is predicated is in him, 8. while their negation is appropriate insofar as they are conceived by us and are grasped from sensible objects. 9. The combining of subject and predicate belongs only to our reasoning. To our reasoning also belongs multiplicity. 10. In God, however, the predicated category and multiplicity are brought into unity. But enough about this.

7 1. It is true, however, that God is named only from his actions. This does not eliminate God truly being the things he is said to be. 2. For the things we predicate of the divine essence are taken from its works. 3. Necessarily, then, something in itself, befitting God, corresponds to them. 4. Among these predicates are idea and paradigm, and they are said to be what a thing itself is. But there is also the idea's image or simulacrum, which is the furthest from what a thing is said to be. 5. Indeed, it is not possible for the thought of the First Principle to be other substances or an accident. 6. The reason is that the divine mind thinks nothing other than itself. For it necessarily thinks what is best and most divine, and does not change. 7. But only it itself is such.[124] It therefore thinks only itself. If, in fact, it does not change, then its mind and its thought are the same thing. 8. But thought is what is thought, just as in the same way sensation is what is sensed. Therefore, God's thought and what he thinks are the same thing. 9. Furthermore, Aristotle expressly states in book 12 of the

124. I.e., the best and most divine.

τῶν Μετὰ τὰ Φυσικά. οὐκ ἄρα ἑτέρας οὐσίας εἰσὶν ὅ τε νοῦς καὶ ἡ τούτου
νόησις. 10. ἀλλὰ μὴν οὐδὲ | συμβεβηκὸς ἐνδέχεται τούτου εἶναι. διότι ἡ νόησις 111v
αὐτή ἐστιν ἡ ζωὴ τοῦ νοῦ, ὡς ἐκεῖσέ φησιν ὁ φιλόσοφος. 11. «ἡ γὰρ νοῦ ἐνέργεια
ζωή. ἐκεῖνος δὲ ἡ ἐνέργεια». ἐνέργεια δὲ ἡ καθ᾽ αὑτὴν ἐκείνου ζωὴ ἀρίστη καὶ
ἀΐδιος. 12. ἡ δὲ ἐκείνου ζωὴ οὐκ ἔστι συμβεβηκός. οὔκουν οὐδὲ ἡ νόησις. διακρίνεται δὲ αὐτοῦ ᾗ τὸ μέν ἐστι δι᾽ αὑτοῦ, ἡ δὲ νόησις δι᾽ ἐκείνου. 13. τοῦτο γὰρ
οὐσίας μὲν διαφορὰν οὐ ποιεῖ, ἀριθμὸν δὲ μόνον ἀναφορᾶς. 14. εἰ δὲ οὐσίας
ἐποίει διαφοράν, ἦν ἂν ἑαυτοῦ ἕτερον ὁ νοῦς, εἴπερ αὐτός ἐστιν ἡ νόησις αὑτοῦ,
ὅπερ ἀδύνατον. 15. τὰ αὐτὰ δέ ἔστιν εἰπεῖν | καὶ περὶ τῆς θελήσεως ὅτι ἀνάγκη 112r
εἶναι θέλησιν ἐν τῷ θεῷ. καὶ διακρίνεσθαι αὐτοῦ καὶ τοῦ λόγου τῷ ἀριθμῷ. καὶ
εἶναι τῆς αὐτῆς οὐσίας παντάπασιν αὐτοῖς. 16. νοῦς ἄρά ἐστιν ὁ θεός, ὡς
δέδεικται. καὶ λόγος ἔστιν ἐν αὐτῷ καὶ θέλησις, καὶ τρία μὲν ταῦτα τυγχάνει, μιᾶς
δὲ οὐσίας τῷ ἀριθμῷ. 17. καὶ διὰ τοῦτο εἷς μὲν θεὸς τρεῖς δὲ ἰδιότητες, ᾗπερ
αὐτοὶ δοξάζομεν.

XLII 1 1. **Ὁ Κρατῶν.** Οὐδὲν θαῦμα, ἔφη, σεμνοῖς, ὡς οἷόν τε, λόγοις, οὐκ
ἀληθῆ κρατύνειν ὑπόθεσιν. 2. ἐπεὶ καὶ λόγων τέχνην ἴσμεν ἐφ᾽ ἑκάτερα τῆς
ἀντιφάσεως δυναμένην ἐπιχειρεῖν, ἐκεῖνο μέντοι θαυ|μάζειν ἄξιον εἰ τούτοις 112v
πείθεις σαυτὸν ὥστε καὶ πιστεύειν ἢ ἀληθῆ πάντα εἶναι τὰ οὕτω λεγόμενα οἴει.
3. ἀλλὰ καὶ τούτου ἴσως τὸ ἔθος αἴτιον. «τοῦτο γὰρ ἡλίκην ἰσχὺν ἔχει. οἱ νόμοι
δηλοῦσι», φησὶν Ἀριστοτέλης, «ἐν οἷς τὴν μυθώδη καὶ παιδαριώδη μεῖζον ἰσχύειν
τοῦ γνῶναι τὸ ἀληθές». 4. ἀλλὰ ταῦτα μὲν ἐᾶν δεῖ. ἐκεῖνο δὲ πυθέσθαι βούλομαι,

2 τούτου] ταύτου T || νόησις[2]] νόσις corr. T^1 **4** ἐκεῖνος] ἐκεῖνο T **5–6** διακρίνεται . . . αὐτοῦ] in marg. annot. T^1: ἴσθι **6** ἐκείνου] ἐκεῖνου corr. T^1 et in marg. δι᾽ ἐκείνου iterat **9** αὐτὰ . . . ἔστιν] δὲ αὐτὰ ἔστιν corr. T^1 et in marg. annot.: γράφεται· τὰ αὐτὰ δέ ἐστιν εἰπεῖν **15** Ὁ Κρατῶν] in marg. scr. T **18** οἴει] εἴη in textu sed in marg. οἴει scr. T **20** ἰσχύειν] ἰσχύει corr. T/T^1 **21** ἐᾶν] sc. ἐάαν

Metaphysics that mind also is all these things.[125] Therefore, we are not dealing with different substances when there is mind and mind's thought. 10. But neither can mind be an accident of God. The reason is because the life of the mind is thought, as the philosopher says in the passage cited above: 11. "For the act of mind is its life. God, however, is that act."[126] Conversely, the life of the mind in itself, as the best and eternal, is act. 12. God's life, however, is not an accident. Neither, then, is his thinking. The latter is distinguished from mind insofar as mind is the basis of its own existence while thought exists through mind. 13. For that distinction does not create a difference of substance, but rather only a numerical difference in a relationship. 14. If, however, it did create a difference of substance, mind would be other than itself—if in fact God is God's thought—which is impossible. 15. The same, moreover, can be said in respect to the Will, since by necessity there is will in God. It is numerically distinguished from God and the Word, but is of the same substance in every way as they are. 16. Mind therefore is God, as has been shown. And Word and Will are in God as well. And while these are numerically three, they are of a single substance. 17. Consequently, God is one, but three properties, just as we have shown.

XLII 1 1. **The Conqueror.** It is no surprise, he said, that you made your case not with truth but, as much as possible, with fine words. 2. Since we know that the art of words is able to argue either side of an argument, what would be really surprising is if you persuaded yourself by these fine words, or if you thought it were all true. 3. But habit is probably the explanation here. "The powerful effect of habit is clearly shown by the laws," Aristotle says, "in which fanciful and puerile survivals prevail against our recognition of the truth."[127] 4. But let us

125. Amiroutzes seems to be thinking not of the *Metaphysics*, but of Aristotle's statement in *On the Soul* 3.5.430a10–17 that mind becomes all things; but he could also be pointing to *Metaphysics* 12.7.1072b20–21 and 12.9.1074b35–1075a5, where thinking and the object of thought are identified.

126. Aristotle, *Metaphysics* 12.7.1072b27–28 ("For the actuality of thought is life, and God is that actuality" [trans. Tredennick]). In addition to the reference to book 12 of the *Metaphysics* just before this quotation, Amiroutzes cites the lines immediately following this statement (12.7.1072b29–30) at XXIX.1.15 and the lines immediately preceding this statement (12.7.1072b14–16, 24–26) at XXXIX12.5–7.

127. Aristotle, *Metaphysics* 2.3.995a4–6. I have adapted the translation of Tredennick to suit Amiroutzes' version of the quotation.

εἰ καὶ αὐτοὶ νομίζετε ἀνάστασιν τῶν νεκρῶν καὶ τίνα ζωὴν τοὶς ἀναβιώσκουσιν
ἀποδίδοτε. 5. πότερον ταύτην τὴν κατ᾽ αἴσθησιν ἅμα καὶ νοῦν ἢ μόνον | τὴν 113r
κατὰ νοῦν καὶ τίνα παρὰ ταύτην ἑτέραν;

XLIII 1 1. **Ὁ Φιλόσοφος**. Πολλάκις, ἔφην ἐγώ, ὅτι οὐκ ἀπὸ τούτων αὐτοὶ
τῶν λόγων ἐφ᾽ ἣν νομίζομεν ἥκομεν πίστιν, ἀλλ᾽ ἀπὸ τῶν προφητῶν καὶ τοῦ
εὐαγγελίου. 2. οὓς καὶ αὐτοὶ παρὰ θεοῦ ἥκειν ὁμολογεῖτε. 3. ἔτι δὲ ἀπὸ τῶν
θαυμάτων καὶ τῶν ἔργων αὐτῶν, οἷς ἡ οἰκουμένη πρὸς τὸν ἕνα θεὸν ἀπὸ τῆς
πλάνης ἐπέστρεψεν. 4. εἰ μὴ γὰρ μὴ συνέβαινε τὰ ἔργα τοῖς λόγοις, ἐνῆν ἴσως
ἀμφιβάλλειν. 5. εἰ δὲ τὰ ἔργα οὐ συμβαίνει μόνον, ἀλλὰ καὶ κήρυκος σαφέστερον
μαρτυρεῖ, τίς ἀμφιβολίᾳ καταλείπεται τόπος; | 6. μὴ οὐχὶ παρὰ θεοῦ τὴν 113v
ἡμετέραν πίστιν ἀφῖχθαι; οὐ διὰ πάσης τῆς οἰκουμένης παραχρῆμα διῆλθε τὸ
κήρυγμα; 7. οὐκ ἐν πάσῃ τῇ γῇ καταλιπόντες οἱ ἄνθρωποι τὴν πατρῴαν
θρησκείαν; προσέδραμον τῇ πίστει τῇ εἰς Χριστόν; 8. οὐ γῆ πάσα καὶ θάλασσα
ἐπέγνω διὰ τοῦ εὐαγγελίου τὸν ἕνα θεόν; οὐ δῆμοι καὶ πόλεις ἀφέντες τὸν
ἀνειμένον καὶ τὸν καθ᾽ ἡδονὴν εἵλοντο τὸν μετ᾽ ἀρετῆς βίον; 9. καὶ πρὸς τὸ
ἔσχατον ἐπέστρεψαν τέλος. καὶ ταῦτα πάντα ἐπράχθη διὰ τίνων ἀνθρώπων
ἰδιωτῶν καὶ ἀγροίκων, καὶ οὐδὲν σεμνὸν | οἴκοθεν οὐδ᾽ ἔνδοξον κεκτημένων. 114r
10. καὶ γὰρ εὐτελεῖς τε ἦσαν καὶ ἄδοξοι, καὶ πενίᾳ συνέξων ἐσχάτῃ. οὐδὲ γὰρ
πολυτεῖν ἐβούλοντο. 11. καὶ τὸ δὴ μεῖζον ὅτι καὶ ἐδιώκοντο καὶ ἠλαύνοντο, καὶ
ὅμως ἐκράτουν καὶ περιεγένοντο τοσαύτης κακίας ἢ τῷ τῶν ἀνθρώπων ἐπεπό-
λαστε βίῳ. 12. καὶ μετὰ ταῦτα δὲ οἱ τῶν Ῥωμαίων βασιλεῖς, γῆς, ὡς εἰπεῖν, ὄντες
ἁπάσας κύριοι, σπουδὴν ἔθεντο ταύτην τὴν πίστιν τῆς οἰκουμένης ἐξελεῖν.
13. ἀλλ᾽ ὅμως οὐδὲν ἤνυσαν. ἀλλ᾽ ἀπέκαμον ἀναιροῦντες μέν, οὐδὲν δὲ ἀνύον-
τες. 14. οἱ γὰρ ἑκά|στοτε προσερχόμενοι τῇ πίστει, πλείους ἐγίνοντο τῶν 114v
ἀναιρουμένων. 15. ταῦτα τοίνυν εἴ τις ἄνευ θείας δυνάμεως εἴποι γενέσθαι,
πάντα μᾶλλον ἢ τ᾽ ἀληθὲς ἐρεῖ. 16. τούτοις ἐγὼ πείθομαι. τοῖς δὴ λόγοις
ἐκείνοις ἐκ περιουσίας χρώμεθα. καὶ ἅμα πρὸς ταῦτα μὴ δεχομένους οὐκ ἔστιν
ἄλλοθεν ἢ ἐντεῦθεν ὁρμᾶσθαι. 17. οὐ μὴν ἀλλ᾽ εἰ μὲν ἑώρων τοὺς ἐναντίους
λόγους μεῖζον ἰσχύοντας καὶ τὴν ἀλήθειαν παρ᾽ ἐκείνοις εἶναι δοκοῦσαν,
18. εἰκότως ἂν ᾐσχυνόμην ἄλλῳ τῷ πλέον ἢ τῷ ἀληθεῖ νέμων καὶ μὴ τὸ φαινόμε-
νον πρὸ παντὸς | αἱρούμενος. 19. νῦν δὲ οὐδένα λόγον τοῦδε βεβαιότερον ὁρῶν 115r

---

3 ταύτην] ταύτης corr. T[1] **4** Ὁ Φιλόσοφος] in marg. scr. T **6** οὓς] οἳ T; in marg. ὃ ἢ ἃ scr. T[1] **15** μετ᾽ ἀρετῆς] in marg. iterat T[1]

leave this aside. What I want to know, rather, is whether you yourself believe in the resurrection of the dead. Also, what sort of life do you ascribe to those who have been restored to life? 5. Do they have a life of the senses and of the mind, or only of the mind, and, even then, a life of the mind other than that here below?

XLIII 1 1. **The Philosopher.** Often, I said, we ourselves do not come to the faith we believe from rational arguments, but from the prophets and the Gospel. 2. You yourself agree that that the prophets come from God. 3. Furthermore, our faith comes from their miracles and works, because of which the whole world turned from error to the one God. 4. If their works do not harmonize with their words, you can reasonably be skeptical. 5. If, however, their works not only agree, but rather clearly witness to what they proclaimed, what room is left for doubt? 6. Did our faith not come from God? Did not the preaching [of the Gospel] extend straight away through the whole world? 7. Did not men in every land desert their ancestral worship? Did they not rush headlong to a faith in Christ? 8. Did not every land and sea acknowledge the one God because of the Gospel? Have not peoples and cities given up a dissolute and hedonistic life and chosen the life of virtue? 9. They also turned toward their final end. And all these things happened through the agency of uneducated bumpkins who had no dignity or influence of their own. 10. For they were simple, inconspicuous people, burdened by extreme poverty and not looking to get rich. 11. And what makes it all the more amazing is that they were hunted down and persecuted, and yet they conquered and prevailed over the great evil that dominated the lives of men. 12. Besides all these hurdles, the Roman Emperors, being, so to speak, the lords of the whole earth, took extraordinary measures to eradicate the faith from the earth. 13. Nonetheless, they failed. Instead, they wearied of the killing and futile effort. 14. For each time they attacked the faith, more believers sprang up than had been executed. 15. If someone says that these things happened without divine power, he is speaking completely contrary to the truth. 16. I myself believe these things. We use these arguments as a supplement. But at the same time, it is not possible to engage those who do not accept these beliefs in any other way than by these arguments. 17. Still, if they deemed the counterarguments to be stronger and thought that truth seems to lie with these opposing arguments, 18. I would quite reasonably be shamed as someone who paid honor to some other thing more than the truth, and who did not embrace what is patently obvious. 19. But since right now I see nothing sounder than the case I have presented, I

ἔχομαι τοῦ κρατίστου φαινομένου. 20. καὶ οἶμαι ἀνεμέσητόν τι πράττειν καὶ ἀνεύθυνον τῷ μάλιστα ἀληθεῖ φαινομένῳ τιθέμενος. 21. ἐπεὶ εἴ γε μὴ ἀληθῶς ἐπεπείσμην, ὡς οἷς αὐτοὶ νομίζομεν πρόσεστι τἀληθές, οὐκ ἂν οὐδ᾽ ἂν ἀποθανεῖν ἐχρῆν, 22. εὖ ἴσθι ὤκνησα μὴ οὐχὶ ἐπὶ τὸ ἄμεινον καὶ ἀληθέστερον φαινόμενον προσδραμεῖν. 23. περὶ μὲν οὖν τῆς ἐμῆς ἐνστάσεως καὶ τοῦ πεπεῖσθαι οὐδὲν πλέον ἐρῶ.

2 1. Ἀνάστασιν δὲ τῶν σωμάτων αὐτοὶ νομίζομεν, οὐ τῶν μὲν, τῶν δ᾽ οὔ, | 115v
ἀλλὰ πάντων ὁμοίως τῶν ἀνθρωπίνων. 2. τὴν μέντοι τούτων ζωὴν οὐ κατὰ τὴν
παροῦσαν οἰόμεθα, ἀλλ᾽ ἄλλην λοιπὸν πρέπουσαν τῇ τότε σφῶν λήξει, ἐπεὶ μὴ
δ᾽ ἐν τῷ τῆς γενέσεως ἔσεσθαι τόπῳ, 3. ἀλλὰ θειότερον αὐτοῖς ἀποδίδοσθαι
χῶρον, οὗ μήτε τὴν φυτικὴν ζωὴν μήτε τὴν αἰσθητικὴν εἰκὸς ἔτι ζήσειν. 4. διότι ἡ
μὲν αἰσθητικὴ ζωὴ οὐ δύναται εἶναι ἄνευ τῆς φυτικῆς. 5. ἐπεὶ μηδὲν αἰσθάνεται
ἄμοιρον τῆς τοιαύτης τυγχάνον ζωῆς, αὕτη δὲ τότε εἶναι οὐ δύναται. 6. «ἕκαστον
γάρ ἐστί, ὧν ἔργον ἐστίν, ἕνεκα τοῦ ἔργου», ὡς ὁ φιλόσοφος ἐν τῷ β΄ Περὶ | 116r
Οὐρανοῦ λέγει. 7. τῆς δὲ τοιαύτης ζωῆς ἔργον, τὸ τρέφειν, τὸ αὔξειν, τὸ γεννᾶν,
ἃ τοῖς ἀναβιώσκουσιν οὐκ ἀποδίδοται. 8. οὗ γὰρ χάριν ταῦτα ἐστίν. ἐκεῖθεν
ἄπεστιν. οὐκ ἄρα δύναται τοῖς ἀναβιώσκουσιν ἡ κατ᾽ αἴσθησιν ὑπάρχειν ζωή.
9. τροφῆς μὲν γὰρ οὐκ ἔτι χρεία ὅτι πέπαυται λοιπὸν ἡ τῶν σωμάτων ῥοή. καὶ
οὐκ ἔτι δεῖ προσφέρειν ἕτερον ἀντὶ τοῦ ἀπιόντος ἀεί. 10. αὐξάνειν δὲ τὸ τέλειον
οὐκ εἰκός, ἐπεὶ ἡ μὲν αὔξησις ἐπὶ τοῦτο φέρει. 11. κινεῖσθαι δὲ οὐκ ἔνι. τοὺς ἔνθα
δεῖ κινεῖσθαι καθεστηκότας. 12. ἢ εἰς ἄπειρον ἡ αὔξησις ἔσται, ἀτελευτήτου τῆς
ζωῆς | ὑποτιθεμένης. 13. τὸ δὲ γεννᾶν καὶ παντάπασιν ἐκεῖθεν ἀπελήλαται. οὔτε 116v
γὰρ ὁ ἀριθμὸς αὔξεται τῶν ἀνθρώπων. 14. ἔτι οὔτε θάνατος ἔσται ἵνα καὶ τὸ τούτου φάρμακον ᾖ. 15. καὶ ὁ χῶρος ἐστὶ τῆς ἑκάστου λήξεως. οὐδαμῇ προσίεται γένεσιν. ὑπὲρ γὰρ τὸν τόπον ἔσται τῆς γενέσεως. 16. λείπεται δὲ μόνην τὴν κατὰ νοῦν ζωὴν τότε εἶναι, προσήκουσαν τοῖς μακαρίοις, ἀθανάτοις λοιπὸν καὶ θείοις γεγενημένοις.

---

4 ἐχρῆν] in marg. scr. T **7** Ἀνάστασιν] in marg. annot. T^1: περὶ ἀναστάσεως **8** ἀνθρωπίνων] ἀνθρώπων corr. T^1 (Acciaiuoli: *humanorum corporum*) **15** λέγει] in marg. scr. T^1 || γεννᾶν] ν finalem supra lin. scr. T^1

maintain what seems to me to be the winning argument. 20. I also consider myself acting blamelessly and unimpeachably in adhering to what most seems to me to be the truth. 21. Since I would not be ready to die if I were not really persuaded that it was the truth and did not think that the truth was inherent in these arguments, 22. understand well that I have not shrunk from committing myself to what seems the better and the truer case. 23. Concerning my commitment and conviction, then, I have nothing more to say.

2 1. We ourselves believe in the resurrection of the body, not just for some and not for others, but for all human bodies in like fashion. 2. Furthermore, we think that the resurrected life will not be like the present one, but different, corresponding to what will then henceforth be their final lot, since this life will not be in the place of their birth. 3. Rather, a more divine locale has been allotted to the dead, where they will plausibly still live neither a vegetative life nor a sensitive life. 4. The reason is because the sensitive life cannot exist without the vegetative. 5. Since nothing has sensation if it has no share in the vegetative life, the sensitive life is not possible after death. 6. For, as the philosopher says in book 2 of *On the Heavens*, "Everything which has a function, exists for the sake of that function."[128] 7. The functions, however, of the present life (to grow, increase, beget) do not belong to the resurrected. 8. For these things have no purpose in the resurrected life. They are absent there. Therefore it is not possible for the resurrected to have a life of sensation. 9. For they will not still have need of nourishment, since bodily flux will henceforth cease, and it will no longer be always necessary to replenish what is being lost with something else. 10. What is complete does not lend itself to increase, since increase would add to it. 11. Nor would motion be possible. What has been fixed in place there would have to be moving. 12. Alternatively, increase would go on indefinitely, which presupposes that life there is incomplete. 13. And begetting is totally out of the question there, for the number of men will not increase. 14. Furthermore, there will be no death there, which would justify its antidote, birth. 15. Also, as it is the place of everyone's final lot, it in no way admits birth. For it transcends the place of birth. 16. We are left to conclude that life there is that of the mind, as befits the blessed, who have henceforth become immortal and God-like.

128. Aristotle, *On the Heavens* 2.3.286a6–7 (trans. Guthrie).

XLIV 1 1. **Ὁ Κρατῶν.** Καὶ τίς ἡ τῶν σωμάτων ἐκείνων ἔσται, ἔφη, ζωὴ μήτε
τῆς φυτικῆς ψυχῆς ἐνεργούσης, μήτε τῆς αἰσθητικῆς; 2. τὸ γὰρ ζῆν τῷ σώματι | 117r
οὐ κατὰ τὴν λογικὴν δήπου τυγχάνει ζωήν, ἀλλὰ κατὰ τὴν φυτικὴν πρῶτον,
ἔπειτα τὴν αἰσθητικήν, ὧν ἀναιρουμένων οὐ δυνατὸν ἔτι τῷ σώματι ζῆν. 3. ἀλλὰ
παρέλκον λοιπὸν συνέσται τῷ νῷ. αὐτὸ μὲν ἐντεῦθεν οὐδὲν ὀνούμενον. μάτην δὲ
ἐκείνῳ συνεξευγμένον. 4. πρὸς δέ, καὶ ἐπηρεάζον ἴσως. οὐ γάρ ἐστιν ὅπως οὐκ
ἀφίξεταί τι ἐντεῦθεν ἐμποδὼν ἐσόμενον τῇ τοῦ νοῦ ἐνεργείᾳ. 5. οὐ περιττὴ
τοίνυν μόνον ἡ τῶν σωμάτων ἀνάστασις οὕτω γίνεται, ἀλλὰ καὶ ἐπὶ τὸ χεῖρον
τῆς λογικῆς ψυχῆς. 6. ἀλλὰ μὴν οὐδὲ τῷ σώματι ἄμεινον ἕξει ἀνισταμένῳ | 117v
μηδεμιᾶς οὔσης μήτε τροφῆς μήτε αἰσθήσεως μήτε τινὸς αὐτῷ ἡδέος. 7. εἰδώλου
δὲ δίκην ἄλλως ὑπὸ τοῦ νοῦ περιαγομένῳ. 8. ἦν τ᾽ ἂν βέλτιον ἴσως ἐν τοῖς
στοιχείοις αὐτὸ καταλιπεῖν τὸν θεὸν καὶ μὴ τοσοῦτον ἐπ᾽ οὐδενὶ δέοντι καινοτο-
μεῖν, 9. ἐπεὶ τί αὐτῷ πλέον ἔσται ἀθανάτῳ γεγενημένῳ, μήτε τινὸς ἡδέος
ἀπολαύοντι, μήτ᾽ ἐπαΐοντος ὅλως; 10. ὁ λίθος γὰρ οὕτω γε καὶ τὰ στοιχεῖα
ἀθάνατα ἔσται. 11. ἔτι πότερον μετὰ τῶν μορίων αὐτοῦ πάντων ἀναστήσεται ἢ
μή; 12. εἰ μὲν γὰρ τούτων χωρίς, οὐκ ἔσται ἐν τῇ προτέρα μορφῇ, ἀλλ᾽ ἀλλό|κο- 118r
τόν τι σῶμα ἀναστήσων. 13. εἰ δὲ μετὰ τούτων, μάτην ἐκεῖ ὀφθαλμὸς ἔσται, καὶ
τὰ λοιπὰ αἰσθητήρια μηδεμιᾶς οὔσης αἰσθήσεως. 14. μάτην δὲ οὐχ ὅπως θεός,
ἀλλ᾽ οὐδ᾽ ἡ φύσις ποιεῖ. τὸ δ᾽ αὐτό ἐστιν εἰπεῖν καὶ περὶ τῶν μορίων, ὧν ἡ
φυτικὴ δεῖται ζωή. 15. ἢ γὰρ μάτην ἔσται ἀναιρουμένου τοῦ σφῶν ἔργου ἢ ἄνευ
τούτων ἀναστήσεται τὸ σῶμα. 16. οὐδέτερον δὲ εὔλογον. οὐδ᾽ εἰκός. ὅλου
τοίνυν ἡ τοῦ σώματος ἀνάστασις μάτην ἔσται, μηδεμιᾶς ζωτικῆς ἐνεργείας
ἀποδιδομένης αὐτῷ. 17. οὐ γὰρ δήπου, τὰς μὲν αὐτῷ ἀποδώσετε, τὰς δ᾽ οὔ;
τοῦτο γὰρ | οὐκ ἔχει λόγον. 18. ὁμοίως αὐτῷ πασῶν ὀφειλομένων. οὐκ ἄρα 118v
τοιαύτην δεῖ τιθέναι τὴν τῶν ἀνισταμένων ζωήν, ἀλλ᾽ ἄμεινον λέγειν ἥπερ ἡμεῖς
φαμέν. 19. ζῆν τὲ γὰρ καὶ αἰσθάνεσθαι καὶ ἥδεσθαι ἢ ἀνιᾶσθαι καὶ τ᾽ ἄλλα

2 τῆς[1]] τοὺς corr. T **5** παρέλκον λοιπὸν] in marg. annot. T[1]: τὸ σῶμα δῆλον ἐστί
10 μήτε τινὸς] μήτέ τινος T **13** μήτε τινὸς] μήτέ τινος T **14** ἐπαΐοντος] ἐπ᾽ ἀίοντι T[1]
16–17 ἀλλόκοτόν] ἀλοκ- corr. T[1] **23** ἀποδώσετε] ἀποδώσεται corr. T[1]

XLIV 1 1. **The Conqueror.** And what will be, he said, the life of those bodies without a functioning vegetative soul and without a sensitive one as well? 2. For to live in a body is not to live intellectually, but first of all to live vegetatively, then sensitively, since if the senses are eliminated it is not possible to live in a body. 3. Rather, in accompanying the mind, these other components are linked to it. The mind itself receives no blame from this association. There would be no purpose, however, for them to be yoked to it. 4. In addition, it would be rather harmful.[129] For there is no way that something will come from these components and not be an impediment to the activity of the mind. 5. Not only would the resurrection of the body therefore be superfluous, but it would also impose a worse condition upon the rational soul. 6. But the resurrected body will not be better off, without any substance, nutrition, sensation, or anything that is pleasurable to it. 7. Rather, in the manner of a phantom, it will be led around fruitlessly by the mind. 8. It would be better off, in fact, if God let it dissolve into the elements and did not remake it into such a useless thing. 9. Indeed, what advantage would it be for someone to become immortal? He would not enjoy any pleasure and would be totally without perceptions. 10. For he would thus be a stone and like the immortal elements. 11. Furthermore, would he resurrect with all his bodily parts or not? 12. For if he resurrects without them, he will not have his prior physical appearance. Rather, some other body will resurrect. 13. If, however, he resurects with his bodily parts, his eye will be in vain there, and so too will the rest of his sense organs, since there will be no sense perception. 14. But God does not act in vain this way and neither does nature. The same can be said about a person's bodily parts, which a vegetative life needs. 15. For life would be in vain if these parts were deprived of their function or if the body would be resurrected without them. 16. Neither outcome makes sense. Nor is it plausible. The resurrection of the whole body, then, would be in vain if it were deprived of its activity as functioning life. 17. For is it not the case that you ascribe some functions to the resurrected body and some not? That does not make sense. 18. The same is true if you were to eliminate everything that a resurrected life ought to have. We should therefore not suppose such a life for the resurrected, but a better one, precisely in the way we assert it. 19. For we think

129. I.e., to the mind, if these components were yoked to it.

πράττειν ἢ πάσχειν οἷς τι ἡδὺ ἕπεται ἢ ἀνιαρὸν νομίζομεν.

XLV 1 1. **Ὁ Φιλόσοφος**. Καλοὶ μὲν οἱ λόγοι καὶ πιθανοί, ἔφην ἐγώ, οὐ μὴν καὶ οἷς περὶ τῆς ἀναστάσεως κοινῇ δοξάζομεν ξυνῳδοί. 2. καίτοι δεῖ τοὺς λόγους ἑκάστους συμφώνους εἶναι τοῖς ὑποκειμένοις καὶ μὴ ἀπᾴδειν. 3. τοῦτο γὰρ τοῦ ψεύδους ἐστὶ μόνου. τὸ δὲ ἀληθὲς ἅπαν ξυνάδει. ὧδε δὲ σκοπῶμεν. | 119r 4. ἀμφότεροι νομίζομεν τοὺς ἀνισταμένους μηκέτι ἐν τῷ τῆς γενέσεως εἶναι τόπῳ, ἀλλὰ τοὺς μὲν μακαρίους ἐν οὐρανῷ, 5. τοὺς δὲ ἀθλίους ὑπὸ τὴν γῆν ἐν τῷ τῶν ἀσεβῶν χώρῳ δίκας τίνοντας ὧν ἐξήμαρτον. 6. ἔτι ἀμφοτέρους ἀθανάτους λοιπὸν ἔσεσθαι καὶ ἀγήρους. γεννᾶν τε αὐτοὺς μηκέτι μὴ δὲ τίκτειν ἅτε τοῦ τῶν ἀνθρώπων ἀριθμοῦ ὁρισθέντος. 7. τούτοις τοίνυν ἐκεῖνα οὐ ξυνάδει. ἡ τελειότης γὰρ τῆς φυτικῆς ζωῆς τὸ γεννᾶν ἐστιν ἕκαστον ὅμοιον αὐτῷ. 8. διὸ καὶ τελεουμένοις ἐπιγίνεται. αἱ δ᾿ ἄλλαι τῆς τοιαύτης ψυχῆς ἐνέργειαι διὰ ταύτην | 119v εἰσίν. 9. αὕτη δὴ τότε ὑπόκειται μὴ εἶναι. σχολῇ τοίνυν αἱ ἄλλαι ὧν αὕτη τελειότης ἐστί. 10. εἰ γὰρ τὸ μᾶλλον ἂν ὂν μὴ εἴη, οὐδὲ τὸ ἧττον ἂν ὑπάρχοι. 11. ἔτι δὲ καὶ ὧδε δῆλον ὅτι μήτε τρέφεσθαι μήτε αὐξάνειν μήτε γεννᾶν ἐνδέχεται τοὺς ἀναβιοῦντας. 12. αἱ γὰρ τοιαῦται ἐνέργειαι πᾶσαι διὰ κινήσεως γίνονται, ἥ τε ἀλλοίωσις καὶ ἡ πέψις καὶ ἡ πρόσφυσις καὶ ἡ ἐξομοίωσις. 13. ἔτι δὲ ἐπίδοσις καὶ ἡ τοῦ ὁμοίου πρόοδος, ὥς ἐστιν ἀφ᾿ ἑαυτοῦ φανερόν. 14. κίνησιν δὲ τότε οὐδὲ μίαν ἐνδέχεται εἶναι καὶ οὐδὲ μεταβολήν, οὐδὲ ἐνέργειαν ἄρα διὰ κινήσεως ἀποτελου|μένην. 120r 15. ὅτι δὲ τότε κίνησιν οὐκ εἰκὸς εἶναι, οὐδὲ συμβαίνει τοῖς ὑποκειμένοις, ὃ δὴ φυλάττεσθαι τοὺς φρονεῖν πανταχοῦ τἀληθῆ βουλομένους. 16. ὧδε ἂν γένοιτο δῆλον. πᾶσαι γὰρ αἱ φυσικαὶ κινήσεις εἰσὶ διὰ τὴν πρώτην τοῦ οὐρανοῦ κίνησιν καὶ δεῖ ταύτην προϋποκεῖσθαι, 17. ἅτε ἀρχὴν οὖσαν καὶ αἰτίαν πάσης κινήσεως, ὡς δείκνυται ἐν τῷ η´ Περὶ τῶν Φυσικῶν Ἀρχῶν. 18. ἡ δὲ

---

2 Ὁ Φιλόσοφος] in marg. scr. T **3** ξυνῳδοί] ω supra lin. iterat T^1 **5** ἅπαν] ἅπα corr. T^1 **14** ὑπάρχοι] η supra οι scr. T **16** ἀναβιοῦντας] ἀναβιῶντας corr. T^1 **17** καὶ^3 . . . ἐξομοίωσις] in marg. scr. T^1 **21** δὴ] δεῖ in marg. scr. T^1 **24** Περὶ] τὴν ante del. T/T^1

that it is to live and feel, and to enjoy pleasure or to be distressed, and to do and suffer other things, from which we derive some pleasure or feel some grief.

XLV 1 1. **The Philosopher.** Fine and persuasive arguments, I said, but they do not reflect what we teach in common concerning the resurrection. 2. Indeed, what we need to do is have each of our arguments conform to the subject matter and not be at odds with it. 3. For the latter is only the way of falsity. Truth, on the other hand, is consistent in all respects. Let this be the way we carry out our examination. 4. Both of us believe that those who are resurrected no longer abide in the place of their birth. Rather, the blessed are in heaven, 5. and the wicked under the earth, that is, in the place of the impious, where they pay for their sins. 6. We also believe that both will be thenceforth immortal and incapable of aging. Also, in no way can they be born or give birth, inasmuch as the number of men is fixed. 7. Your arguments, however, do not harmonize with these statements. For the purpose of vegetative life is generation, each thing producing what is like itself. 8. Hence, this purpose falls to those who were born from such a purpose. There are other activities of the vegetative soul that exist because of this purpose. 9. The vegetative soul, it has been stipulated, does not exist then [in the afterlife]. These other activities, therefore, of which giving birth is their purpose, scarcely exist there as well. 10. For if what is greater does not exist, neither does what is lesser. 11. Furthermore, it is thus clear that neither rearing, nor growing, nor being born are possible for those who come to life again. 12. For all such activities come about through motion, as would be true for alteration, ripening, growth by attachment, and assimilation. 13. Also, this is true of increase and the progression of similar action, as is self-evident. 14. But no motion or change is possible in the afterlife, nor, therefore, is any activity achieved through motion. 15. Since it is reasonable to suppose that there is no motion in the afterlife, asserting it would not be consistent with our presuppositions, something that those who are absolutely inclined to the truth will guard against. 16. The inconsistency becomes apparent as follows. For all natural motions stem from the motion of the first heavenly sphere, and this fact must be established as an axiom from the start, 17. inasmuch as it is the principle and cause of all motion, as is shown in book 7 of the *Physics*.[130] 18. This motion of the first sphere is

130. Cf. Aristotle, *Physics* 7.1.241b24–243a2; but also *Metaphysics* 12.8.1073a23–b3; and *On the Heavens* 2.12.292b22–32.

τοιαύτη κίνησις ἀναιρεῖται τότε. εἰ γὰρ εἴη, καὶ αἱ τῶν ἄλλων σφαιρῶν ἂν εἶεν.
19. τούτων δὲ ὑποτιθεμένων, ἀνάγκη καὶ γέννησιν εἶναι καὶ φθορὰν | καὶ ἁπλῶς 120v
τὴν παροῦσαν τοῦ κόσμου τάξιν. 20. ὄντος γὰρ τοῦ τε ποιητικοῦ καὶ τοῦ παθητι-
κοῦ καὶ ἐχόντων ὡς νῦν ἔχουσιν, ἀνάγκη τὸ ἔργον γίνεσθαι. 21. τοῦτο δὲ οὐδετέ-
ροις δοκεῖ. οὐκ ἄρα ἐνδέχεται τότε τὴν φυτικὴν ζωὴν εἶναι. 22. καὶ ἀπὸ τοῦ
χώρου δὲ ἐν ᾧ ἔσονται οἱ ἀνιστάμενοι τὸ αὐτὸ δείκνυται. 23. ἑκάστῳ γὰρ τόπῳ
ἀποδίδοται καὶ τὰ ἀνήκοντα ἔργα. τῇ δὲ τότε λήξει τὰ τοιαῦτα οὐκ ἀνήκει.
24. ἔστι γὰρ τοῦ ἐνθάδε τόπου. ὅτι μὲν οὖν ἡ φυτικὴ ζωὴ ἐκποδὼν ἔσται τότε
φανερόν.

2 1. Λείπεται δὴ περὶ τῆς αἰσθητικῆς ἰδεῖν. 2. ἀλλὰ καὶ τοῦτο δέδεικται πρότε-
ρον | ὅτι αὕτη οὐχ ὑφίσταται δίχα τῆς φυτικῆς, ὡς ὁ φιλόσοφος δείκνυσιν ἐν τῷ 121r
α´ Περὶ Ψυχῆς. 3. ταύτης οὖν ἐκποδὼν γινομένης, οἴχεσθαι κἀκείνην ἀνάγκη.
4. ἔτι αἱ αἰσθήσεις ἐν μὲν τοῖς ἀλόγοις ζώοις εἰσὶ διὰ τὸ ὀρεκτὸν ἵνα ἐπ᾽ αὐτὸ
ἴωσιν ἢ φύγωσιν. 5. τὸ δὲ ὀρεκτὸν τοῦτο οὐκ ἐκτείνεται εἰ μὴ ἐφ᾽ ὅσον τὴν
τοιάνδε ζωὴν συντηρεῖν. 6. ἔργον γὰρ ἕτερον τοῖς τοιούτοις ζώοις οὐκ ἀποδίδο-
ται εἰ μὴ ὅσον ἀνήκει πρὸς τὴν σφῶν σωτηρίαν. 7. τοῖς δὲ λογικοῖς οὐ διὰ τοῦτο
μόνον, ἀλλ᾽ οὐχ ἥκιστα καὶ διὰ τὸν νοῦν. 8. ὑποβάλλουσι γὰρ αὐτῷ τὰ εἴδη τῶν
αἰσθητῶν. | 9. ὁ δὲ ἐκ τούτων ἀφαιρεῖται τὸ νοητὸν εἶδος καὶ τὸ καθόλου 121v
ἀφελὼν τὴν ὕλην καὶ τὰς ἀτομικὰς ἰδιότητας, καὶ οὕτως ἐπὶ τὴν γνῶσιν ἔρχεται
τῶν ὄντων. 10. ἐν δὲ τῇ ἀναστάσει τούτων οὐδέτερον δύναται εἶναι. 11. οὐ γὰρ
ἔτι δεῖται τῶν αἰσθήσεων ὁ νοῦς οὔτε διὰ τὸ ὀρεκτὸν ὃ τέτακται πρὸς τὴν τῶν
ζώων σωτηρίαν, οὔτ᾽ ἐπὶ τὸ τὰ εἴδη νοεῖν· 12. ἀλλ᾽ οἶδεν αὐτὰ ἐξ αὑτοῦ καὶ ἐκ
τῆς μιᾶς ἀρχῆς ᾗ σύνεστι καὶ ἣν ὡς εἰκὸς θεωρεῖ. 13. οὐκ ἄρα ἐκεῖ τῶν αἰσθή-
σεων χρεία οὔτε τοῖς μακαρίοις οὔτε | τοῖς ἀθλίοις. 14. οὐδὲ τὴν αἰσθητικὴν 122r
τοίνυν ζωὴν τοὺς ἀναβιοῦντας ἐνδέχεται ζῆν ἀλλὰ τὴν κατὰ νοῦν μόνην. 15. ὅτι
δὲ ἐνδέχεται καὶ κατὰ νοῦν μόνον τῷ σώματι ζῆν δῆλον ἐντεῦθεν. 16. τὸν γὰρ
οὐρανὸν καὶ τὰς σφαίρας ἁπάσας ἔτι δὲ καὶ τοὺς ἀστέρας μετέχειν, φησὶν

4–5 οὐδετέροις] οὐ δὲ τέροις corr. T^1 **7** λήξει] λῆξει corr. T/T^1 **11** δίχα] δι corr. T/T^1 **14** ἐφ᾽ ὅσον] ἐφόσον T **22** ζώων] ζώντων corr. T || αὑτοῦ] ἀὐτοῦ T **25–26** ὅτι . . . ἐνδέχεται] signo (manu monstrante) in marg. denotat T^1

eliminated in the afterlife. For if it were there, so too would be the motions of the other spheres. 19. If those are posited, then necessarily there also would be generation, corruption, and, simply put, the arrangement we presently have in the world. 20. For when there is an active element and a passive one, and conditions are as those that presently hold, an action necessarily follows. 21. But that strikes neither of us as plausible. Therefore, it is not possible in the afterlife for vegetative life to exist. 22. And those who are resurrected demonstrate this very same thing from the locale where they will dwell. 23. For each place is assigned its proper functions. Functions such as these are inappropriate to the afterlife. 24. For they belong to a place in the world here below. Clearly then, vegetative life is alien to the afterlife.

2 1. It remains for us to look at the sensitive life. 2. But it has already been shown that it has no substantive existence without vegetative life, as the philosopher demonstrates in book 1 of *On the Soul*.[131] 3. With the latter eliminated, so too necessarily is the former swept away. 4. Furthermore, the senses exist in irrational animals on account of appetite, so that at its prompting they approach or flee [things]. 5. This appetite, however, does not extend beyond that which sustains life here in this present life. 6. For no other action is assigned such animals but what is proper to their preservation. 7. To rational beings, however, actions have been assigned not only because of this purpose, but also, and not least of all, because of their mind. 8. For the forms of sensible things fall under the purview of mind. 9. It abstracts from them the intelligible form by separating out from matter the universal and the individual proprieties, and thus arrives at a knowledge of things. 10. In the resurrection, however, neither of these things can happen. 11. For the mind no longer needs the senses nor an appetite ordered toward the preservation of animals, nor for thinking the forms. 12. Rather, it knows forms from within itself and from the single principle with which it dwells, and which, it is reasonable to suppose, it contemplates. 13. Consequently neither the blessed nor the wicked have any need of the senses there. 14. Hence, it is not possible for the resurrected to live a sensitive life, only the life of the mind. 15. Clearly, then, in the afterlife the body also can only live a life of the mind. 16. For, Aristotle says, the heavens and all the spheres as well as the stars

131. Cf. Aristotle, *On the Soul* 2.2.413a25–b2.

Ἀριστοτέλης, πράξεως καὶ ζωῆς. 17. τὸ αὐτὸ δὲ καὶ Πλάτων, καὶ ὅσοι κατὰ
φιλοσοφίαν διέλαμψαν τίθενται. 18. ταῦτα δὲ οὔτε τὴν φυτικὴν οὔτε τὴν αἰσθη-
τικὴν εἰκὸς ἔχειν ψυχήν, ὥς ἐστιν ἀφ᾽ ἑαυτοῦ φανερόν. 19. μόνος γὰρ ὁ νοῦς
πρόσεστιν αὐτοῖς. ἐνδέ|χεται ἄρα τῷ σώματι καὶ διὰ τὸν νοῦν μόνον ὑπάρχειν τὸ 122v
ζῆν. 20. εἰ δέ τινες οἴονται τὰ τοιαῦτα μὴ μετέχειν ζωῆς, οὐδὲν πρὸς τὸν νῦν
λόγον. 21. οὐ γὰρ διότι ἀδύνατον τοῦτο, φασίν, ἀλλ᾽ ὅτι μὴ συμβαίνειν ἴσως
οἴονται οἷς κατὰ δόξαν τίθενται. 22. οὐκ ἄρα ἀδύνατον τὸν νοῦν ζωὴν τῷ σώματι
χορηγεῖν. εἰ δὴ τοῦτο ἐνδέχεται, οὐ μάτην ἀναβιώσεται τὸ σῶμα. 23. ἀλλ᾽ ἐπὶ τῷ
μετέχειν ζωῆς οὐδὲ καθάπερ κωφὸν εἴδωλον. ἄλλως ὁ νοῦς αὐτὸ περιάξει, ἀλλὰ
ζωῆς αὐτῷ μεταδοὺς καὶ οἰκεῖον ὄχημα ποιησάμενος. 24. εἰ δὲ μηδὲν ἐνεργεῖ δι᾽
αὐτοῦ τοῦ, | θαυμαστὸν οὐδέν. 25. οὐ γὰρ διὰ τοῦτο αὐτὰ ἀποδίδοται, ἀλλὰ διὰ 123r
μόνην τὴν τοῦ θεοῦ δικαιοσύνην ὅτι πρὸς ἑκάτερον καὶ τἀγαθὸν καὶ τὸ κακὸν
ὑπηρέτησεν. 26. δίκαιον οὖν ὅλον τὸν ἄνθρωπον τὸ ὀφειλόμενον ἀπολαμβάνειν.
27. ἴσως δὲ οὐδὲ παντάπασι χωριστὸν εἶδος παρήγαγε, τὴν λογικὴν ψυχήν, ὁ τοῦ
παντὸς τοῦδε δημιουργός, 28. ἀλλὰ καθ᾽ αὐτὴν μὲν τὴν οὐσίαν ἔχον, συνεζευ-
γμένον δὲ σώματι, ἐπεὶ καὶ ὁ ἄνθρωπος τὸ συναμφότερόν ἐστιν, οὐ τὸ εἶδος
μόνον. 29. εἰ δὲ χωριστὸν εἶδος καθάπαξ ἦν ἡ λογικὴ ψυχή, τί δήποτε συνεζύγη
τῷ σώματι; 30. ἣν γὰρ ὁ | Πλάτων αἰτίαν οἴεται δέδεικται οὖσα οὐκ ἀληθής. 123v
31. οὔκουν διὰ τὴν τοῦ θεοῦ μόνον δικαιοσύνην αὖθις ἀπολαμβάνει τὸ ἴδιον ἡ
ψυχὴ σῶμα, 32. ἀλλὰ καὶ ὅτι μὴ χωριστὸν εἶδος παντάπασιν ἐστὶν ἴσως. 33. εἰ δὴ
δεῖ σῶμα ἔχειν ἄμεινον, τὸ αὐτῆς αὖθις ἀπολαβεῖν ἀποδίδοται δὲ αὐτῇ τὸ σῶμα,
34. οὐχ ᾗ ὀργανικόν (τοιοῦτον γὰρ ἐνταῦθα αὐτῇ ἀπεδίδοτο μόνον), ἀλλ᾽ ᾗ ποτε
γέγονεν αὐτῆς. 35. τοῦ γὰρ τέλους ἀναιρουμένου, οὐκ ἂν ἔτι εἴη τὰ πρὸς τὸ
τέλος· 36. ἀλλὰ τὸ τέλος δι᾽ ὃ ταῦτα πάντα ἀναγκαῖα κατὰ τὴν παροῦσαν εἰσὶ
ζωὴν ἀναιρεῖται λοιπὸν τότε, ὡς δέδεικται πρότερον, 37. καὶ ἃ τοίνυν | δι᾽ ἐκεῖνα 124r

4 τὸν . . . μόνον] τοῦ νοῦ μόνου supra lin. scr. T^1 **5** νῦν] νοῦν corr. T/T^1 **6** φασίν] φυσίν corr. T^1 **8** χορηγεῖν] χορηγείν corr. T/T^1 || τῷ] τὸ supra lin. scr. T^1 **15** ἔχον] ἔχων corr. T^1 **16** ἐστιν] ἐστὶν corr. T/T^1 **18** ὁ] bis T || οὖσα] ούσα corr. T^1, et annot.: γράφεται· δείκνυται οὖσα **22** ἀλλ᾽ ᾗ] ἀλλῇ T **24** τέλος^2] aliquid supra scr. T^1 sed del.

enjoy activity and life.[132] 17. Plato says the same thing,[133] as does everyone who reckons in accord with an enlightened philosophy. 18. As is self-evident, it is fair to say that these entities have neither a vegetative nor a sensitive soul. 19. For only mind is present in them. Therefore it is possible for body to have life through mind alone. 20. If, however, some people think that these entities do not partake of life, that view does not affect the present argument. 21. The reason is that they say it is not impossible for such entities to have life, but they think that such an attribution of life does not perhaps agree with what they believe as a matter of dogma. 22. It is therefore not impossible for the mind to supply life to the body. If in fact this is possible, then the body does not vainly live again. 23. But in enjoying life it is not like a dumb phantom. The mind will lead it differently, sharing its life with it and making it the mind's own vehicle.[134] 24. If, however, the mind does not act through the body, there is nothing startling about that. 25. For it did not receive the afterlife on account of the body, but exclusively on account of God's justice, since his justice attends to both good and evil. 26. It is just that the whole man pays his debt then [in the afterlife]. 27. The maker of this world rightly created a rational soul that was not separated in every respect, 28. but rather yoked to a body while retaining its own substance, since man is a composite, not just a form. 29. If, however, the rational soul were absolutely a separated form, why would it ever be yoked to the body? 30. For the reason Plato gives we have shown to be false. 31. Therefore it was not only because of God's justice that the soul gets back again its own body, 32. but also because it is rightly not a completely separated form. 33. If, then, it necessarily has a better body, the body it is given is the body which it receives back, 34. but not as an organ (for such a body was given it only for here below), but in the sense that it once belonged to the soul. 35. For when an end is removed, the things intended for that end no longer have any use; 36. but the end for which all these things were necessary in the present life would then be eliminated in the afterlife, as has already been shown, 37. and necessarily then so too would be

132. Cf. Aristotle, *On the Heavens* 2.12.292a18–b3.

133. Cf. Plato, *Timaeus* 30–37.

134. On the Neoplatonic vehicle of the soul, the ὄχημα, which Proclus ascribed to Aristotle, see Dodds in Proclus, *The Elements of Theology*, 304–9 and 313–21; and Blumenthal, *Aristotle and Neoplatonism*, 28–29, 84–85, 112–13, 125–26.

ἣν ἐκποδῶν ἀνάγκη γενέσθαι. 38. οὔκουν ἢ ὀργανικὸν τότε τὸ ἀνιστάμενον ἔσται σῶμα, ἀλλ᾽ ᾗ ποτὲ τῆς λογικῆς ὑπῆρξε ψυχῆς 39. ὥστε δὲ ἀεισυνεῖναι καὶ ζῆν ἀθάνατον καὶ ἀνώλεθρον ἀποτετελεσμένον. 40. ἔτι δὲ ἀναλλοίωτον καὶ ἀμετάβλητον. τότε μηδὲν ἐνεργεῖν ἐπὶ τὸ ἄμεινον ὑπάρξει αὐτῷ. 41. τοιαῦτα γὰρ ὁ φιλόσοφος καὶ τὰ τῶν ἀστέρων σώματα τίθεται διὰ τὸ θεῖα εἶναι. οὐ γὰρ οἴκοθεν αὐτὰ κινεῖσθαι, ἀλλ᾽ ὑπὸ τῶν σφαιρῶν, ὡς δείκνυται ἐν τῷ ιβ´ τῶν Μετὰ Φυσικά. 42. τὸ δὲ μάτην οἴεσθαι τὸ σῶμα ἀνίστασθαι εἰ μὴ τῆς κατ᾽ αἴσθησιν ἡδονῆς ἀπολαύει, | οὑτωσὶν εὐφήμως εἶπον, οὔτ᾽ ἀναγκαῖον, οὔτ᾽ 124v εὔλογον ἄλλως. 43. ἡ γὰρ ἡδονὴ οὐκ ἔστι προηγούμενον τῆς κατ᾽ αἴσθησιν ἐνεργείας τέλος. ἀλλ᾽ ἕπεται μόνον ποθεινὸν τὸ τέλος ποιοῦσα. 44. οὔκουν ἔστι δι᾽ ἑαυτήν, ἀλλὰ διὰ τὸ τέλος, ὃ τοῖς ἐξ ἀναστάσεως οὐχ ἁρμόζει. 45. πῶς οὖν ἔσται τί μάτην διὰ ταῦτην ὅταν ἐκεῖνο μὴ δεῖται οὗ ἕνεκα αὕτη ἦν ᾗ ἐπεφύκει; 46. ὅτι δὲ ἡ ἡδονὴ οὔκ ἐστι δι᾽ αὑτήν αἱρετή, ἀλλὰ διὰ τὸ τέλος δῆλον. 47. ἦν γὰρ ἂν ἅπασα τοιαύτη, καὶ οὐκ ἂν διέφερον αἱ πράξεις τῷ καλῷ ἢ μὴ τοιούτῳ, ἀλλὰ μόνῃ τῇ ἡδονῇ, ὥσπερ ὑπέλαβεν Ἐπίκουρος. 48. ἀλλ᾽ οὗτος ὁ λόγος ἀναιρεῖ τὸν | τῶν ἀνθρώπων βίον. 49. πάντα γὰρ ἔδει τολμᾶν καὶ ποιεῖν ὅθεν 125r ἔμελλεν ἔσεσθαί τις ἡδονή. 50. ἔτι τοῦ τέλους ἀπιόντος, παύεται τὸ ἥδεσθαι ὡς φαίνεται δι᾽ ἐπαγωγῆς. 51. ἥ τε γὰρ τρυφὴ μέχρι τοσούτου ἡδεῖα, μέχρις ἂν ἐπιγένηται πλήρωσις. 52. τά τε ἄλλα πάντα τὰ κατ᾽ αἴσθησιν ἡδέα μέχρι τούτου τοιαῦτα δοκεῖ, μέχρις ἂν ἐν ἐνδείᾳ τὸ σῶμα ὧν ἂν ὀρέγηται ᾖ. 53. περαιτέρω δὲ οὐκ ἔτι. ἡ ἡδονὴ ἄρα οὐκ ἔστι δι᾽ ἑαυτήν, ἀλλὰ διὰ τὸ τέλος τῆς ἐνεργείας ᾗ ἐπιγίνεται. 54. οὐκ ἄρα μάτην οἵα τε ποιεῖν ἐστιν οἷς ἂν μὴ παρῇ. 55. καίτοι καὶ τὸ ἥδεσθαι αὐτὸ οὔκ ἐστι τοῦ | σώματος, ἀλλὰ τῆς ψυχῆς κατὰ τὸ σῶμα. 56. οὔ- 125v κουν γίνεται μάτην τῆς ψυχῆς ἐν ταῖς ἰδίαις ἐνεργείαις καθ᾽ αὑτὴν ἀγαλλομένης. 57. ἱκανὸν δὲ τὸ τοῦ εἴδους τέλος καὶ τὸ ὑποκείμενον αὐτὸ καλὸν ποιῆσαι καὶ

3 ἀναλλοίωτον] -αλοι corr. T^1 **4** μηδὲν] μὴδὲν T **6** δείκνυται] δείκται corr. T^1 **14** οὐκ] οὐ- bis, sed corr. T/T^1 **17** παύεται] παύεσθαι corr. T^1 et in marg. iterat **22** οἵα] οἱά T **23** τοῦ] bis T

removed whatever depended on these things for existence. 38. The body, therefore, is not resurrected because it is an organ in the afterlife, but because it once belonged to the rational soul. 39. It will always accompany the soul, and now, since it is perfected, it will lead an immortal and indestructible life. 40. Furthermore, it will undergo no alterations and will be unchangeable. In the afterlife it will function in a way that cannot in any sense be improved upon. 41. For such is how the philosopher depicts the bodies of the stars, because they are divine. For they do not move of their own power, but through that of the spheres, as is shown in book 12 of the *Metaphysics*.[135] 42. To think, however, that the body is resurrected in vain if it does not enjoy the pleasures of the senses is not, I would say with all due respect, a necessary conclusion nor an otherwise reasonable one. 43. For pleasure does not take the lead as the end of sense activity. Rather, it is only a consequence of that activity achieving its desired end. 44. Therefore pleasure does not exist for its own sake, but for the sake of an end that does not fit the conditions that arise with resurrection. 45. How, then, is anything in vain on these grounds, when what was the reason for its existence or its being engendered is not needed? 46. It is clear then that pleasure is not chosen for its own sake, but for an end [other than itself]. 47. For if pleasure were completely for its own sake, actions would not differ in terms of their goodness or lack of goodness, but only in terms of their pleasure, as Epicurus maintained. 48. But that line of argument destroys the life of men. 49. For it would require having the effrontery to do everything and anything that would result in some pleasure. 50. Furthermore, when the end is absent, the sensation of pleasure itself ends, as is shown from experience. 51. For wantonness is pleasurable up to such a point, namely, up to when satiety occurs. 52. All other sensual pleasure seems to be like this up to such a point, namely, as long as the body is in need of what it craves. 53. Beyond that there is no further pleasure. Pleasure, therefore, is not for its own sake, but for the sake of the activity of which it is a consequence. 54. Therefore it is not the case that activities, for which pleasure is not present, take place in vain [in the afterlife]. 55. Rather, the sensation itself of pleasure is not of the body, but of the soul throughout the body. 56. Therefore nothing is in vain when the soul takes delight in its own activities in its own self. 57. It is the sufficient end of form

135. Cf. Aristotle, *Metaphysics* 12.8.1073a23–24; see Wolfson, "Plurality of Immovable Movers," 238.

εὔδαιμον. 58. ἐπεὶ δὲ τὸ τέλος τοῦ νοῦ τὸ τυχεῖν ἐστι τῆς πρώτης ἀληθείας καὶ τοῦ πρώτου νοητοῦ, τοῦτο δὲ ὑπάρχει τότε τοῖς μακαρίοις καθ᾽ ὑπερβολήν. 59. δίχα τινὸς διόδου καὶ μεταβολῆς ἆθλον ἀναφαίρετον αὐτοῖς τοῦτο δίδοται ὑπὸ τοῦ θεοῦ. 60. οὐδενὸς ἔτι δεῖ τῷ σώματι πρὸς εὐδαιμονίαν συνημμένῳ μὲν τῇ λογικῇ ψυχῇ καὶ ζωῆς ἀναλόγου μετέχοντι, 61. ἀπαθεῖ δὲ καὶ ἀθανάτῳ | 126r γεγενημένῳ. οὐ γὰρ τοιοῦτον οἷον νῦν ἐστιν. 62. ἀλλὰ ἀνίσταται θεῖον καὶ ἔνδοξον κοῦφον καὶ λαμπρὸν καὶ ἀναλλοίωτον ἀποτετελευμένον καὶ πρέπον ὄχημα τῆς λογικῆς ψυχῆς καὶ οἷον ἄξιον τῆς μακαρίας ἐκείνης ζωῆς. 63. τὸ δὲ τῶν ἀθλίων ἀθάνατον μὲν καὶ ἀναλλοίωτον οὐ μὴν ἔνδοξον οὐδ᾽ ἐπὶ τὸ ἄμεινον αὐτῷ ἀλλ᾽ ἐπὶ τὸ χεῖρον, τῇ ψυχῇ συναπτόμενον ὅπως ὧν ἐξύβρισεν τίσῃ δίκην.

3 1. Ταῦτα ἐστιν ἃ περὶ τῆς ἀναστάσεως αὐτοὶ δοξάζομεν εἰς ἣν οὐκ ἀπὸ τῆς φιλοσοφίας ἥκομεν. 2. ἔστι γὰρ τὸ δόγμα τοῦ κυρίου μου τοῦ Ἰησοῦ πρώτου. οἱ δὲ προφῆται οὐ διαρρήδην αὐτὸ | 126v εἶπον. 3. τὰ μέντοι ἑπόμενα καὶ ἀπὸ τῆς φιλοσοφίας δείκνυμεν, καὶ οὐδὲν ἂν δεξαίμεθα ᾧ μὴ καὶ αὕτη συνάδει ἀπὸ τῶν ὑποκειμένων ἀρχῶν. 4. οἱ γὰρ διαφωνοῦντες αὐτῇ φιλοσοφίᾳ καὶ τοῖς ὑποκειμένοις οὐδὲν ὑγιὲς νομίζουσι. 5. δεῖ γὰρ τοῖς γοῦν ὑποκειμένοις συνᾴδειν καὶ μὴ «μαχόμενα λέγειν καὶ ἑαυτοῖς καὶ τοῖς εὐλόγοις κατὰ τὸν Σιμωνίδου μακρὸν λόγον». 6. τοῦ μὲν γὰρ ἀληθεῖς τὰς ἀρχὰς εἶναι σημεῖον, τὸ προϊόντων μηδὲν ἄλογον συμβαίνειν, τοῦ δὲ ψεύδους τοὐναντίον.

3 ἀναφαίρετον] ἀναφρέντον corr. T[1] **6** ἀλλὰ ἀνίσταται] transposui **7** ἀναλλοίωτον] ἀναλοί-T **9** ἀναλλοίωτον] ἀναλοί- corr. T[1]

to have made the subject itself beautiful and happy. 58. Since, however, the end of mind is to have found the first truth and the first thought, this befalls the blessed beyond measure in the afterlife. 59. The prize remains inseparably theirs, given to them by God, without any mediation or change. 60. The body [in the afterlife], inasmuch as it is joined to the rational soul and analogously sharing its life, has need of nothing else for happiness, 61. since it has been made free of suffering and has become eternal. For such a state is not possible now [on earth]. 62. But when it has risen, the body is divine, glorious, light, and luminous, and the unchangeable, perfect, and fitting vehicle of the rational soul, and, as such, worthy of that blessed life. 63. The body of the wicked, however, though eternal and unchangeable [in the afterlife], is not neither glorious nor better than this one here, but worse off, joined to the soul in order to pay the price of wanton insolence.

3 1. This is what we have to teach concerning the resurrection. We have not come to it from philosophy. 2. For it is the teaching of my first lord, Jesus. The prophets, however, do not announce it with any clarity. 3. We demonstrate its consequences, though, from philosophy, and we would accept nothing that does not accord with it on the basis of our premises. 4. For those who disagree with this philosophy and our premises believe that nothing is sound. 5. We ought to agree on our premises and not say that "they are contradictory with themselves and with good reasoning, as is the case in Simonides' 'long story.'"[136] 6. For the sign that principles are true is that nothing being proposed is found to be irrational, which is the opposite of falsity.

136. Aristotle, *Metaphysics* 14.3.1091a7–9.

APPENDIX I

George Amiroutzes' Letter to Cardinal Bessarion of 10 December 1461

First published in 1833 by Jean-François Boissonade in his collection of Greek texts, *Ἀνέκδοτα: Anecdota graeca e codicibus regiis*, the letter was reprinted by Jacques-Paul Migne in volume 161 (the final volume) of his Patrologiae cursus completus, Series graeca, in 1866. Boissonade used two fifteenth-century manuscripts of the Bibliothèque nationale de France, gr. 2966 and gr. 3043. Both lack the letter's date at the end, something that two Vatican manuscripts, Vat. gr. 1416 and Ott. lat. 181, do have. But the Ottobonianus is a copy of the Vaticanus and of no independent value. The same is true of the manuscript in Rome's Biblioteca Vallicelliana, Allacci CXVII, which also is a copy of Vat. gr. 1416. In 1915, Lambros ("Ἡ περὶ ἁλώσεως Τραπεζοῦντος ἐπιστολή") supplied the date from Vat. gr. 1416. My partial edition is based on the three independent manuscripts, namely, BnF gr. 2966, BnF gr. 3043, and Vat. gr. 1416.

I have edited and translated the start of the letter and its last part, where Amiroutzes appeals to Bessarion and explains his situation in Adrianople. What is omitted is Amiroutzes' description of the fall of Trebizond, where he has nothing to say about his role in the event.

Sigla:

A Paris, BnF, MS gr. 2966, ff. 2v–4r = Gallica, https://gallica.bnf.fr/ark:/12148/btv1b10723719b/f8.image

B Paris, BnF, MS gr. 3043, ff. 4v–7v = Gallica, https://gallica.bnf.fr/ark:/12148/btv1b10723193p/f5.image

O BAV, MS Vat. gr. 1416, ff. 143r–149r

V BAV, MS Ott. gr. 181, ff. 107r–110r

Vall Bibl. Vallicelliana, MS Allacci CXVII, ff. 541r–549r (= text no. 40)

Boiss Boissonade, *Anecdota*, 5:389–401, from AB

—

1. Αἰδεσιμώτατε καὶ σεβασμιώτατε ἐν Χριστῷ πάτερ καὶ δέσποτα, εἴης μοι ὑγιαίνων καὶ εὖ ἔχων ἐν ἅπασιν.

2. Ἃ πάλαι προύλεγον καὶ διεμαρτυρόμην πρὸς τοὺς ἡμετέρους πολίτας, ἔγραφον δὲ καὶ πρὸς τὴν σὴν κυριότητα, δεόμενος ἕνα γοῦν μοι τῶν παίδων δεξάμενον διασῶσαι, γέγονε καὶ πέρας ἔχει. 3. Καίτοι δεινὰ μὲν ἀγγέλλων οἶδα καὶ οἷα οὐκ ἂν ἀδακρυτὶ παρέλθοις, ἀλλὰ μικράν σοι καταθείμην ἂν χάριν, τὰς κοινὰς ἀποκρυψάμενος συμφοράς. Τίς γὰρ ὄνησις ἀγνοίᾳ συνεῖναι τῶν οἰκείων κακῶν; 4. ἅμα δὲ καὶ μάτην ἂν εἴην αὐτὸς σιωπῶν ἃ πανταχοῦ νῦν, οἶμαι, διεβόησε καὶ διετραγῴδησεν ἡ φήμη.

. . .

5. Ἐπεὶ δὲ τῆς πόλεως ἐκράτησαν καὶ πάντας ὥσπερ ἐν μιᾷ σαγήνῃ τοὺς Κομνηνοὺς ἔσχεν ὑποχειρίους, παῖδάς τε εὐθὺς καὶ κόρας ἐλάμβανον, ἀνδραποδιζόμενοι σχεδὸν ἅπαντας ὅσοις ὥρας τι προσῆν. 6. Ἐν οἷς καὶ τὸν ἐμὸν φεῦ! υἱόν, ὃν αὐτὸς διὰ τῆς ματρὸς ἐκ τοῦ θείου λουτροῦ λαβὼν υἱὸν ἐποιήσω, τὸν καλὸν Βασίλειον· 7. ἔτι δὲ καὶ τὸν τῆς θυγατρὸς νυμφίον, ὅτι νέος τε ἦν καὶ καλὸς ἐδόκει, ἐλάχιστον χρόνον ἀπολελαυκότα τοῦ γάμου. 8. Τὸν δὲ βασιλέα σὺν πάσῃ τῇ συγγενείᾳ καὶ τοὺς ἐν τέλει σχεδὸν ἅπαντας εἰς τὰς τριήρεις ἐμβαλόντες, εἰς τὴν Κωνσταντινούπολιν ἤγαγον· ἐκεῖθεν δὲ πάλιν εἰς τὰ Ἀδριανοῦ ἀγαγόντες κατῴκισαν.

9. Καὶ νῦν εἰμὶ ἐνταῦθα, «κορυφῆς» ἀτεχνῶς «ὑπερτέλλοντα δειμαίνων πέτρον». Καίτοι πολλάκις παρὰ τὴν πολιορκίαν ἠφείδησα ἐμαυτοῦ ὥστε θανεῖν·

---

2 πάτερ] πάτερε O **7** ἂν[2]] om. AB **10** φήμη] φίνη O **18** Κωνσταντινούπολιν] Κωνσταντίνου πόλιν AB

GEORGE AMIROUTZES' LETTER TO CARDINAL BESSARION OF 10 DECEMBER 1461

1. Most venerable and reverend in Christ father and lord, may you think kindly of me and fare well in all things.

2. The things that I foretold some time back and called our countrymen to witness have happened and come to pass. These I also put in writing to your lordship when I begged that you ransom at least the one of my sons who has been taken prisoner. 3. I know that I was reporting frightful things, the sort that you would not look past without tears, but I was offering you this small benefit in revealing our common suffering. For what profit comes from ignorance of one's very own misfortunes? 4. Moreover, at the same time I would be pointlessly silent about things the notoriety of which, I think, has now been spread abroad everywhere and is seen as a tragedy.

. . .

5. When they [the Turks] had captured the city and swept up in their control all the Comneni as if in a single dragnet, he [Mehmed II] immediately took the boys and girls and made slaves of almost all of those who had attained any sexual maturity. 6. Among that number is—alas!—my son, the beautiful Basil, whom you made your son, having lifted him up from the divine bath [of baptism] through your mother. 7. Furthermore, they enslaved my daughter's husband right after they got married because he is young and handsome. 8. Putting the Emperor [of Trebizond] with almost his whole extended family on triremes, they carried them off to Constantinople, whence then they herded them to Adrianople and settled them there.

9. And now this is where I am, absolutely "quailing at the rock that looms over my head."[1] And since the siege [of Trebizond] I have often not cared

1. Euripides, *Orestes* 6.

ἀλλ᾽ οὕτως ἐγένετο τούτου τυχεῖν, τῆς προνοίας, οἶμαι, ἐπὶ τὸ χεῖρον φυλαττούσης, ὅπως, ἐπὶ πολὺν τιμωρηθεὶς χρόνον, ἔπειτα ἀποθάνω. 10. Καὶ τὰ μὲν ἄλλα φέρειν οἷός τε εἰμί, πενίαν φημὶ καὶ τὴν ἐν ἀλλοδαπῇ ἀνελεύθερον διατριβήν· 11. ἡ δὲ τοῦ παιδὸς στέρησις ἐμπιπρᾷ μου τὰ σπλάγχνα. Πρὸς γὰρ τοῖς ἄλλοις αἰκιζόμενον αὐτὸν ὑπὸ τοῦ πάντων κρατοῦντος καὶ μαστιζόμενον ἑκάστοτε μανθάνων, ἔκφρων γένομαι· 12. αἴτιον δὲ, ὅτι φρονήματος ἐπειλημμένος οὑμὸς παῖς ὤν τε ἄλλως φύσει περὶ ἀρετὴν θερμός, τὴν πάτριον οὐ προδίδωσι δόξαν, τὴν μὲν οὖν ἀρχὴν λόγοις αὐτὸν ἐπεχείρει πείθειν καὶ δώροις ὁ κρατῶν· 13. ὡς δὲ ἦν τούτοις ἀνάλωτος, ἐπὶ τὰς βασάνους ἐτράπετο. ἐπεὶ δὲ πάντα ποιήσας οὐδὲν ἴσχυσε, τὴν μὲν ἀρετὴν ἐθαύμασε τοῦ παιδὸς καὶ τὴν μετὰ φρονήματος ἔνστασιν· 14. οὐ μὴν ᾗ προσῆκεν ἐλεύθερον αὐτὸν ἐποίησεν· ἀλλ᾽ ἀπογνοὺς τὴν μεταβολήν, ἀποδόσθαι ἔγνωκε· τοσαύτης αὐτὸν φιλανθρωπίας ἠξίωσε. πλείστου δὲ αὐτὸν ὅμως ἀποδίδωται, καὶ ὅσον αὐτοὶ οὐκ ἄν ποτε ἱκανοὶ ἐσόμεθα λυτρώσασθαι.

15. Τὰ μὲν οὖν ἡμέτερα ἐν τούτοις καὶ πολλῷ χείροσιν ἔτι· δεῖσθαι δέ σου βουλόμενοι χεῖρα ὀρέξαι, οὐ πολλῶν ἡγοῦμαι δεήσεσθαι λόγων. 16. ὁ γὰρ πολλοῖς τῶν ἀθλίων Ῥωμαίων τὴν αἰχμαλωσίαν λυσάμενος οὐ δή που πολίτην ἕνα δεόμενον περιόψει. καίτοι τὸν πρόσθεν χρόνον εὐλαβὴς ἦν αἰτεῖν τι παρὰ τῆς σῆς κυριότητος· 17. ἀλλὰ νῦν οὐκ ἂν αἰσχυνοίμην τὸ πρᾶγμα. δέομαι τοίνυν τῆς σῆς κυριότητος, αἰδεσιμώτατε δέσποτα, μεμνημένον τῆς πολλῆς ἡμῶν ἀεὶ περὶ σὲ εὐνοίας καὶ τῶν πολλῶν ἐπὶ σοὶ καὶ μεγάλων ἐλπίδων, ὧν ἔχοντες ἡδέως διεβιώσαμεν τὸν μέχρι τῆς ἁλώσεως χρόνον, ὡς οἶδεν ὁ πάντα ἐφορῶν ὀφθαλμός, ἔτι δὲ τῆς παρὰ σοῦ εἰς ἡμᾶς εὐεργεσίας, ἣν εἴ τις τῶν ἡμετέρων ἀφέλη, οὐκ

---

1 οὕτως] οὕτω AB **4** σπλάγχνα] σπλάχνα O **8** τὴν μὲν] καὶ τὴν AB **10** ἐθαύμασε] ἐθαύμαζε Boiss **11** ἔνστασιν] At this point V and its two apographs, O Vall, place a completely irrelevant figure of a square divided into four quadrants and also divided by a diagonal into two triangles with each corner of the square and the midpoint of each side marked by a numeral, i.e., from α΄ to θ΄. A notation on its right side calls the figure τετράγωνον, while the top half of square has the notation παραπλήρωμα γνωρίμον and the lower half simply παραπλήρωμα (cf. Euclid, *Elements*, vol. 5, part 1, 146, line 27, and 147, line 14: scholia 135 and 136 ad prop. μγ΄). The text of V's source must have been written on a sheet where, for whatever reason, this geometrical figure was written, and V assumed that it was part of the letter. || μὴν] μετὰ O **13** ἀποδίδωται] ἀποδίδοται B Boiss **16** δεήσεσθαι] δεήσασθαι AB **17** οὐ δή] οὐδί OV **18** περιόψει] περιριόψη O

whether I died, but [have left things] to happen as they might, since providence, I believe, is preserving me for worse so that after having suffered for a long time, I shall then die.[2] 10. I am up to enduring other miseries—I mean, I am up to enduring this destitution and slavery in a foreign land. 11. The loss of my son, however, strikes to the core of my being. Among other things, I lose my mind each time I see him being tortured and flogged by the ruler of all.[3] 12. The reason is that my son is a totally serious minded person, by nature on fire for virtue. He is not abandoning the belief of his fathers. In the beginning, the ruler attempted to persuade him by arguments and gifts. 13. When he did not succumb to these tactics, he turned to physical punishment. When he still did not subdue him after trying all these things, he marveled at the virtue of the boy and his thoughtful determination. 14. He did not in fact set the boy free as he deserved. But after giving up on converting him, he decided to sell him; he did deem him worthy of such a humane act, but all the same, he would sell him for an extremely high price. I myself would never be capable of paying this ransom.

15. Thus, then, is our situation in these matters and in matters still much worse. In wishing to beg you to extend a hand, I do not think I have to use many words. 16. For having effected the release from captivity of many of the forlorn Romans, you will not overlook an individual countryman in need. Indeed, I was restrained before in asking something from your lordship. 17. But I would not be ashamed now, given my situation. I therefore beg your lordship, most honorable despot, being mindful of our constant goodwill toward you and our many and great hopes for you which we sweetly entertained until the time of the conquest,[4] as the all-seeing eye[5] knows, and being mindful as well of your goodwill toward

2. Cf. Plutarch, *Consol. ad Apoll.* 118C6

3. A common honorific used, for instance, by Bessarion himself in addressing Demetrius, the Despot of Mistra (Mohler, *Kardinal Bessarion*, 3:425.9), but here to mean Mehmed II.

4. Of Constantinople rather than Trebizond, presumably.

5. A common epithet for God, sanctioned already by the Septuagint in 2 Macc. 12:22, 15:2.

οἶδ᾽ εἴ τι περιλειφθήσεται, καὶ τῆς καθαρᾶς ἐκείνης καὶ εἰλικρινοῦς φιλίας, ἣν οὐ χρόνος, οὐ πραγμάτων μεταβολαί, οὐ τοσοῦτον διάστημα ἴσχυσεν ὁπωσοῦν ἀμαυρῶσαι, τὰ προσήκοντα τῇ παρούσῃ τύχῃ βοηθῆσαι 18. καὶ πρῶτον μὲν ἡμῖν τὸν Βασίλειον ἐλευθερῶσαι, ὅς, τούτου τυχών, εὐθὺς παρὰ σὲ ἕξει, δοῦλος ἐσόμενος· ἔπειτα καὶ ἡμῖν τινὰ χορηγίαν εἰς τὸ μέλλον πορίσασθαι, ἀφ᾽ ἧς ἐν τῇ παρούσῃ τύχῃ διαβιώσομεν. 19. εἰ δὲ μεγάλα ταῦτα καὶ ἀμφότερα οὐ ῥᾴδιον τὸ νῦν ἔχον γενέσται, σὺ δὲ τὸν παῖδε λυσάμενος τὰ μέγιστα εὖ ποιήσεις καὶ οὗ μεῖζον ἡμῖν οὐκ ἂν γένοιτο, 20. αὐτοὶ δὲ τὴν ἄλλην τύχην οὐ χαλεπῶς οἴσομεν, ὁρῶντες τοὺς ἀθλίους Ῥωμαίους οἳ ἅπαντα πράττουσιν ὅπως τῆς ἐφημέρου τροφῆς εὐπορήσωσιν.

21. Ἀλλά σοι ὁ πάντα διέπων θεὸς μακρὸν μὲν αἰῶνα δοίη, ἐρρωμένον δὲ ἡμῖν καὶ εὔθυκον διαφυλάττοι· σὲ γὰρ ἔχοντες καὶ αἰχμαλωσίαν καὶ πενίαν καὶ πᾶσα τύχην οὐ χαλεπῶς οἴομεν. πρὸς θεοῦ δὲ μὴ ἀπαξιώσῃς ἡμῖν ἀεὶ γράφειν· ὡς ἡμῖν καὶ τὰ σὰ γράμματα μόνα μεγίστην φέρει παραμυθίαν. 22. ἐνταῦθα δὲ ἡμῖν ἐπιστέλλειν ῥᾴδιον· πολλοὶ γὰρ ἐκ Βενετίας, οἱ δὲ καὶ ἐκ Φλωρεντίας εἰς τὴν Κωνσταντινούπολιν ἀφικνοῦνται· ἐντεῦθεν δὲ εἰς τὴν Ἀδριανοῦ τριῶν ἡμερῶν ὁδός ἐστιν· ὥστε ἔστι καὶ γράμματα καὶ ἄλλο τι ἀσφαλῶς πέμπειν. καὶ γὰρ αὐτὸς μαθών τι παρὰ σοῦ ἥκειν, τάχιστα εἰς τὴς Κωνσταντίνου ἀφίξομαι.

23. Ὁ παρὼν ἄνθρωπος ὁ τὰ γράμματα κομίζων ἔστιν ἡμέτερος πολίτης, συγγενὴς καὶ οἰκεῖος τοῦ Παρασκευᾶ, τοῦ τῆς μητρὸς θεράποντος· ἀπώλεσε δὲ καὶ αὐτὸς παῖδα καὶ γυναῖκα, ὃν εἰ βοηθείας τῆς δυνατῆς ἀξιώσεις, τῇ μητρὶ καὶ θανούσῃ δόξεις χαρίζεσθαι· καὶ γὰρ αὐτὸς δι᾽ ἐκείνην πρὸς σὲ ἔδραμεν.

24. Ἐν Ἀδριανουπόλει, δεκεμβρίου ια´ τῆς Ἰνδικτιῶνος ἐνάτης, τῆς σῆς αἰδεσιμότητος ἐλάχιστος δοῦλος Γεώργιος ὁ Ἀμιρούτζης.

1 τῆς] post add. et deinde del. OV εἰς ἡμας || φιλίας] φιλείας O **2** τοσοῦτον] τὸ τοσοῦτον O **9** ὁρῶντες] post OV add. εἰς || οἳ] om. A || ἅπαντα] πάντα OV **11** αἰῶνα] τὸν αἰῶνα OV **14** σὰ] om. OV **15** καὶ] om. AB **16** Κωνσταντινούπολιν] Κωνσταντίνου πόλιν AB **20–21** δὲ καὶ] δέ τε καὶ OV **21** εἰ] om. AOV **23–24** Ἐν . . . Ἀμιρούτζης] OV; Ἔρρωσο AB

us (if someone took that away from us, I do not know if there would be anything left), and being mindful of that pure and exquisite friendship that neither time, nor changes of circumstances, nor such a great distance have been strong enough to diminish in any way: help our situation in the present misfortune, 18. first of all liberating for us Basil, who, if he were liberated, would forthwith come to you to be your servant,[6] and then providing us some funds that would allow for an improvement in the situation we presently endure. 19. If these daunting things cannot both be done with ease at the present time, the most important thing you can do is ransom the boy. No greater benefaction can be done for us than this. 20. We ourselves, however, will not take it badly if we suffer a different fate, seeing how the forlorn Romans endure all sorts of miseries in order to procure their daily bread.[7]

21. But may the God who disposes all things grant you a long life. May he preserve you in good health and with a good disposition toward us. For we, who are suffering from imprisonment, penury, and ill fortune, will not view you harshly. For God's sake, do not ever disdain to write to us, since only your letters to us offer the greatest consolation. 22. To send a letter to us here is easy, for there are many who have come to Constantinople from Venice and Florence. From there to Adrianople is a three days' journey. Hence you can send me a letter and anything else quite safely. For once I learn that something from you has arrived, I shall speedily travel to Constantinople.

23. The man who has now traveled to you with my letter is our fellow countryman, a kinsman and an official of the Paraskeve monastery, which shelters [the tomb] of your mother. He himself has lost his son and his wife. If you deem him worthy of effective help, you will be reputed as doing a service for your deceased mother. For it was on her account that he fled to you.

24. In Adrianople, the tenth of December of the ninth Indiction, your Most High Reverence's humblest slave, George Amiroutzes.

6. Amiroutzes hyperbolically uses the world *doulos*, which can mean "slave," here.

7. Cf. *The Philosopher* I.1.2.

APPENDIX II

Johannes Werner's Preface to George Amiroutzes' Treatise *De his quae geographiae adesse debent*

Amiroutzes' treatise in a Latin translation by an anonymous scholar appeared as one of the appendices in Johannes Werner's Latin translation of book one of Ptolemy's *Geography* published in Nuremberg in 1514.[1] A digital version of the volume is available at https://reader.digitale-sammlungen.de/resolve/display/bsb11199369.html. Antonio Rigo, "Interessi astronomici," 108, offers a photograph of sign. l, ff. 1v–2r (on f. 1v there is an image of the sphere labeled *Formula metheoroscopii Ioannis de Regiomonte*, and on f. 2r the opening of Regiomontanus's preface to Cardinal Bessarion for Regiomontanus's treatise *De compositione et usu cuiusdam meteoroscopii*). I extract below the relevant passages in Werner's preface to Cardinal Matthew Lang for Amiroutzes' treatise, followed by an English translation. I also provide the *incipit-desinit* of the Latin translation of Amiroutzes's treatise in the hope that someday it will lead to the discovery of the Greek text in an adespotic manuscript. The preface is found on sign. 1, ff. 1r–v, and the treatise on sign. 1, ff. 2r–7v.

1. The best description I know of Amiroutzes' work is Dalché, "Reception of Ptolemy's *Geography*," 337: "The content here is purely mathematical, and the essential problem considered is that of the variation in the degree of longitude, the resolution of which was considered indispensable for the resolution of two further issues, one scientific and the other practical: how to establish the relative distance between cities and between cities and the ends of the world and how to provide means for planning swift and efficient military opertions. This is the only fifteenth-century treatise to deal with such questions." See also ibid., 357: "Amiroutzes's explanations of how to calculate the distance between places whose spherical coordinates known."

—

1. Pientissimum id reor officii genus, antistes reverendissime, illustrissime princeps, bonarum artium opuscula quae in abstrusis bibliothecarum angulis, pulverulento conspersa situ diu latuerant propensius inquirere atque pro viribus curare ut ea pro ingenti studentium profectu in lucem prodeant. . . . 2. Hoc itaque officii genere cunctis de litteris nostra aetate Ioannem Stabium, domini nostri imperatoris divi Maximiliani geographum historiographumque, profecto liquet optime mereri, qui Germaniae plerasque perlustrans librarias haud modica bonarum opuscula artium, et ea quidem utilissima, carie tineisque pene consumpta, suis etiam fere consepulta auctoribus investigavit. . . . 3. Sed redeo ad Ioannem Stabium, mei amantissimum, qui Graecorum inventis mirummodum afficitur. 4. Is mihi iam pridem obtulerat de his quae geographiae debent adesse opuscolum cuiusdam Amirucii Constantinopolitani hoc ferme aevo recenter compositum et in Latinam paulopost linguam a quodam utriusque linguae haud mediocriter perito traductum. 5. Monuit insuper iussitque ut idem opusculum, detersis ei mendis aliquot etiam adiectis appendicibus reddere lucidius. Haec itaque iussa monitaque ad ingenioli mei mensuram libentius implevi. 6. Propensius enim dedi operam ut quaecumque Graecus ille vir crassiore, ut aiunt, Minerva tractaverat ad calcalum revocata conarer altius repetere. Nam in eodem opusculo nonnulla reperiunt assumpta quae a vero haud parum discrepare videntur. . . . 7. Graeco tamen auctori ea [*sc.* vitia] non sunt usque adeo

12 opuscolum] oposculum *editio*

JOHANNES WERNER'S PREFACE TO GEORGE AMIROUTZES' TREATISE *DE HIS QUAE GEOGRAPHIAE ADESSE DEBENT*

1. I consider it the most sacred sort of duty, most reverend bishop and illustrious prince, to be especially keen to seek out writings in the liberal arts that have long lain strewn about in dusty ruin in obscure corners of libraries,[1] and, as much as one can, to see to their publication to the great profit of scholars. . . . 2. And thus it is eminently clear that in this kind of duty, toward every kind of literature, in our time, Johannes Stabius, the geographer and historiographer of our lord the divine Emperor Maximilian, has rendered exceptional service. He has explored most of the libraries of Germany and discovered not a small number of works of literature, and indeed exceptionally useful ones, that were nearly consumed by decay and worms,[2] and almost even buried along with their authors. . . . 3. But let me return to my dearest Johannes Stabius, who takes pleasure to a wonderous degree in the discovery of Greek texts. 4. He had already earlier passed on to me the opuscule of a certain Amirucius of Constantinople concerning what should be in a work of geography. It had been composed recently, almost in our own day, and a little later translated into Latin by someone learned in both languages to no small degree. 5. Furthermore, he advised—indeed, commanded—that I purge this same opuscule of its flaws and even render it clearer by the addition of appendices. And so I complied quite willingly with this advice and command to the degree my abilities allowed. 6. For I was all the more inclined to do this work in order that whatever that Greek gentleman had drawn out from Minerva, as they say, in rough and ready fashion, I might try to bring to a greater degree of accuracy by redoing the calculations. For one finds some things assumed in this opuscule that do not seem to square with the facts. . . . 7. Nonetheless, I do not

1. A standard Renaissance trope when speaking of the discovery of manuscripts and texts; cf. Rice, *Prefatory Epistles of Jacques Lefèvre d'Etaples*, 242.14: *e situ ac squalore redemit*.

2. Another Renaissance trope; cf. ibid., 337.21–22: *ne diutius inter blattas et tineas moretur situmve ducat*.

imputanda, qui animum suum, veluti coniicio, circa modica tantum agitavit intervalla. . . . 8. Hoc denique Amirucii Constantinopolitani opusculum a me fideliter recognitum atque ipsius appendices, reverendissime domine et illustrissime princeps, celsitudini tuae devotissime dedico. . . . 9. Ex Nurenberga anno nostrae salutis millesimoquingentesimodecimoquarto.

DE HIS QUAE GEOGRAPHIAE ADESSE DEBENT

[inc.] Quoniam necessarium quidem est scienter de terrae situ scribenti cognoscere circumferentiam quae inter duo puncta secundum verticem locorum datorum in Geographia quanta sit secundum proprium circulum, quanta, videlicet, pars eius sit et secundum maximum. . . . [des.] Quas sane partes, si orientalior secundum b. locus eo qui secundum a. fit, addere opportet existentibus quoniam posita est cognita longitudo secundum a. loci. Sin autem occidentalior auferre ab existentibus, et quod reliquum fuerit aut quod ab additione fit ponere longitudinem secundum b. loci.

think that these errors should be so much imputed to the Greek author who, as I would venture to guess, was intent on treating only modest intervals. . . . 8. This opusculc of Amirucius of Constantinople, then, faithfully revised by me along with its appendices, I, in my profound devotion to your Highness, dedicate to you, most reverend lord and illustrious prince. . . . 9. From Nuremberg, in the year of our salvation 1514.

BIBLIOGRAPHY

Primary Works

Acta et diplomata graeca — F. Miklosich and J. Müller, eds. *Acta et diplomata graeca: Medii Aevi sacra et profana.* Vols. 1–2, *Acta Patriarchatus Constantinopolitani.* Vienna, 1860–62.

Alexander of Aphrodisias, *Mantissa* — I. Bruns, ed. *Supplementum Aristotelicum.* Vol. 2, part 1, *Praeter commentaria; Scripta minora: De anima liber cum Mantissa.* 101–86. Berlin, 1887.

———, *On the Soul* — I. Bruns, ed. *Supplementum Aristotelicum.* Vol. 2, part 1, *Praeter commentaria; Scripta minora: De anima liber cum Mantissa.* 1–100. Berlin, 1887.

———, *Supplement* — R. W. Sharples, trans. *Supplement to "On the Soul."* Ithaca, NY, 2004.

Amiroutzes, George, *Dialogus de fide* — Zenobio Acciaiuoli, trans. *Dialogus de fide.* 1518.

A. Argyriou and G. Lagarrigue. "Georges Amiroutzès et son 'Dialogue sur la foi au Christ tenu avec le Sultan des Turcs.'" *Byzantinische Forschungen* 11 (1987): 29–221.

Ó. de la Cruz Palma, ed. and trans. *El Diálogo de la Fe con el Sultán de los turcos.* Nueva Roma: Bibliotheca Graeca et Latina Aevi Posterioris 9. Madrid, 2000.

Aquinas, Thomas, *De ente et essentia* — L. Baur, ed. *Sermo seu tractatus De ente et essentia.* Münster, 1933. https://www.corpusthomisticum.org/oee.html.

———, *De potentia* — P. M. Pession, ed. *Quaestiones disputatae de potentia.* Turin, 1953. https://www.corpusthomisticum.org/qdp1.html.

———, *Summa contra gentiles* — C. Pera, P. Marc, and P. Carmello, eds. *Summa contra gentiles.* Rome, 1961. https://www.corpusthomisticum.org/scg1001.html.

——, *Summa theologiae* R. Busa, ed. *Summa theologiae.* 9 vols. London, 1888–1906. https://www.corpusthomisticum.org/sth1001.html.

Aristotle, *Metaphysics* W. D. Ross, trans. *Aristotle's Metaphysics: A Revised Text with Introduction and Commentary.* 2 vols. Oxford, 1924.

H. Tredennick, trans. *Metaphysics: Books 1–9.* Loeb Classical Library 271. Cambridge, MA, 1933.

H. Tredennick and G. C. Armstrong, trans. *Metaphysics: Books 10–14. Oeconomica. Magna Moralia.* Loeb Classical Library 287. Cambridge, MA, 1935.

——, *Nicomachean Ethics* H. Rackham, trans. *Nicomachean Ethics.* Loeb Classical Library 73. Rev. ed. Cambridge, MA, 1934.

——, *On Plants* W. S. Hett, trans. *Minor Works.* Loeb Classical Library 307. 141–233. Repr. Cambridge, MA, 1936.

——, *On Sense and Sensible Objects* W. S. Hett, trans. *On the Soul. Parva Naturalia. On Breath.* Loeb Classical Library 288. Repr. Cambridge, MA, 1957.

——, *On the Heavens* W. K. C. Guthrie, trans. *On the Heavens.* Loeb Classical Library 338. Cambridge, MA, 1939.

——, *Physics* P. H. Wicksteed and F. M. Cornford, trans. *Physics: Books 1–4.* Loeb Classical Library 228. Repr. Cambridge, MA, 1957.

P. H. Wicksteed and F. M. Cornford, trans. *Physics: Books 5–8.* Loeb Classical Library 255. Repr. Cambridge, MA, 1957.

——, *Posterior Analytics* H. Tredennick and E. S. Forster, trans. *Posterior Analytics. Topica.* Loeb Classical Library 391. Cambridge, MA, 1960.

——, *Topics* H. Tredennick and E. S. Forster, trans. *Posterior Analytics. Topica.* Loeb Classical Library 391. Cambridge, MA, 1960.

Avicenna, *De Almahad*	A. Alpago, trans. *Compendium de anima. De mahad, idest, de dispositione, seu loco, ad quem revertitur homo, vel anima eius post mortem. Aphorismi de anima. De diffinitionibus, et quaesitis. De divisione scientiarum.* 40–102. Venice, 1546. Repr. Westmead, 1969.
———, *De philosophia prima*	S. van Riet, ed. *Liber de Philosophia prima, sive, Scientia divina I–IV.* 3 vols. Leiden, 1977–83.
———, *Epistola sulla vita futura*	F. Lucchetta, ed. and trans. *Epistola sulla vita futura.* Pubblicazioni dell'Istituto di storia della filosofia e del Centro per ricerche di filosofia medioevale, n. s. 5. Padua, 1969.
———, *The Metaphysics of* The Healing	M. E. Marmura, ed. and trans. *The Metaphysics of* The Healing. Provo, UT, 2005.
Chalcocondyles, Laonicus, *The Histories*	A. Kaldellis, trans. *The Histories.* 2 vols. Dumbarton Oaks Medieval Library 33–34. Cambridge, MA, 2014.
Critobulus, Michael, *Histories*	D. R. Reinsch, ed. *Critobuli Imbriotae Historiae.* Corpus fontium historiae byzantinae 22. Berlin, 1983.
	C. T. Riggs, trans. *History of Mehmed the Conqueror.* Princeton, 1954.
Ecthesis chronica	S. P. Lambros, ed. *Ecthesis chronica and Chronicon Athenarum.* London, 1902.
	M. Philippides, ed. *Emperors, Patriarchs and Sultans of Constantinople, 1373–1513: An Anonymous Greek Chronicle of the Sixteenth Century.* Brookline, MA, 1990.
Euclid, *Elements*	I. L. Heiberg and E. S. Stamatis, eds. *Elementa Euclidis.* 5 vols. Leipzig, 1969–77.
Eugenicus, John, *Consolation to Constantine Palaeologus*	S. P. Lambros, ed. *Παλαιολόγεια καὶ Πελοποννησιακά.* Vol. 1: 117–22. Athens, 1912.
Filelfo, Francesco, *Ep.*	J. De Keyser, ed. *Collected Letters: Epistolarum Libri XLVIII.* 2nd corrected reprint. 4 vols. Turin, 2017.

George of Hungary, *Tractatus de moribus, conditionibus et nequicia Turcorum* — R. Klockow, ed. and trans. *Tractatus de moribus, conditionibus et nequicia Turcorum. Traktat über die Sitten, die Lebensverhältnisse und die Arglist der Türken*. Schriften zur Landeskunde Siebenbürgens 15. Cologne, 1993.

Gregory of Nazianzus, *Or.* — *Orationes*. PG 36:9–664.

C. G. Browne and J. E. Swallow, trans. *S. Cyril of Jerusalem: Catechetical Lectures. S. Gregory of Nazianzum: Select Orations and Letters*. Nicene and Post-Nicene Fathers, Second series. Vol. 7: 203–434. Buffalo, NY, 1894.

Historia politica — I. Bekker, ed. *Historia politica et patriarchica Constantinopoleos. Epirotica*. Corpus Scriptorum Historiae Byzantinae 49. Bonn, 1849.

Horace, *Ep.* — H. R. Fairclough, trans. *Satires. Epistles. Art of Poetry*. Loeb Classical Library 194. Repr. Cambridge, MA, 1929.

Iorga, *Notes et extraits* — N. Iorga, ed. *Notes et extraits pour servir à l'histoire des croisades au XV*[e] *siècle*. 6 vols. Paris, 1899–1916. Originally published in *Revue de l'Orient latin* 4–8 (1896–1900).

John of Salisbury, *Policraticus* — J. A. Giles, ed. *Joannis Saresberiensis postea episcopi Carnotensis opera omnia*. Vol. 3, *Polycratici libri I–IV*. Oxford, 1848.

Lascaris, Theodore II Ducas, *Ep.* — N. Festa, ed. *Epistulae CCXVII*. Florence, 1898.

Manuel II Palaiologus, *Dialogue with a Persian* — E. Trapp, ed. *Dialoge mit einem "Perser."* Vienna, 1966.

T. Khoury, ed. and trans. *Entretiens avec un Musulman: 7*[e] *controverse*. Sources chrétiennes 115. Paris, 1966.

K. Förstel, ed. and trans. *Dialoge mit einem Muslim*. 2 vols. Wurzburg, 1993.

Martí, Ramón, *De secta Machometi* — J. Hernando I Delgado, ed. and trans. "Ramón Martí (s. XIII), *De seta Machometi* o *De origine, progressu, et fine Machometi et quadruplici reprobatione prophetiae eius*." *Acta historica et archaeologica mediaevalia* 4 (1983): 9–63.

Nicetas Byzantius, *Refutation of the Koran*	K. Förstel, ed. and trans. *Schriften zum Islam: Griechisch-deutsche Textausgabe*. Würzburg, 2000.
Orientalium documenta minora	G. Hofmann, T. O'Shaughnessy, and I. Simon, eds. *Orientalium documenta minora*. Volume 3, part 3. Concilium Florentinum: Documenta et Scriptores, ser. A. Rome, 1953.
PG	Patrologiae cursus completes, Series graeca, ed. J.-P. Migne. 161 vols. Paris, 1857–66.
Photius, *Bibl.*	*Bibliotheca*. PG 103.
Plutarch, *Moralia*	F. H. Sandbach, trans. *Moralia*, vol. 15. Loeb Classical Library 429. Cambridge, MA, 1969.
Porphyry, *Introduction*	J. Barnes, trans. *Porphyry: Introduction*. Oxford, 2003.
Proclus, *The Elements of Theology*	E. R. Dodds, ed. and trans. *The Elements of Theology: A Revised Text with Translation, Introduction and Commentary*. Oxford, 1963.
Psellus, Michael, *Hagiographical Orations*	E. A. Fisher, ed. *Orationes hagiographicae*. Stuttgart, 1994.
———, *Funeral Oration on the Patriarch Michael Cerularius*	K. N. Sathas, ed. *Ἐπιτάφιοι Λόγοι*, vol. 4, 303–87. Bibliotheca Graeca Medii Aevi. Athens, 1874.
Scholarius, George [Gennadius II], *Oeuvres complètes*	L. Petit, X. A. Sidéridès, and M. Jugie, eds. *Oeuvres complètes de Gennade Scholarios*. 8 vols. Paris, 1928–36.
Simplicius, *On Aristotle's Physics*	H. Diels, ed. *In Aristotelis Physicorum libros quattuor priores commentaria*. Commentaria in Aristotelem graeca 9. Berlin, 1882.
Surius, Laurentius, *De probatis sanctorum historiis*	*De probatis sanctorum historiis*. 6 vols. Cologne, 1576–81.
Tursun Beg, *The History of Mehmed the Conqueror*	H. Inalcik and R. Murphey, ed. and trans. *The History of Mehmed the Conqueror*. Minneapolis, 1978.

Secondary Works

Accad, M. "Corruption and/or Misinterpretation of the Bible: The Story of the Islâmic Usage of Tahrîf." *Near Eastern School of Theology Theological Review* 24 (2003): 67–97.

Allacci, Leone. *De ecclesiae occidentalis atque orientalis perpetua consensione, libri tres*. Cologne, 1648.

Angelou, A. D. "'*Who am I?*' Scholarios' Answers and the Hellenic Identity." In *Φιλέλλην: Studies in Honour of Robert Browning*. Edited by C. N. Constantinides, N. M. Panagiotakes, E. Jeffreys, and A. D. Angelou. 1–19. Istituto ellenico di studi bizantini e postbizantini di Venezia, Bibliotheke 17. Venice, 1996.

Argyriou, A., and G. Lagarrigue. "Georges Amiroutzès et son 'Dialogue sur la foi au Christ tenu avec le Sultan des Turcs.'" *Byzantinische Forschungen* 11 (1987): 29–222.

Arnakis, G. G. "Gregory Palamas among the Turks and Documents of His Captivity as Historical Sources." *Speculum* 26 (1951): 104–18.

Ayoub, M. M. "Towards an Islamic Christology, II: The Death of Jesus, Reality or Delusion (A Study of the Death of Jesus in Tafsīr Literature)." *The Muslim World* 70.2 (1980): 91–121.

Babinger, F. *Aufsätze und Abhandlungen zur Geschichte Südosteuropas und der Levante*. 3 vols. Südosteuropa-Schriften 3, 8. Munich, 1962–76.

———. "Ja'qūb-Pascha, ein Leibarzt Mehmed's II: Leben und Schicksale des Maestro Jacopo aus Gaeta." *Rivista degli studi orientali* 26 (1951): 87–113. Repr. in idem, *Aufsätze und Abhandlungen*, 2:240–62.

———. "Maometto il Conquistatore e gli umanisti d'Italia." In *Venezia e l'Oriente fra tardo Medioevo e Rinascimento*. Edited by A. Pertusi. 433–49. Civiltà europea a civiltà veneziana 4. Florence, 1966. Repr. in idem, *Aufsätze und Abhandlungen*, 3:291–307.

———. "Mehmed II., der Eroberer, und Italien." *Byzantion* 21 (1951): 127–70. Repr. in idem, *Aufsätze und Abhandlungen*, 1:172–200.

———. *Mehmed the Conqueror and His Time*. Edited by W. C. Hickman; translated by R. Manheim. Bollingen Series XCVI. Princeton, 1978.

———. "Notes on Cyriac of Ancona and Some of His Friends." *Journal of the Warburg and Courtauld Institutes* 25 (1962): 321–23. Repr. in idem, *Aufsätze und Abhandlungen*, 3:123–25.

Balivet, M. "Le soufi et le basileus: Haci Bayram Veli et Manuel II Paléologue." *Medioevo greco* 4 (2004): 19–30.

Bănescu, N. "Le conflit entre Gênes et l'empire de Trébizonde à la veille de la conquête turque (1418–1449)." *Studi bizantini e neoellenici* 5 (1939): 4–10.

Beldiceanu, N. "Biens des Grands Comnènes en 1461 d'après un registre ottoman." *Byzantion* 49 (1979): 21–41.

Beldiceanu, N., and I. Beldiceanu-Steinherr. "Biens des Amiroutzès d'après un registre ottoman de 1487." *Travaux et mémoires* 8 (1981): 63–78.

Bianchi, L. *Pour une histoire de la "double vérité."* Paris, 2008.

Blumenthal, H. J. *Aristotle and Neoplatonism in Late Antiquity: Interpretations of the* De anima. Ithaca, NY, 1996.

Böhm, T. *Die Christologie des Arius: Dogmengeschichtliche Überlegungen unter besonderer Berücksichtigung der Hellenisierungsfrage.* Studien zur Theologie und Geschichte 7. St. Ottilien, 1991.

Boissonade, J.-F. *Ἀνέκδοτα: Anecdota graeca e codicibus regiis.* 5 vols. Paris, 1829–33.

Bouamama, A. *La littérature polémique musulmane contre le christianisme depuis ses origines jusqu'au XIII*[e] *siècle.* Islamochristiana 17. Algiers, 1988.

Bryer, A. "Rural Society in Matzouka." In *Continuity and Change in Late Byzantine and Early Ottoman Society. Papers Given at a Symposium at Dumbarton Oaks in May 1982.* Edited by A. Bryer and H. Lowry. 53–95. Washington, DC, 1986. Repr. in idem, *Peoples and Settlement in Anatolia and the Caucasus, 800–1900* (London, 1988), as article XII.

———. "Trebizond and Serbia." *Ἀρχεῖον Πόντου* 27 (1965): 29–40.

Bryer, A., and D. Winfield. *The Byzantine Monuments and Topography of the Pontos.* Dumbarton Oaks Studies 20. Washington, DC, 1985.

Bussanich, J. "Plotinus's Metaphysics of the One." In *The Cambridge Companion to Plotinus.* Edited by L. P. Gerson. 38–65. Cambridge, 1996.

Bynum, C. W. *The Resurrection of the Body in Western Christianity, 200–1336.* New York, 1995.

Campbell, C., and A. Chong, eds. *Bellini and the East.* London, 2005.

Caspar, R. "Les versions arabes du dialogue entre le catholicos Timothée I et le calife al-Mahdī (IIe/VIIIe siècle) 'Mohammed a suivi la voie des prophètes.'" *Islamochristiana* 3 (1977): 107–75.

Clark, E. A. *The Origenist Controversy: The Cultural Construction of an Early Christian Debate.* Princeton, 1992.

Collins, J. J. *The Apocalyptic Imagination: An Introduction to Jewish Apocalyptic Literature.* 2nd ed. Grand Rapids, 1998.

Dalché, P. G. "The Reception of Ptolemy's *Geography* (End of the Fourteenth to Beginning of the Sixteenth Century)." In *Cartography in the European*

Renaissance. Edited by D. Woodward. Vol. 1, 285–364. The History of Cartography 3. Chicago, 2007.

Daneloni, A. "Nuovi contributi su Zanobi Acciaiuoli." *Studi medievali e umanistici* 3 (2005): 375–400.

de la Cruz Palma, Ó., ed. and trans. *El Diálogo de la Fe con el Sultán de los turcos*. Nueva Roma: Bibliotheca Graeca et Latina Aevi Posterioris 9. Madrid, 2000.

Demetracopoulos, J. A. "Demetrius Cydones' Translation of Bernardus Guidonis' List of Thomas Aquinas' Writings and the Historical Roots of Byzantine Thomism." In *1308: Akten der 36. Kölner Mediaevistentagung, Köln, 9.–12. September 2008*. Edited by A. Speer and D. Wirmer. 827–81. Berlin, 2010.

———. "Latin Philosophical Works Translated into Greek." In *The Cambridge History of Medieval Philosophy*. Edited by R. Pasnau and C. Van Dyke. Vol. 2, 822–26. Cambridge, 2010.

Diels, H., ed. *Die Fragmente der Vorsokratiker: Griechisch und Deutsch*. Rev. ed. by W. Kranz. 3 vols. Berlin, 1961.

Di Matteo, I. "Confutazione contro i cristiani dello Zaydita al-Qāsim b. Ibrāhīm." *Rivista degli studi orientali* 9 (1922): 301–64.

———. "Il 'taḥrīf' od alterazione della Bibbia secondo i musulmani." *Bessarione* 38 (1922): 64–111, 223–60.

———. *La divinità di Cristo e la dottrina della Trinità in Maometto e nei polemisti musulmani*. Biblica et orientalia 8. Rome, 1938.

Frangedaki, A. "On Fifteenth-Century Cryptochristianity: A Letter to George Amoiroutzes from Michael Apostolis." *Byzantine and Modern Greek Studies* 9 (1984–1985): 221–24.

Fritsch, E. *Islam und Christentum im Mittelalter: Beiträge zur Geschichte der muslimischen Polemik gegen das Christentum in arabischer Sprache*. Breslauer Studien zur historischen Theologie 17. Breslau, 1930.

Fyrigos, A. "Tomismo e antitomismo a Bisanzio (con una nota sulla *Defensio S. Thomae adversus Nilum Cabasilam* di Demetrio Cidone)." In *Tommaso d'Aquino († 1274) e il mondo bizantino*. Edited by A. Molle. 27–72. Venafro, 2004.

Gaudeul, J.-M., and R. Caspar. "Textes de la tradition musulmane concernant le taḥrîf (falsification) des Écritures." *Islamochristiana* 6 (1980): 61–104.

Gill, J. "A Tractate about the Council of Florence Attributed to Georges Amiroutzes." *The Journal of Ecclesiastical History* 9 (1958): 30–37. Repr. in idem, *Personalities of the Council of Florence and Other Essays* (Oxford, 1964), 204–21.

Goddu, A. "Medieval Natural Philosophy and Modern Science—Continuity *and* Revolution." In *Philosophy and Theology in the Long Middle Ages: A Tribute to Stephen F. Brown*. Edited by K. Emery, R. Friedman, and A. Speer. 213–33. Studien und Texte zur Geistesgeschichte des Mittelalters 105. Leiden, 2011.

Graux, C., and A. Martin. *Notices sommaires des manuscrits grecs d'Espagne et de Portugal*. Paris, 1892. Reprint of A. Martin, "Rapport sur une mission en Espagne et en Portugal," *Nouvelles Archives des Missions scientifiques et littéraires* 2 (1892): 1–322.

Greshake, G., and J. Kremer. *Resurrectio mortuorum: Zum theologischen Verständnis der leiblichen Auferstehung*. Darmstadt, 1986.

Griffith, S. H. "Arguing from Scripture: The Bible in the Christian/Muslim Encounter in the Middle Ages." In *Scripture and Pluralism: Reading the Bible in the Religiously Plural Worlds of the Middle Ages and the Renaissance*. 29–58. Studies in the History of Christian Traditions 123. Leiden, 2005.

Grössing, H. "Stabius (Stöbere), Johannes." In Worstbrock, *Deutscher Humanismus*, 2:947–57.

Grypeou, E., M. Swanson, and D. Thomas, eds. *The Encounter of Eastern Christianity with Early Islam*. The History of Christian-Muslim Relations 5. Leiden, 2006.

Gwynn, D. M. *The Eusebians: The Polemic of Athanasius of Alexandria and the Construction of the "Arian Controversy."* Oxford, 2007.

Hanson, R. P. C. *The Search for the Christian Doctrine of God: The Arian Controversy, 318–381*. Edinburgh, 1988.

Henle, R. J. *Saint Thomas and Platonism: A Study of the* Plato *and* Platonici *Texts in the Writings of Saint Thomas*. The Hague, 1956.

Henne, P. *Introduction à Origène*. Paris, 2004.

Hoffmann, T. "Intellectualism and Voluntarism." In *The Cambridge History of Medieval Philosophy*. Edited by R. Pasnau and C. Van Dyke. Vol. 1, 414–27. Cambridge, 2010.

Holmes Katz, M. *The Birth of the Prophet Muhammed: Devotional Piety in Sunni Islam*. London, 2007.

Jacoby, D. "Un agent juif au service de Venise." *Thesaurismata* 9 (1972): 68–96.

Janssens, B., and P. Van Deun. "George Amiroutzes and His Poetical Oeuvre." In *Philomathestatos: Studies in Greek Patristic and Byzantine Texts Presented to Jacques Noret for his Sixty-Fifth Birthday*. Edited by B. Janssens, B. Roosen, and P. Van Deun. 297–324. Orientalia Lovanensia Analecta 137. Leuven, 2004.

Jugie, M. "Écrits apologétiques de Gennade Scholarios à l'adresse des musulmans." *Byzantion* 5 (1929/30): 295–314.

Kaldellis, A. "The Interpolations in the *Histories* of Laonikos Chalkokondyles." *Greek, Roman, and Byzantine Studies* 52 (2012): 259–83.

Karpov, S. P. *Ιστορία της αυτοκρατορίας της Τραπεζούντας*. Translated by E. Krichevskaya and A. Efstathiou. Athens, 2017.

———. *L'impero di Trebisonda, Venezia, Genova e Roma: Rapporti politici, diplomatici e commerciali*. Translated by E. Zambelli. Rome, 1986.

Khoury, A.-T. *Les théologiens byzantins et l'Islam: Textes et auteurs (VIIIe–XIIIe s.)*. Louvain, 1969.

———. *Polémique byzantine contre l'Islam (VIIIe–XIIIe s.)*. Leiden, 1972.

Kristeller, P. O. *Iter Italicum: A Finding List of Uncatalogued or Incompletely Catalogued Humanistic Manuscripts of the Renaissance in Italian and Other Libraries*. 7 vols. Leiden, 1963–97.

Lambros, S. P. "Γεωργίου Ἀμηρούτζη ἀνέκδοτος εὐχὴ πρὸς τὸν Θεόν." *Νέος Ἑλληνομνήμων* 3 (1906): 51–55.

———. "Ἡ περὶ ἁλώσεως Τραπεζοῦντος ἐπιστολὴ τοῦ Ἀμηρούτζη." *Νέος Ἑλληνομνήμων* 12 (1915): 476–78.

Lazarus-Yafeh, H. *Intertwined Worlds: Medieval Islam and Bible Criticism*. Princeton, 2014.

Lewis, B. "The Privilege Granted by Meḥmed II to His Physician." *Bulletin of the School of Oriental and African Studies* 14.3: *Studies Presented to Vladimir Minorsky by his Colleagues and Friends* (1952): 550–63.

Lilla, S. "Introduzione allo studio dello Ps. Dionigi l'Areopagita." *Augustinianum* 22 (1982): 533–77.

Lowe, C. G. "A Byzantine Manuscript of the University of Illinois." *Speculum* 4 (1929): 324–28.

Macé, C., and P. Van Deun. "L'intellect n'est pas commun à tous les hommes: L'*Opuscule philosophique* de Georges Amiroutzès († vers 1470)." *Medioevo greco* 9 (2009): 1–6.

Maiorino, M. "Il bibliotecario-archivista di Leone X: Zanobi Acciaiuoli (1518–1519)." In *Studi in onore del cardinale Raffaele Farina*. Edited by A. M. Piazzoni. Vol. 1, 639–62. Vatican City, 2013.

Mercati, G. "Sopra alcuni autografi di Giovanni Eugenico." *Bessarione* 35 (1919): 155–58. Repr. in idem, *Opere minori raccolte in occasione del settanesimo natalizio* (Studi e testi 79; Vatican City, 1937), vol. 4, *1917–1936*, 61–64.

Michel, A. "Résurrection des morts." In *Dictionnaire de théologie catholique*. Edited by A. Vacant et al. Vol. 13.2, 2501–71. Paris, 1937.

Michel, T. F., ed. and trans. *A Muslim Theologian's Response to Christianity, Ibn Taymiyya's* Al-Jawab al-Sahih. Delmar, NY, 1984.

Milgrom, J. *Numbers: The Traditional Hebrew Text with the New JPS Translation.* The JPS Torah Commentary. Philadelphia, 1990.

Mohler, L. *Kardinal Bessarion als Theologe, Humanist und Staatsmann: Funde und Forschungen.* 3 vols. Paderborn, 1923–42. Repr. Paderborn and Aalen, 1967.

Mondrain, B. "Jean Argyropoulos professeur à Constantinople et ses auditeurs médecins, d'Andronic Éparque à Démétrios Angelos." In *Πολύπλευρος νοῦς: Miscellanea für Peter Schreiner zu seinem 60. Geburtstag.* Edited by C. Scholz and G. Makris. 223–50. Munich, 2000.

Monfasani, J. "The Bessarion Missal Revisited." *Scriptorium* 37 (1983): 119–22. Repr. in idem, *Byzantine Scholars in Renaissance Italy: Cardinal Bessarion and Other Emigrés: Selected Essays* (Aldershot, 1995), as essay V.

———. "Bessarionea." *Byzantinische Zeitchrift* 113 (2020): 81–92.

———, ed. *Collectanea Trapezuntiana: Texts, Documents, and Bibliographies of George of Trebizond.* Binghamton, NY, 1984.

———. "Diodorus Siculus." In *Catalogus translationum et commentariorum: Medieval and Renaissance Latin Translations and Commentaries.* Edited by G. Dinkova-Bruun, J. Haig Gaisser, and J. Hankins. Vol. 11, 61–152. Toronto, 2016.

———. *George Amiroutzes the Philosopher and His Tractates.* Recherches de théologie et philosophie médiévales 12. Leuven, 2011.

———. *George of Trebizond: A Biography and a Study of His Rhetoric and Logic.* Columbia Studies in the Classical Tradition 1. Leiden, 1976.

———. "The 'Lost' Final Part of George Amiroutzes' *Dialogus de Fide in Christum* and Zanobi Acciaiuoli." In *Humanism and Creativity in the Renaissance: Essays in Honor of Ronald G. Witt.* Edited by C. S. Celenza and K. Gouwens. 197–229. Leiden, 2006.

———. "A Note on George Amiroutzes (c. 1400–c. 1469) and His Moral Argument against the Transmigration of Souls." *Bulletin de philosophie médiévale* 54 (2012): 125–35.

———. "Pletone, Bessarione e la processione dello Spirito Santo." In *Firenze e il Concilio del 1439. Convegno di Studi, Firenze, 29 novembre–2 dicembre 1989.* Edited by P. Viti. Vol. 2, 833–59. Florence, 1994. Repr. in idem, *Byzantine Scholars in Renaissance Italy: Cardinal Bessarion and Other Emigrés: Selected Essays* (Aldershot, 1995), as essay VIII.

———. Review of Ó. de la Palma, *El Diálogo de la Fe con el sultán de los turcos.* *Speculum* 79 (2004): 1024–25.

Moulakis, A. "Leonardo Bruni's Constitution of Florence." *Rinascimento* 26 (1986): 141–90.

Nau, M. F. "Un colloque du patriarche Jean avec l'émir des Agaréens et faits divers des années 712 à 716 d'après le ms. du British Museum *Add.* 17193." *Journal Asiatique* 11.5 (1915): 225–79.

Navascués Benlloch, P. de. *Pablo de Samosata y sus adversarios: Estudio histórico-teológico del cristianismo antioqueno en el s. III*. Studia ephemeridis Augustinianum 87. Rome, 2004.

Newman, N. A., ed. *The Early Christian-Muslim Dialogue: A Collection of Documents from the First Three Islamic Centuries (632–900 A.D.). Translations with Commentary*. Hatfield, PA, 1993.

Noiret, H. *Lettres inédites de Michel Apostolis*. Paris, 1889.

Papadopoulos-Kerameus, A. "Θεοφάνους Μηδείας καὶ Γεωργ. Ἀμηρούτση [sic]: Ἐπιστολαί." *Ὁ ἐν Κωνσταντινουπόλει Ἑλληνικὸς Φιλολογικὸς Σύλλογος, Σύγγραμμα περιοδικόν* 14 (1884): *Μαυρογορδάτειος Βιβλιοθήκη* suppl., 18–29.

Patrinelis, C. G. "Mehmed II the Conqueror and His Presumed Knowledge of Greek and Latin." *Viator* 2 (1971): 349–54.

———. *Ὁ Θεόδωρος Ἀγαλλιανὸς ταυτιζόμενος πρὸς τὸν Θεοφάνην Μηδείας καὶ οἱ ἀνέκδοτοι λόγοι του*. Athens, 1966.

Pelikan, J. *The Shape of Death: Life, Death, and Immortality in the Early Fathers*. New York, 1961.

Perl, E. "Pseudo-Dionysius the Areopagite." In *The Cambridge History of Philosophy in Latin Antiquity*. Edited by Lloyd P. Gerson. Vol. 2, 767–87. Cambridge, 2010.

Pertusi, A. "Gli studi latini di Manuele Caleca e la traduzione del De Trinitate di Boezio." In *Miscellanea Giovanni Galbiati*. Vol. 3, 283–312. Fontes ambrosiani 27. Milan, 1951.

Philippidis-Braat, A. "La captivité de Palamas chez les Turcs: Dossier et commentaire." *Travaux et mémoires* 7 (1979): 109–222.

Pietras, H. *Council of Nicaea (325): Religious and Political Context, Documents, Commentaries*. Rome, 2016.

Podskalsky, G. "Die Rezeption der thomistischen Theologie bei Gennadios II. Scholarios (ca. 1403–1472)." *Theologie und Philosophie* 49 (1974): 305–23.

———. *Theologie und Philosophie in Byzanz: Die Streit um die theologische Methodik in der spätbyzantinischen Geistesgeschichte (14./15. Jh.), seine systematischen Grundlagen und seine historische Entwicklung*. Byzantinisches Archiv 15. Munich, 1977.

Raby, J. "Mehmed the Conqueror's Greek Scriptorium." *Dumbarton Oaks Papers* 37 (1983): 15–34.

———. "Pride and Prejudice: Mehmed the Conqueror and the Italian Portrait Medal." In *Italian Medals*. Edited by J. G. Pollard. 171–94. Studies in the History of Art 21. Washington, DC, 1987.

Ramelli, I. L. E. "Origen's Anti-subordinationism and Its Heritage in the Nicene and Cappadocian Line." *Vigiliae christianae* 65.1 (2011): 21–49.

Reinsch, D. R. "Byzantinisches Herrscherlob für den türkischen Sultan: Ein bisher unbekanntes Gedicht des Georgios Amirutzes auf Mehmed den Eroberer." In *Cupido legum*. Edited by L. Burgmann, M. T. Fögen, and A. Schminck. 195–220. Frankfurt, 1985.

———. "Reichsidee und Sprache nach der Halosis: Georgios Amirutzes und Georgios Sphrantzes." In *Geschehenes und Geschriebenes: Studien zu Ehren von Günther S. Henrich und Klaus-Peter Matschke*. Edited by S. Kolditz and R. C. Müller. 329–35. Leipzig, 2005.

Rice, E. F., Jr., ed. *The Prefatory Epistles of Jacques Lefèvre d'Etaples and Related Texts*. New York, 1972.

Riedmatten, H. de. *Les actes du procès de Paul de Samosate: Étude sur la christologie du IIIe au IVe siècle*. Paradosis: Études de littérature et de théologie ancienne 6. Fribourg, 1952.

Rigo, A. "Gli interessi astronomici del cardinal Bessarione." In *Bessarione e l'Umanesimo: Catalogo della mostra*. Edited by G. Fiaccadori. 105–17. Saggi e ricerche 1. Naples, 1994.

Sahas, D. J. "Captivity and Dialogue: Gregory Palamas (1296–1360) and the Muslims." *Greek Orthodox Theological Review* 25 (1980): 409–36.

Said Reynolds, G. "On the Qur'anic Accusation of Scriptural Falsification (*taḥrīf*) and Christian Anti-Jewish Polemic." *Journal of the American Oriental Society* 130.2 (2010): 189–202.

Saleh, W. A. "A Fifteenth-Century Muslim Hebraist: Al-Biqāʿī and His Defense of Using the Bible to Interpret the Qur'an." *Speculum* 83 (2008): 629–54.

Sirry, M. *Scriptural Polemics: The Qur'ān and Other Religions*. Oxford, 2014.

Sophocles, E. A. *Greek Lexicon of the Roman and Byzantine Periods (From B.C. 146 to A.D. 1100)*. 2 vols. Cambridge, MA, 1914.

Spyridon of the Laura and S. Eustratiades. *Catalogue of the Greek Manuscripts in the Library of the Laura on Mount Athos, with Notices from Other Libraries*. Cambridge, MA, 1925.

Stavrides, T. *The Sultan of Vezirs: The Life and Times of the Ottoman Grand Vezir Mahmud Pasha Agelović (1453–1474)*. The Ottoman Empire and Its Heritage 24. Leiden, 2001.

Stefec, R. *Die Briefe des Michael Apostoles*. Schriften zur Kulturgeschichte 29. Hamburg, 2013.

Stelzer, W. "Cuspinianus (Spieshaymer, Spieß-, -heimer), Johannes." In Worstbrock, *Deutscher Humanismus*, 1:519–37.

Stéphanou, E. "Théophane de Médie: Opuscules philosophiques." *Échos d'Orient* 31 (1932): 165–76.

Strnad, A. A. "Die Rezeption von Humanismus und Renaissance in Wien." In *Humanismus und Renaissance in Ostmitteleuropa vor der Reformation*. Edited by A. A. Strnad and W. Eberhard. 71–135. Cologne, 1996.

Suermann, H. "Copts and the Islam of the Seventh Century." In Grypeou, Swanson, and Thomas, *Encounter of Eastern Christianity with Islam*, 97–109.

Swanson, M. N. "Folly to the Hunafā: The Crucifixion in Early Christian-Muslim Controversy." In Grypeou, Swanson, and Thomas, *Encounter of Eastern Christianity with Islam*, 237–56.

Tinnefeld, F. "Georgios Gennadios Scholarios." In *La théologie byzantine et sa tradition*. Edited by C. G. Conticello and V. Conticello. Vol. 2, 477–549. Turnholt, 2002.

TLG = Thesaurus Linguae Graecae. Online version, produced by the Department of Classics, University of California at Irvine, http://stephanus.tlg.uci.edu/.

Toenies Keating, S. "Revisiting the Charge of *Taḥrīf*: The Question of Supersessionism in Early Islam and the Qur'ān." In *Nicholas of Cusa and Islam: Polemic and Dialogue in the Late Middle Ages*. Edited by I. C. Levy, R. George-Tvrtković, and D. Duclow. 202–17. Studies in Medieval and Reformation Traditions 183. Leiden, 2014.

Tomadakis, N. B. "'Ετούρκευσεν ὁ Γεώργιος Ἀμιρούτζης." *Ἐπετηρὶς Ἑταιρείας Βυζαντινῶν Σπουδῶν* 18 (1948): 99–143.

Wallis, R. T. *Neoplatonism*. 2nd ed. Foreword and bibliography by L. P. Gerson. London, 1995.

White, H. G. E., and W. Hauser. *The Monasteries of the Wadi 'n Natrûn*. 3 vols. New York, 1926–33.

Wolfson, H. A. "The Plurality of Immovable Movers in Aristotle and Averroës." *Harvard Studies in Classical Philology* 63 (1958): 233–53.

Worstbrock, F. J., ed. *Deutscher Humanismus 1480–1520, Verfasserlexicon*. 3 vols. Berlin, 2005–15.

———. "Werner (Vernerus, Bernerus), Johannes." In idem, *Deutscher Humanismus*, 2:1266–77.

Wulf, M. de. *Philosophy and Civilization in the Middle Ages*. Repr. New York, 1953.

GENERAL INDEX

Specific works will be found under the name of the author, unless anonymous or otherwise indicated.

INDEX OF SCRIPTURAL CITATIONS